# Macroeconomic Essentials for Media Interpretation

Peter Kennedy

Simon Fraser University

# Macroeconomic Essentials for Media Interpretation

The MIT Press

Cambridge, Massachusetts

London, England

Second printing, 1997

This book was set in Times New Roman and Helvetica on the Monotype "Prism Plus"
PostScript Imagesetter by Asco Trade Typesetting Ltd., Hong Kong.

Printed and bound in the United States of America.

Library of Congress Cataloging-in-Publication Data

Kennedy, Peter, 1943–
  Macroeconomic essentials for media interpretation / Peter Kennedy.
    p.  cm.
  Includes index.
  ISBN 0-262-11221-3 (alk. paper). — ISBN 0-262-61128-7 (pbk. : alk. paper)
  1. Macroeconomics. 2. Economic policy. I. Title.
HB172.5.K457   1997
339—dc21                                                      96-39199
                                                                  CIP

*Dedicated, with love, to N. C.*

# Contents

# Preface

This book is designed to serve as a supplement to macroeconomics textbooks, although some instructors may wish to use it as a text on its own. It has three distinguishing features: it is concise, nontechnical, and applied. As such it should appeal to instructors and students swamped by the encyclopedic approach of traditional principles texts, to instructors teaching mainly business students interested in relevance, and to instructors teaching a policy- or applications-oriented macroeconomics course.

*Why and how is it concise?* Educational psychologists have been telling instructors for years that it is better to teach students a small amount of important material well than to cover a large amount of material less thoroughly. Accordingly, this book concentrates on the important concepts of macroeconomics, foregoing pages of interesting and useful but not essential supplementary material. This book summarizes the essentials of what students need to know and provides numerous examples of applications.

*Why and how is it nontechnical?* What do we want our students to be able to do upon completing their macroeconomics course: manipulate a 45° line diagram and derive the multiplier, or interpret and evaluate media commentary on the macroeconomy? I am not alone in believing that for many students the latter is preferable and that in terms of meeting this latter goal there is a high opportunity cost associated with pressing students to learn algebraic and graphical derivations. Only graphs with exceptional pedagogical value, such as the aggregate demand/aggregate supply diagram and its alter ego the Phillips curve, are employed in this book. This less-technical approach does not mean a loss of rigor, but merely a different kind of rigor, involving critical thinking skills that most students find very challenging.

*Why and how is it applied?* Although those seeking a degree in economics need to become conversant with the technical skills and theoretical nuances of professional economists, this approach need not dominate introductory courses, where so many students—particularly business students—are not committed economics majors and the opportunity cost is so high. The application orientation of this text is accomplished by providing over five hundred two- or three-sentence news clips, the vast majority based on actual news reports, as illustrations or student exercises. Much can be learned from working through these clippings—institutional facts, policy nuances, common misunderstandings, perspective on magnitudes, alternative viewpoints, and political realities, as well as how theoretical concepts are applied.

Chapter 1 describes what readers will find in this text, but several features should emphasized.

1. Do not be fooled by the "nontechnical" flavor of the book. The material is presented at a high conceptual level and is intellectually demanding—necessary criteria for successful interpretation and evaluation of media commentary. Some challenging topics, such as real versus nominal interest rates and international phenomena, are given much more emphasis than in traditional texts because they play such a prominent role in media interpretation.

2. Some of the most common technical material has made its way into the text via optional end-of-chapter appendices. Appendices 4.3, 4.4, and 5.1 exposit the 45°-line diagram, the algebraic derivation of the multiplier, and the graphical derivation of the aggregate demand (AD) curve, for example. Appendix A at the end of the book provides an overview of supply/demand analysis of the four major macroeconomic submarkets and how the aggregate supply/aggregate demand diagram summarizes activity in these four markets. For students not yet versed in supply/demand analysis, appendix A also contains an introduction to microeconomic supply and demand curves.

3. In each chapter I have set some material aside in boxed areas called *curiosities*—short expositions of important related topics that should be considered integral parts of the chapter.

4. Each chapter ends with examples of news clippings and answers to related questions, followed by several exercises based on news clips. Many chapters also have a set of numerical exercises asking students to test their understanding of concepts by calculating implications in terms of numerical examples. Appendix B at the end of the book contains additional questions, but without any indication of which chapter's material is relevant. To aid independent study, answers to all even-numbered questions are provided in appendix C at the end of the book.

5. Some end-of-chapter questions are easy, but many can be quite difficult, primarily because news clips seldom announce the macroeconomic concept relevant to their interpretation and journalists never spell things out as completely as do textbooks. Consequently, these excursions into the real world sometimes seem ambiguous to students. In light of all this, some instructors may wish to tailor the difficulty level by providing extra infor-

mation. Most of the more difficult exercises are even-numbered exercises so that their solutions can be found in appendix C.

No author is without debts. My thanks to Jim Marlin, Erik Poole, Lance Shandler, Bill Scarth, Bill Watson, and especially Ann Sochi for reading through part or all of initial versions. As usual, though, my biggest debt is to the generations of my students who have struggled with this manuscript as it has developed.

# 1 Introduction

There are three kinds of economics: curve shifting, pop art, and media. Formal theorizing favored by academic economists usually involves shifting curves on diagrams, so it is called *curve-shifting economics*. Its technical character makes it suitable mainly to those seeking a university degree in economics. *Pop-art economics* is found in economics best sellers. Although fun, it is too often harebrained. *Media economics* is the economics encountered on the business pages of newspapers or on television. This is what business people and interested laypersons need to know about economics and what undergraduate students should be learning about economics in addition to curve shifting. It is the kind of economics a reader will learn from this book.

Each type of economics has two variants: microeconomics and macroeconomics. The former analyzes the behavior of individual firms and consumers, with attention focused on issues such as how consumers make choices, how firms determine prices, and the implications of government-imposed sales taxes or quotas. The latter, the subject of this book, looks at the big picture, analyzing economy-wide variables such as inflation, unemployment, interest rates, and exchange rates, and focusing on issues such as what determines business cycles, how interest rates are set and the implications of the government printing more money or fixing the exchange rate.

The purpose of this chapter is to introduce the reader to media economics and provide a summary of the major macroeconomic concepts exposited in this book.

---

**Upon completion of this chapter you should**

- know what kind of economics you will learn from reading this book; and
- have an overview of the important macroeconomic ideas it contains.

---

## 1.1 Media Economics

Textbooks written for economics majors present economics using the language and perspective of professional economists. Students learn to analyze economic phenomena through economic models, formalized with graphs and, at advanced levels, with algebra and calculus. Much time is devoted to learning how to manipulate various graphical or algebraic models that have come to serve as an intellectual framework for economists.

In one respect, it is entirely appropriate that such textbooks have this flavor because it reflects accurately what academic economists do: they build, manipulate, and estimate economic models to aid in explanation, prediction, and policy formulation. Possession of a degree in economics means one is familiar with the terminology of these models and the technical means by which they are manipulated. At the undergraduate textbook level, the technical dimension is predominantly in the form of graphical analysis, so this type of economics is accordingly referred to as *curve-shifting economics*. At advanced levels the technical dimension is dominated by algebraic formulas in which Greek letters play prominent roles. Hence this type of economics is sometimes called *Greek-letter economics*, a term introduced by Paul Krugman in the preface to his book *The Age of Diminished Expectations*.

At the other end of the spectrum from curve-shifting economics is the entirely nontechnical *pop-art economics* found in books sold to the general public, some of which actually become best sellers. Krugman calls this *airport economics* because these books are most prominently displayed at airport book stores where business travelers are likely to buy them. They usually have some axe to grind. Most tell tales of imminent disaster, and a few advocate specific panaceas. In general, they do not teach their readers much about economics and, in any event, are not designed as textbooks.

Between these two extreme approaches is the economics that appears in the media, most notably on the business pages of newspapers. This is *media economics*, which has two varieties: (1) what Krugman calls *up-and-down economics*—news reports preoccupied with what latest economic numbers are up or down, and (2) *economic policy evaluation*—news commentary directed at explaining, praising, or condemning government macroeconomic policies. The main purpose of this book is to teach macroeconomic principles and how they can be used to interpret these two varieties of media economics.

## 1.2  Up-and-Down Economics

The following examples illustrate ways in which up-and-down economics appears in the media:

*According to the latest statistics, housing starts are up, indicating unexpected strength in the economy. Bond prices fell on the news . . .*

*In his eyes the battle is between the rate-lowering effect of the U.S. recession and the high rate of inflation. That sums up the problem now facing the interest rate forecasters.*

*News that U.S. job creation in January was more robust than anticipated sent a signal to currency markets to expect a stepped-up fight against inflation, unleashing a bout of buying fervor for the U.S. dollar.*

These examples are typical of commentary on newspaper business pages because they are relevant to money-making activity on bond or foreign exchange markets, or because they deal with variables such as interest rates that business people or mortgage renewers would be keen to forecast. Despite its practical value, however, most economists find up-and-down economics "stupefyingly boring" (to use Krugman's term) and are upset that most people think that up-and-down economics is what economists do.

Why do economists disclaim up-and-down economics? A major reason is that it is too simpleminded. The predictions of up-and-down economics result from applying macroeconomic principles in conjunction with simplifying assumptions that are not quite true. This approach allows quick and easy calculation of predictions that may be good first approximations, particularly for those forced to take immediate action. However, the process lacks the intellectual rigor so prized by academic economists. There is no recognition of how economic forces from a variety of sources interact to influence the variable in question; economic "laws" of questionable empirical validity are employed with unjustified confidence; long-run guides to economic behavior are used to predict results in the short run; and nuances of modern macroeconomic theorizing are ignored.

Despite this condemnation by academic economists, a major goal of this book is to teach readers up-and-down economics. There are several reasons for doing this. First, and most important, by learning how to interpret news clips such as those cited above, students will genuinely learn, understand, and remember fundamental macroeconomic principles. Second, although boring to academic economists, up-and-down economics is useful to those involved or just interested in the business world. For example, knowing that a rise in inflation will increase interest rates and thereby cause bond prices to fall can help one avoid capital losses on bond holdings. Third, by focusing on applications as they appear in the media, students will as a natural by-product learn much about the institutional structure of our economy. And fourth, it is necessary to understand up-and-down economics to be able to evaluate media commentary on policy issues, the second dimension of media economics.

## 1.3   Policy Evaluation

The second variety of media economics is economic policy evaluation. The following examples illustrate ways in which it appears in the media:

*What cannot be done, various reformers in the U.S. notwithstanding, is to impose on any government the obligation to balance its budget annually. Consider the consequences. If it did work, it would introduce a major destabilizing element.*

*The monetarists will allow you to go ahead and ruin people and countries, but when eventually in good and common sense you say, "enough is enough," the monetarists say, "well, you spoiled the experiment."*

*This is the reason that the fixed exchange rate system was scrapped in 1971. The United States had been pursuing an inflationary monetary policy to help pay for the Vietnam War and new social programs, and its trading partners did not all want to participate in it.*

In contrast to up-and-down economics, media commentary on economic policy is of considerable interest to academic economists, primarily because most feel strongly that policy analysis is one of the main reasons for studying macro-economics. This book emphasizes this dimension of media economics by providing hundreds of short, two- or three-sentence news clips such as those above, asking students for interpretion and evaluation.

Students are not asked, however, to interpret or evaluate the news clips using the technical curve-shifting art of the professional economist. With one significant exception, our presentation of media economics avoids using graphs.

## 1.4   A Picture Can Be Worth a Thousand Words

The curve-shifting approach does have one advantage we would be foolish to throw away: sometimes a graph can greatly facilitate exposition and understanding. The aggregate supply/aggregate demand diagram and its alter ego, the Phillips curve, are so valuable in this respect that they are shamelessly exploited. All other diagrams—most notably the supply/demand diagrams for money, labor, and the exchange rate—are bypassed; for those interested, appendix A at the end of the book exposits these diagrams to provide perspective on the curve-shifting approach and a sense of what makes the aggregate supply/aggregate demand diagram so useful.

This book is very short; attention is focused on the "really important" ideas of macroeconomics, with much of the encyclopedic and technical detail of traditional texts ignored. This should ensure that these really important ideas are properly learned and remembered. What are these really important ideas?

## 1.5  Really Important Macroeconomic Ideas

Listing the really important macroeconomic ideas is a challenging task because so many macroeconomic ideas are important that any one person's selection of a few as "really important" is bound to be controversial. The first step in creating such a list is to address the question, "Really important for what?" The list below stems from the answer, "Really important for understanding media commentary on the macroeconomy." It includes ideas important to those interested in how macroeconomics is relevant, ideas that students should be sure to understand and take with them when they complete their course.

The list below is included here to provide an overview of what can be expected throughout the rest of the book, though the reader may be unfamiliar with some of the terminology employed; a second reading, after completing the book, is advised. For convenience, one major idea has been drawn from each of the remaining chapters.

**Chapter 2: Gross Deceptive Product.** Gross domestic product, GDP, figurehead of our national economic accounts and the measure of our total annual output of goods and services, has many defects as a measure of our economic well-being or as a means of comparing standards of living across countries.

**Chapter 3: Discouraged/Encouraged Workers.** Unemployed people who become discouraged by their unsuccessful search for work, and therefore stop searching, are suddenly no longer counted as unemployed. When the economy picks up, they can become encouraged and begin looking for work again, thus becoming counted as unemployed. This discouraged/encouraged worker phenomenon helps explain paradoxical movements in the measured rate of unemployment and is an example of the more general problem of difficulties in measuring economic variables.

**Chapter 4: The Multiplier.** An increase in government spending can ultimately cause a greater increase in national income. This multiplied impact of fiscal policy is one basis for the Keynesian view that the government can and should intervene in the operation of the economy to maintain full employment, even if it means creating a budget deficit.

**Chapter 5: The Natural Rate of Unemployment.** The institutional structure of an economy gives rise to a "natural" rate of unemployment consistent with a steady rate of inflation. Unfortunately, the natural rate is neither known nor constant over time. It is currently thought to be about 6 percent, although recent experience suggests it has fallen to a lower level. An important implication is that efforts to lower unemployment below this natural rate can succeed only in the short run and only by accelerating inflation. (See also chapter 12.)

**Chapter 6:   Productivity.**   In the long run, increases in our economic standard of living depend primarily on productivity increases. To achieve higher growth in productivity we must increase national saving: present generations must sacrifice current consumption to improve productivity for future generations. Productivity increases often come about through "creative destruction," a process in which existing jobs are destroyed through the creation of new jobs embodying technological advances.

**Chapter 7:   Crowding Out.**   The means used to finance an increase in government spending set in motion a variety of secondary forces that decrease aggregate demand. This crowding out of aggregate demand diminishes the impact of fiscal policy, in the long run perhaps offsetting it entirely.

**Chapter 8:   Printing Money.**   The U.S. central bank, the Federal Reserve (the Fed), "prints" money by buying bonds, enabling commercial banks to increase their loans and thereby expand the nation's money supply. Irregular relationships between economic activity and measures of the money supply create problems for monetary policy.

**Chapter 9:   Inflation and Money-Supply Growth.**   In the long run, an economy's inflation is equal to the difference between the rate of growth of its money supply and its rate of growth of output. This reflects the monetarist belief that, in the long run, inflation is always and everywhere a monetary phenomenon, which leads to their prescription that the Fed should be replaced by a robot programmed to increase the money supply at a low, steady rate, the genesis of the prominent "rules-versus-discretion" policy debate.

**Chapter 10:   Interest Rates and Bond Prices.**   A genuine economic "law" is that there is an inverse relationship between the interest rate and the price of bonds. One implication of this law is that if the interest rate is forecast to rise, those holding bonds will try to sell them to avoid suffering a capital loss.

**Chapter 11:   Real versus Nominal Interest Rates.**   The interest rate affecting aggregate demand is the real interest rate. The observed interest rate—the nominal interest rate—differs from the real interest rate in that it has a premium for expected inflation built into it. For practical purposes, the main determinant of change in the nominal interest rate is change in the expected rate of inflation. The difference between real and nominal interest rates helps explain many seeming anomalies, such as an increase in the money supply causing a rise rather than a fall in the interest rate.

**Chapter 12: Inflation Asymmetry.** Inflation accelerates quickly, with only a small temporary reduction in unemployment below its natural rate, but lowering inflation requires an extended period of high unemployment, primarily because it takes so long for expectations of inflation to fall. It is this asymmetry that causes governments to fight inflation so tenaciously.

**Chapter 13: The Real Cause of Inflation.** Although an excessive rate of money-supply growth is the driving force behind inflation, the real cause of inflation is the reason the monetary authorities are increasing the money supply at an excessive rate. Such behavior is policy error. Examples of such errors include misinterpreting the consequences of a negative supply shock, misjudging the natural rate of unemployment, fixing the nominal interest rate, fixing the exchange rate, and financing too much government spending.

**Chapter 14: The Structural Deficit.** The long-run impact of a government's budget deficit is better measured by calculating its effect in the long run on the ratio of the publically held national debt to GDP because this measure reflects the economy's capacity to service its national debt. It involves corrections for cyclical factors, growth, and money creation. The burden on future generations of this debt depends primarily on how the deficit spending is used. Spending on capital goods could make future generations better off.

**Chapter 15: Trade Deficit.** A continuing trade deficit is due not to a lack of competitiveness, but rather to a sustained capital inflow, possibly caused by a high real interest rate created by a large government budget deficit.

**Chapter 16: Monetary Policy Lost under Fixed Exchange Rates.** When a small economy fixes its exchange rate with a large economy, monetary policy must maintain the exchange rate and thus cannot be used for other goals, such as controlling inflation. The small country must experience whatever monetary policy and inflation characterizes the large country.

**Chapter 17: Purchasing Power Parity.** Although changes in our real exchange rate occur because of phenomena such as natural resource discoveries, in the long run movements in our nominal exchange rate primarily reflect differences between our inflation rate and the inflation rates of our major trading partners. One implication is that a country with higher inflation than its trading partners should experience a steady depreciation of its nominal exchange rate.

**Chapter 18: Interest Rate Parity.** Save for a risk premium, real interest rates tend to be approximately equal throughout the world, but nominal interest rates are not. The latter differ according to inflation rate differences or, equivalently, to expected exchange rate movements. One implication is that a country wishing to maintain a nominal interest rate below that of its trading partners must accept a continual rise in its exchange rate.

Several of these and other macroeconomic principles give rise to formal equations that can be used as rules of thumb for predicting long-run macroeconomic behavior. Along with the aggregate demand/aggregate supply and Phillips curve diagrams, as well as some definitions that can be written in equation form, these principles form the technical dimension of this book, providing sufficient background for students to move on to more advanced courses in macroeconomics.

Readers must be warned, however: the nontechnical nature of this book does not imply that its contents will be easy to learn or use. There are several reasons for this.

1. The media illustrations and the questions based on them are challenging; they require problem-solving skills and demand that the student thoroughly understand the economic principles. Only rarely can questions be answered simply by looking up material in the book.

2. Many of the concepts on which this book concentrates are more advanced than those emphasized by traditional texts, reflecting the focus on media interpretation. For example, most traditional texts do little more than define the difference between real and nominal interest rates, but because this difference plays a crucial role in interpreting media commentary related to interest rates, it is a key concept here.

3. Unfamiliar terminology pops up frequently. All readers can seek help in the glossary at the end of the book, and those for whom this book is a supplement to a traditional text can turn to it for help. Often, however, readers must employ "street smarts" to make sense of a journalist's metaphor or use of unfamiliar terminology. To aid student efforts to develop their street smarts, answers to all even-numbered questions appear in appendix C at the end of the book.

4. The concise nature of this book means that its pace is fast. New concepts are presented more quickly than in traditional texts, and easy concepts are given little elaboration. Readers accustomed to longer expositions may wish on occasion to refer to a traditional text for more detail.

## Chapter Summary

- Media economics consists of *up-and-down economics*, focusing on understanding what causes economic numbers such as interest rates, unemployment, or inflation to go up or down, and *economic policy evaluation*, focusing on adjudicating the merit of government policy. This book exposits macroeconomic principles important for media economics; some economic concepts prominent in traditional texts are dealt with very briefly, and other concepts, some not emphasized in traditional texts, are highlighted.

- The book's conciseness implies that it must focus on "really important macreoeconomic ideas," where "really important" refers to their role in media interpretation. A list of several such ideas was presented as a preview of this book's contents.

- Traditional textbooks emphasize curve-shifting, an approach to economic analysis in which curves are shifted on diagrams to illustrate economic results. With the exception of the aggregate supply/aggregate demand and the Phillips curve diagrams (unfamiliar terms can be found in the glossary), which are truly worth a thousand words, this book avoids such technical material. Despite its nontechnical nature, it is nevertheless intellectually demanding.

- Appendix A at the end of the book presents an overview of how supply-and-demand curves are used in a macroeconomic context. The macroeconomy consists of four aggregate markets—for goods and services, for money, for labor, and for foreign exchange—that interact to determine the character of the economy. This interaction is very complicated, creating headaches for students. The aggregate supply/aggregate demand diagram was developed to consolidate many of these interactions and thereby to simplify the exposition of macroeconomic phenomena. Readers can gain perspective on the curve-shifting dimension of macroeconomics by examining this appendix before and then again after reading the rest of the book.

# 2 Measuring GDP and Inflation

For at least five centuries systematic accounting systems have existed for private business, and data on individual behavior have always been available for collection. Microeconomics cannot complain of a lack of empirical data with which to verify its theories, quantify its conclusions, or suggest new directions for research. For macroeconomics, however, the situation is different: the financial, institutional, and legal resources of the government are necessary to collect aggregate data. Although governments have provided this data-collecting service for many years, until recently it was simply a convenient by-product of other government activities such as tax collecting. Until the beginning of the Second World War, all these data consisted either of indices of price levels, production activity, and employment, or of trends in financial activity.

In the 1930s, the Keynesian approach to macroeconomics (described in chapter 4) was introduced, offering an explanation and policy advice for the Great Depression. As the popularity of this new approach to macroeconomics grew, economists beseeched the government to collect data relevant to the testing and use of Keynesian theory. In response, the government developed the *National Income and Product Accounts* to measure economic activity, the figurehead of which—GDP—appears frequently in the popular press.

The purpose of this chapter is to explain the basic structure of the national income accounts and offer some perspectives on the interpretation and use of the GDP measure.

---

**Upon completion of this chapter you should**

- understand what GDP is and how it is measured;
- know what price indices are and how they are used;
- recognize the difference between real and nominal variables; and
- realize that using GDP to measure social welfare or to compare countries must be heavily qualified.

---

## 2.1  What Is GDP?

Gross domestic product (GDP), is the total dollar value of all final goods and services produced in a country during a year. Several things about this definition should be noted:

1. Both goods, such as automobiles and top hats, and services, such as the help of lawyers and plumbers, are included.
2. Current market prices, reflecting the value society places on items, are used to aggregate different outputs to a dollar total. Government purchases, many of which do not occur on markets, are valued at their cost of production.
3. Only final goods and services are included. Intermediate goods, such as steel that has yet to be made into hammers and shovels, are not included. This avoids double counting the steel.
4. This measure is an annual flow, a rate of production. A GDP of $6 trillion implies that the economy is producing $6 trillion worth of goods and services per year.
5. U.S. GDP measures production by U.S. citizens and foreigners alike inside the geographic borders of the United States and thus unequivocally reflects economic activity in the United States.

Economists and the media use many names besides GDP to refer to the nation's annual output of goods and services: output, total output, national output, income, total income, national income, and aggregate supply. (Algebraic representations use the capital letter $Y$.) These names suggest that economists use the terms *output* and *income* interchangeably; it is important to understand why.

Consider one element of GDP, a loaf of bread worth a dollar. With only a few exceptions, every penny of this dollar's worth of bread can be traced back into somebody's pocket as income. Some of the dollar is profit/proprietor

---

**Curiosity 2.1:   What Is the Difference between GDP and GNP?**

In 1992, the United States joined the rest of the world and made gross domestic product (GDP) the figurehead of its national economic accounting system, replacing gross national product (GNP). GDP measures output produced inside the United States, whether by foreigners or U.S. citizens. GNP measures output of U.S. citizens, no matter where they are located in the world. GNP is slightly higher (about 0.3 percent) than GDP, mainly because U.S. corporations abroad earn more than foreign corporations located in the United States, but this difference has been diminishing slowly as year after year more foreign investment flows into the United States than U.S. investment flows abroad.

---

income to the grocer, baker, miller, and farmer (or dividend income to their stockholders); some is wage and salary income to their employees; some is interest income to the banker who has financed their loans (or interest income to those who purchased their corporate bonds); and some is rental income to their landlords. It is because of this that *total output*, GDP, is referred to as *total income*.

Laypersons' use of the word *income* is slightly different in that it reflects what we receive as income, regardless of whether or not it corresponds to output. There are three differences of note. First, of the dollar's worth of bread, some money will be set aside by the grocer, baker, miller, and farmer to cover depreciation—to pay for replacing their buildings and equipment when they have worn out—and thus will never make it into anyone's pocket as income. Second, if the grocer, baker, miller, or farmer pays any indirect taxes, such as sales taxes as the bread makes its way through the production process, then this money goes directly to the government and thus will not make it into anyone's pocket as income. And third, transfer payments make up part of our income, but do not correspond to output produced—for example, government production subsidies, welfare and unemployment insurance payments, gifts, and interest on government and consumer debt. A subset of the national income accounts reports data on these kinds of measures.

As a nation, our annual income—what we have available to distribute to our citizens—is what we have produced during the year. Despite the fact that individual incomes do not quite match the concept of a nation's aggregate income we will use the terms *aggregate output* and *aggregate income* interchangeably, suggesting that GDP could be measured by adding up all incomes and making adjustments for the phenomena noted above. For those interested, appendix 2.1 at the end of this chapter shows how this would be done. Some countries use this method to help in estimating GDP, but the United States uses a different method.

## 2.2   Estimating GDP

Suppose that everything produced during the year was bought during the year. By adding up all expenditure on final goods and services during the year we would have a measure of GDP, what was produced during the year. This is the rationale behind the expenditure approach to measuring GDP, and, with three major adjustments, it is the method by which U.S. GDP is estimated.

First, what if some of what was produced was not bought during the year? Suppose a million dollars worth of furniture, manufactured during the year and so part of that year's GDP, was not purchased during the year. The national accounts statistician views this extra furniture as having been purchased by the manufacturers themselves for the purpose of augmenting their inventory. In this way, by imaginative accounting, items that were not bought become bought, which causes the adding-expenditures approach to measure what was actually produced, namely GDP. Similarly, of course, if during the year people bought more than what was produced so that inventories fell, the national accounts statistician records this as a negative investment in inventories, lowering the adding-expenditures measure to measure accurately what was actually produced.

Second, what if some things bought during the year were used products, such as antiques, and so do not correspond to that year's production? Such items are not counted when adding all expenditures, but the fraction of such sales that reflects a purchase of the services provided by the antique dealer is counted.

Third, what if some of the spending during the year was on imported goods and services, or on goods with imported components? Adding up all spending would then overestimate what was actually produced in the United States. This problem is solved by subtracting all imports.

Table 2.1 reports GDP measured via the expenditure approach. Total expenditure on goods and services is broken into four general categories, corresponding to those formulated by Keynes: consumption expenditure (denoted $C$), investment expenditure ($I$), government expenditure ($G$), and foreign expenditure or exports ($X$). An extra category, imports ($M$), is subtracted from exports to produce net exports, which removes the import component inherent in all categories so that we end up with total expenditure on domestically produced goods and services. It must be stressed that all spending here is on actual goods and services, so that investment is spending on such things as lathes, delivery trucks, factories, and shopping centers, rather than on financial investments such as stocks and bonds; government spending is on things such as highways and IRS accountants, not on transfer payments such as welfare payments that do not correspond to output.

Table 2.1 is a simplified version of a national accounts expenditure table; more detail can be found in the monthly publication *Survey of Current Business* published by the Bureau of Economic Analysis (BEA—a branch of the Commerce Department). Notice that in the table spending on inventory appears as

**Table 2.1**   U.S. gross domestic product, 1995 ($ billions)

| | | |
|---|---:|---:|
| **Consumption** | | **4,925** |
| Durable goods | 606 | |
| Nondurable goods | 1486 | |
| Services | 2833 | |
| **Investment** | | **1,066** |
| Nonresidential structures | 199 | |
| Nonresidential equipment | 539 | |
| Residential | 290 | |
| Change in inventories | 37 | |
| **Government** | | **1,358** |
| Federal defence | 346 | |
| Federal nondefence | 171 | |
| State and local | 841 | |
| **Net exports** | | **−95** |
| Exports | 807 | |
| Imports | 902 | |
| **Gross domestic product** | | **7,254** |

Source: *Survey of Current Business*, August 1996.

"change in inventories," which could be negative if inventories fell because more output was bought than was produced during the year.

## 2.3   Real versus Nominal GDP

One way the GDP measure can increase is if the nation produces a larger physical quantity of goods and services, implying that more goods and services are available for distribution to participants in the economy. Such a change would be of importance to our standard of living, but GDP can also change simply because the prices of all goods and services rise, as they do during an inflation. In this case, a larger GDP does not correspond to a larger physical quantity of goods and services. Typically, each year GDP increases for both reasons, so we need some way of distinguishing changes in GDP due to physical changes in output from changes due to price level fluctuations.

This is accomplished by distinguishing between *real* and *nominal* GDP. Nominal GDP is GDP valued at current prices, the number reported in the national accounts. Real GDP is GDP valued at prices prevailing during some base year, currently chosen by the national accounts statisticians to be 1992. For example, if we take the physical quantities of goods and services produced during 1994 and add them together by valuing them at 1992 prices, we obtain 1994 GDP measured in 1992 prices, otherwise known as 1994 real GDP.

Suppose we take nominal GDP for 1994 and divide it by real GDP for 1994. The numerator expresses 1994 output in 1994 prices, and the denominator

**Table 2.2**  Nominal and real GDP

| Year | Nominal GDP (billions of current $) | GDP deflator (1992 = 100) | Real GDP (billions of 1992 $) |
|---|---|---|---|
| 1990 | 5,546.1 | 93.7 | 5,919.0 |
| 1991 | 5,724.8 | 97.3 | 5,883.7 |
| 1992 | 6,020.2 | 100.0 | 6,020.2 |
| 1993 | 6,343.3 | 102.2 | 6,206.8 |
| 1994 | 6,738.4 | 104.3 | 6,460.6 |

Source: *Survey of Current Business*, July 1994 and August 1995.

expresses this same physical output in 1992 prices, so the ratio reflects the extent to which overall prices have risen from 1992 to 1994. If this ratio is 1.123, say, we conclude that prices have risen during this period by 12.3 percent. When this calculation is done for each year, we obtain a series representing the change of the overall price level over time. By tradition, the numbers in this series are multiplied by 100 so that, for example, the 1.123 above becomes 112.3. Such a series is called a price index, usually denoted $P$. This particular price index is called the *GDP deflator* because to convert from nominal to real GDP we divide by the price index, thus deflating nominal GDP to base year dollars. It can be expressed as

$$\text{GDP deflator } P = \frac{\text{GDP valued at current prices}}{\text{GDP valued at 1992 prices}} \times 100.$$

To check your understanding of price indices, convince yourself that in the base year the price index must be 100 and that to convert nominal GDP to real GDP we should divide by P and multiply by 100:

$$\text{real GDP} = \frac{\text{nominal GDP}}{P} \times 100.$$

This is illustrated in table 2.2, which reports for selected years nominal GDP, the GDP deflator, and real GDP. Notice that although nominal GDP rises from 1990 to 1991, real GDP falls.

Percentage change in real GDP is the usual measure of an economy's real growth rate; percentage change in the GDP deflator is one way, but not the usual way, of measuring inflation.

## 2.4  Measuring Inflation

Inflation is defined as a persistent rise in the general price level. This price level is usually measured by the *consumer price index*, the CPI, a price index designed to reflect growth in prices of consumer goods and services. If the prices of all consumer goods and services rise by 10 percent, the CPI rises by 10 percent to reflect this. The CPI is calculated by observing changes in the cost of purchasing a typical bundle of consumer goods and services. As the cost of buying this bundle rises (falls), the CPI rises (falls). Thus the CPI is a weighted average of all prices, with the weights given by the relative importance of different goods or services in the typical bundle of purchases. The approximate general breakdown of the typical bundle currently in use is housing 39 percent, food and beverage 20 percent, transportation 20 percent, clothing 6 percent, medical care 5 percent, entertainment 4 percent, and other 6 percent. The CPI can be expressed as

$$\text{Consumer price index CPI} = \frac{\text{current cost of typical bundle}}{\text{1992 cost of typical bundle}} \times 100.$$

Although conceptually everyone "knows" what inflation is, from having to deal with it in their everyday lives, few recognize that two main measurement problems affect its interpretation: what to do about changes in relative prices and what to do about quality changes.

A change in relative prices means that not all prices have changed by the same percentage amount. When relative prices change, consumers tend to buy less of items that have become relatively more expensive and more of items that are now relatively cheaper. The typical bundle changes in a way that causes the CPI calculation based on a fixed bundle to overestimate the change in the cost of living associated with the price changes. If inflation measures are used to measure changes in the cost of living, as they invariably are, they are overestimates. In practice, statisticians carefully choose a typical bundle and use that bundle as a base from which to measure changes in the cost of living. Whenever this bundle becomes glaringly out of date, it is revised, and the old index is spliced smoothly to the new in some suitable fashion.

Changes in quality are difficult to incorporate into the price index. Their importance stems from the use of price indices to reflect changes in the "purchasing power" of a dollar. If the quality of a good or service increases and its price rises to cover the higher cost of producing the higher quality product, the rise in price increases the price index, but the rise in the price index in this case does not reflect a fall in the value of what is purchased with a dollar. Similarly, if a computer becomes many times more powerful but its price does not change, the purchasing power of a dollar has increased because it can buy more computing, but the price index does not decrease to reflect this. In practice, statisticians deal with this problem by monitoring quality changes by a variety of means and making suitable adjustments.

An interesting example is often used to clarify this point. Suppose you were given $10,000 and told that you may spend it on 1990-quality goods and services at 1990 prices or on 1994-quality goods and services at 1994 prices. If you choose the latter option, you are implicitly saying that quality increases between 1990 and 1994 have offset the price increases, so "inflation" between

---

**Curiosity 2.2:   How Do the GDP Deflator and the CPI Differ?**

The GDP deflator and the CPI are both price indices. The CPI is particularly well known because it measures changes in the cost of living and so is of more personal interest to individuals; for that reason, it is the price index normally used to calculate the rate of inflation. There are three major differences between the two indices. First, the CPI reflects prices of only consumer goods and services, whereas the GDP deflator calculation includes prices of all output. Second, the CPI incorporates prices of imports, excluded from the GDP deflator calculation. And third, the CPI is calculated by tracking over time the cost of a fixed basket of goods and services, whereas the GDP deflator allows the output basket to change. One other difference is that, once published, the CPI is never revised, as are other statistics, because it is often used in contracts to measure cost-of-living wage adjustments.

---

1990 and 1994 is zero or negative insofar as it affects the purchasing power of your dollar.

Most people and governments are unequivocally of the opinion that inflation is undesirable. Measurement problems, however, indicate that measured inflation may not be a good guide to the extent to which inflation should be considered undesirable. Some experts believe, for example, that current measurement overestimates "true" inflation by between one-half and one percentage point. Furthermore, an examination of why inflation is undesirable suggests that, surprisingly, inflation is not nearly as severe a social ill as it is generally thought to be.

---

## 2.5   The Costs of Inflation

Economists do not pay much heed to the usual complaints about inflation. For most people, the impact of rising prices is offset by rising wages. Those living on fixed incomes, such as welfare recipients or old-age pensioners, can (although may not) be protected through appropriate policy action. Arbitrary redistribution of wealth, such as rises in real estate values, come about mainly if an inflation is unanticipated, in which case economists would condemn it.

From their study of microeconomics economists know that our economic system works well because prices act as signals to induce producers to produce the things we value most at the lowest cost—the right prices ensure that the economy maximizes the total welfare of its participants. This is what is meant when it is said that the price system is a very *efficient* way of allocating and distributing goods and services. To economists, the main cost of inflation is the resource misallocation it causes—the loss of efficiency that results because inflation distorts price signals. This happens in many different ways, some examples of which follow.

- During periods of inflation, people are more interested in investing their savings in assets designed to protect them against inflation, such as real estate, rather than in productive investments that enhance the growth and efficiency of the economy. A classic example is people in Brazil holding wealth in the form of Volkswagens during high inflation periods.

- During high inflation, business finds it worthwhile to collect bills more promptly, using resources for this purpose that could otherwise have been used to produce goods or provide other services.

- Individuals reduce money holdings to cut wealth losses caused by rising prices lowering the purchasing power of their cash and checking accounts. Getting along with fewer money holdings is inconvenient and misallocates the individual's personal resources of time, energy, and leisure.

- In the extreme case of hyperinflation, inflation of over 100 percent per year, the currency system breaks down and the economy reverts to the far less efficient barter system.

Offsetting these arguments, however, is the fact that many prices are inflexible or "sticky" in the downward direction. Many prices that should fall tend not to do so and instead remain constant. For the price system to operate efficiently, relative prices must change through selected price increases, rather than through the rise of some prices and the fall of others. In reality, the efficiencies of the price system can be gained only by allowing some inflation.

Most laypersons are amazed to discover that economists' measure of the harm done by inflation reflects phenomena of such seemingly little severity. It

---

**Curiosity 2.3:  What Level of Inflation Should We Aim For?**

In the early 1990s, Governor John Crow of the Bank of Canada aimed for 0 percent inflation. Many economists felt that this target was extreme, as did the Canadian government, which did not reappoint Crow. Alan Greenspan, chairman of the Board of Governors of the Federal Reserve System, the U.S. central bank, offered a more flexible target in a statement to the U.S. Committee on Banking, Housing and Urban Affairs in February 1989:

*Maximum sustainable economic growth over time is the U.S. Federal Reserve's ultimate objective. The primary role of monetary policy in the pursuit of this goal is to foster price stability. For all practical purposes, price stability means that expected changes in the average price level are small enough and gradual enough that they do not materially enter business and household financial decisions.*

He did not make the mistake of aiming for an unrealistic inflation level that in any event would be inappropriate, nor did he pin himself down to a specific level, the better to deal with criticism. An inflation rate of 2 or 3 percent seems to be an acceptable target.

seems there are few substantive costs and some benefits to modest inflation. Why, then, do we fear inflation?

For reasons explained at length later in this book, inflation is very quick to rise but very slow to fall. Although a low, steady rate of inflation does not carry significant cost, to bring inflation down to this level a high cost must be paid in the form of a prolonged period of high unemployment. We fear inflation because if it rises above the modest level we are willing to live with, we will have to pay a high unemployment cost to bring it back down.

## 2.6   GDP as Gross Deceptive Product

Correcting GDP for inflation by converting nominal GDP to real GDP avoids one important defect in using GDP to draw conclusions about the state of the economy, but many others remain. GDP is often used to measure an economy's level of well-being and to compare one economy's welfare to another's. A proper perspective must be brought to the analysis of such uses of GDP. Some examples illustrating this follow.

1.  Some things are produced but never sold and so are not included in GDP. A classic example is the work of a homemaker, an omission from GDP that has angered women's rights activists. Another classic example is the case of a lawyer marrying her gardener. Suddenly she does not pay for gardening done on her property, so this service is no longer counted in GDP. A third example is an electrician wiring a plumber's home in return for which the plumber plumbs the electrician's home. Such barter exchanges do not find their way into the GDP measure. Comparisons between countries with different portions of their economy appearing on formal markets are suspect for this reason. National accounts statisticians impute to home owners the rent implicitly paid to themselves (and include this rent as expenditure on housing), thus adjusting for one of the worst of these omissions, but no other imputations are attempted.

2.  Some expenditures are hidden from data gatherers—illegal activities such as selling drugs and prostitution, and underground economic activity such as services provided for unrecorded (and so untaxable) cash transactions. Some people feel that illegal activities provide considerable benefit to society (as evidenced by the fact that so many people are so eager to participate in them), so that their exclusion causes GDP to understate the benefit society derives from annual economic activity.

3.  Some items are included in GDP that do not reflect net benefits to society. The Exxon Valdez oil spill required over $2 billion of cleanup expenditure to bring us back to the prespill state. This expenditure is added into GDP, with no offsetting reduction of GDP to reflect the pollution cost to society. A crime-ridden country spends a lot more on police protection, all added into

GDP, to obtain the same state of security as that enjoyed by a more law-abiding country.

4. Government expenditure on goods and services is valued at cost, despite the fact that the benefit produced by this expenditure could be valued quite differently by the market forces used to value other components of GDP. If entry fees were charged to the Smithsonian museums, for example, the output thereby measured would probably exceed the museums' cost. On the other hand, everybody has a favorite example of what they consider to be wasteful government spending.

5. GDP does not account for nonrenewable natural resources used up in production processes. In Kuwait, for example, because so much of GDP takes the form of oil exports, the GDP measure is misleading as an indicator of the economy's sustainable output level.

6. Cross-country comparisons are rendered difficult by several factors: some countries spend a lot on housing to deal with a harsh climate; leisure-loving societies do not have their leisure valued; exchange rates used to express GDP figures in common currencies do not reflect accurately cost-of-living differences; and differences in income distributions are ignored.

Despite the problems in using GDP to measure an economy's welfare and to compare it to the welfare of other economies, most economists are comfortable using GDP figures for comparisons over time—measuring an economy's growth rate, for example. As long as the size of the underground economy is stable, no dramatic changes in crime and pollution occur, and the fraction of economic activity that appears on markets is relatively constant, growth measures should paint an adequate picture of economic progress.

## Media Illustrations

**Example 1**

**The oil crisis caused U.S. oil companies' overseas profits to shoot up, producing a jump in _____ that could mislead policymakers.**

*Should the blank be filled in with GDP or GNP?*
Income produced by U.S. citizens outside the geographic boundaries of the United States, such as in overseas oil profits, is counted in GNP but not in GDP, so the blank should be filled in with GNP.

*Explain why it could mislead policymakers.*
One reason why the United States switched from GNP to GDP as its measure of output is that GNP movements can arise for reasons unconnected with domestic economic activity, as this example illustrates. Using GNP, policymakers may be misled into thinking that the U.S. economy is thriving and, as a consequence, may undertake inappropriate policy action.

### Example 2

**Suppose, to use a not unrealistic example, a new computer is invented that costs one-fourth of existing computers and performs as well. Now, when GDP is calculated, production of the same number of computers creates only one-fourth as much dollar output, and GDP falls!**

*This suggests that the great technological leaps in computing we have been experiencing have served to decrease GDP, which doesn't seem right. Is it right? If no, why not? If yes, what would you suggest be done to deal with this problem?*

There is no problem here. Nominal GDP falls, but interest should center on real GDP. The fall in the price of computers is built into the GDP deflator, so real GDP should remain unchanged. This ignores changes in the quantity of computers purchased because of the change in relative prices, so the typical bundle used by the national accounts statisticians would have to be changed.

### Example 3

**For the same price, I can now buy a computer with four times as much power. Surely this means that our GDP has increased, but I don't see how: the same number of computers at the same price adds up to the same dollar output!**

*Suppose exactly the same number of computers is being produced, but now they are more powerful. Should GDP increase? Does it actually increase?*

This illustrates the problems national accounts statisticians have with changes in quality. Quality changes are often neglected by the national accounts statistician, but because of the magnitude of recent computer price and quality changes, the case of computers is an exception to this usual practice of neglect. In computing GDP, the statistician values computers in terms of the implicit price of buying computer power equivalent to that of older computers. In this example, the national accounts statistician would impute a new, lower "computing power" price, so although nominal GDP does not change, real GDP would increase to properly reflect the higher quality of output.

### Example 4

**Society needs an index that incorporates the measures of economic welfare that GDP leaves out. If such an index came to replace GDP as the definitive measure of our general economic health, we could begin to look beyond the narrow definition of economic growth when formulating economic policy.**

*What measures of economic welfare does GDP leave out?*

Economic welfare is affected by many things that GDP does not capture adequately: quality changes in goods and services, leisure, income distribution, environmental quality, crime levels, work performed outside the marketplace, underground and illegal activities, climate, natural beauty, and personal freedoms, for example.

## Chapter Summary

- GDP, the amount of final goods and services produced by an economy during a year is equal to the income generated in that economy during that year. It is measured by adding up all expenditures, correcting for inventory change, omitting expenditure on used items, and subtracting imports.

- Nominal GDP is GDP valued at current prices; real GDP is a measure of GDP that has the influence of the price level removed; it is calculated by dividing nominal GDP by a price index. Price indices, such as the GDP deflator or the CPI, measure changes in the overall price level.

- To economists, the main cost of a steady inflation is the resource misallocation it creates by distorting price signals. Increases in inflation are fought tenaciously because it is so costly in terms of unemployment to bring inflation back down to an acceptable level.

- Using GDP to measure social welfare or to compare countries is subject to many criticisms.

## Formula Definitions

- GDP deflator

$$P = \frac{\text{GDP valued at current prices}}{\text{GDP valued at 1992 prices}} \times 100.$$

- $\text{real GDP} = \frac{\text{nominal GDP}}{P} \times 100.$

- consumer price index

$$\text{CPI} = \frac{\text{current cost of typical bundle}}{\text{1992 cost of typical bundle}} \times 100.$$

- inflation = percentage change in CPI = % $\Delta$CPI.

## Media Exercises

1. **The Commerce department announced that it is shifting from 1987 to 1992 as the base year for calculating the nation's real GDP and price index. The new figures will account for changes in consumers' tastes, technological advances and other phenomena.**

a. In the new official figures, will the number for real GDP for 1987 become larger or smaller, or stay the same as it was before the base was changed to 1992?

b. In the new official figures, will the 1992 real GDP number be larger, smaller, or the same as the 1992 nominal GDP?

c. What will the new 1992 price index number be?

d. Will the new 1987 price index number be larger, smaller, or the same as it was before?

e. The announcement claims that consumer tastes and technological advances will be accounted for. How would this be done?

2.  **Homemakers often feel that their work is taken for granted, and advocates in the women's movement argue that the statistical invisibility of homemakers' work has substantive policy implications.**

    What is meant by "statistical invisibility" here?

3.  **A government report traces the economy's stagnation in the last fifteen months to massive declines in spending on commercial construction, while residential construction grew at only half the pace of previous recoveries. Of recent note, however, is a fall in inventories.**

    a. In which category or categories of the national expenditure accounts—$C$, $I$, $G$, or $X$—would these spendings be recorded?

    b. Does the fall in inventories appear in the accounts as a positive or a negative number? Why?

4.  **Note that the percent change in the GDP deflator rather than the more familiar CPI is being used as the measure of inflation. The GDP deflator is a price index that samples _____, not just those paid by _____.**

    a. What does CPI mean?

    b. Fill in the blanks.

5.  **It's amazing. If the government hires a completely useless paper shuffler, GDP increases, but if General Motors hires this person GDP remains unchanged, as it should.**

    Is this correct? Explain your reasoning.

6.  **So all of these apples just rotted because of the producers' storage error! What a waste of GDP!**

    Do these apples get counted into GDP? Explain your reasoning.

7 . **For many people, a rise in the consumer price index is not an accurate measure of how much their cost of living has increased. What about for a nonsmoking vegetarian who walks to work, for example?**

Why might the CPI not be applicable to this person?

8. **Experts keen on the concept of Green GDP have offered a variety of suggestions to make economic statistics more environmentally friendly.**

Give an example of such a suggestion.

9. **It's all very well to make the accounts balance by calling unsold goods "investment in inventory," but what if these unsold goods are perishable?**

   a. What account is being "balanced" by calling unsold goods investment in inventory?

   b. How would you answer the question posed at the end of the clip?

10. **Wilson claimed that a better measure of Turkish national income could be obtained by including money sent back to their families by Turks living and working in Germany, a practice currently ignored in the national accounts.**

Comment on this statement.

11. **Although these seasonally adjusted GDP figures show nothing untoward, a different story is told if we look at the seasonally *un*adjusted figures: real GDP dropped by 8 percent from the fourth to the first quarter!**

   a. What does this information suggest is the normal behavior of unadjusted quarterly GDP when moving from the fourth to the first quarter? How can you tell?

   b. What do you think is causing this?

12. **He argues that business spending on activities such as research and development, management consulting, and employee training, health and safety—now counted as intermediate business services—should be added directly to the investment component of GDP, perhaps placing it in a new subcategory called intangible capital or service capital. His figures suggest this would increase GDP by about $200 billion. He also wants to shift consumer spending on education and on consumer durables from consumption to investment, and calculates that this would involve about $980 billion.**

What do you think would happen to GDP if these proposals were adopted?

13. **And so the debate continues. Some feel that capital gains are undeserved and should be taxed at one hundred percent, whereas others**

believe that doing so would destroy entrepreneurial incentives. As for including them in GDP, that has already been decided by the national accounts statisticians.

Are capital gains included in GDP? Why or why not?

14. **Although GDP casts much light on the functioning of the economy, it has a blind spot for ecological concerns.**

Explain the nature of this blind spot.

15. **He asked the government to explain why the relative weight of food was being reduced in the new price index in spite of recent rapid increases in food prices.**

How would you explain this change?

16. **The government insists that the CPI measures consumer prices, not the cost of living. But don't shoot the CPI—whether bringing good news or bad, it's the best messenger we've got.**

a. What's the difference between the CPI and the cost of living?

b. Which of the two rises by more during inflationary times?

17. **The rapid development of computers makes it difficult to determine how much of the rise in measured prices of computers is due to pure price change or due to the change in quality of the product. It is clear that the cost of obtaining a given amount of computing capability has been falling.**

What does this imply about how rising computer prices should affect the CPI?

18. **The bank estimates that the annual inflation rate in January would have been only 3.5 percent rather than 4.1 percent had it not been for sales tax increases, and that estimate does not include any income tax increases.**

How are sales tax increases incorporated in the price index?

19. **As best as we can tell, responded the central bank governor, the center of the 2 percent inflation target, namely 1 percent, appears to correspond to genuine price stability once the various sources of bias in the CPI are allowed for.**

Give an example of bias in the CPI measure.

20. **The economists who set up GDP also established a number of rather arbitrary conventions to distinguish between the investment and consumption components of GDP. Generally, goods and services purchased by households are treated as consumption expenditures. _____ purchases are**

the major exception to this rule and are included in the investment category of GDP.

Fill in the blank. What is the rationale behind this exception?

21. **The Commerce Department revised its estimate of real GDP to $3.877 trillion, up from the earlier estimate of $3.835 trillion. Before adjusting for inflation, GDP was $4.603 trillion, up from $4.523 trillion.**

What GDP deflators were used for these two calculations?

## Numerical Exercises

N1.  Suppose the sum of consumption, investment, and government spending is $620 billion, where investment includes involuntary inventory accumulation of $2 billion in addition to expenditure on both plant and equipment. Suppose also that government spending includes $5 billion interest payments on the national debt, $5 billion unemployment insurance payments, $10 billion social security payments, $2 billion in salaries to elected politicians, $14 billion in salaries to government employees, and $25 billion expenditure on goods and services produced by the private sector. If we imported $3 billion more than we exported, what is measured GDP?

N2.  Which of the following raise measured GDP by $200?

   a.  A steel company sells $200 of steel to an automobile manufacturer.

   b.  You are hired by the government to shuffle paper uselessly for $200.

   c.  You are hired by General Motors to shuffle paper uselessly for $200.

   d.  An antique dealer sells a $2,000 armoire, pocketing a 10 percent commission.

   e.  You receive a $200 unemployment insurance check from the government.

   f.  Your firm's inventories fall by $200.

   g.  You win $200 at the race track.

N3.  Suppose that inventories fall by $2 billion, consumption increases by $8 billion, unemployment insurance payments decline by $4 billion, and imports rise by $1 billion. By how much should measured GDP change?

N4.  If a typical market basket of goods and services cost $150 in 1992, the base year, and $180 in 1995, what is the price index in 1995?

N5.  Suppose hamburgers cost $1.50 last year and $1.65 this year, and the overall price index (the GDP deflator) rose from 125 last year to 150 this year.

a. How much will 1,000 hamburgers contribute to this year's nominal GDP?

b. How much will 1,000 hamburgers contribute to this year's real GDP?

c. What was the rate of inflation during the past year, as measured using the GDP deflator?

N6.  If in 1994 nominal GDP is 600 and real GDP is 500, what is the price index for 1994?

N7.  Suppose the price index is 130 and a typical basket of goods and services costs $520. What would this typical basket have cost in the base year?

N8.  If the CPI changes from 110 in 1993 to 120 in 1994, what is the rate of inflation?

N9.  Suppose nominal GDP is $566 billion in 1992, $600 billion in 1993, and $642 billion in 1994. If 1992 is the base year, the price index is 105 in 1993, and real growth in 1994 is 3 percent, what is the price index in 1994?

N10. Suppose the CPI is 100 in 1992, its base year. In 1993 and 1994, it is equal to 112 and 120, respectively. During 1995 the economy experienced an inflation of 10 percent.

a. What rate of inflation characterized this economy during 1994?

b. If national consumption in 1994 was $300 billion in 1994 dollars, what is this consumption expressed in 1992 dollars?

c. What is the 1995 value of the CPI?

N11. Suppose that in 1992 the price and quantity of energy were 1.00 and 50, respectively, and that in 1993 they were 1.04 and 60, respectively. In 1992 the price and quantity of all other goods and services were 1.10 and 40, respectively, and in 1993 they were 1.20 and 30, respectively.

a. Using 1992 as a base year, what is the CPI in 1993?

b. What is the rate of inflation between 1992 and 1993?

N12. Suppose the CPI is calculated assuming that one-quarter of expenses is for health, transportation, and entertainment, and three-quarters is for all other items. When the prices of items in the first category double and the prices of all other items quadruple, then does the CPI change overstate, understate, or measure accurately the change in the cost of living?

N13. If GDP increases in nominal terms from $600 billion in 1994 to $663 billion in 1996, and if the price index (1992 = 100) rises from 120 to 130, how much real growth (in 1992 dollars) in GDP occurred between 1994 and 1996?

N14. Suppose that last year the price index (base year 1992) was 119 and income was $900 billion. The corresponding numbers for this year are 123 and $950 billion.

a. What is this year's income expressed in 1992 dollars?

b. What was inflation this year?

c. What was real growth this year?

## Appendix 2.1:  Measuring GDP by Adding Up Incomes

Because with only a few exceptions every dollar of output produced makes its way into someone's pocket as income, it should be possible to measure GDP by adding up all incomes and making a few adjustments for the exceptions. This is the thinking that lies behind the adding-up-incomes approach to measuring GDP, an alternative to the adding-up-expenditures approach.

Incomes are placed into five categories: compensation of employees (about 74 percent of incomes); proprietors' incomes (about 8.5 percent); corporate profits (about 8 percent); interest incomes (about 9 percent); and rental incomes (about 0.1 percent). Only interest payments associated with productive activity are included; interest on government bonds and consumer loans are not included. These incomes are added and then the following four adjustments are made:

1. *Depreciation.*  Firms set aside earnings to cover depreciation of their buildings and equipment; this part of output produced never makes it into anyone's pocket as income and so must be added on.

2. *Indirect taxes.*  Firms may pay indirect taxes to the government, such as sales taxes. This part of output produced does not make it into anyone's pocket as income, so it must also be added on.

3. *Subsidies.*  Some firms might receive subsidies from the government, in which case the income they earn is overstated. Some of their income does not correspond to output produced, so subsidies must be subtracted.

4. *Foreign production.*  Income received from foreign sources must be subtracted because it does not correspond to domestic production. Income paid to foreigners must be added.

Table 2A.1 presents an example of how GDP is measured using this approach. The statistical discrepancy item is included to force this means of

**Table 2A.1**   GDP by adding income payments, 1994 ($ billions)

| | | |
|---|---:|---:|
| Employee compensation | 4,223 | |
| Proprietors' incomes | 478 | |
| Corporate profits | 587 | |
| Rental income | 122 | |
| Net interest | 404 | |
| **National income** | | **5,814** |
| plus: indirect taxes | 626 | |
| less: subsidies | 18 | |
| plus: statistical discrepancy | −1 | |
| **Net national product** | | **6,421** |
| plus: depreciation | 826 | |
| **Gross national product (GNP)** | | **7,247** |
| plus: income payments to foreigners | 215 | |
| less: income payments from foreigners | 208 | |
| **Gross Domestic Product (GDP)** | | **7,254** |

Source: *Survey of Current Business*, August 1996.

measuring GDP to produce the same number as the adding-up-expenditures measure shown in table 2.1. Some countries, Canada for example, believe that these means of measuring GDP are equally reliable and so produce their official GDP measure by averaging the two measures. This is accomplished by taking half of the difference between the two measures, calling it a statistical discrepancy, adding it to the smaller number, and subtracting it from the larger number. The United States feels that the adding-up-expenditures method is unequivocally superior and so uses it alone to produce its GDP measure.

# 3    Unemployment

During the 1970s and 1980s, the U.S. economy was remarkably successful in creating jobs for new entrants to the workforce, entrants whose numbers were exceptionally high—baby boomers were coming of age, women were leaving the home to work, and immigration had grown. This increase in U.S. employment is particularly impressive when contrasted with the minimal employment growth that characterized Europe during the same period. The strong growth in employment was complemented by a good performance on the unemployment front. With the exception of the recessions of the early 1980s and early 1990s, unemployment in the United States, in sharp contrast to Europe, remained at reasonable levels, between five and six percent. However, this relationship between employment growth and unemployment performance need not necessarily hold. During this period, Canada was even more successful on a per capita basis than the United States in creating jobs, but it nonetheless experienced a growing unemployment rate. One purpose of this chapter is to explain why employment creation and the unemployment rate are not as closely related as might be expected.

Unemployment is implicitly if not explicitly a major topic of several later chapters, most notably chapter 4, which explains how government spending policy affects employment, and chapter 12, in which the infamous trade-off between inflation and unemployment is discussed. The content of these later chapters will be enhanced by the perspective on unemployment provided by this chapter.

> **Upon completion of this chapter you should**
>
> - be aware that growth in employment reduces the rate of unemployment only if it exceeds the growth in the number of people wanting a job;
> - know what is meant by the "natural" rate of unemployment; and
> - understand how the way in which unemployment is measured can explain paradoxical movements in the measured unemployment rate.

## 3.1   Defining and Measuring Unemployment

The unemployment rate is defined as the number of *unemployed*, people who want to have a job but do not have one, expressed as a percentage of the *labor force*, the total number of people over age fifteen who want to have a job:

$$\text{unemployment rate} = \frac{\text{unemployed}}{\text{labor force}}.$$

Several qualifications are incorporated in the official definition of unemployed such as that it refers to the "noninstitutionalized" (i.e., people not in prisons or

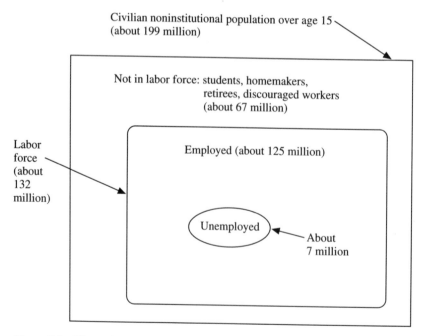

**Figure 3.1**   Illustrating unemployment concepts
Source: *Monthly Labor Review*, July 1996.

---

**Curiosity 3.1:   How Is Unemployment Measured?**

Each month about 1,500 employees of the Bureau of the Census, on behalf of the Bureau of Labor Statistics (BLS), interview 59,500 households. Each civilian household member over age fifteen is first asked if he or she did any work for pay during the last week. If the answer is yes, even if he or she worked just for an hour, that person is counted as employed. Those answering no are asked if they worked fifteen hours or more without pay for a family business or farm, and if the answer is yes, they are counted as employed. Those answering no are asked if they are waiting to begin a confirmed job or to be called back to a job from which they have been laid off; if the answer is yes, they are counted as unemployed. Those answering no are asked if they have been doing anything to find work during the last four weeks, and if they answer yes, they are counted as unemployed. The others, those who have not been looking for work (because they are students or homemakers, for example, or because they have given up hope of finding a job) are classified as not in the labor force. The official unemployment rate is calculated as the ratio of the unemployed to the sum of the employed and unemployed. To its credit, the BLS also publishes a measure called the total unemployment rate, which includes as unemployed those wanting work but too discouraged to look for it, and those wanting full-time work but only able to obtain part-time work. This measure is typically about two percentage points higher than the official rate of unemployment, a difference that widens during recessions.

---

mental institutions) civilian population over the age of fifteen, but such qualifications do not affect its basic meaning. Figure 3.1 shows how these concepts are related.

The measured rate of unemployment can be an underestimate or an overestimate of this "true" unemployment rate. Underestimation occurs because part-time workers are counted as employed, even if they really want full-time work. Overestimation occurs when people who do not want work pretend to want work in order to collect unemployment benefits. The biggest problem with measuring unemployment, however, is the discouraged/encouraged worker phenomenon.

The unemployed are people who want a job but don't have one. The main problem in measuring unemployment is finding some reliable way of determining who really wants a job. For lack of a better way, this is done by classifying as unemployed only those actively looking for work. Thus, to be counted officially as unemployed someone must be without work and looking for work.

But what about people without work who have looked long and hard for jobs and have become convinced that there are no jobs out there for them? They become discouraged in their search and stop looking. Suddenly, these *discouraged workers* are no longer counted as being in the labor force, and the measured unemployment rate falls. Many would claim that this results in an underestimate of the "true" rate of unemployment.

This is not the only problem caused by the discouraged worker phenomenon. Whenever the economy recovers from a recession, discouraged workers notice that times are better and that acquaintances have obtained jobs, signs that encourage them once again to look for work. These *encouraged workers* suddenly become counted as unemployed, causing a paradoxical rise in unemployment just when income and employment are increasing.

## 3.2   The Employment/Unemployment Connection

One would think that an increase in employment must surely mean a decrease in unemployment, but we have just seen that movements of discouraged/encouraged workers out of and into the labor force can cause unemployment to change in a direction opposite to that in which employment is changing. This is a special case of a more general phenomenon. Each year thousands of new jobs are created, but also each year thousands of new members of the labor force appear, wanting these jobs. What happens to the unemployment rate depends on the relative magnitudes of the growth in jobs and the growth in the labor force.

The creation of jobs is determined by the demand for the goods and services we produce, which in turn is affected by prices charged and by government policies, among other things. The growth of the labor force is affected by population growth and changes in the *participation rate*—the percentage of the civilian noninstitutional population over age fifteen in the labor force, currently about 67 percent:

$$\text{participation rate} = \frac{\text{labor force}}{\text{population over age 15}}.$$

This dimension of unemployment is of particular interest because it is so often overlooked in discussions of unemployment.

The role of population growth is predictable. One can look ahead and see a wave of baby boomers leaving school, and the number of immigrants is a known quantity. The role of changes in the participation rate is not so easy to predict, however. The women's liberation movement was one factor leading to annual increases in the participation rate for women (called the *female participation rate*), increases which were difficult to predict with any accuracy. During the last thirty years the female participation rate has increased from 40 percent to about 58 percent. (The male participation rate is about 75 percent.) Perhaps most difficult to predict are changes in the participation rate due to the discouraged/encouraged worker phenomenon.

## 3.3   What Is Full Employment?

To an economist, full employment does not mean a zero unemployment rate. Zero unemployment is not realistic, for several reasons. First, at any point in

---

**Curiosity 3.2:   Why Is Unemployment So High in Europe?**

Unemployment in Europe is about twice that of the United States. The most persuasive explanations claim that this is due to institutional differences, such as higher minimum wages, more unionization, generous unemployment benefits, and various government regulations. Layoff regulations and plant-closing laws, for example, make it very expensive for a firm to reduce its work force, so managers are reluctant to hire new workers, choosing instead to meet demand fluctuations by adjusting overtime. Laws forcing Sunday closures and limitations on shop hours mean that fewer employees are hired. At one university, fire regulations require that a staff member be present on each floor of the library, making it too expensive to keep extended hours. In short, it seems the natural rate of unemployment is higher in Europe because of institutional phenomena.

---

time some people are temporarily unemployed because they are in the midst of changing jobs or looking for an initial job. The unemployment corresponding to this ongoing process of improving the occupational and geographical match of workers and jobs is referred to as *frictional unemployment*.

Second, many people may be unemployed because technological progress has made their skills obsolete or because new trade agreements have changed the nature of what is produced domestically. They must retrain to obtain jobs. Both frictional unemployment and this *structural unemployment* are healthy because they show that the economy is responding to the forces of change. Some workers are switching jobs to produce the goods and services that the changing tastes of society are demanding or to find jobs they will be happier doing. Other workers are retraining to keep up with the technological innovations that improve productivity. Part of frictional and structural unemployment, however, reflects demographic factors such as the increased participation rate of women and the young. Many of the former need more training, having spent time as homemakers, and the latter are both unskilled and at a stage in life when switching jobs is more common.

The third reason that zero unemployment is unrealistic is that institutional phenomena may affect unemployment. For example, minimum wage laws may make it too costly to hire extra labor; generous unemployment benefits may make it easier to stay or become unemployed; government regulations, such as restrictions on how many hours per day a store can be open, may decrease job availability; and there may be racial or gender discrimination.

Unemployment arising from these three causes creates the *natural rate of unemployment* (NRU), what economists mean by "full employment." This rate of unemployment is thought currently to be about 6 percent, but is not a fixed or known number. The NRU varies across countries and over time within a single country. It is affected, for example, by the current pace of technological change, the rate at which public tastes change, participation rate changes, and government policies affecting labor mobility, job vacancy information, and

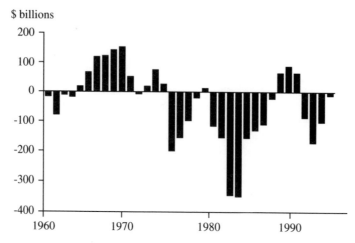

**Figure 3.2**   Output gap
Okun's Law (see curiosity 3.3) measured the output gap. Negative numbers mark a loss of actual output relative to potential output; positive numbers mark periods of boom when the economy produced more than its "full-employment" output.
Source: *Economic Report of the President*, 1995.

labor retraining programs. The fact that the U.S. economy has recently been experiencing an unemployment rate below 6 percent with no apparent inflationary tendency suggests that the 6 percent estimate of the NRU is now too high.

At any point in time, an economy's unemployment rate can be below or above its natural rate of unemployment, as the economy cycles through booms and recessions. Such cycles are called *business cycles*, with the economy viewed as moving through four stages: an expansionary stage, a peak, a contractionary stage, and a trough. Loosely speaking, we could consider the economy to be in a recession whenever the unemployment rate is above the NRU and in a boom whenever the unemployment rate is below the NRU. Much macroeconomic theorizing is concerned with generating an explanation for the business-cycle phenomenon. Unemployment above the NRU is referred to as *cyclical* unemployment, which is often used to measure the cost to society of unemployment.

## 3.4   The Cost of Unemployment

When operating at full employment (the natural rate of unemployment), the economy is said to be producing its *potential* GDP. Figure 3.2 shows the difference between actual output and the potential level of output. This difference, called the *output gap*, can be either positive or negative, depending on whether the economy is in a boom or a recession. During a recession, when unemployment exceeds the natural rate, the gap reflects output lost forever because of a

---

**Curiosity 3.3:   What Is Okun's Law?**

A rule of thumb called Okun's Law is used to translate unemployment greater than the natural rate into an output gap and thereby to measure the cost to society of excessive unemployment. An extra percentage point of unemployment above the natural rate corresponds to an output gap of 2.5 percentage points of GDP. This implies, for example, that if the NRU is 6 percent, an unemployment rate of 8 percent gives rise to an output gap of 5 percent of GDP, or about $300 billion!

It may seem odd that an extra 1 percent of unemployment is associated with *more* than a 1 percent change in GDP. This happens because firms find it more profitable to meet demand fluctuations by varying the workload of current workers rather than by varying the number of employees. Firms have a tendency to hoard labor as the economy moves into a recession, electing not to lay off as many workers as the drop in their sales would dictate, mainly because they do not want to risk losing workers whose skills and experience make them of particular value to their firm when the recession ends and because it allows them to avoid the costs of hiring and training new workers. Consequently, output falls by more than unemployment rises when the economy moves into a recession; during a recovery, output can increase by making fuller use of the hoarded labor. Furthermore, when hoarded labor no longer exists, firms meet many fluctuations in demand by varying overtime, rather than by varying the number of employees. This also reflects rational behavior on the part of the firm: because existing employees are more productive than new employees, hiring and training costs can be avoided, fringe benefit costs are unaffected, and layoff costs are not incurred.

---

failure to operate at full employment, and is thus a popular way of measuring the cost of unemployment to society. Notice in figure 3.2 how large this loss was in 1982 and 1983 when unemployment was so high. Notice also how figure 3.2 shows clearly the cyclical behavior of the economy, something macroeconomists are keen to explain.

Some claim that the output gap measure of the cost of unemployment is too facile in that it does not account for the human suffering that unemployment also entails. Although true, the failure of the unemployment measure to capture human suffering is not easily remedied. In contrast to twenty years ago, a much greater fraction of the unemployed are now members of the peripheral work-force—irregular or part-time participants in the job market, rather than skilled adult workers who are the sole breadwinners of their family.

---

## Media Illustrations

### *Example 1*
**The unemployment rate moved up to 7.8 percent (seasonally adjusted) in May from April's 7.7 percent, but not because of job losses. Indeed, employment rose by a big 0.6 percent or 700,000 during the month. However, that wasn't as big as ...**

*Why would the unemployment rate be seasonally adjusted?*
Seasonal adjustment removes changes that habitually occur during that month in order to see if there is any novel change in the unemployment figure.

*Complete the last sentence:*
... as big as the growth in the labor force—the number of people looking for a job.

### Example 2
**Employment is projected to revive at 3.5 percent per year. Because the trend rate of increase in the labor force is just less than 2 percent per year, that would seem to produce a healthy decline in the unemployment rate of 1.5 percentage points per year. Unfortunately, matters are not so simple because, as is by now well understood, the normal official unemployment rate does not include all the sources of slack in the labor market.**

*How has the 1.5 percentage point decrease in the unemployment rate been calculated?*
The difference between the 3.5 percent growth in employment and the 2 percent growth in the labor force produces the 1.5 percentage point fall in the unemployment rate.

*Give an example of a "source of slack," referred to in the clip, and explain what impact it would have on the 1.5 percentage point figure.*
The discouraged/encouraged worker phenomenon is relevant here. The recovery may cause some discouraged workers to become encouraged workers and begin looking for work, causing the actual growth of the labor force to exceed its trend rate of 2 percent. This would decrease the 1.5 percentage point figure.

### Example 3
**A closer look at the numbers shows little to cheer about. The unemployment rate fell, but not because more jobs were created, as implied by the press release, which called it "good news" and a "good trend."**

*How could the unemployment rate fall if more jobs weren't created?*
Job seekers could have become discouraged and stopped looking for work. This increase in the number of discouraged workers could have decreased the unemployment rate.

*Why might the author of this clipping feel that there is "little to cheer about"?*
It is difficult to view favorably a situation in which job prospects are so poor that people have given up even looking for a job.

### Example 4
**In a typical recession, the unemployment rate moves up sharply, although it can take a few months for this to happen because employers are loath to lay off people until they're sure sales are really down. Once the recession is over, the rate usually moves down again, although again there is a lag as employers don't start hiring until they re confident of the recovery.**

*Explain why it would be in employers' long-term interest to "hoard labor"—not to lay off as many workers as short-term considerations would suggest.*

Firms are reluctant to lay off workers because they are afraid that these skilled and experienced workers may not be available after the recession. It is costly to hire and train new workers.

*Use the concept of labor hoarding to offer an alternative explanation for why the unemployment rate is slow to move down after the recession ends.*

When the recession ends and sales increase, the extra labor hoarded by the firm can meet the increased demand for the firm's output. There is no need for the firm to hire extra labor until demand for its output increases substantially.

## Chapter Summary

- The unemployment measure is affected both by the number of new jobs created and by the number of people joining the labor force to seek jobs.

- Measured unemployment is for some reasons an underestimate and for other reasons an overestimate of the "true" rate of unemployment.

- The discouraged/encouraged worker phenomenon can explain paradoxical movements in measured unemployment.

- Full employment corresponds to the natural rate of unemployment (NRU), measured as the sum of frictional, structural, and institutionally induced unemployment.

- The output gap, often calculated by a rule of thumb called Okun's Law, is used to measure the cost of unemployment to society.

## Formula Definitions

- unemployment rate $= \dfrac{\text{unemployed}}{\text{labor force}}$.

- participation rate $= \dfrac{\text{labor force}}{\text{population over age 15}}$.

- Okun's law: output gap as % of GDP $= 2.5(\text{unemployment rate} - \text{NRU})$.

## Media Exercises

1. **In any economic slowdown, the unemployment rate rises, first and foremost, because employment growth slows or actually goes into negative**

territory. How high the jobless rate goes, however, can also depend very crucially on exactly how fast the labor force decides to grow.

Explain how labor-force growth plays a role here.

2. **Labor-force growth is the great unknown in forecasting unemployment rates because people's reactions are very difficult to gauge. For example, during recessions, will people not bother looking for a job because of the difficulty in finding one, or will they look even harder because of the need for additional family income when wage increases are coming in below the inflation rate?**

   a. Explain how labor-force growth influences the unemployment rate.

   b. What impact will the two cited examples have on the measured unemployment rate?

3. **This council—an advisory body with business and union representation—decided to rethink the concept of unemployment. It was intent on unraveling the paradox of substantial new job creation coupled with a high and largely unyielding jobless rate.**

   How could this paradox come about?

4. **Labor-force growth has, in the past, tended to reflect the general economic situation. In almost all postwar recession years, the participation rate fell slightly, with the result that . . .**

   Complete this clipping by explaining how this phenomenon would affect the level of unemployment as the economy moved into recession.

5. **In fairness, the strong job growth for women occurred partly because so many more women were available to work. The female participation rate rose to 55 percent from just 45 percent a decade earlier. That translated into an extra 17 million women in the labor force. In contrast, the male participation rate fell during the period, to 76 percent from 77 percent, which meant that there were only an extra ten million men in the labor force.**

   a. What is meant by the female participation rate?

   b. If the male participation rate fell, why are there more men in the labor force?

   c. Can we conclude from this information that the female unemployment rate must have fallen relative to the male unemployment rate? Why or why not?

6. **Pretty sluggish job growth during the rest of the year is likely to keep the unemployment rate stagnant, particularly as the recent increases**

in employment will probably encourage more people to join the labor force.**

    a. Why would the recent increase in employment encourage people to join the labor force?

    b. How will this affect the unemployment rate?

    c. What terminology do economists use to refer to this phenomenon?

7. **The reduction in the unemployment rate projected to take place as a result of the budget proposals is expected to be moderated as participation rates continue to _____ .**

Fill in the blank in this clip and explain your rationale.

8. **This is the critical assumption in the projection. If participation rates turn out to be _____ , the unemployment rate will be higher and vice versa for participation rates.**

Fill in the blanks in this clip and explain your rationale.

9. **We consider it entirely possible that an encouraged worker effect will set in when employment picks up, which could lead to a paradoxical rise in the unemployment rate.**

Explain how this paradox could come about.

10. **Our jobless rate fell last month to its lowest level in three years. But if you think it's a sign that the economy is suddenly moving up, look again.**

Why wouldn't a fall in the unemployment rate be a sign that the economy is moving up?

11. **More job losses in the manufacturing sector helped pull employment down by 390,000 in November. Only the fact that this seasonally adjusted employment drop was matched by a _____ in the labor force kept the unemployment rate steady.**

Fill in the blank and explain your rationale.

12. **Unemployment insurance may increase the incidence and length of joblessness and has certain inflationary attributes, but these drawbacks are outweighed by the positive social factors, according to a new study published by the Brookings Institution.**

How does unemployment insurance

    a. increase the incidence of joblessness, and

    b. increase the length of joblessness?

13. **There are some subsidy features to unemployment insurance, primarily for jobs that are unattractive or that offer seasonal or unstable employment. Without this subsidy, paid mainly by the government, many unskilled jobs would go begging.**

    a. Explain how unemployment insurance subsidizes certain kinds of jobs.

    b. What do you think would happen to wages paid for these jobs if unemployment insurance ceased to exist?

14. **He is critical of the flat rate contribution schedule for unemployment insurance, which he says acts as a subsidy from companies with more stable employment levels to those which frequently lay off workers. This subsidy encourages firms to rely more heavily on layoffs of workers than other methods of adjusting to fluctuations in the demand for their output. He suggests that the excessive and inefficient bias toward layoffs in the system could be eliminated by adopting a system of experience rating, as is done in some states: a company's contributions would be related to the amount of benefits drawn by its employees in the past.**

    a. Does this subsidy mean that firms prone to laying off employees are paying lower wages than they would otherwise? Explain why or why not.

    b. Would adoption of experience rating cause unemployment to become more or less sensitive to recessions? Explain.

15. **Nationally, the monthly survey of U.S. households found 387,000 more people at work in February than in January, but many of the new jobs were only part-time, the Labor Department reported.**

    a. Does the creation of part-time jobs affect unemployment in the same way as the creation of full-time jobs?

    b. What can you say about the unemployment rate from this information?

16. **Despite the changed composition of the jobless ranks, today's high unemployment level is portrayed by some as a disaster of Great Depression proportions.**

    Of what relevance here is the changed composition of the jobless?

17. **Three percent real GDP growth is just about enough to keep the unemployment rate constant.**

    Why wouldn't a zero growth rate keep unemployment constant?

18. **Unfortunately, the work force in the 1990s is projected to expand much more slowly in coming years both because the population is not increasing as rapidly and because it is unlikely that the participation of women will keep _____.**

a. Why would a slower growth in the work force be regarded as unfortunate? Why might some view it as fortunate? Hint: Compare short- and long-term implications.

b. Fill in the blank.

19. **The Bureau of Labor Statistics said Friday that the country lost 190,000 jobs in August and noted that the unemployment rate would be more than two percentage points higher than a year ago if there weren't so many …**

Complete this clipping.

20. **Even if employment continues to climb, the jobless rate will likely stay around its current level for the balance of this year, Cramer said. That's because …**

Complete this clipping.

21. **If the participation rate had remained steady instead of falling since the recession began, the unemployment rate would be 1.8 percent _____ .**

Fill in the blank and explain your reasoning.

22. **The number of jobs created, rather than the unemployment rate, gives a more timely indication of the state of the economy.**

Explain what thinking must lie behind this claim.

23. **Job creation in October was much more robust than most forecasters had predicted, but the number of people either working or looking for work increased even more sharply.**

a. What is happening to the unemployment rate?

b. Should this news be viewed as positive or negative? Why?

24. **And so we find ourselves in the strange situation in which employment is rising and at the same time unemployment is rising.**

Explain this phenomenon.

## Numerical Exercises

N1. If the population over age fifteen is 160 million, the number of discouraged workers is 10 million, the labor force is 110 million, and total employment is 90 million, what is the measured unemployment rate?

N2. Suppose the population over age fifteen is 150 million, the number of discouraged workers is 5 million, the participation rate is 70 percent, and the unemployment rate is 10 percent. How many officially unemployed are there?

N3. Suppose the population over age fifteen is 140 million, the participation rate is 60 percent, and the unemployment rate is 10 percent. If the number of discouraged workers increases by 2 million, what does the unemployment rate become?

N4. Suppose the population over age fifteen is 150 million, the number of discouraged workers is 5 million, the unemployment rate is 10 percent, and there are 90 million employed. What is the participation rate?

N5. Suppose frictional unemployment is 1 percent, structural unemployment is 2 percent, cyclical unemployment is 3 percent, and unemployment due to unemployment insurance and minimum wage legislation is 4 percent. Based on this information, what is the NRU?

N6. Suppose the population over age fifteen is 25 million, the participation rate is 80 percent, the number of discouraged workers is one million, the number of people with full-time jobs is 16 million, and the number of people with part-time jobs is two million. What is the measured unemployment rate?

N7. Suppose the population over age fifteen is 150 million, the participation rate is 60 percent, and the unemployment rate is 10 percent. If the number of encouraged workers increases by 2 million, what does the participation rate become?

N8. Suppose the population over age fifteen is 150 million, the participation rate is 60 percent, and the unemployment rate is 10 percent. If the labor force grows by 3 percent and employment grows by 2 percent, what does the unemployment rate become?

N9. Suppose GDP is $900 billion and current unemployment is 10.5 percent. What would GDP be if unemployment were only 7.5 percent? Hint: Use Okun's Law.

# 4    The Keynesian Approach

With the publication of *The General Theory of Employment, Interest and Money* in the midst of the Great Depression, John Maynard Keynes revolutionized macroeconomic thinking in many ways. He introduced a model he thought capable of explaining the existence of prolonged unemployment, something that previous macroeconomic models did not do. He stimulated research on fundamental economic relationships, such as the consumption function (how consumption demand responds to income changes), heretofore overlooked. He argued persuasively for the need for government intervention in the operation of the economy, an issue that is still contentious, and he placed the level of aggregate demand for goods and services at center stage of macroeconomic analysis, a position it has maintained to this day, although now in tandem with other macroeconomic variables. Appendix 4.1 at the end of this chapter offers some perspective on Keynes's contribution by describing the classical approach to macroeconomics—the school of macroeconomic thought dominant prior to publication of Keynes's theory.

The purpose of this chapter is to examine the role played by aggregate demand for goods and services in determining the economy's level of national income, and thus to explain the heart of the Keynesian approach to macroeconomics

---

**Upon completion of this chapter you should**

- understand the central role played by aggregate demand in determining the level of national income;
- be comfortable with the concept of the multiplier and so understand why a change in aggregate demand of $x$ dollars changes national income by a multiple of $x$ dollars; and
- know why changes in inventories can be used as a forecasting device.

---

## 4.1   Aggregate Demand

The general idea behind the Keynesian approach is that natural forces cause our output of goods and services (i.e., our national income) to match the level of aggregate demand for our goods and services. This match is called an *equilibrium* because at such a position there are no pressures for change. (Further discussion on the equilibrium concept can be found in appendix A at the end of this book.) The automatic movement of income to match aggregate demand has two implications. First, to predict the level of national income, we should look at what is happening to the level of aggregate demand for our goods and services. Second, to influence the level of national income, we can change any component of domestic aggregate demand over which we have control.

Keynes viewed aggregate demand for goods and services as being comprised of four major types of demand: demand by consumers for things such as toys and haircuts, referred to as $C$ for consumption demand; demand by business firms for things such as factories, machinery, and delivery trucks, referred to as $I$ for investment demand; demand by the government for things such as hospitals and armies, referred to as $G$ for government demand; and demand by foreigners for goods we send abroad, such as wheat and lumber, referred to as $X$ for exports. Demand in each of these sectors includes demand for imported as well as domestic goods and services. To obtain what is important for the Keynesian view, aggregate demand for *domestically produced* goods and services, imports must be subtracted from the sum of $C$, $I$, $G$, and $X$. Textbooks often use a circular-flow diagram to illustrate how these components of aggregate demand contribute to equilibrium. For those interested, this diagram (figure 4A.1) is presented in appendix 4.2 at the end of this chapter.

Keynes split demand up into these different categories for a good reason. He believed that it would be easier for economists to analyze these categories of demand separately rather than as an aggregate. For example, the factors that determine the level of consumption demand are different from those that determine investment demand; recognizing this difference should provide better insight into the operation of the economy and how it might respond to policy.

---

**Curiosity 4.1:   What about Unwanted Investment in Inventories?**

Keynes specified the four demands—consumption demand, investment demand, government demand, and exports—as being what sectors of the economy—consumers, business firms, the government, and foreigners—would *want* to purchase during any year. "Investment in inventories," introduced in chapter 2, does not reflect desired demand and so is not included in these demand categories. Inventory investment is merely an accounting device, devised by the national accounts statisticians to allow the adding up of demands to produce a measure of national output by reconciling what demanders bought with what producers made.

---

Much of the historical development of the Keynesian approach has taken the form of investigating in detail the economic forces that determine demand in one of these sectors and then seeing what implications this analysis has for the operation of the economy as a whole.

One of the simplest of Keynes's insights is that the level of consumption demand is affected by the level of income. As income increases, so does consumption, but not by as much because income earners save some income and set aside some to pay taxes. Economists usually capture this by specifying that consumption is a function of after-tax (or *disposable*) income. The slope of this function is referred to as the *marginal propensity to consume* (MPC). The MPC tells us what fraction of an additional dollar of disposable income will be spent on consumption. The fraction not spent on consumption is called the *marginal propensity to save*. This *consumption function*, as it is known, is a major ingredient in the Keynesian explanation of the determination of income. Much more complicated variants of the consumption function have been developed, involving additional explanatory variables, but this simple version suffices to illustrate the Keynesian approach. The other three categories of aggregate demand also have functions that explain their levels, but for now we will ignore these functions and assume the categories are fixed at constant levels.

---

## 4.2   Determining National Income

Keynes believed that natural forces operating in the economy cause the level of aggregate supply of domestically produced goods and services (AS), also known as national income, to move in order to meet the level of aggregate demand for goods and services (AD). What are these forces?

Suppose that aggregate demand exceeds national income/output, a situation referred to as *excess aggregate demand*. In this case, the output produced by the economy is not enough to satisfy all the aggregate demand, so that firms producing and selling goods should experience a fall in inventories or a loss in sales from lack of inventories. Firms providing services should discover that some customers must be turned away. Profit maximizing firms could react to this in one of three main ways:

1. They could increase output to meet the higher level of aggregate demand by using existing employees and equipment more productively, by hiring additional workers, or by increasing workers' hours. Such firms are *quantity adjusters*.

2. They could increase prices to induce people to decrease aggregate demand to the level of output that is being produced. Such firms are *price adjusters*.

3. They could adopt some combination of the two options above, adjusting both price and quantity at the same time.

Let us look at each of these options in turn.

**Quantity Adjusting.**   By increasing production the firm directly addresses the problem of shrinking inventories or lost business. This is an especially appealing strategy if the firm is currently operating at less than full capacity, so that increasing output can be accomplished at little additional cost.

**Price Adjusting.**   This option is forced on a firm when it is operating at full capacity, so that it is not possible to increase output.

**Adjusting Both Price and Quantity.**   It could be that the firm is not operating at full capacity, so that it is possible to increase output, but it is operating close to full capacity, so that output can be increased only by incurring a higher per unit cost than the prevailing price. For example, workers may have to be paid overtime wages that are higher than normal wages, or new, inexperienced (and therefore less productive) workers may have to be hired. In this case, a firm can increase output only if the price also increases, giving rise to a combination of price and quantity adjustments.

This discussion of quantity and price adjusting suggests that if firms are operating well below full capacity, so that output can be increased without raising unit cost, then quantity adjustment is appropriate. If firms are operating at full capacity, so that output cannot be increased, price adjustment is appropriate. If the firm is at an intermediate stage, in which output increases raise unit costs, both prices and output should be increased to maximize profit.

In the most simplified version of the Keynesian analysis, which we adopt in this chapter, the economy is specified to be operating well below full capacity, so that quantity adjustment occurs and thus national income/output moves to equate itself to aggregate demand.

A similar result occurs when national income exceeds aggregate demand. In this case, not all of the output produced by the economy is bought, so that firms producing and selling goods should experience a buildup of inventories, and firms providing services should discover that some employees are often idle. Profit-maximizing firms can react to this in one of three main ways:

1. Adjust quantity: lay off workers or cut back workers' hours to stop producing the unwanted output.

2. Adjust price: decrease prices to induce people to increase aggregate demand by enough to buy all of the output being produced.

3. Adopt some combination of the two options above, adjusting both price and quantity at the same time.

Quantity adjustment is the most natural reaction because it directly attacks the inventory buildup and the problem of idle employees. Cutting price is not likely to be a profit-maximizing move, even in tandem with output reduction, unless costs fall as well. The most likely scenario is that national income/output will adjust to match aggregate demand. As noted above, this is the heart of the Keynesian analysis: aggregate demand is the driving force that determines the level of national income.

## 4.3    The Multiplier

The policy conclusion of this Keynesian analysis is that by increasing aggregate demand the government can increase national income. An obvious way of doing this is by increasing government spending, $G$.

Suppose $G$ is increased by $8 billion, creating an excess demand of $8 billion. Inventories fall and business is turned away, signaling to producers that there is excess demand, so they react by increasing output/income. Suppose national output/income increases by $8 billion. Will this stop the forces pushing up output/income?

Although the initial excess demand of $8 billion has now been met by $8 billion of extra output, and it would seem that the forces pushing up income/output would be eliminated, this is not so. This $8 billion increase in income itself creates extra demand. Consumers will want to increase consumption demand now that their income is higher, reopening the excess demand gap. This renews the forces that stimulate the economy, causing this process to repeat itself and thus leading to an ever larger income level.

This process is outlined in figure 4.1, where the notation should be obvious. (For example, ↑ agg D for g & s stands for an increase in aggregate demand for goods and services.) For those interested, this process can also be illustrated on a classic macroeconomic diagram, the 45° line diagram, shown in appendix 4.3 at the end of this chapter.

At first glance it seems as though the process outlined in figure 4.1 could go on forever, but it does not. Although the excess demand is continually being renewed, the magnitude of this renewal is shrinking, so this iterative process eventually dies out. The numerical example began with $8 billion excess demand. This led to an income increase of $8 billion, which in turn caused aggregate demand to increase, but by less than $8 billion. Why? Consumers use part of

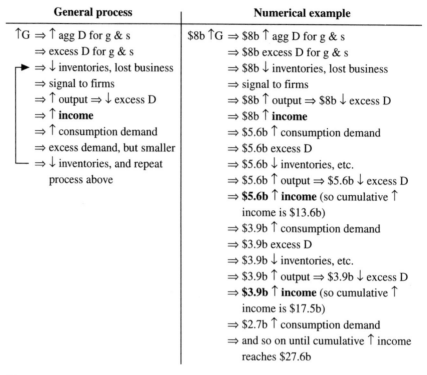

| General process | Numerical example |
|---|---|
| ↑G ⇒ ↑ agg D for g & s | $8b ↑G ⇒ $8b ↑ agg D for g & s |
| ⇒ excess D for g & s | ⇒ $8b excess D for g & s |
| ⇒ ↓ inventories, lost business | ⇒ $8b ↓ inventories, lost business |
| ⇒ signal to firms | ⇒ signal to firms |
| ⇒ ↑ output ⇒ ↓ excess D | ⇒ $8b ↑ output ⇒ $8b ↓ excess D |
| ⇒ ↑ **income** | ⇒ $8b ↑ **income** |
| ⇒ ↑ consumption demand | ⇒ $5.6b ↑ consumption demand |
| ⇒ excess demand, but smaller | ⇒ $5.6b excess D |
| ⇒ ↓ inventories, and repeat process above | ⇒ $5.6b ↓ inventories, etc. |
| | ⇒ $5.6b ↑ output ⇒ $5.6b ↓ excess D |
| | ⇒ **$5.6b** ↑ **income** (so cumulative ↑ income is $13.6b) |
| | ⇒ $3.9b ↑ consumption demand |
| | ⇒ $3.9b excess D |
| | ⇒ $3.9b ↓ inventories, etc. |
| | ⇒ $3.9b ↑ output ⇒ $3.9b ↓ excess D |
| | ⇒ **$3.9b** ↑ **income** (so cumulative ↑ income is $17.5b) |
| | ⇒ $2.7b ↑ consumption demand |
| | ⇒ and so on until cumulative ↑ income reaches $27.6b |

**Figure 4.1**  The multiplier process
In the numerical example, a dollar increase in income increases consumption by 0.7 dollars.

any increase in income to pay taxes and augment savings, causing the increase in consumption demand to fall well short of $8 billion. In this numerical example, consumption increases by 70 percent of the income increase. The next time the economy cycles through this iterative process, income increases again, but by less than $8 billion, and the third time through it increases by still less, as shown in the numerical example.

Because of the renewal of aggregate demand, the ultimate increase in national income resulting from the $8 billion increase in government spending is more than $8 billion. If we had continued the iterative calculations in our numerical example, the ultimate cumulative increase in income would have turned out to be $26.7 billion. (For those interested, appendix 4.4 at the end of this chapter shows how this can be deduced algebraically.) In this example, each dollar increase in government spending serves eventually to increase income by 3.3 dollars. The *income multiplier with respect to government spending*, or the increase in equilibrium income due to a dollar increase in government spending—referred to casually as "the" multiplier—is said to be 3.3. The iterative process whereby an increase in government spending leads to an extended increase in income is called the *multiplier process*.

**Curiosity 4.2:   What Is the Multiplier?**

A formal definition of the multiplier is the change in the equilibrium level of income per change in government spending. (The equilibrium level of income, discussed in appendix A, is that income level at which aggregate demand for goods and services equals aggregate supply of goods and services.) It is calculated as

$$\text{multiplier} = \frac{\Delta \text{GDP}}{\Delta G}.$$

where $\Delta GDP$ is the change in equilibrium income resulting from a change in government spending of size $\Delta G$. A common use of the multiplier is to enable calculation of what increase in government spending is needed to push the economy to a desired income level. Suppose, for example, that we wish to increase the income level by $10 billion, and the multiplier is 4. From the definition of the multiplier we obtain $4 = 10/\Delta G$, implying that the required $\Delta G = 2.5$ billion dollars.

   This example of a multiplier of 4 should not be taken literally. The multiplier value varies across countries and within a single country over time. Furthermore, its actual value is difficult to measure. As will be seen in chapter 7, some economists believe its value is very small, perhaps less than one.

   To be careful, we should really call the multiplier "the income multiplier with respect to government spending," so as not to confuse it with other multipliers, but we follow tradition and call it "the" multiplier, seldom using the quotes. Many other multipliers exist, all giving the change in something of interest per change in something over which we have control. Some examples are the income multiplier with respect to the money supply, giving the change in equilibrium income per change in the money supply, and the employment multiplier with respect to the tax rate, giving the change in equilibrium employment per change in the tax rate. The latter multiplier should be negative because an increase in the tax rate should decrease disposable income and thus lower consumption demand, decreasing aggregate demand for goods and services.

The heart of the multiplier process is consumption demand induced by income increases. These consumption demand increases keep the multiplier process going. A government decision to build an airplane-producing plant in a small town should have a significant multiplier effect on that town as incomes earned by those building the plant and employed in the plant are spent in town shops and restaurants. In turn, these businesses and new businesses drawn in by this prosperity will need to hire more workers, who will spend part of their incomes in local shops, and so on, expanding this prosperity through the multiplier process.

## 4.4   Inventories and Forecasting

In figure 4.1, inventory changes play an important role, mainly serving as a signaling device that alerts producers to changes in aggregate demand. They also play two other important roles in macroeconomics.

First, desired inventory changes are a component of aggregate demand that affects the dynamics of an economy's reaction to disequilibrium, thereby playing an important role in the propagation and maintenance of business cycles. Consider a stimulating dose of fiscal policy. As the economy goes through the multiplier process, inventories are constantly falling because aggregate demand is continually a bit higher than output. If firms do nothing about this, after the multiplier process has worked itself out, inventories will have fallen to an undesirably low level. To prevent this from happening, firms must produce some extra output during the multiplier process. The time path followed by the economy during the multiplier process is affected by when and how quickly the firm decides to do this. If, for example, the firm elects to increase output to restore inventory levels at a late stage in the multiplier process, the level of national income could temporarily overshoot its final level.

Second, inventory changes can help in forecasting the direction of the economy. Their use in this regard occurs frequently in newspaper commentary, where they play a more prominent role than complex economic models built expressly for forecasting purposes.

When inventory levels are unusually high or are rising rapidly, firms should react by cutting back on production—meeting demand out of inventory—to decrease inventory levels to a more desirable level. This production cutback decreases income, however, setting the multiplier process in motion and pushing the economy towards a recession. We should forecast a downturn in the economy.

When inventory levels are unusually low or are falling rapidly, firms should react by increasing production to build inventories up to a more desirable level. The production increase also increases income, however, setting the multiplier process in motion and thereby pushing the economy to an even higher level of income. We should forecast an upturn in the economy.

## 4.5   Policy Implications

Although our earlier example of the multiplier process was couched in terms of a policy of increasing government spending, any policy that influences aggregate demand has similar effects. An alternative way of increasing aggregate demand is to decrease taxes, which increases aggregate demand indirectly by increasing consumers' disposable income, thereby enticing them to increase consumption demand, *C*.

Changing government spending or taxation is referred to as *fiscal policy* because each involves a direct change in the government budget deficit. (*Fiscalis* is Latin for "pertaining to the public purse.")

In particular, an *expansionary fiscal policy* (an increase in government spending or a decrease in taxes) creates a government budget deficit. Keynesians believe this is a natural side effect of a fiscal policy designed to maintain an

---

**Curiosity 4.3: What Is a Leading Indicator?**

Inventory behavior is an example of a leading indicator—a variable that consistently changes a few months in advance of changes in macroeconomic activity and that thus can be used to forecast business cycles. Experience has shown that depending on a single leading indicator is unwise, but combining several leading indicators into a composite index produces much better forecasts of business cycles. One such composite is the Index of eleven Leading Indicators, compiled monthly by the Bureau of Economic Analysis and published in the *Survey of Current Business*.

This composite index provides on average a thirteen-month advance warning of an impending recession. Its components vary as improvements are made. As reported recently in the *Survey of Current Business*, they were:

1. Average weekly hours of nonsupervisory workers in manufacturing
2. Average weekly new claims for unemployment insurance (inverted to produce a number that increases in expansions)
3. Manufacturers' new orders for consumer goods
4. Vendor performance—percentage of companies reporting slower deliveries from suppliers
5. New orders for plant and equipment
6. New private housing authorized by local building permits
7. Change in manufacturers' unfilled orders
8. Change in sensitive materials prices (prices that change quickly with changes in supply and demand)
9. Standard and Poor's index of 500 common stocks
10. Real money supply (M2, explained in chapter 8)
11. University of Michigan Index of Consumer Expectations

This index of eleven leading indicators is reported as a monthly percentage change calculated as a weighted average of the changes in its components.

---

economy at full employment—a side effect that should be reversed when in boom times governments cut back on spending or increase taxes to cool off the economy. In the Keynesian view, running a deficit is a small price to pay for jump-starting the economy so that the multiplier process can pull it out of a recession. They believe that the deficit can be offset later by a budget surplus when the economy is strong.

Keynesians also believe that an economy can become stuck in a recession when its natural recovery forces operate far too slowly, creating prolonged periods of high unemployment. They further believe that, through fiscal policy the government is able to move the economy out of a recession and that it should do so. This advocacy of government intervention in the economy has been opposed by others who believe that as a matter of principle the government has no business interfering in the economy, and that government intervention, however well intentioned, too often makes things worse, not better. The choice between increases in government spending and decreases in taxes reflects this difference of opinion: the former involves more government influence over the production and distribution of goods and services in the economy, whereas the latter involves less.

Keynesians and their modern counterparts, New Keynesians, believe that judicious government intervention in the economy is appropriate. The beliefs of those on the left of the political spectrum—socialists, liberals, and Democrats—can also be characterized this way. Classical economists (see appendix 4.1), monetarists (see chapter 9), and their modern counterparts, New Classicals, believe that government intervention is to be avoided. The beliefs of those on the right of the political spectrum—conservatives and Republicans—can also be characterized this way. This issue is revived in chapter 9 when discussing the "rules-versus-discretion" debate: should policy authorities be permitted to enact policy as they see fit?

## Media Illustrations

### *Example 1*

**All this frugality is producing a consumer-generated recession. What is needed is some policy action to stimulate consumer spending to move the economy out of its current lassitude. Consumer attitude surveys indicate that the time is ripe for such a move, and the high savings rate of recent years has led many economy watchers to predict an upturn.**

*What is a consumer-generated recession?*
There has been a fall in consumer spending, decreasing aggregate demand and, through a contractionary multiplier process, causing a recession.

*What kind of policy action could stimulate consumer spending?*
A decrease in taxes could increase consumer spending.

*How would stimulating consumer spending move the economy out of its current lassitude?*
Stimulating consumer spending would increase aggregate demand, which—through a multiplier process—would move the economy to a higher level of income.

*What is the relevance of consumer attitude surveys?*
If consumer attitudes towards spending are negative, policy actions to increase consumer spending and the multiplier process, which relies on higher incomes increasing consumption demand, may not work.

*Why has the high savings rate of recent years led to a prediction of an upturn?*
The high savings rates have increased people's wealth. Feeling wealthy, consumers may increase their spending.

### Example 2

**Under present circumstances there is such a thing as a "free lunch." In effect, all of the ingredients of that lunch are already there—the people who want to work, the factories and equipment standing idle, and the raw materials not being used. It is just a question of injecting a little spending power to prevent the free lunch from going to waste.**

*What kind of government policy is this a plea for?*
The statement "injecting a little spending power" suggests it is a plea for a stimulating dose of fiscal policy: increasing government spending or reducing taxes.

*Explain how a stimulating fiscal policy would work to create a free lunch.*
By increasing aggregate demand, firms would be motivated to use idle resources to produce output to meet this aggregate demand.

*What would happen if this policy were undertaken without the ingredients listed above?*
The list of ingredients indicates that the resources needed to produce the extra output are presently idle; the economy is operating at less than full capacity. Were this not the case, price increases rather than output increases would result from the stimulating fiscal policy.

### Example 3

**Most economists these days are preaching that consumers had better start spending. Fears of unemployment have curtailed consumer spending and starved the federal government of tax revenues needed to reduce the deficit.**

*Why would economists urge consumers to start spending?*
If consumers increase their spending, the increase in aggregate demand will set in motion the multiplier process, which would move the economy out of recession.

*Does the fact that unemployment fears curtail consumer spending serve to stabilize or destabilize the economy? Explain.*
If consumer spending drops as unemployment increases, then aggregate demand falls, setting in motion a multiplier process that pushes the economy to an even lower level of output and employment, thus destabilizing the economy.

*How has a curtailment of consumer spending starved the government of tax revenues?*
By curtailing consumer spending, a multiplier process pushing the economy to a lower level of income is set in motion. The lower level of income automatically reduces the government's income tax receipts.

### Example 4

**Changes in inventories go a long way, for instance, toward explaining why first-quarter real GNP was ahead of a year earlier by a meager 1.7 percent.**

*What must have been happening to inventories during the first quarter?*
It seems that GNP did not grow by as much as one would normally expect. One way in which this could happen is if firms cut back production to decrease inventories. A good guess here is that inventories were falling.

**Example 5**
**Economists expect to see some further liquidation of inventories this quarter, but at a slower rate. The change from rapid to slow—from negative to less negative—shows up as a plus for the economy.**

*What is a liquidation of inventories, and how would it be accomplished?*
Liquidation of inventories is getting rid of inventories, accomplished by decreasing production levels in order to have more sales met by inventories.

*Why would a slower rate of inventory liquidation be a "plus for the economy"?*
To slow down the rate of inventory liquidation, a firm would have to increase production so that not quite so many sales would be met by inventories. The increase in production increases income and sets in motion the multiplier process, stimulating the economy.

## Chapter Summary

- In a major break with tradition, Keynes focused on aggregate demand as the primary determinant of economic activity, illustrated in this chapter by assuming that producers were quantity rather than price adjusters.

- An increase in aggregate demand, created for example by an increase in government spending, induces producers to increase output to restore fallen inventories. The resulting increase in income causes consumption demand to increase, thus extending the expansion. This is the essence of the multiplier process, whereby an increase in government spending leads eventually to a much larger increase in income. The strength of this process is captured by the multiplier, which tells us the increase in equilibrium income caused by a dollar increase in government spending.

- Inventory changes send signals to producers that indicate what is happening to aggregate demand and that foretell subsequent changes in output and employment. Consequently, they are often used for forecasting purposes.

## Formula Definition

- "the" multiplier $= \dfrac{\Delta \text{GDP}}{\Delta G}$.

## Media Exercises

1. **There are specific reasons, of course, why a downturn may have been aborted in the past few months. With the Russian invasion of Afghanistan and the long confinement of U.S. diplomats as hostages in Iran, the United States began to strengthen the armed forces. Defense contracts work in the old-fashioned Keynesian way to stimulate the economy.**

   Explain how this old-fashioned Keynesian way operates to stimulate the economy.

2. **The federal government will be prevented by the size of the deficit from taking any action to stimulate the economy. The only possible source of stimulus is a decrease in the personal savings rate.**

   a. What action could the government take to stimulate the economy? Explain why the size of the deficit may prevent this.

   b. How would a decrease in the personal savings rate serve as a source of stimulus?

3. **We saved 17 percent of our disposable income during the recession, the highest rate since World War II. The level of savings has fallen off since then to less than 10 percent of disposable income.**

   Would the higher savings rate have eased or exacerbated the recession? Explain how.

4. **The only other potential bright spots observers spy on the horizon are lower personal tax rates and higher take-home pay under the federal tax reform package, which will begin in July.**

   Why would these changes be viewed as "bright spots"?

5. **Weak markets will lead to a rapid drop in the rate of business capital spending during the next year, which in turn will increase unemployment.**

   Explain how a drop in capital spending will increase unemployment.

6. **In a loose sense, we are all Keynesians now—all of us, at any rate, who reject the notion that a sick economy heals itself by "natural" recuperative powers, without government action.**

   a. Explain why rejecting this notion makes us Keynesians.

   b. What kind of government action is being referred to at the end of this clip?

7. **For Canada, the demand pressures generated by the U.S. tax cut and the spillover effects of increased U.S. defense spending will push the Canadian economy further into an excess demand situation.**

a. How will the U.S. tax cut and the increased U.S. defense spending influence the U.S. economy?

b. Why would these pressures influence the Canadian economy and create an excess demand situation?

8. **The report attributed the strength of the recovery during the first three months of this year to increased consumer spending and residential construction, as well as a reduced rate of inventory liquidation.**

a. Explain how increased consumer spending contributes to the recovery.

b. Explain how a reduced rate of inventory liquidation contributes to the recovery.

9. **For the people around here, the $2 million increase in government spending means 84 direct jobs and, depending on the employment multiplier you prefer, another 240 or 320 indirect jobs. In the bush. On the booming grounds. On the highways. In the drugstore down the street.**

a. What is meant by an "employment multiplier"?

b. Calculate the magnitude of this multiplier.

10. **There have been times when the federal government has kept pumping fiscal stimulus into the economy when it was already growing vigorously and did not need the boost. The result was ...**

a. What is meant by fiscal stimulus?

b. Complete the last sentence.

11. **Manufacturers ended last year on a strong note with both shipments and orders rising to record levels in December. At the same time there was an ominous buildup of inventories, which also rose to a record level.**

Why is the buildup in inventories described as "ominous."

12. **When the news of Wednesday's numbers on GDP was made public, stocks and bonds immediately rose, and the U.S. dollar strengthened. Then, when analysis of the numbers came in, the markets went into reverse. The reason for this was that the greater part of the improvement in the quarter—$33.7 billion out of a total GDP advance of $39.2 billion—came from additions to business inventories.**

Explain why markets would go into reverse upon learning about the additions to inventories.

13. **The extent of the downturn surprised many analysts. Real GDP fell at an annual rate of 4 percent, but if an apparently unplanned buildup of inventories is taken into account, the rate of decline is estimated at 7.6 percent.**

a. Explain what logic is being used to arrive at the 7.6 percent figure.

b. What is the relevance of the *unplanned* buildup of inventories?

14. **As consumer spending slackened, stocks began to pile up, so an inventory correction is underway, and it will reduce this quarter's real GDP by more than 10 percent at an annual rate.**

a. What is an inventory correction?

b. Why would an inventory correction cause GDP to fall in this case?

15. **What cannot be done, various reformers in the United States notwithstanding, is to impose on any government the obligation to balance its budget annually. Consider the consequences. If it did work, it would introduce a major destabilizing element.**

Explain how forcing the government to balance its budget would be destabilizing.

16. **Two hundred years ago Adam Smith said, "What is prudence in the conduct of every private family can scarce be folly in that of a great kingdom." With the advent of a "Keynesian revolution" since World War II, principles of fiscal responsibility were abandoned—in fact, they were reversed. The message of Keynesianism might be summarized as, "What is folly in the conduct of a private family may be prudence in the conduct of the affairs of a great nation."**

a. Exactly what is the "folly" referred to here?

b. Explain the rationale behind the "message of Keynesianism" given here.

17. **The U.S. Department of Commerce has estimated that if U.S. manufacturers use metric measures, their increased ability to compete on world markets should increase exports by about $600 million and thus benefit the U.S. economy by between $1.2 billion and $1.8 billion.**

Where are the $1.2 billion and $1.8 billion numbers coming from?

18. **Some claim that the fact that both deficits and unemployment have increased together since 1979 proves that fiscal stimulus doesn't work. It's true that our jobless rate rose from 1979 to 1984, while the federal deficit doubled as a percentage of GDP, but the inference about the ineffectiveness of fiscal stimulus is nevertheless wrong because ...**

Complete the argument about to be developed here. Hint: What is happening to tax revenues?

19. **Countercyclical policy is about filling in holes and shaving off peaks— exactly what John Maynard Keynes prescribed.**

Exactly what "filling in holes and shaving off peaks" did Keynes prescribe?

20. **Unemployment is contagious: people who lose their jobs cut their spending, causing other workers to be laid off. With sales lagging, business firms lose confidence; they cut back on investment, so that more people are out of work.**

    What terminology do economists use to describe this phenomenon?

21. **The Japanese economy is putting on the brakes, and this should inhibit U.S. economic recovery.**

    Why would a slowdown of the Japanese economy affect U.S. economic recovery?

22. **The U.S. economy should have enough vigor to continue growing for the rest of the decade, despite the braking effect of budget deficit reduction.**

    Explain "the braking effect of budget deficit reduction."

23. **GDP grew at a much faster 4.8 percent rate in the October–December quarter, but analysts said that growth masked some dangerous imbalances not present in the first quarter report. Almost all of the fourth-quarter increase in GDP wound up as unsold inventory sitting on shelves.**

    a. If inventory doesn't get sold, how could it get counted into GDP?

    b. Why is this phenomenon described as a "dangerous imbalance"?

24. **The conference was told that the country is headed for a big inventory liquidation that will keep the recession going well into the next year.**

    Explain how an inventory liquidation will keep the recession going.

25. **In the first two quarters of the year, consumer spending was somewhat sluggish, but there was a strong buildup of inventories by business, which boosted economic output.**

    a. Are weak consumer spending and strong inventory buildup consistent with one another? Explain why or why not.

    b. Does it matter if output is boosted by strong consumer spending or by strong inventory buildup? Explain why or why not.

26. **The inventory buildup, the major source of strength in the first quarter, will not be repeated and will actually be a source of weakness as production is reduced to work down unwanted stockpiles in the face of slumping sales, analysts said.**

    How can an inventory buildup be both a source of strength and a source of weakness?

27. **The Commerce Department has just reported that manufacturers' stock of raw materials, goods in process, and finished items fell by 1 percent in**

May, the latest month for which figures are available. It was the biggest drop in seventeen years. But it isn't just the sheer size of the May decline that excites the experts. Rather, it is the fact that the figure extends a trend that has been going on for most of the year. The cumulative impact has now reached the point where it has become a more potent force for recovery.

a. Does the 1 percent fall in stock in May imply that aggregate demand and income are the same, that demand exceeds income, or that income exceeds demand?

b. Why should the May decline "excite the experts"?

c. What is the "cumulative impact" referred to in the final sentence, and why is it a potent force for recovery?

28. Business inventories could have accumulated because sales fell below expectations. On the other hand, firms may have stockpiled inventories because they anticipated a surge in sales. The distinction is important because 87 percent of the stronger-than-expected 3.4 percent annualized growth in real GDP in the second quarter came from inventory accumulation. Those who offer the first explanation are forecasting _____, whereas those who offer the second explanation are forecasting _____.

Fill in the blanks.

## Numerical Exercises

N1. Do you think an economy is better off having an income multiplier with respect to government spending equal to 2 or equal to 8? Defend your answer.

N2. Suppose that the income multiplier with respect to government spending is 3.

a. The government wants to stimulate the economy to increase its income level by $12 billion. What increase in government spending is required?

b. If the government increased spending and thereby increased income by $63 billion, what must the increase in government spending have been?

N3. Suppose you notice that a $7 billion tax cut was accompanied by a $9 billion increase in consumer spending in the same year. How would you explain why consumer spending increased by more than the tax cut?

**Table 4.1**  Output and expenditure ($ billions)

| Output | Consumption | Investment | Government spending | Net exports |
|--------|-------------|------------|---------------------|-------------|
| 100 | 80 | 26 | 20 | 10 |
| 150 | 120 | 26 | 20 | 8 |
| 200 | 160 | 26 | 20 | 6 |
| 250 | 200 | 26 | 20 | 4 |
| 300 | 240 | 26 | 20 | 2 |
| 350 | 280 | 26 | 20 | 0 |
| 400 | 320 | 26 | 20 | −2 |

N4.  Suppose that the income multiplier with respect to government spending is 2.5 and the marginal tax rate is 25 percent. If the government increases spending by $8 billion, what will happen to the budget deficit?

N5.  Suppose the current level of income is $600 billion, "the" multiplier is 4, the marginal tax rate is 20 percent, and the current budget deficit is $20 billion.

   a.  What change in the level of government spending would be required to push the economy to an income level of $630 billion?

   b.  What impact would this have on the budget deficit?

N6.  Suppose "the" multiplier is 4 and the government increases spending by $5 billion, but the economy is at full employment at nominal income level $600 billion, so that an increase in government spending elicits price increases rather than output increases.

   a.  By how much will the price level increase?

   b.  By how much will nominal income increase?

   c.  By how much will real income increase?

N7.  Using the data in table 4.1, what will be happening to inventories when the level of income is $350 billion?

N8.  What is the equilibrium level of income for the economy described in table 4.1?

N9.  Using the data in table 4.1, by how much should the level of income have increased after two rounds of the multiplier process if the economy begins at its equilibrium position and increases government spending by $50 billion?

N10.  Suppose that last year consumption was $570 billion, tax receipts were $240 billion, and income was $900 billion. The corresponding numbers for this year are $600 billion, $250 billion, and $950 billion.

a. What is the MPC (marginal propensity to consume out of disposable income)?

b. What is the marginal tax rate?

---

## Appendix 4.1: Macroeconomics before Keynes: The Classical School

The classical school dominated macroeconomic thinking before Keynes published his famous book *The General Theory of Employment, Interest and Money* in 1936. The purpose of this appendix is to lend some perspective to this chapter's exposition of the Keynesian approach by providing a brief description of the classical view, which has three distinguishing characteristics, and by contrasting them with Keynes's view.

### Wage and Price Flexibility

Classical economists believed that prices and wages were quite flexible, so that disequilibria were uncommon. They explained unemployment, a disequilibrium in the labor market, as a temporary reluctance of wages to fall. This view of wages and prices as flexible was reinforced by a tendency to focus on the long-run equilibrium of the economy with little regard for how the economy might behave when out of equilibrium. Implicitly, they assumed that disequilibrium forces operated reasonably quickly to prevent phenomena such as prolonged recessions. A crucial policy implication of classical economics is that there is no need for government intervention via fiscal or monetary policy. (Monetary policy is discussed in chapter 8.)

Keynes, in contrast, claimed that it was the failure of disequibrium adjustments to occur speedily that explained phenomena such as the Great Depression. He complained that the classical economists' tendency to focus on long-run equilibrium had led them to overlook the important role of short-run disequilibrium dynamics in explaining economic phenomena. He concluded that there was a need for government policy intervention to speed the adjustment process.

### Say's Law

The classical school believed that supply creates its own demand, a claim known as *Say's Law*. The rationale behind Say's Law is that production of a billion dollars of output (supply) creates exactly a billion dollars of income payments that end up financing a billion dollars of spending. This causes aggregate demand automatically to match aggregate supply.

How does this happen? Any income not spent is saved and so is available to finance investment spending. Suppose there is an increase in saving, which causes aggregate demand to fall short of aggregate supply. The higher saving increases supply in the market for investment funds, causing the interest rate (the "price" of such funds) quickly to fall (classical economists believed market adjustments were swift), and thus increasing investment demand because it is now cheap for firms to borrow to undertake investment projects. This ensures that any fall in aggregate demand due to higher saving is offset by extra investment demand. The result suggests that deficient aggregate demand should never be a concern, one reason why Keynes's focus on aggregate demand was so innovative.

Keynes did not believe in Say's Law. One of his major objections is that a fall in the interest rate causes people to increase the amount of cash they wish to hold in their pockets and in their checking accounts. With a lower interest rate, a smaller interest return is foregone by holding more wealth in the form of cash, so people hold more cash for the convenience it provides. Consequently, not all of an increase in saving makes its way to financing higher investment; some is siphoned off into people's cash holdings. In short, according to Keynes it is quite possible that aggregate demand falls short of aggregate supply, implying a need for monetary or fiscal policy to boost aggregate demand.

**Money Is Neutral**

Classical economists believed that the quantity of money created by the economy's central bank (see chapter 8) has no long-run influence on real variables in the economy, such as the level of output. Instead, they believed that money-supply increases in the long run cause only price increases. This belief is often referred to as the *money neutrality* proposition. This view is formalized in the quantity theory of money equation, discussed later in chapter 8. In this theory, the relationship between money and income is captured by the formula $Mv = PQ$, where $M$ is the money supply, $v$ is a constant called velocity, $P$ is the overall price level, and $Q$ is output. The classical economists viewed output in the long run as being maintained at its full-employment level by the flexing of wages, so $Q$ is considered fixed. Velocity also was thought to be fixed, reflecting the nature of the economy's payments system. Because $v$ and $Q$ are fixed, a doubling of the money supply by the quantity theory equation in the long run merely doubles the price level: money is neutral, playing no role in affecting the real dimension of the economy, such as output and employment levels.

Keynes did not agree that it was legitimate to view output $Q$ as constant. Although $Q$ may be constant in the long run, movement to that long-run position may be so slow that prolonged recessions could develop, permitting an increase in the money supply to affect output. (How this happens is described in chapter 8.) Furthermore, because the interest rate can affect people's desired cash holdings, velocity should not be considered constant.

Modern schools of economic thought do not ignore the short run and its associated dynamics. They do not believe in Say's Law, and they have reinterpreted the quantity theory to make it more palatable. But one difference between the classical and Keynesian views described above continues to divide modern macroeconmic theorists: the classical school believed that wages and prices are quite flexible and that, because of this, government should not intervene in the operation of the economy, whereas Keynes believed the opposite. The same difference characterizes New Classicals and New Keynesians, the modern counterparts to the classical and Keynesian schools, discussed later in curiosity 12.1.

## Appendix 4.2:  The Circular Flow of Income

A popular way of illustrating the Keynesian analysis of aggregate demand is through the circular-flow diagram. This diagram shows how from year to year the income earned producing things enables people to buy these things and thereby permits the process to continue in a never-ending circular flow of income earning and spending.

The flow of income and spending is shown circulating clockwise in figure 4A.1. In the bottom box are producers who pay income in the form of wages, profits, interest, and rent, which flow up to the left to households in the top box. These households use this income to finance spending, which flows down to the right to the producers, providing them with the means to continue producing and paying incomes. Along the route of this circle, however, are several leakages from and injections into this circular flow.

The first leakage is taxes taken from income as it flows to households. A second leakage is saving, which goes to financial markets where it is made available to investors. (Saving is also made available to governments selling bonds to finance budget deficits. To keep figure 4A.1 simple, however, this and other complications are omitted.) A third leakage is spending on imports, a demand for goods and services which never reaches producers.

Offsetting the leakages are injections into the circular flow, shown in figure 4A.1 as investment, government, and export demand for goods and services. When these injections equal the leakages, aggregate demand for goods and services equals aggregate supply of goods and services, and the economy is thus in equilibrium. Keynes argued that when leakages are greater than injections, an increase in the government spending injection can restore equilibrium.

Another purpose played by the circular-flow diagram is to illustrate the equality between national income and output stressed in chapter 2. In the bottom box producers produce national output (GDP). The entire value of this output is paid out in income of one kind or another, going up to the left on the diagram. It is also sent up to the right on the diagram to those demanding it. To measure national income, then, one can add up either all income payments or all spending on domestically produced goods and services.

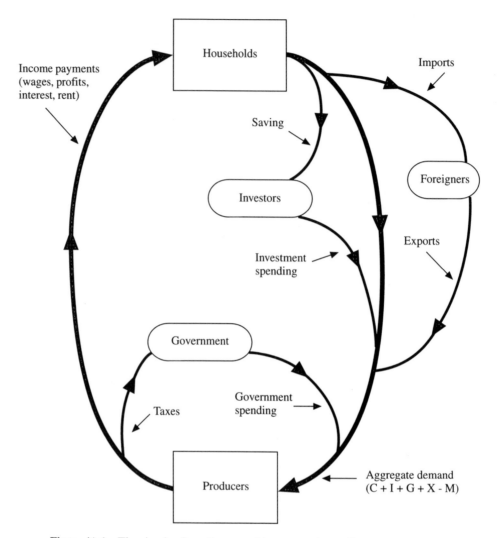

**Figure 4A.1**   The circular flow diagram of income and spending
Income flows up to the left to households and circulates back down to producers through
a variety of spending channels.

## Appendix 4.3:   The 45° Line Diagram

The first of the infamous curve-shifting diagrams to which macroeconomics
students are introduced is the 45° line diagram, designed to illustrate the elements of Keynesian analysis. All points on a 45° line are equidistant from both
axes. In figure 4A.2, the 45° line is labeled AD = AS because everywhere along
that line, aggregate demand for goods and services (measured on the vertical
axis) is equal to aggregate supply of goods and services (measured on the horizontal axis). Such points are possible equilibrium positions.

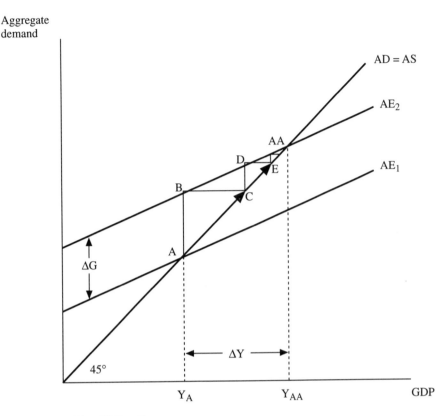

**Figure 4A.2** The 45° line diagram
Government spending is increased by $\Delta G$—shifting AE$_1$ up to AE$_2$, moving the economy ultimately from A to AA, and increasing income by $\Delta Y$.

We begin with an economy represented by the aggregate expenditure line AE$_1$, showing how increases in income ($Y$) increase aggregate demand for goods and services through the consumption function (i.e., as income increases, consumption demand increases). This implies that the economy will be at position A, corresponding to income level $Y_A$. Verify this by choosing an income level larger/smaller than $Y_A$ and seeing that aggregate supply will be larger/smaller than aggregate demand, so that income will fall/rise. It may seem odd to call the AE line an aggregate expenditure line rather than an aggregate demand line. The reason for this is that economists reserve the adjective "demand" to characterize curves drawn as a function of price.

Next, increase government spending by $\Delta G$, shifting the AE$_1$ line up by $\Delta G$ to AE$_2$, creating a new equilibrium at AA, corresponding to income $Y_{AA}$. The change in equilibrium income resulting from this jump in government spending is $\Delta Y = Y_{AA} - Y_A$ and the multiplier is given by $\Delta Y/\Delta G$. If the change in government spending were one dollar, $\Delta Y$ would portray the magnitude of the multiplier. The movement from A to C to E portrays the adjustment process from A to AA, as described earlier in figure 4.1. The initial increase in government spending creates an excess demand of AB, so output increases by this amount, moving the economy to C; at position C, however, there continues to be excess demand, given by the smaller amount CD. Output increases by the amount CD, thus moving the economy to E. This process continues until the economy reaches position AA, where the excess demand has finally been squeezed off.

## Appendix 4.4:   Algebraic Derivation of the Multiplier

Among the first of the infamous algebraic manipulations to which macro-economics students are introduced is the derivation of the multiplier. This is accomplished by using a mathematical model to represent the Keynesian view of the economy.

The equilibrium condition—aggregate supply of goods and services equals aggregate demand for goods and services—is written as

$$Y = C + I_0 + G_0$$

where $Y$ is GDP, $C$ is consumption demand, $I$ is investment demand, and $G$ is government demand. The zero subscripts on $I$ and $G$ indicate that they are determined *exogenously*: they are not affected by the interaction of supply-and-demand forces as are the *endogenous* variables $Y$ and $C$. In this simple model of the economy, it is traditional to view $G$ as determined by government policy and $I$ as determined by what Keynes called "animal spirits"—changes in technology or profit expectations. $C$ is specified as a linear function of the level of income:

$$C = a + bY,$$

where $b$ is the MPC, the marginal propensity to consume.

These two equations form a set of *simultaneous equations* that can be solved to yield the equilibrium level of income. This is done by substituting the second equation into the first to get

$$Y = a + bY + I_0 + G_0,$$

and solving for equilibrium $Y$ to get

$$Y^e = (I_0 + G_0)/(1 - b).$$

Those versed in calculus can take the derivative of this expression with respect to $G_0$ to find the multiplier. Those not versed in calculus can find the multiplier by finding the change in equilibrium income caused by increasing government spending. If government spending is increased to $G_0 + \Delta G$, then equilibrium income becomes

$$Y^{e'} = (I_0 + G_0 + \Delta G)/(1 - b)$$

and the change in equilibrium income, $Y^{e'} - Y^e$, is easily calculated to be

$$\Delta Y = Y^{e'} - Y^e = \Delta G/(1-b)$$

so the multiplier is

$$\Delta Y/\Delta G = 1/(1-b).$$

Using this or any formula to calculate the multiplier can be misleading because the algebraic result for the multiplier depends on what equations have been used to derive it. Suppose, for example, we wish to recognize that consumption is a function of after-tax income, not before-tax income. The consumption function above would become

$$C = a + b(Y - T),$$

where $T$ is tax revenues, in turn expressed as a linear function of income

$$T = d + tY,$$

where $t$ is the marginal tax rate. Now we have a set of three simultaneous equations in three endogenous variables: $Y$, $C$, and $T$. These can be solved to find a new expression for equilibrium income, which can be used to find that the multiplier is given by $1/(1 - b + bt)$.

Recognizing taxes makes the multiplier smaller. Why? At each round of the multiplier process, income increases are partly taxed away, implying that consumption increases and thus aggregate demand increases are smaller, so the resulting income increases are smaller.

# 5    The Supply Side

In microeconomic analysis, economists rely heavily on supply-and-demand curves. They would never attempt to explain an economic phenomenon or offer policy advice without examining both the supply and the demand side of the market. In light of this, it is remarkable that the Keynesian view of the macroeconomy, which focused almost exclusively on the demand side, was accepted so completely by the profession. In retrospect, this was a grievous error for three main reasons.

1. When the large supply-side shocks of the early 1970s, such as OPEC-enforced increases in the price of oil, hit the economy, the Keynesian analysts were caught unprepared. Their economic models could not be employed to analyze the macroeconomic problems this created, so they were not able to offer useful advice.

2. Without the supply side of the economy, economists could not produce convincing analyses of business cycles, or explain anomalous facts such as simultaneous increases in inflation and unemployment.

3. Neglecting the supply side deflected economists' attention from economic growth and increasing living standards—from what is happening to aggregate supply in the very long run. In the early 1970s, when the economy's growth rate slowed dramatically, they were inadequately prepared to analyze this phenomenon or prescribe policy to deal with it.

The purpose of this chapter is to discuss the supply side of the economy and how it can be integrated into macroeconomic analysis in the short and long runs. Discussion of the very long run, the topic of economic growth, is postponed until the next chapter.

**Upon completion of this chapter you should**

- understand how an aggregate supply/aggregate demand diagram can be used to portray business cycle behavior;
- explain how to analyze a supply-side shock; and
- be familiar with "supply-side economics."

## 5.1   The Aggregate Supply Curve

The supply side in the Keynesian analysis introduced in the preceding chapter can be represented by an aggregate supply curve with three distinct zones, as illustrated by AS in figure 5.1. This curve shows how the quantity of output from firms increases as the overall price level increases.

1. At low levels of output, with excess capacity, firms are able to increase output without requiring price increases. Hoarded labor and idle machinery can be used to increase output without any increase in per unit costs. In this zone the aggregate supply curve is flat, corresponding to the flowchart explanation given in figure 4.1 in chapter 4.

2. At intermediate levels of output, firms find that to produce more output they must pay current workers overtime, hire inexperienced, less-productive workers, pay higher wages to attract additional workers, and use older, less efficient machinery. Consequently, they increase output only if price increases to cover higher per unit costs. The aggregate supply curve becomes upward-sloping.

3. At some very high level of output, firms can no longer increase output because they have reached the physical limit of their capacity to produce output. The aggregate supply curve becomes vertical.

Anything that increases firms' costs shifts the AS curve in the upward direction. This happens because firms will supply the same output only if they are compensated for their higher costs by a higher price. A wage increase is an example of an increase in an input cost shifting the AS curve upward. Oil price increases engineered by OPEC in the 1970s is another prominent example. Readers are reminded that a change in the price level moves the economy along the AS curve; changes in all other variables cause shifts.

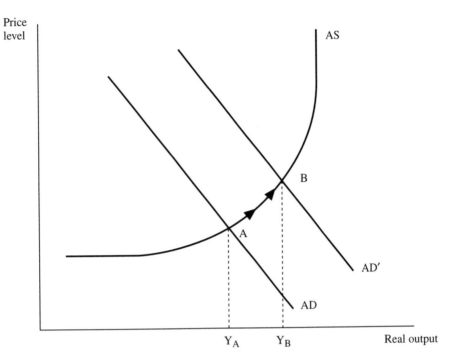

**Figure 5.1**  The AS/AD diagram
An increase in government spending shifts AD to AD′, moving the economy from A
to B.

## 5.2  The Aggregate Demand Curve

To be useful, a supply curve must be paired with a demand curve. In this case,
an aggregate demand curve is developed by specifying that when the overall
price level decreases, real demand for goods and services increases. The negative relationship between the overall price level and aggregate demand for
goods and services comes about for three reasons.

1. *The wealth effect.*   A fall in the price level causes the wealth of those who
   have loaned money to rise, inducing them to increase their consumption
   spending. Conversely, borrowers experience a decrease in their wealth and,
   feeling poorer, decrease their consumption. The decrease is quite small, however, because the dominant borrower, the government, is assumed not to
   change its spending. Consequently, the lenders' reaction generates this net
   wealth effect on consumption. Suppose, for example, you are a lender and
   own a bond worth ten thousand dollars. If the price level falls so dramatically that a sports car originally costing $50,000 dollars now costs only
   $5,000 dollars, wouldn't you feel wealthy enough to buy such a car?

2. *International forces.*    A fall in the price level causes our goods to be cheaper to foreigners and foreign goods to be more expensive to us. Consequently, demand for our exports increases, and we shift some of our demand for imports to domestically produced goods and services, which compete against imports.

3. *The real money supply.*    A fall in the price level causes the real supply of money in the economy to rise, which (as will be seen in chapter 9) serves to increase aggregate demand through several channels. For example, a rise in the real supply of money causes its price, the interest rate, to fall. This, in turn, causes people to increase spending because borrowing costs have fallen.

A fall in the price level causes an increase in aggregate demand. The Keynesian multiplier effect is thus invoked, further increasing aggregate demand, so that a modest fall in the price level ends up increasing aggregate demand by a substantial amount, creating the downward-sloping aggregate demand curve AD portrayed in figure 5.1. For those interested, a graphical derivation of this curve appears in appendix 5.1 at the end of this chapter. Appendix A at the end of the book provides a more general overview of this curve and how it relates to other macroeconomic curves. The intersection of AD and AS, point A, is an equilibrium for the economy, so we visualize the economy as being at price level $P_A$ and at corresponding output level $Y_A$.

An increase in aggregate demand for goods and services due to government policy shifts the AD curve horizontally to the right by an amount equal to the multiplier times this increase. A prominent example of such policy shifts is an increase in government spending—an expansionary fiscal policy. Tracing the economy's reaction to such a shock can illustrate how the aggregate supply/aggregate demand diagram is used.

## 5.3   Using the Aggregate Supply/Aggregate Demand Diagram

An increase in government spending of $\Delta G$ increases spending at every price level by $\Delta G$ times the multiplier, so the entire AD curve shifts to the right by this amount, as shown in figure 5.1 by the shift to AD'. The equilibrium moves to point B and real income increases from $Y_A$ to $Y_B$. Notice that the new equilibrium position involves a rise in the price level, which, through wealth effects, international effects, and a fall in the real money supply, decreases real aggregate demand, causing the change in income ($Y_B - Y_A$) to be smaller than would have been the case had the price level not risen. The multiplier becomes smaller than the multiplier of the previous chapter. This process is illustrated in figure 5.2, an updated flowchart incorporating the role of the price level.

Now the initial excess demand is squeezed off through two sources—increases in output and increases in prices—so the multiplier in real terms is smaller than when we did not recognize the role of the price level.

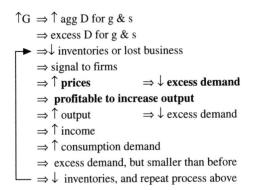

$\uparrow$G $\Rightarrow$ $\uparrow$ agg D for g & s
      $\Rightarrow$ excess D for g & s
      $\Rightarrow\downarrow$ inventories or lost business
      $\Rightarrow$ signal to firms
      $\Rightarrow$ $\uparrow$ **prices**          $\Rightarrow$ $\downarrow$ **excess demand**
      $\Rightarrow$ **profitable to increase output**
      $\Rightarrow$ $\uparrow$ output          $\Rightarrow$ $\downarrow$ excess demand
      $\Rightarrow$ $\uparrow$ income
      $\Rightarrow$ $\uparrow$ consumption demand
      $\Rightarrow$ excess demand, but smaller than before
      $\Rightarrow$ $\downarrow$ inventories, and repeat process above

**Figure 5.2**  The multiplier process with price changes
Incorporating price changes into the multiplier process makes the multiplier smaller in real terms.

The three zones of the AS curve give rise to three different reactions to a dose of fiscal policy. When the AS curve is flat, the economy reacts primarily by increasing output; in the intermediate range both output and prices increase; and when the AS curve is vertical, only price increases follow expansionary fiscal policy. The lesson should be clear. Expansionary policy is appropriate when the economy is in a severe recession, but is inappropriate in a boom.

## 5.4    Where Is Full Employment?

The analysis of the preceding section is antiquated and misleading, mainly because it contains a very naive view of what is happening in the labor market. In particular, there is no indication in figure 5.1 of what output level would be generated by an economy at its NRU, the natural rate of unemployment, or what economists call full employment. Let us remedy this by drawing in figure 5.3 a vertical line at the level of output $Y_{NRU}$ that the economy would produce if it were at its natural rate of unemployment. This line is labeled LRAS because, as will be seen shortly, it represents the aggregate supply curve of the economy in the long run when contractual and informational barriers to adjustment no longer exist. The upward-sloping line SRAS, akin to the intermediate section of the AS curve in the preceding section, is the short-run aggregate supply curve. For convenience, the AD curve is drawn to pass through point A, the intersection of LRAS and SRAS.

Placing the full-employment position on this diagram allows a more realistic portrayal of an economy's reaction to a spending shock. Two such shocks are of interest: (1) an increase in aggregate demand for goods and services pushing the economy into a boom, and (2) a decrease in aggregate demand for goods and services pushing the economy into recession. Analyzing each of these shocks permits exposition of the modern view of the economy's supply side and

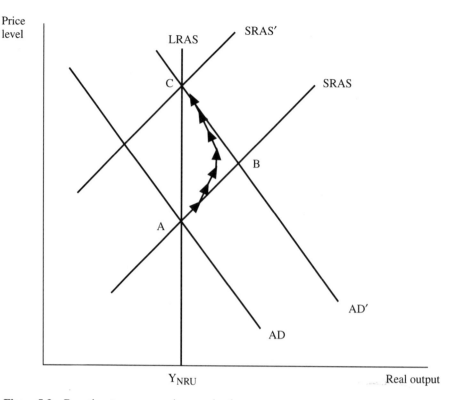

**Figure 5.3**    Reaction to an expansionary shock
The shock shifts AD to AD', and the economy reacts by moving from A toward B as price rises, thereby decreasing the real wage and enticing firms to hire more workers. When workers become aware that their real wage has fallen and are able to do something about it, the economy moves towards C. Higher wages shift SRAS up to SRAS'.

of how the aggregate supply/aggregate demand diagram is used to portray business-cycle behavior.

## 5.5   Moving into a Boom

Suppose an exogenous increase in aggregate demand shifts the AD curve to AD'. (*Exogenous* means resulting from an action that is external to the supply and demand forces under investigation; government policy actions are exogenous.) Inventories fall and business in the service industry is turned away, indicating to firms that demand for their good or service has risen. Two basic reactions are possible.

1. *Perfect competition.*   Some firms may be in industries that produce a homogeneous good or service with perfect competition prevailing. Entry of new firms and expansion of existing firms has pushed price and output of the

good or service to the point at which the price just covers the cost of producing an extra unit of output. At the current price, no firm is willing to increase output because it is not profitable to do so. Consequently, in this industry extra demand bids up price. This prompts these firms to increase output and induces new firms to enter. Some firms may be able to increase output by getting current workers to work overtime, but competition among firms and entry of new firms will not make this a profitable way of meeting this demand in the longer run. New firms and most existing firms will want to hire more workers.

2. *Imperfect competition.* Firms that are not in perfectly competitive industries have more leeway in their possible reactions to the higher demand. Their output is not perfectly substitutable for competitors' outputs, so they have not been pushed by competitors to produce to a point at which price just covers the cost of producing an extra unit of output. Consequently, they have the option of meeting the extra demand by increasing output rather than by allowing prices to rise. For many of these firms, this option is attractive for two reasons: (1) the costs of adjusting prices, so-called "menu costs" such as printing new catalogues and annoying loyal customers, and (2) a danger that competitors may not follow this price increase, creating considerable loss of demand for the price initiator. Consequently, firms may react initially by adjusting quantity to meet extra demand. Many firms can do this by getting workers to work overtime, but some may find it necessary to hire extra workers. Once this extra demand is seen to be permanent, most firms will want to hire extra workers, and price increases should occur. These price increases may prompt new firms to enter this industry, and they will need to hire new workers.

At this stage the reader should see two important things happening. First, although some prices may not rise immediately, overall, prices rise and so does output. In figure 5.3 the economy starts to move out towards point B. Second, although some firms may not want to hire extra workers right away, overall firms will want to hire extra labor. When they try to hire these extra workers, however, they discover to their surprise that the workers are hard to come by. Because the economy is at its natural rate of unemployment, a pool of unemployed eager to work at the going wage does not exist. To solve this problem, firms bid up the wage rate slightly, inducing some students to quit school, some homemakers to leave home, and some job searchers to find more quickly a job with the wage they feel they deserve. In terms of figure 5.3, the wage increase shifts the SRAS curve upwards a bit, so that the movement out towards point B turns slightly in an upward direction.

In essence, firms are willing to employ extra workers because it is profitable for them to do so. The rise in the price of their product has more than compensated firms for the higher wage they are now paying: the real wage has fallen. Ordinarily, workers would not put up with this. At a real wage lower than that corresponding to the natural rate of unemployment, some workers would withdraw their services, choosing instead to become students or home-makers, or to search the job market for a better job. Consequently, for the movement out towards point B in figure 5.3 to occur, workers must for some reason be willing to supply more labor at a lower real wage. Economists offer two main explanations for this.

1. *Information problems.* Workers may not realize what is happening, genu-inely mistaking a higher money wage for a higher real wage. They know exactly what the money wage is, but do not have a clear idea of what is happening to the overall price level.

2. *Contract obligations.* Workers may be obliged by a formal or informal contract to supply labor at a fixed money wage until the expiration of that contract. Some contracts are renegotiated sooner than others, implying that overall wages do not rise in step with overall price increases. Formal con-tracts last on average about three years. Those covered by informal con-tracts typically experience a wage increase once per year.

What is notable about both of these explanations is that they explain only a temporary fall in real wages. Workers eventually realize that their real wage has fallen and demand a rise in the money wage to compensate them fully for higher prices, and eventually all contracts are renegotiated, bringing the real wage back to its original level. Consequently, the economy's movement toward point B is only temporary. In time, money wages rise as much as prices. As money wages rise, the SRAS curve shifts upwards, reflecting firms' increased costs, so the economy moves along the curved arrowed line from A out towards B but eventually back to the NRU at point C, and the SRAS curve ends up eventually at SRAS'.

By now it should be clear why the vertical line at the NRU is called the long-run aggregate supply curve. An important policy lesson should also be evident. Any policy designed to move the economy below its NRU can succeed in the short run, but in the long run the economy will return to the NRU, leaving a higher price level as a legacy.

Another policy lesson might not be so evident. Suppose the government underestimates the NRU, believing for example that it is 5 percent when it is actually 6 percent. A 5 percent unemployment rate corresponds to a higher level of output than a 6 percent unemployment rate, so the government thinks that the LRAS curve lies to the right of the actual LRAS curve. Policy de-signed to push the economy to this underestimated NRU (and corresponding higher output level) requires continued rightward shifts of the AD curve to counteract the economy's movements back to the actual LRAS curve. This creates continued price increases—an inflation—and is the first of several examples we will encounter of how inappropriate government policy can lead to inflation.

---

**Curiosity 5.1:   How Do AD and AS Curves Differ from Microeconomic Curves?**

Unfortunately, despite superficial similarities, microeconomic demand curves and the aggregate demand curve are quite different concepts, a fact often hidden from students. A microeconomic demand curve is defined as showing how demand for the good or service in question changes as price changes, ceteris paribus (i.e., holding all other influences on demand constant). This ceteris paribus condition is not maintained for the aggregate demand curve, which shows how aggregate demand for all goods and services changes as the overall price level changes, *allowing the economy's output level to change to maintain equality with aggregate demand.* Consequently, the aggregate demand curve is more accurately described not as a demand curve but as a curve that shows combinations of price and output that correspond to equilibrium in the goods and services market.

Use of the aggregate supply/aggregate demand diagram in analyzing the economy should also have made clear that the aggregate supply curve was really concerned with what was going on in the labor market: were workers misinformed? did they have contractual obligations? and so on. Consequently, the aggregate supply curve is more accurately described not as a supply curve but as a curve that shows combinations of price and output that correspond to equilibrium in the labor market.

The beauty of the aggregate supply/aggregate demand diagram is that it allows two markets—the goods-and-services market and the labor market—to be illustrated in one diagram, simplifying our discussion of the macroeconomy. In fact, it does more than this. Contributions to aggregate demand from activity in the money/bond market and the foreign exchange market (discussed in chapters 9 and 16, respectively) are also incorporated in the aggregate demand curve, allowing this single diagram to represent simultaneous activity in the four major macroeconomic submarkets. Further discussion of this can be found in appendix A at the end of this book.

---

## 5.6   Moving into a Recession

Let us now look at an economy in equilibrium at point AA in figure 5.4 and postulate an exogenous fall in aggregate demand for goods and services shifting AD to AD′. The fall in aggregate demand should lead firms to lay off workers to avoid accumulating inventories and to cut prices to stimulate demand for their products. Laid-off workers may bid down the wage rate in an effort to regain employment, and this fall in cost may be passed on by firms as a further lowering of price. In figure 5.4 the economy would move from AA out towards BB and then down to CC as the falling wage shifts the SRAS curve down to SRAS′.

This is, of course, a mirror image of the reaction described in figure 5.3, but the image is deceptive. The reaction of an economy entering a boom can

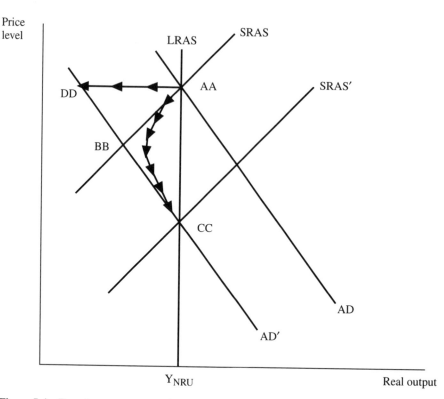

**Figure 5.4** Reaction to a contractionary shock
The shock shifts AD to AD′, and the economy reacts by moving from AA toward BB as price falls and firms lay off workers. If unemployed workers bid down the money wage, the economy moves toward CC. Lower wages shift SRAS down to SRAS′. A quantity adjustment to DD, where the economy is stuck in a less-than-full-employment equilibrium, is more likely, however.

reasonably be expected to occur fairly quickly. The economy in figure 5.3 moves from A towards B and then up to C back at the NRU within about three years because few labor contracts in the United States are for longer than three years and may be shorter if labor unions are worried about such shocks and sign only short-term contracts.

The reaction of an economy entering a recession is much different in that although wages and prices may eventually fall, they do so very reluctantly, so much so that it is more reasonable to postulate that the economy initially moves not towards point BB but to point DD, and stays there for a long time before wages and prices eventually fall, slowly moving the economy down towards point CC, where full employment is recovered. Although wages and prices fell during the Great Depression, during ordinary recessions drops in wages and prices have not been experienced on any significant scale. It seems that recoveries from recession happen not because prices and wages fall, but rather because of a major stimulus to aggregate demand—such as a war

increasing government spending, a technological innovation increasing investment spending, or a buildup of saving increasing consumption spending—all of
which lead to multiplier effects.

Why are wages and prices "sticky" downward? Earlier arguments suggest
that menu costs and fears of price wars are reasons why prices are sticky
downward. Wages are sticky downward for several reasons.

1. *Contracts.* Union contracts are fixed until expiration, so wages will be
   sticky for that reason. More important are "implicit contracts," informal
   understandings firms have with their workers that wages will be steady
   through both good and bad times unless such changes are proved to be
   permanent, with deficient demand met by laying off temporary workers,
   part-timers, and recent hires. Most workers and all firms find this agreement
   advantageous. Most workers get income security and, in exchange, are willing to accept a slightly lower wage than the firm would otherwise have to
   pay; firms are assured of keeping its best workers. Temporary workers, part-
   time workers, and recent hires (sometimes called "outsiders" as opposed to
   the "insiders" who have the attractive implicit or union contract) are willing
   to put up with this layoff system for two reasons. First, being for a time
   subject to layoff may be part of the price one pays to become eventually an
   insider. Second, some of these people believe that their skills are not attractive enough to secure a good job elsewhere. They may feel better off with
   this job even if it is subject to layoff. Both reasons are strengthened by the
   existence of unemployment insurance.

2. *Relative wages.* Workers are concerned about relative wages: how their
   wages stand in relation to those of friends and workers in other occupations.
   Consequently, nobody is willing to be the first to agree to work for a lower
   wage for fear of moving to a lower rung on the ladder of relative wages. If
   everyone were to agree in unison to lower wages, a speedy fall in wages
   might be possible. This could happen, for example, in a country such as
   Japan where each year there is a coordinated, economy-wide wage determination process. In the United States, only the pain of a prolonged period of
   high unemployment is likely to force unions and individual workers to agree
   to wage reductions.

3. *Temporary recession.* Workers may believe that the recession is temporary
   and decide to get by on unemployment insurance or welfare until the economy recovers, rather than agree to work for a lower wage. This belief has
   been reinforced over the years by government commitment to full employment. Workers have been led to believe that soon the government will take
   policy action to pull the economy out of recession.

4. *Efficiency wages.* Firms are afraid of alienating their workers. They find it
   in their profit-maximizing interest to pay a real wage higher than the real
   wage that is consistent with full employment, so in the face of deficient

---

**Curiosity 5.2: Are Real Wages Countercyclical?**

Some of the arguments presented in this chapter suggest that real wages are countercyclical: they rise during recessions and fall during booms. A fall in real wages, for example, induces firms to hire more labor, decreasing unemployment, increasing output, and pushing the economy into the expansionary phase of the business cycle. This does not necessarily happen, however. Other arguments have suggested that firms are primarily quantity adjusters, increasing output via overtime as the economy goes into a boom and decreasing output via hoarding labor and layoffs as the economy enters a recession. Price reactions take place only after the boom or recession has continued for some time, with price changes preceding, matching, or following wage changes, depending on circumstances. Firms in perfectly competitive industries, for example, are likely to have price changes precede wage changes; firms in imperfectly competitive industries may follow a markup pricing strategy and so may not increase price until wages increase. Furthermore, cyclical movements initiated by aggregate demand shocks will have different characteristics than movements initiated by supply-side shocks, so there is no guarantee that real wages are countercyclical. The empirical evidence suggests that they follow no consistent pattern over the cycle.

---

demand they do not press workers for lower wages. There are several reasons for this. First, by paying an abnormally high real wage, a firm may be able to hire a better quality of worker. Second, workers may react by putting forth more work effort, either because they feel morally bound to do so or because they could be fired from an attractive insider job if they are caught shirking. And third, the high wage should reduce labor turnover, lowering hiring and training costs. The classic example of such behavior is Henry Ford's 1914 successful offer of $5 per day, a huge jump in the going wage.

All this suggests that a negative demand shock will most likely move the economy to point DD, where the goods-and-services market is in equilibrium, but the labor market is not. If the unemployed workers do not cause wages to fall, no forces are set in motion to push the economy back to full employment. Keynes explained this simply by stating that the unemployed do not bid down wages, so the economy is stuck at point DD, sometimes called a less-than-full employment equilibrium. Modern interpretations draw the same conclusion, but provide reasons why economic agents act in rational, maximizing ways to cause wages to be sticky. This has earned them the name New Keynesians.

The upshot of all this is that although the economic forces of supply and demand may eventually operate to bring an economy out of recession and back to full employment, they operate too slowly to satisfy participants, so there is a need for policy action. This is the essence of the Keynesian message.

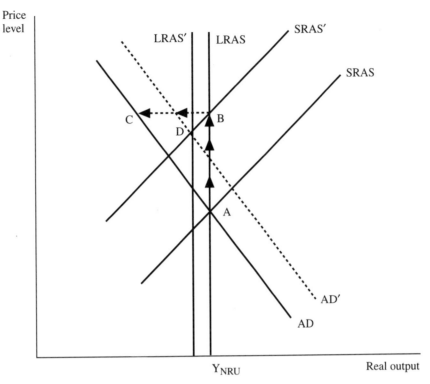

**Figure 5.5**  Reaction to a supply-side shock
The shock of higher energy costs shifts SRAS to SRAS′ and LRAS to LRAS′. Firms
pass on the higher cost by increasing prices, moving the economy from A to B. The price
rise lowers demand, and firms cut output, thereby moving the economy to C. Further
reaction depends on how workers respond to the fall in their real wage and on the nature
of government policy action.

## 5.7  Analyzing Supply Shocks

Although we can now recognize that Keynesian analysis did contain an implicit
supply curve, prior to the 1970s this supply curve was kept hidden. Rather than
using an aggregate supply/aggregate demand diagram such as those portrayed
in figures 5.2 through 5.4, economists used alternative diagrams that did not
show explicitly the supply side of the economy. As a result, they tended to forget about or unintentionally denigrate the role of the supply side in affecting
economic activity.

The suppression of the role of aggregate supply became painfully evident
when Keynesian analyses were unable to suggest appropriate policies to deal
with the major supply shocks of the early 1970s. With the aggregate supply/
aggregate demand diagram, the impact of a supply-side shock can be analyzed
more easily. Suppose the economy is at position A in figure 5.5, and a negative

supply-side shock—perhaps an increase in the price of energy—hits the economy. (Since 1970 the world has experienced four major energy price shocks, resulting from the following events: 1973 OPEC oil embargo, 1979 Iranian revolution, 1985 OPEC price crash, and 1990 Iraq-Kuwait war.) The resulting higher production costs cause the SRAS curve to shift upward to SRAS′. The LRAS curve should also shift slightly to the left to LRAS′, for two reasons. First, less energy will be used per worker, so workers will become less productive, implying that output produced by a given quantity of labor will be less. Second, the fall in worker productivity causes the real wage in the labor market to fall, prompting some workers to leave the labor force. In the new long-run equilibrium, the number of workers becomes smaller. The LRAS curve reflects long-run activity in the labor market. In the long run, a fewer number of less productive workers correponds to equilibrium in the labor sector, so the LRAS curve must be further to the left.

In this situation, firms may begin to pass on the higher cost of energy by increasing prices, thus moving the economy to point B. The higher price decreases aggregate demand, and firms react by cutting back production, laying off workers, and moving the economy over to point C. At this stage, the government may adopt a fiscal policy that shifts AD rightward to AD′.

Care must be taken not to overstimulate and try to push the economy all the way back to the original LRAS. The biggest complication, however, arises from workers' reaction to the price increase. If workers recognize their decreased productivity and accept the fall in their real wage, the economy could settle at D in figure 5.5. More realistically, however, workers may demand wage increases to prevent their real wage from falling. This would shift the *SRAS* further upward (not shown in figure 5.5), leading to more price increases and frustrating the fiscal policy. Unemployment will be maintained (i.e., the economy will remain to the left of LRAS′ at a position like C) as long as employed workers prevent the real wage from falling to reflect their decreased productivity.

## 5.8  Supply-Side Economics

Some economists came to believe that economic forces springing from the supply side were strong enough to play a major role in determining the level and character of economic activity. Such economists developed what has become known as *supply-side economics*.

The most distinguishing characteristic of supply-side economics is the importance placed on economic incentives. For example, a rise in the tax rate is thought to influence significantly the work/leisure decision, the consumption/saving decision, the investment decision, and the market/nonmarket activity decision. This, in turn, affects the quantity of goods and services supplied in the economy in both the short and the long run. Economists who believe that the strength of economic incentives is considerable are called *supply-siders*. They

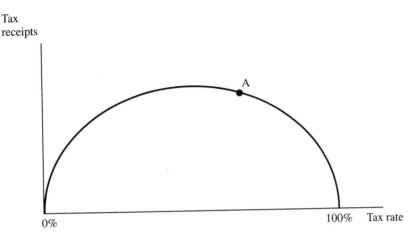

**Figure 5.6**  The Laffer curve
An increase in the tax late initially increases tax receipts, but the disincentive effects of higher taxes eventually cause a fall in tax receipts. Note that at point A lowering the tax rate would increase tax receipts.

advocate the adoption of supply-oriented policies that operate through changing incentives.

Supply-side economics forces economists to rethink their advocacy of traditional policies in three ways:

1. When an economy is subjected to a supply-side shock, such as an increase in the price of oil, the traditional demand-oriented remedies for economic problems may be inappropriate. Consider, for example, a negative supply-side shock that makes the economy less productive, such as the example analyzed earlier in figure 5.5. An increase in government spending to move the economy back to its original level of income would only serve to increase prices.

2. Traditional demand-oriented policies have impacts on the supply side that can alter substantively their influence on the economy. Consider, for example, an increase in taxes enacted to decrease aggregate demand and fight inflation, traditionally captured by a leftward shift of the AD curve. But higher taxes also shift the AS curve upward/leftward by raising costs and reducing incentives: firms view taxes as costs to be passed on, and workers supply less labor when after-tax remuneration falls, compounding the impact on income and making the impact on the price level uncertain.

3. Previously neglected policy options, which affect mostly the supply side, are being reconsidered. Such options include: reducing import tariffs on intermediate goods; preventing generous wage increases in the public sector from acting as a standard for the private sector; encouraging expansion of the capital stock through investment tax credits, accelerated depreciation allowances, and lower interest rates; increasing worker productivity by means of

> **Curiosity 5.3:   What Is Real Business-Cycle Theory?**
>
> Another legacy of economists' revitalized interest in the supply side of the economy is *real business-cycle theory*: the belief that real (as opposed to nominal) changes such as technology shocks, new products, new government regulations (regarding such things as pollution), weather changes, changes in consumer preferences, natural resource discoveries, labor supply changes, tax rate changes, large changes in relative prices (such as that of oil), and other supply-side factors are primarily responsible for fluctuations in economic activity. Also, according to this theory, traditional demand-side shocks play a secondary and very transitory role in affecting the economy. Real business-cycle theory could be viewed as the most recent variant of supply-side economics. Although few economists feel that business cycles can be explained adequately by such supply-side phenomena alone, real business-cycle theory has undoubtedly improved our understanding of business cycles.

goverment spending on social overhead such as transportation systems, communication infrastructure, and basic research activity; and eliminating or reducing unnecessary health, safety, or environmental regulations.

The greatest attribute of these supply-side policies is that they can raise output and employment while lowering the price level, whereas demand-side policies must raise the price level while increasing output and employment. Supply-siders make much of this difference, claiming that its exploitation can create policy actions capable of attacking "stagflation."

The spirit of supply-side economics has come to be represented by the Laffer curve, illustrated in figure 5.6, which shows how the tax rate affects tax receipts. With a zero tax rate, tax receipts are also zero. Increasing the tax rate at first increases tax receipts, but eventually causes a fall in tax receipts as the incentive effects of higher taxes cause people to work and invest less and to participate more heavily in the underground economy. Supply-siders believed that the U.S. economy in the early 1980s was at a point like A, so that a reduction in the tax rate would lead to a rise in tax receipts. This was part of the rationale behind the Reagan tax cuts.

The enthusiasm of the supply-siders is not shared by many economists, for several reasons:

1. Although incentives matter in theory, in practice their empirical magnitude has been shown to be very small.
2. Many supply-side policies, such as changing tax rates, have minor effects on aggregate supply but major effects on aggregate demand, shifting the AD curve by more than the AS curve, creating results very similar to those of traditional demand-side policies.

3. Supply-side tax cuts have led to dramatic increases in the government budget deficit and the national debt. In figure 5.6, the economy was to the left of the hump when the Reagan tax cuts were enacted, and thus tax receipts actually decreased.

4. Many supply-side policies, such as lowering import tariffs or reducing taxes on the rich, are politically unacceptable or have undesirable distributional effects.

Because of these objections, supply-siders are not viewed with favor in the economics profession. They have left an important legacy, however—that the supply-side should not be ignored in macroeconomic analyses.

## Media Illustrations

### Example 1

**Michael Spence of Harvard University fears the high risks involved in some supply-side policies: "The Reagan people are currently arguing over what level of tax cuts should be implemented. What if they're wrong? What if the supply side doesn't respond enough to at least take care of the foregone revenues?"**

*Why can tax cuts be viewed as a supply-side policy?*
By cutting tax rates, people's after-tax return from working and investing is greater, so there is greater incentive to work harder and invest more. This should increase aggregate supply.

*What are the "foregone revenues"?*
These are the reductions in tax revenues from the original income level due to the lower tax rate.

*What is meant by the supply side not "respond[ing] enough to … take care of the foregone revenues"?*
The tax cut would need to cause a sufficiently large increase in income to make the rise in tax revenues due to higher income offset the fall in tax revenues due to the initial tax cut.

*What is the specific high risk that Spence is worried about here?*
The risk that the tax cut will increase the budget deficit.

### Example 2

**Professor Arthur Laffer's famous freehand curve showing the effect of tax reduction on tax revenue, the magic logo of the supply-siders, was also not taken seriously by the profession. For some, Laffer was a figure of fun. Most others held that the Kleenex, paper napkin, or toilet paper on which, according to varying legend, the curve was first drawn, could better have been put to its regular use.**

*Where on the Laffer curve in figure 5.6 is the possibility of tax rate reduction increasing tax revenue illustrated?*

Consider any tax rate to the right of the top of the hump on this curve. A reduction in this tax rate moves the economy up toward the top of the hump and thus to a higher tax revenue.

*What reasoning creates this possibility?*

Lower tax rates increase after-tax income, which should stimulate consumption demand and, through the Keynesian multiplier process, increase income. This increases tax revenue, but ordinarily not by enough to offset the original reduction in tax revenue due to the lower tax rate. The supply siders noted, however, that lower tax rates create incentives for work, which cause aggregate supply to increase. The extra force increasing income could create extra tax revenues sufficient to cause net tax revenues actually to increase.

### Example 3

**Secretary of the Treasury William E. Simon, on behalf of President Ford's administration, has submitted a proposal to the House Ways and Means Committee to reduce taxes on corporate profits. It seems the nation is faced with a trade-off between growth and redistribution: does it want to split a smaller pie equally or a larger pie less equally? The "difference principle," advocated by Harvard philosopher John Rawls in his book *A Theory of Justice*, holds that inequality can be justified only if it works to the absolute benefit of the least advantaged.**

*Explain what rationale must lie behind Simon's proposal and how it gives rise to the "trade-off."*

Simon must feel that reducing taxes on corporate profits will cause corporations to respond by increasing investment spending, which increases both aggregate demand and the economy s productive capacity, and thus stimulates growth. The trade-off is between this growth and the redistribution of income towards the wealthy owners of corporations.

*Under what circumstances would Rawls's difference principle be met in this context?*

The difference principle would be met if the inequality created by the lower profits taxes causes the low-income and unemployed in the economy to benefit. Such benefits could come about because of higher employment and higher real wages due to productivity increases.

## Chapter Summary

- Keynesian neglect of the supply side of the economy handicapped analysis of supply-side shocks, business-cycle behavior, and long-run economic growth.
- The AD curve is most appropriately interpreted as a series of possible equilibrium positions for the economy in which aggregate demand for goods and services matches aggregate supply of goods and services. The AS curve is

most appropriately interpreted as a series of possible equilibrium positions for the labor market. Short-run equilibria in the labor market differ from long-run equilibria because of contract obligations and information failures, so short- and long-run AS curves differ. The long-run AS curve is a vertical line at the level of output corresponding to the NRU.

- An expansionary policy at full employment moves the economy in the short run to a higher price level and a higher output level, but in the long run the economy returns to its original full-employment (NRU) level of output, implying that in the long run the only effect of this policy is to raise the price level. The temporary increase in output occurs because workers are induced to provide more labor at a lower real wage; formal or informal contract obligations may prevent them from quickly adjusting their money wage to offset price level increases, or they may not quickly perceive that these price increases have lowered their real wage. Two results of note are that (1) during the second half of this reaction, the economy is moving back up to the NRU while continuing to experience price increases (unemployment and prices are increasing together); and (2) if the government tries to maintain the economy at an unemployment level below the NRU, a continually rising price level will develop.

- A contractionary policy at full employment moves the economy into a recession that is made worse by "downward-sticky" wages and prices. Modern Keynesians, called New Keynesians, have provided several reasons why this is consistent with rational, maximizing behavior. The wage and price stickiness exacerbates and prolongs the recession, causing Keynesians to call for government policy action.

- A negative supply-side shock can make the economy less productive and thus require a fall in the real wage if full employment is to be maintained. The economy's reaction to such a shock depends on how workers react to price increases that lower their real wage and on whether government recognizes any change in the full-employment level of output.

- Supply-side economists stress the role of incentives (disincentives) created by policies. An infamous example is the Laffer curve, which shows how disincentives cause tax revenues eventually to decrease as the tax rate increases. Supply-side economics has been discredited mainly because the empirical magnitude of the incentive effects is so small.

## Media Exercises

1. **For years, the scale has tipped toward controlling the economy by controlling federal spending and consumption. Now, it may begin to lean toward stimulating production through incentives.**

   What names are usually given to these policies?

2.  **Inevitably, says Laffer, economic growth will raise enough tax revenues to more than offset the original tax cut, thus shrinking the federal deficit and reducing inflation.**

    a. Where on the Laffer curve must Laffer believe the economy is located?

    b. What is the logic behind the feeling that this tax cut would serve to reduce inflation?

3.  **The European Union's jobless rate is nudging 12 percent. A few die-hard Keynesians might reckon that this leaves room for a demand stimulus to create jobs, but most economists believe that ...**

    a. What is the logic of the die-hard Keynesians?

    b. Complete this clipping to explain why most economists do not agree with the die-hard Keynesians.

4.  **Indeed, there was a remarkable concensus among economists at the conference that most of the rise in unemployment over the past two decades does not reflect deficient demand, but rather a rise in the ...**

    Complete this sentence.

5.  **If a "stimulative deficit" were deliberately undertaken to prime the pump of the economy, then the debt might liquidate itself.**

    a. How could a deficit "prime the pump" of the economy?

    b. How could this cause the debt to liquidate itself?

6.  **The trouble is that workers became accustomed to real wage increases of about 3 percent per year, and when productivity growth crashed in the 1970s, they refused to cooperate by lowering real wage growth. Firms acquiesced in order to avoid lower productivity due to worker dissatisfaction. The end result was similar to that of the oil price increases.**

    a. How would this be portrayed on an *AS/AD* diagram?

    b. What terminology do economists use to refer to the phenomenon described in the second sentence?

7.  **When the British in 1979 cut top tax rates of 83 percent on earned income and 98 percent on investment income to 60 percent and 75 percent respectively, they were accused of hugely reducing the share of tax paid by the rich. Instead, the top 5 percent of British taxpayers today contribute a third as much again in real terms as they did in 1978. This is because ...**

    Complete this clipping.

8. **The calculations governments make about tax revenues are always based on the assumption that taxpayers are dutiful sheep who will raise not a bleat as they are led to the fleecing pen. They will all continue to stay where they are, work just as hard, produce just as much, and pay their taxes on the same basis as they always have.**

   Do these claims imply that a government will underestimate or overestimate the extra tax revenue that a tax increase will generate?

9. **At a pragmatic level, my colleagues take the view that if a rich man paying a lower tax rate makes it possible for a low-income family to have a good house to live in, useful and secure employment, access to good and affordable medical care, and a good education for their children, then society as a whole is richer.**

   a. What great trade-off is being described here?

   b. What name might economists use to describe this spokesperson and her colleagues?

10. **One striking challenge came from supply-side economists, who contended that the sheer waste and perverse incentives associated with high tax rates created opportunities to cut tax rates without cutting ...**

    Complete this sentence.

11. **Supply-side economics, packaged and popularized as "Reaganomics," has become a big deal in the current policy debate over the fight against stagflation. To counteract this phenomenon of persistent high inflation, unemployment, and stagnant growth, supply-side policies emphasize increasing production to take the pressure off prices.**

    Use an *AS/AD* diagram to show how supply-side policies could accomplish the results claimed in the second paragraph.

12. **If adverse supply shocks (escalating oil prices, crop failures) were so influential in creating stagflation in the 1970s, it is difficult to believe that we cannot create favorable supply shocks in the 1980s.**

    Use an *AS/AD* diagram to show how adverse supply shocks create stagflation (rising prices and rising unemployment).

13. **With the economy mired in recession, it is almost a classic case of room for government stimulus without damage.**

    What is meant here by government stimulus "without damage"?

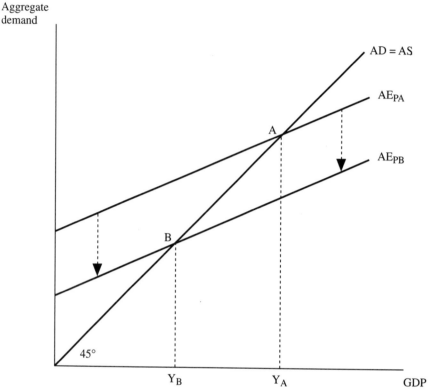

**Figure 5A.1a**  Deriving the AD curve
A rise in price from $P_A$ to $P_B$ shifts the AE curve down to $AE_{PB}$, changing the equilibrium point from A to B. The higher price level $P_B$ is matched with the lower income level $Y_B$ in Figure 5A.1b.

---

## Appendix 5.1:   Deriving the AD Curve

The purpose of this appendix is to present the graphical derivation of the AD curve in its simplest form. This derivation utilizes the 45° line diagram (exposited in appendix 4.2) in figure 5A.1a to derive the AD curve in figure 5A.1b.

In figure 5A.1a we begin with price level $P_A$, which gives rise to aggregate expenditure line $AE_{PA}$, putting the economy at equilibrium point A. At point A the price level is $P_A$ and income is $Y_A$, shown in figure 5A.1b as point AA. Suppose now that the price level increases to $P_B$. This causes the wealth effect and other phenomena to operate to decrease aggregate demand for goods and services, shifting the AE curve down to $AE_{PB}$, lowering equilibrium income to $Y_B$. Thus, the higher price level $P_B$ corresponds to the lower equilibrium income level $Y_B$, shown in figure 5A.1b as point BB.

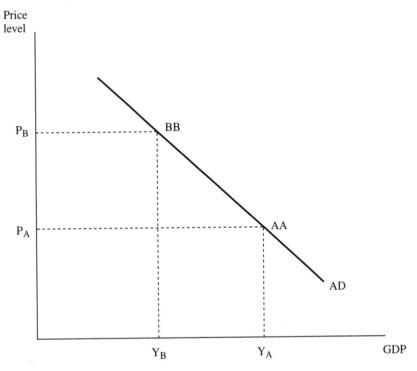

**Figure 5A.1b**   Deriving the AD curve
The movement from A to B in Figure 5A.1a a corresponds to a movement from AA to BB, producing a downward-sloping AD curve.

Figures 5A.1a and 5A.1b show that the AD curve is downward-sloping. It also makes clear that the AD curve is better described as an "equilibrium" curve: for each price level it tells us what level of income would have to prevail to create equilibrium in the goods and services submarket of the macro-economy. This version of the AD curve is very simple; it represents equilibrium in only one macroeconomic submarket, the goods and services market; more elaborate versions of the AD curve also represent equilibrium in the money market or in both the money and the foreign exchange markets.

# 6 Growth

In the 1950s and 1960s, the rate of growth of U.S. productivity, and hence of the domestic standard of living as measured by per capita output of economic goods and services, was between 2.5 and 3.0 percent per year. In the 1970s and 1980s, however, this rate fell to less than half its former level. At the higher rate of growth, the standard of living doubles every generation, about every twenty-five years, but at the lower rate the standard of living increases only by half during a generation. What appears to be a small difference in growth rates has surprisingly dramatic implications for the standard of living in the long run.

It is difficult for politicians and even policymakers to become excited about doing something to raise the rate of productivity growth by, say, 0.7 percentage points. Doing so would double per capita real income over one hundred years from what it would otherwise be, but the number of percentage points seems so small, and the payoff so far away, that politicians are easily distracted by issues with bigger numbers and more immediate payoffs, such as keeping the economy at full employment. The misery of unemployment and the drama of short-run swings from recession to boom can seduce policymakers into focusing on unemployment issues and theorists into concentrating on business-cycle fluctuations. Both groups too easily forget that our material standard of living—what many believe to be most important dimension of economics—is determined by forces only peripherally associated with the issue of full employment.

The previous chapter discussed the supply side of the economy, emphasizing the distinction between the short and long runs, but focused on the business cycle—fluctuations of output around potential output. The purpose of this chapter is to discuss how potential output is itself growing, a supply-side phenomenon of a different sort, what determines the rate of growth of potential output and what determines productivity growth, which is the prime determinant of our material standard of living.

---

**Upon completion of this chapter you should**

- realize that most of macroeconomics focuses on what keeps the economy operating at its potential output rather than on what causes potential output to grow rapidly;

- know the main determinants of economic growth and possible explanations for the recent slowdown in productivity growth; and

- be aware of the important role played by the nation's saving rate and how it is affected by the government budget deficit.

---

## 6.1   The Determinants of Growth

The rate of growth of output varies dramatically over the business cycle. As we emerge from a recession, the economy can grow very quickly, at rates exceeding five or six percent per year, as unemployed labor as well as idle plants and equipment are put to work. "Economic growth" refers not to such short-run spurts in an economy's growth rate, but to growth in an economy's *potential* or full-employment output, measured over quite long periods of time. Economic growth depends on increases in the quantity and quality of the two basic inputs of the macroeconomic production process—capital and labor—and on improvements in the way in which they are combined. This gives rise to the following five main sources of GDP growth:

1. *An increase in the size of the labor force.*   Examples of supply-side policies that affect the size of the labor force are immigration regulations, day care subsidies, retirement benefits, and tax incentives.

2. *An increase in the quality of the labor force.*   Examples of supply-side policies that influence labor quality are subsidies for retraining programs and the development of technical schools oriented more closely to the needs of industry.

3. *An increase in the size of the stock of physical capital.*   (Physical stock equals the number of buildings and the amount of equipment that firms have to work with.) Examples of supply-side policies that affect the size of the capial stock are tax incentives for investment and saving.

4. *An increase in the quality of the capital stock.*   Examples of supply-side policies that influence the quality of capital are tax incentives for research and development, and the promotion of competition.

5. *Improvements in the way in which capital and labor are combined to produce output.*   Improvements could be due to better worker/management relations, just-in-time inventory policies, economies of scale, and the movement of farm workers to the cities.

**Table 6.1**   Relative contributions to U.S. growth, 1929–1982

| Source | % contribution to total growth of 2.9% per year on average | % contribution to per person growth of 1.5% per year on average |
|---|---|---|
| Labor input except education | 32 | −12 |
| Education per worker | 14 | 27 |
| Capital | 19 | 20 |
| Advances in knowledge | 20 | 38 |
| Improved resource allocation | 8 | 16 |
| Economies of scale | 9 | 18 |
| Land | 0 | −3 |
| Changes in legal and human environment | −1 | −3 |

Source: Edward F. Denison, *Trends in American Economic Growth 1929–1982* (Washington, D.C.: Brookings Institution, 1985).

Technological change, thought by many to be the most important determinant of growth, is embodied in labor and capital, so it is included with the improvements in their quality.

The middle column of table 6.1 shows the relative contributions to actual growth in the United States during the 1929–1982 period. The negative contribution of changes in legal and human environment is due to regulatory legislation involving worker safety and environmental protection, which directs resources away from the production of output counted in the GDP measure. The category "advances in knowledge" is calculated as a residual; it represents technical change.

Associated with the concept of economic growth is an increasing material standard of living enjoyed by people in the economy, the main determinant of which is an economy's *productivity*, usually measured as output per working hour. Growth in productivity results from increases in physical capital, higher quality of labor and capital, and improvements in how capital and labor are combined. The role of each of these is affected by institutional features of the economy such as the work ethic of the culture, the entrepreneurial drive of the populace, and its ability to adapt to change. The righthand column of table 6.1 offers some insight into past contributions to productivity growth. The negative number for labor input reflects decreases in hours worked per week. Note the size of the unexplainable residual "advances in knowledge" that reflect technical change.

Productivity growth in the United States has slowed dramatically in recent years. Several explanations have been offered for this slowdown:

1. *A return to normal.*   The rate of productivity growth experienced during the thirty years following the Second World War was anomolously high when

---

**Curiosity 6.1:   What Is Endogenous Growth Theory?**

Keynesian analysis viewed investment spending as a component of aggregate demand and focused on its multiplier impact on income. A longer-run view, however, recognizes that investment affects the supply side of the economy by increasing the capital stock and making the economy more productive. In round terms, 60 percent of investment offsets depreciation of existing plant and equipment, 20 percent increases capital in line with annual labor-force growth, and the remaining 20 percent serves to increase capital per worker, thus enhancing productivity.

   Early attempts to formalize this role of investment viewed GDP as being determined by a formula such as

$$GDP = AL^{.7}K^{.3}.$$

where $L$ and $K$ are labor and capital stocks, respectively, and $A$ is a constant. GDP grew because each year the labor force grew, and the capital stock also grew thanks to investment. Growth in productivity was captured by postulating that $A$ grew each year by about 2 percent, reflecting technical change brought about by a continuous stream of innovations. A key assumption was that this rate of technical change is unaffected by the saving and investment levels that it helps determine through its influence on the growth rate. The independence of the rate of technical change from investment and saving activity is what is meant by the statement that technical change is exogenous. The lack of such independence means that technical change is determined endogenously by the interaction of saving, investment, growth, and technical change.

   Modern growth theory questions this exogenous view of technical change, claiming that technical change is determined endogenously: the level of technical change can be influenced by investment in education to improve the quality of labor and by investment in research and development to improve the quality of capital. Furthermore, the success of such investments could induce more such investment and higher saving to finance it. It is therefore possible that a virtuous cycle could develop in which investment creates more knowledge, which in turn spurs more investment. This endogenous growth theory raises the profile of national saving and investment.

---

viewed in a broader historical context. It may be that recently we have fallen back to a more normal rate of productivity growth or are experiencing a normal cyclical downturn in the rate of discovery of new technology.

2. *Decreases in investment.*   A smaller rate of investment implies lower growth in the amount of capital (plant and equipment) with which each worker has to work, as well as a slower rate at which technical change becomes embodied in the capital stock. It also implies lower spending on research and development, decreasing the rate at which technological innovations are developed. Decreases in government investment in infrastructure (roads, airports, and water supply systems, for example) affect the productivity of private capital and thereby affect growth. A decrease in the national rate of saving affects the amount of funding available for investment.

3. *Measurement problems.*   Many productivity increases manifest themselves in a higher quality of output rather than in a higher quantity of output per worker. If quality changes are not measured properly, which is often the case, the growth slowdown may be an illusion. Increases in government regulations to enhance worker safety and environmental protection are another source of measurement problems. To the extent that such regulations achieve their desired ends, traditional measures of productivity are usually underestimates, and thus the productivity growth slowdown is an illusion, but if they reflect unnecessary bureaucracy, productivity growth is dissipated.

4. *Inflexibilities.*   For productivity increases to occur, both labor and output markets must be flexible, allowing competition to force old, inefficient industries to die out and new, more efficient industries to replace them. In Europe, many countries have enacted policies to protect existing industries and jobs, making the introduction of technological change very costly. The United States is thought to have a relatively flexible labor market in this respect. From 1973 to 1983, the U.S. economy created eighteen million jobs, whereas the German economy lost almost a million jobs.

5. *Structural changes.*   Over time, changes in tastes and technology affect what is produced, where it is produced, how it is produced, and the skills required of the labor force. Although such structural changes reflect the needed flexibility noted earlier, they can also lead to slowdowns in further growth. Examples of such changes include a shift of economic activity into the service industries, where productivity increases are more difficult to attain; a change in the composition of the workforce, including more young people and former homemakers with less experience and market-oriented skills; and a slowdown in the movement of labor from the farm to the city as the great technological advances in agriculture become fully integrated into the economy. Increases in energy prices require that the economy shift to a new profit-maximizing mix of inputs, reflecting their new relative prices, during which time productivity growth will be inhibited.

6. *Incentive effects.*   Supply-siders claim that we have been taxing work, saving, and output while subsidizing consumption, leisure, unemployment, and retirement. The remarkable economic growth of Japan and the four "tigers" (Hong Kong, Singapore, Taiwan, and South Korea) has been based on allowing free markets to operate—permitting entrepreneurs to reap the fruits of their risk and labor. This has led many economists to believe that, although the supply-siders' incentive effects may not have much impact in the short run, they can be of considerable importance in the long-run growth context.

## 6.2   The Productivity Growth Process

Unfortunately, the process by which productivity increases are incorporated into the economy is not a comfortable one. In 1942, economist Joseph Schumpeter described the essence of capitalism as the continuous mutation of the firm and market, as old industries prospered, died, and then were replaced by new industries. He named the process *creative destruction.*

New technology invariably destroys many more jobs than it creates. Indeed, this is the essence of how productivity increases are injected into the economy. Fewer workers are needed to produce the same output, with the surplus workers put to work, producing a bonus (extra output) that would not be possible without the new technology. This process can be far-reaching. In 1800, nearly 90 percent of the U.S. population was on farms, but today that figure is less than 3 percent. An unfortunate side effect of this process is that new technologies usually require workers with new skills, so that those with old skills become unemployed. For example, blacksmiths cannot easily get jobs as auto mechanics. The newly unemployed find that sweeping technological and institutional change has wiped out firms and entire industries, revolutionized products and human skills, and dramatically altered the nature of the workplace itself. Understandably, workers find it difficult to adapt to such changes, producing long-term unemployment, recession, and slow growth.

Although this process is ongoing as a continual stream of innovations occurs, some periods of innovation are of such importance that they exaggerate any subsequent recession and growth slowdown. The industrial revolution is the best-known example. More recent examples include the period between 1880 and 1930, with the development of electric power, chemicals, the internal combustion engine, and the assembly line; the period between 1940 and 1970, with the creation of plastics, synthetic fibers, the jet engine, television, and multinational corporations; and, most recently, the information revolution based on the personal computer, biotechnology, telecom networks, and lean, flexible, decentralized, nonhierachical workplaces.

Such periods of great innovation give rise to a long-wave cycle. The recession created by significant innovations lingers—with stagnant growth, write-offs of dated capital stock, high structural unemployment, and social tension—until a new generation of workers arises, unencumbered by the old way of doing things. The economy rebuilds itself around the new technology and its associated new infrastructure, creating a protracted period of expansion, within which the normal business cycles occur. Some economists believe that the current productivity slowdown is in part due to the economy passing through the trough of a long-wave cycle.

The creative destruction phenomenon is the process whereby productivity increases are implemented, increasing our standard of living. One policy implication is that governments should not inhibit this process by forcing firms to bear high costs when laying off workers, subsidizing firms to protect jobs, or insulating firms from competition. Another policy implication is that governments should facilitate adjustment by organizing worker retraining programs.

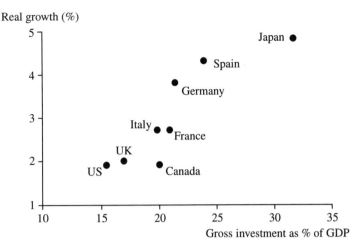

**Figure 6.1**   Real growth and investment
Real growth as measured on the vertical axis is average growth over the 1986–1991 period. Gross investment is for 1991.
Source: *OECD Economic Surveys 1993–1994*

## 6.3   The Role of National Saving

No agreement exists about the causes of the productivity growth slowdown, but economists do agree that the level of investment is a crucial element in the productivity growth process. Figure 6.1 illustrates the connection between growth and investment for selected countries. The relationship between investment and growth is by no means exact, but it is apparent. A major determinant of investment is the level of national saving—that part of GDP not used for private or public consumption. A useful perspective on national saving can be gained by looking at how the various categories of aggregate demand are financed.

Income earners allocate some of their income to pay for their consumption of goods and services and some of it to pay their taxes. What is left over is called *private saving*, which is used to buy financial assets such as government bonds, or stocks and bonds sold by businesses to pay for their investment in plant and equipment. What determines how much of the saving goes to the government and how much to business? The answer, in short, is the interest rate. The government needs to sell enough bonds to finance its deficit, so it bids up the interest rate to get the financing it needs. As the interest rate rises, some businesses decide that it is too expensive to undertake investment plans and so abandon them. In this way, the rising interest rate squeezes business demand for financing down to what is left over after the government has financed its deficit.

**Figure 6.2**   Sources of financing for government and investment spending

This can be illustrated by ignoring the international sector and writing GDP as

$$\text{GDP} = C + G + I,$$

reflecting its aggregate demand components, and writing it again as

$$\text{GDP} = C + T + S,$$

reflecting its use in financing consumption and paying taxes $T$, with what is left over, called private saving $S$. This gives rise to the portrayal in figure 6.2 of $T$ and $S$ serving as the financing sources for $G$ and $I$.

Taxes are used exclusively to finance government spending, with the budget deficit financed by some of our private saving. What private saving is left over is used to finance investment, so investment ends up equal to private saving less the budget deficit. The lesson from this is that there are two fundamental determinants of investment: the level of private saving and the government budget deficit. Between them, they determine the interest rate, which forces investment to a level equal to what is referred to as *national saving*: private saving less the government budget deficit. In formal terms,

investment = national saving = private saving − government deficit.

During the 1980s both determinants of national saving changed markedly. Before 1980, U.S. private saving was about 9.6 percent of GDP, and the government budget deficit was about 1.4 percent of GDP, yielding a national saving rate of about 8.2 percent. By 1990, private saving had fallen to 6.6 percent, and the government deficit had risen to 3.6 percent, dropping national saving to 3 percent. This rate of national saving is low not just in comparison to earlier years, but also relative to the 12 percent of most other industrialized countries and the 17 percent of Japan.

Did the drop in U.S. national saving cause investment in the United States to fall? Surprisingly, not much, mainly because of financing from foreign sources (see curiosity 6.2 on foreign financing). Reliance on foreign financing is not a good long-run strategy, however. It can disappear quickly, causing great disruption, and if it is continued, much of the benefit of the investment accrues to the new foreign owners of our businesses rather than to our own citizens. Consequently, considerable attention has been focused on ways to increase the national saving rate, such as by decreasing the government deficit, an obvious implication of the analysis above.

## 6.4  Policy for Growth

Policies to encourage growth and productivity increases fall into four broad categories.

1. Government should provide an institutional environment conducive to the efficient operation of private enterprise, including protection of property rights, maintenance of law and order, establishment of a sound monetary system, prevention of monopolies in major services such as transportation and communication, and liberalization of trade and investment so that the country does not miss out on new technologies.

2. Government should invest in growth-enhancing public goods. Such goods have overall returns to society that exceed the returns that can be captured via private enterprise. For example, private enterprise cannot collect payment from all those who benefit from a dam that provides flood control. As a result, such goods are not provided adequately by private enterprise. Other examples involve providing infrastructure, such as highways, and spending on education and health. Some have argued that such investment in public goods should be viewed as part of national saving because it augments the nation's stock of human and physical capital.

3. Government should provide appropriate incentives for savers and investors through favorable tax treatment of saving and investment, particularly investment in research and development: tax reductions for individual retirement accounts to increase saving and lower taxes on capital gains to reward investment in entrepreneurial activities, for example. Bringing private saving back up to earlier levels may be difficult, however. Personal savings have fallen for many reasons that government policy is not in a position to affect. For example, improved social security has reduced the need to save for one's old age; insurance and bank loans have reduced the need to save for rainy days; and changes in the age profile of the populace, from younger to older, and in social attitudes, toward self-gratification and less concern for future generations, have reduced saving. Most empirical evidence does suggest, however, that high-growth countries have lower tax rates on average than low-growth countries.

4. Government should ensure that fiscal policy does not create a large government deficit which reduces the financing available for private investment—in other words, national saving. The reduction in national saving is particularly disadvantageous if the deficit corresponds to spending on things such as transfer payments rather than infrastructure.

**Curiosity 6.2:   What about Foreign Financing?**

Domestic financing for investment comes from national saving, which is private saving less the government deficit. Foreigners may also provide financing, which can be examined by including imports $(M)$ and exports among the aggregate demand categories that comprise GDP.

GDP can be written as $C + I + G + X - M$, reflecting its aggregate demand makeup, or $C + T + S$, reflecting its breakdown for financing purposes. Equating these two expressions, we get

$$C + I + G + X - M = C + T + S.$$

Cancel the Cs and move the $X - M$ to the financing side to get

$$I + G = T + S + M - X.$$

$I$ and $G$ are financed by taxes, private saving, and foreign sources $M - X$:

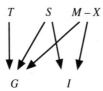

**Figure 6.3**   The role of foreign financing for government and investment spending

How does $M - X$ represent foreign financing? $M - X$ is the excess of U.S. imports over exports. In 1994, this was about \$150 billion and represents US\$150 billion left in the hands of foreigners after they paid for their imports. These dollars are available to be loaned to U.S. citizens, augmenting the sources of financing discussed earlier. More on this topic appears in chapter 15, which discusses the balance of payments. In formal terms we have,

investment = private saving − government deficit + foreign financing.

A prime objective of these government policies is to increase saving and investment. The bottom line here can be expressed in cruder terms that may strike a reader with more force. Raising productivity requires that workers be given more and better capital and education. The only way this can be done is by asking the present generation to sacrifice—consume less to create capital and pay for education that in all likelihood will benefit only future generations. If the present generation is more self-centered than its predecessors, it will be difficult for policy to make much headway in achieving this objective.

## Media Illustrations

### *Example 1*
**Economist McKenzie attacks both U.S. political parties' attraction to what he calls "jobilism"—trying to create jobs mostly by protecting current jobs, thence reducing churn.**

*What is "churn" in this context?*
Churn is another term for creative destruction. It refers to the turnover of jobs—elimination of jobs that have become obsolete because of technical advances and their replacement with new jobs in areas that meet new demands for goods and services and that incorporate new technology. For example, the invention of the automobile required the elimination of jobs in the buggy industry and the creation of jobs in the automobile industry.

*Why would reducing churn be viewed as undesirable?*
Churn causes productivity to improve.

*What implications does churn have for one's view of the North American Free Trade Agreement?*
One would have to recognize that this agreement would require the loss of many jobs, which should be offset by the creation of many new jobs as our economy specializes in what it does best, improving our overall productivity.

### *Example 2*
**Lipsey points to evidence that when demand is held too long below capacity output, "capacity itself may shrink (at least relative to the potential labor force) with disastrous consequences for the inflation-unemployment trade-off." This means that successive demand-induced recessions compound the problem and lead to ever increasing levels of inflation and unemployment.**

*How and why would capacity shrink?*
If demand is below capacity output, there is idle capital stock and thus no incentive for new investment. Over time, the existing capital stock wears out and becomes obsolete. This depreciation of the existing capital stock shrinks capacity.

*Why is the caveat "at least relative to the potential labor force" added?*
The labor force continuously grows as population grows. This growing labor force requires a growing capital stock with which to work. It is not enough for the capital stock to remain unchanged or to grow only slightly; it must grow by enough to match the growth in the labor force.

*Describe how an AS/AD diagram would illustrate the inflation/unemployment problem referred to in the clipping.*
The fall in the capital stock makes the economy less productive, causing the AS curve to shift leftwards/upwards as well as moving the economy to a lower level of income/employment and to a higher price level.

### Example 3

**Personal saving habits peaked in the early 1970s, when average U.S. residents stashed away over 9 percent of take-home pay, and declined through the 1980s to a low of less than 3 percent. It seems that they prefer to cut down on their saving to maintain living standards; the catch is that a low saving rate makes it harder to increase living standards.**

*Explain this seeming paradox.*

By decreasing saving to maintain living standards, we decrease the financing available for investment, causing investment in new plant and equipment and in research and development to fall, thus inhibiting the increases in productivity that increase living standards.

### Example 4

**There is some suspicion that what cuts inflation in the short run may make the economy more inflationary in the long run.**

*Explain the logic of this statement.*

Increasing taxes and decreasing government spending may be used to shift the AD curve to the left to reduce upward pressure on prices, which cuts inflation. Higher taxes, however, may have supply-side effects, such as reducing investment, and decreased government spending may lower investment in infrastructure. Reducing investment causes the capital stock and thus potential output to grow by less than it would otherwise, so that, later, demand expansion will more quickly exceed potential output and thus create price increases.

## Chapter Summary

- Most of macroeconomic analysis is concerned with explaining business-cycle behavior and devising the means of keeping the economy as close to full employment as possible without creating inflation. Comparatively little attention is paid to what many would claim are more important goals of macroeconomic analysis: explaining the process whereby our material standard of living increases and devising the means of enhancing this process.

- GDP growth is due to increases in the quantity and quality of labor and capital, as well as in improvements in the way in which they are combined to produce output.

- Productivity, measured as output per hour worked, is the prime determinant of our material standard of living. Productivity increases are incorporated into the economy via *creative destruction*, a process in which old industries are replaced by new ones, destroying more jobs than are created. Putting to work the resulting jobless creates extra output that produces the increase in our standard of living.

- Several explanations for the recent slowdown in productivity growth have been put forward, but this slowdown remains a puzzle.

- *National saving*, the difference between private saving and the budget deficit, represents domestic financing available for investment. This pool of financing can be increased either by the currrent generation saving more (and thus sacrificing for the benefit of future generations) or by the government decreasing its budget deficit.

## Formula Definitions

- national saving = private saving − government deficit.

- investment = national saving + foreign financing.

## Media Exercises

1. **After a recession, annual growth will probably be 3 percent to 4 percent, rather than the more robust 5 percent to 6 percent typical.**

   Explain why an economy's growth rate is typically so high after a recession.

2. **The nation's core economic problem remains slow growth in productivity— a condition that is worsened, if not caused, by U.S. residents' historically low rate of ...**

   Complete this sentence and explain the logic behind it.

3. **On those rare occasions when the economic benefits of accelerated infra- structure spending are discussed, it is usually in the context of the coun- tercyclical role assigned to such spending by John Maynard Keynes, leading to charges of "make-work projects" with little economic value. Precious little is said about the critical links that exist between quality infrastructure and ...**

   a. Explain what is meant by the countercyclical role and how it works.

   b. In the context of the countercyclical role, are make-work projects of equal value to quality infrastructure? Why or why not?

   c. Complete this clipping.

4. **Given the low level of savings and investment, some economists now fear that the United States will be lucky during the 1990s to match the record of the 1980s when the amount of goods and services produced by each worker rose a scant 0.8 percent a year.**

a. What technical term do economists use to talk about the phenomenon being discussed here?

b. Why are savings and investment important in this context?

5. **Over the longer term, business may be shooting itself in the foot by taking a hard line against government taxing and spending policies if this hard line causes a decline in public spending on the economy's infrastructure—roads, sewers, bridges, and other public works.**

Explain the logic of this claim.

6. **Economists have traditionally concentrated on annual fluctuations in GDP and had little to say about _____. Questions such as why growth in per capita GDP in industrial economies slowed from an average of 3.5 percent in 1950–1973 to 1.9 percent in 1974–1990 have been mostly ignored. That is a shame. If growth had continued at its earlier pace, real incomes today would be a third higher. By comparison, the gains from _____ seem minuscule.**

Fill in the blanks here.

7. **The case for tax breaks for investment rests on the claim that because of big spillover effects, the return on investment in machinery and equipment to the economy as a whole is far greater than . . .**

Complete this clipping.

8. **One popular view is that the best way for governments to stimulate growth is to improve the functioning of markets and to adopt stable and credible macroeconomic policies that encourage firms to take a long-term view. The trouble with this view is that governments, like voters, are more interested in . . .**

Complete this clipping.

9. **Countries with a high level of education tend to absorb new technology more quickly and therefore to grow more quickly. But one problem is that firms and workers cannot take account of external benefits from investing in education, which means that they . . .**

Complete this clipping.

10. **It may make more sense to remove some of the many disincentives to save and invest than to use the tax system to discriminate in favor of investment. For example, tax breaks on mortgage-interest payments divert savings from . . .**

Complete this clipping.

11. **Although policymakers in the United States talked boldly about boosting investment, they mainly ducked the question of how to boost its low rate of _____ . To finance higher investment the United States would have to increase _____ or slash _____ .**

Fill in the blanks here.

12. **They don't seem to be getting the underlying message in the country's failures in domestic and international markets: the United States has been destroying too few jobs.**

What logic could lie behind this statement?

13. **We must view the loss of hundreds of thousands of jobs in the U.S. textile industry over the past two decades as a positive measure of the success of the industry in dramatically improving ...**

Complete the claim in this clipping.

14. **Mr. Stein himself estimates that the growth of budget deficits during the 1980s cut 3 percent from the decade's GDP.**

How would growing budget deficits lower GDP? Shouldn't they increase GDP through the multiplier effect?

15. **The budget deficit diverts domestic savings that could have been directed to productive investment elsewhere. During the 1960s, the budget deficit absorbed about 2 percent of national savings, according to the General Accounting Office. By the 1970s, it absorbed 19 percent, and by 1990, the figure was 58 percent.**

How would budget deficits accomplish this diversion?

16. **Domestic investment did not fall as sharply as did national saving because ...**

Complete this clipping to explain how domestic investment could have been financed if saving fell.

# 7  Crowding Out

The multiplier process causes an increase in government spending, or any other exogenous increase in spending, to have a greater ultimate effect on the nominal level of income through price increases, real income increases, or both, depending on where the economy is relative to full employment. This phenomenon makes fiscal policy attractive for those who believe in government intervention to control the economy, but opponents of this Keynesian view claim that the magnitude of the multiplier, and thus the strength of fiscal policy, is greatly exaggerated. They accuse advocates of the Keynesian approach of not telling the whole story when explaining how the multiplier process operates. In particular, they claim the Keynesians have ignored the effects on the economy caused by the means used to finance an increase in government spending.

The purpose of this chapter is to examine the *crowding out* phenomenon—the process whereby an increase in government spending crowds out, or decreases, other components of aggregate demand, thus making the multiplier smaller. Some empirical estimates suggest that the multiplier may be as small as 0.6.

---

**Upon completion of this chapter you should**

- be able to identify several ways in which an increase in government spending crowds out other types of aggregate demand; and
- understand how different means of financing an increase in government spending lead to different multiplier values.

---

## 7.1  Automatic Stabilizers

When students first learn about the multiplier, they jump to the conclusion that it is better to have a large rather than a small multiplier to enable the government to push the economy out of a recession more easily. There are two main reasons why this conclusion is not warranted:

1. Our knowledge of the economy and how it operates is imperfect, so deciding when and by how much to change government spending is not an exact science. A large multiplier magnifies any mistake by the government.

2. A large multiplier means that *any* change in aggregate demand, not just a change in government spending, has a substantive impact on economic activity. All economies are subject to irregular changes in aggregate demand, such as changes in export demand due to changes in foreign economies, or changes in investment demand due to new inventions. With a high multiplier, these changes have a large impact on economic activity, creating instability.

In light of these two problems, anything that causes the multiplier to become smaller—called an *automatic stabilizer*—is considered desirable because it insulates the economy from the effects of aggregate demand shocks. Several phenomena can serve as automatic stabilizers. Each of the following examples is explained in the context of an increase in aggregate demand. They would operate in reverse if aggregate demand were to decrease.

### Income Taxes

The increase in income at each stage of the multiplier process is not all available for spending; some is required to pay income taxes on the extra income earned. Because taxes inhibit the rise in consumption spending, aggregate demand does not increase by as much at each stage of the multiplier process, so the multiplier process does not stimulate income by as much.

### Unemployment Insurance

As the economy is stimulated, some of the people who receive unemployment insurance will find jobs. The increase in their income is partially offset by lost unemployment insurance payments. Consequently, the increase in consumption demand is smaller than if there had been no unemployment insurance, so the strength of the multiplier process is decreased. Similarly, a negative shock to the economy is cushioned because those losing their jobs collect unemployment insurance and so do not decrease consumption demand by as much as they would otherwise.

### Imports

The increase in consumption demand at each stage of the multiplier process is not all on domestically produced goods and services. Some demand goes to imports. This means that at each stage of the multiplier process aggregate demand for domestically produced goods and services does not increase by as much, so the multiplier process does not stimulate income by as much.

### Interest Rates

As their income increases, people wish to hold more money (cash) for two reasons. First, more money is needed to facilitate a higher level of production (although money is not a physical input to the production process, just try producing anything without money on hand!). And second, more money is needed to facilitate the higher consumption spending induced by the higher income. This extra demand for money, if not met by the monetary authorities, causes the price of money, the interest rate, to rise. (See chapter 10 for more on the interest rate.)

A higher interest rate reduces all four of the major types of aggregate demand:

1. Consumption falls because a higher interest rate tempts people to save rather than to consume. Further, it makes monthly payments on loans to purchase major consumer durables too high for many would-be buyers.

2. Investment falls because the higher costs of borrowing money to undertake an investment project may make that project unprofitable. Further, some firms with money to invest discover they can earn a higher return from loaning it out than from investing it in new equipment.

3. Government spending falls because local governments may decide to wait for lower interest costs before borrowing to finance projects such as a library or a swimming pool.

4. Export demand falls because the rise in interest rates causes foreigners to buy more of our financial assets, which increases the demand for our dollars

on the foreign exchange market. This increases the value of our dollar, making it more expensive for foreigners to buy our exports. (See chapter 15 for more on this international phenomenon.)

The interest rate can play a strong role in reducing the size of the multiplier. One economic model has estimated the multiplier to be about 2.0 if the interest rate is held constant, but only about 0.6 if the interest rate is allowed to rise.

All of the above examples of crowding out operate regardless of whether the initial stimulus to aggregate demand takes the form of an increase in government spending or an increase in some other form of aggregate demand. In the former context, an additional important source of crowding out is the means used to finance the increase in government spending.

## 7.2   Financing an Increase in Government Spending

The Keynesian story of the multiplier phenomenon traditionally sweeps under the rug the fact that the government must somehow finance an increase in spending. This is important because the means chosen to finance spending may have an influence on aggregate demand that to some extent could offset the stimulus of the fiscal action. An increase in government spending can be financed in three basic ways: raising taxes, selling bonds to the public, and selling bonds to the central bank (often referred to as *printing money*). Let us look at the crowding out that may occur with each of these three financing means.

### Taxation

If taxes are raised to finance an increase in government spending, consumers reduce consumption spending to be able to pay the higher taxes. The decrease in consumption demand partially offsets the increase in government spending, reducing the size of the multiplier. The offset is only partial because not all the financing for extra taxes comes from reducing consumption. Some comes from reducing saving, which is not a component of aggregate demand.

### Selling Bonds to the Public

Keynesians implicitly assume the government sells bonds to finance an increase in its spending. Extra crowding out comes about in two ways in this context:

1. *Raising interest rates.*   To sell bonds the government must make them attractive, so it must raise the interest rate. The higher interest rate crowds out all types of spending, as explained above.

2. *Smoothing consumption.*   When the bonds mature, interest and principal must be paid to the bondholders. People may believe that future taxes will

---

**Curiosity 7.1:   What Is the Balanced-Budget Multiplier?**

The multiplier assumes that the increase in government spending is financed by selling bonds to the public. When the increase in government spending is financed by raising taxes, this multiplier is called the *balanced-budget multiplier*, reflecting the fact that, in this case, the fiscal action has no impact on the size of the government's budget deficit or surplus.

An increase in government spending of one dollar increases aggregate demand by one dollar, but an increase of taxes by one dollar decreases aggregate demand by less than one dollar because the extra dollar for taxes comes partly from reducing saving. Consequently, a net positive impact on aggregate demand results from a balanced-budget change in government spending. We can conclude that the Keynesian multiplier process does not necessarily require creation of a budget deficit.

The balanced-budget multiplier is quite small, however, rendering unconvincing the Keynesian plea for fiscal policy in this context. In very simple models of the economy it is easy to show that the balanced-budget multiplier is one. More realistic models of the economy that incorporate automatic stabilizers, however, push this number well below 1.0.

---

be higher because of this and react by increasing saving (decreasing current consumption demand) to build up a reserve so that those anticipated higher taxes can be paid without disrupting future consumption levels. For those interested, more on this "Ricardian equivalence" phenomenon can be found in appendix 7.1 at the end of this chapter.

**Printing Money**

Financing increases in government spending by raising taxes or by selling bonds to the public leaves the supply of money in the economy unchanged, resulting in what is called a *pure* fiscal policy. In contrast, financing by selling bonds to the central bank increases the money supply. When buying a government bond (or any bond, for that matter), the central bank writes a check against itself and thereby creates money out of thin air, which explains why this means of financing is referred to as *printing money*. The U.S. central bank is often referred to as "the Fed," short for the Federal Reserve System. (Chapter 8 explains the money creation process in more detail.)

Financing by printing money mixes a fiscal policy of increased government spending with a monetary policy of increasing the money supply. In this case, there are no crowding out effects due to the financing means. The operation of the multiplier is in fact strengthened by the increase in the money supply because (as explained in chapter 9) an increase in the money supply also stimulates the economy. This leaves open, however, the question of whether the increase in income is due to the fiscal policy or the monetary policy.

Monetarists are prominent critics of the Keynesian approach. They claim that crowding out forces are strong, rendering fiscal policy weak. They also claim that financing a fiscal policy by printing money is the only way any substantive impact can be made on GDP, but that the impact is due not to the increase in government spending, but rather to the increase in the money supply. In their view, the quantity of money in the economy is the proper focus of attention in analyzing the macroeconomy, something we have heretofore ignored. The next chapter begins our examination of the role of money.

## Media Illustrations

### Example 1

**I think a lot of people, particularly in the business community and among economists, have realized that much of the present deficit is of a purely cyclical nature, resulting from what they call the automatic stabilizers.**

*What is a deficit of a purely cyclical nature?*
A cyclical deficit is created by an automatic fall in tax revenues and a rise in certain types of government spending (such as unemployment insurance payments) during recessions.

*From what kind of deficit should a cyclical deficit be distinguished?*
It is to be distinguished from a budget deficit that has arisen from a discretionary change in government spending or taxing.

*What is an automatic stabilizer?*
An automatic stabilizer is an increase or decrease in spending that kicks in automatically to stabilize the economy whenever it moves into a recession or a boom.

### Example 2

**Of course, if Washington needed less cash, it would undoubtedly ease the strain on the states and the corporate sector.**

*What does "Washington needing cash" mean?*
The federal government needs to sell bonds to obtain cash to finance its budget deficit.

*What is the "strain on the states and the corporate sector"?*
Washington's activity in the bond market has pushed up interest rates, making it expensive for state governments and corporations to borrow.

### Example 3

**One question is whether the government can steel itself to bring its fiscal policy into line with the central bank's monetary policy. Will the government be able to borrow the funds it will need to cover this year's deficit out of the existing money supply, which the Fed is trying to restrict?**

*Of what relevance is the Fed's monetary policy here?*

If the Fed is restricting the money supply, it will not be willing to buy any of the government's bonds, so all of these bonds must be sold to the public.

*How can the government make sure it can borrow the funds it needs if the Fed refuses to increase the money supply?*

By raising the interest rate high enough, the government can ensure that it obtains the funds it needs. A higher interest rate causes savers to increase their saving, and causes some firms to cut back on investment so funds that would have been used for this purpose are now available to buy government bonds.

## Chapter Summary

- Several factors—most notably taxes, imports and interest rates—"crowd out" or reduce aggregate demand during the multiplier process. These automatic stabilizers reduce the magnitude of the multiplier, cushioning the economy from aggregate demand shocks.

- Financing an increase in government spending by increasing taxes or by selling bonds to the public causes crowding out forces to reduce the magnitude of the multiplier.

- Financing by selling bonds to the central bank, called *printing money*, averts crowding out forces. Opponents of the Keynesian view claim that, in this case, the rise in GDP is due to the increase in the money supply, not the increase in government spending.

## Media Exercises

1. **So many programs exist that the federal deficit will swell as they are maintained while tax revenues fall as a result of the weak economy.**

   Do these two phenomena serve to stabilize or destabilize the economy when it moves into recession? Explain.

2. **Fears had been expressed that financing of the federal deficit might squeeze private borrowers out of the market.**

   By what mechanism are private borrowers squeezed out of the market?

3. **Economists at the seminar agreed that the U.S. deficit of about $180 billion is severely straining domestic capital markets because private-sector capital demand is proving to be exceptionally bouyant. The result is a classic "crowding out" situation.**

a. What is meant by "severely straining"?

b. What is the main category of aggregate demand being crowded out here? Explain your reasoning.

4. **The bang from a buck of direct government spending—say, highway construction—is far greater than the punch from a tax cut of equal dollar magnitude.**

Explain why this is so.

5. **Clinton has promised to get the economy moving strongly again, but if that requires increased government spending, financial markets may insist on an interest rate premium in anticipation of problems funding an even larger U.S. public debt. Those higher money costs could offset any benefit of higher government spending.**

Explain the rationale behind the last sentence.

6. **About the only benefit ever claimed for the deficit is that it will bring an increase in the level of aggregate demand and therefore a reduction in unemployment. In recent years, however, this very Keynesian notion has begun to be doubted by many economists. The main worry is "crowding out."**

Explain how crowding out can discredit the Keynesian view.

7. **The slack exists, of course, because people continue to save even when the private-sector demand for loans ebbs away. They also tend to save more, not less, in scary times.**

Does the phenomenon referred to in the second sentence serve as an automatic stabilizer or destabilizer?

8. **Not all economists buy the Keynesian story that a cut in government spending reduces income and claim that the multiplier is in effect zero, thanks to falling interest rates and a falling dollar.**

a. How would falling interest rates come about?

b. How could this cause the multiplier to be zero?

9. **The OECD (Organization for Economic Cooperation and Development) data also indicate, for example, that the stimulative effects of tax reductions are considerably smaller than those triggered by government expenditure increases—a fact of life long recognized by economists.**

Explain why this is so.

10. **As soon as the budget is produced, we're likely to hear a lot about the danger that government borrowing will "crowd out" private borrowing.**

How does government borrowing crowd out private borrowing?

11. **A second reason for questioning the employment-generating abilities of the deficit involves how consumers respond to an increase in government borrowing. Rational consumers realize that a higher deficit now means higher taxes in the future. If people ...**

   Complete this clipping to explain what people will do to cause the employment-generating abilities of the deficit to be weak.

12. **In a closed economy, government borrowing "crowds out" household and business investment by pricing them out of available savings, that is, by _____, so fiscal stimulus has no net impact on the economy. In an open economy, however, excess demand for capital is met from ...**

   a. Fill in the blank.

   b. Complete this clipping.

13. **The evidence showed that as the economy moved out of a recession, the interest rate usually rose, and when the economy crashed into a recession, the interest rate usually fell.**

   Explain why this would be so.

14. **This is the "crowding out" theory: increased government borrowing crowds household and business investment out of limited savings, driving up _____, but not raising total demand.**

   Fill in the blank.

---

## Numerical Exercises

N1. Suppose that the government increases its spending by $10 billion but will not allow a deficit, so at the same time it increases taxes by $10 billion. Will the equilibrium level of income rise, fall, or stay the same? Explain your reasoning.

N2. Which of the following policies would a Keynesian expect to produce the largest increase in income?

   a. A tax cut of $200

   b. An increase in transfer payments of $200

   c. An increase in government spending of $200

   d. A "balanced-budget" increase in government spending of $200

N3. Suppose the government has decided to increase spending by $5 billion to buy some helicopters. To prevent this action from having any impact on GDP, must taxes be increased by $5 billion, more than $5 billion, or less than $5 billion?

## Appendix 7.1:    Ricardian Equivalence

When the government taxes to finance higher spending, people decrease consumption because after-tax income falls. When the government borrows to finance higher spending, people may figure that future taxes will increase and may accordingly decrease consumption now to build up a nest egg to enable them to pay these future taxes. *Ricardian equivalence* claims that the fall in consumption is the same, regardless of the government's financing method.

Suppose, for example, that the government increases spending by $10,000 for one year and raises taxes accordingly. A taxpayer may decide to smooth this large hit to consumption over two years, electing to lower consumption by only $5,000 in year one, paying the $10,000 tax bill by borrowing the other $5000 at the current interest rate of 10 percent. In the second year, this taxpayer must repay the loan plus interest, a total of $5,500, so experiences a fall in consumption of $5,500 in that year. Suppose the government had chosen to finance by selling a bond to mature in one year, paying 10 percent. A taxpayer will see that in one year's time she will be taxed $11,000 to pay for this bond redemption (i.e., $10,000 plus $1,000 interest). Can she smooth the hit to consumption over two years in the same way? Yes. By lowering consumption in the first year by $5,000 and investing it at 10 percent, she will have $5,500 returned in the second year, implying that consumption need only fall by $5,500 in the second year to pay the $11,000 tax bill.

Several restrictive assumptions are necessary to derive this result: taxes cannot create incentives to change work behavior; there must be no borrowing constraints; the interest rate at which the government can borrow must match the interest rate at which an individual can borrow; taxpayers cannot be shortsighted; and taxpayers must be as concerned about future generations' welfare as about their own welfare. Most economists do not believe these assumptions are realistic and so do not espouse Ricardian equivalence. The empirical evidence is equivocal. It does seem reasonable, though, that fear of higher future taxes may make some taxpayers save more to ease the burden of paying future taxes, so the Ricardian equivalence argument can be added to the list of crowding out phenomena.

# 8     The Money Supply

Money plays an important role in the operation of the economy, as illustrated in the following excerpt from a 1942 radio broadcast by Keynes:

*For some weeks at this hour you have enjoyed the daydreams of planning. But what about the nightmare of finance? I am sure there have been many listeners who have been muttering, "That's all very well, but how is it to be paid for?" Let me begin by telling you how I tried to answer an eminent architect who pushed on one side all the grandiose plans to rebuild London with the phrase, "Where's the money to come from?" "The money?" I said. "But surely, Sir John, you don't build houses with money? Do you mean that there won't be enough bricks and mortar and steel and cement?" "Oh no," he replied. "Of course there will be plenty of all that." "Do you mean," I went on, "that there won't be enough labor? For what will the builders be doing if they are not building houses?" "Oh no, that's all right," he agreed. "Then there is only one conclusion. You must be meaning, Sir John, that there won't be enough architects." But there I was trespassing on the boundaries of politeness. So I hurried to add, "Well, if there are bricks and mortar and steel and concrete and labor and architects, why not assemble all this good material into houses?" But he was, I fear, quite unconvinced. "What I want to know," he repeated, "is where the money is coming from." To answer that would have got him and me into deeper water than I cared for, so I replied rather shabbily, "The same place it is coming from now." He might have countered (but he didn't), "Of course I know that money is not the slightest use whatever. But, all the same, my dear sir, you will find it a devil of a business not to have any."*

The message here is that although money is not a physical ingredient required for the production of goods and services, its presence greatly facilitates this production. Money serves as a lubricant for the economy, allowing greater specialization of production and labor, and thus creating higher productivity. Imagine how inefficient it would be to do business by bartering one good or service for another!

By controlling the amount of money in the economy, the government can affect the operation of the economy. The purpose of this chapter is to explain how the banking system works and how the government—through its central bank, the Federal Reserve System—influences the supply of money in the economy.

---

**Upon completion of this chapter you should**

- know how the money supply is measured;

- understand how a fractional-reserve banking system operates;

- be aware of how the government can influence the money supply; and

- be familiar with the concept of the money multiplier.

---

## 8.1   What Is Money?

Money is defined as anything widely accepted in payment for goods and services and to pay off debt. Many things can serve this purpose, as evidenced historically by the use of cigarettes in prisoner-of-war camps and large stone wheels on the island of Yap. This definition creates a serious problem in measuring a country's money supply. What should be counted as money? Should we count cigarettes and stone wheels? Different choices of what should be counted as money give rise to different measures of the money supply. These measures are called *monetary aggregates*.

In our society, dollar bills and coins in the hands of the public should definitely be counted as money because they are almost universally accepted as payment. Although not quite so widely accepted as cash, traveler's checks are sufficiently widely accepted as payment that it is reasonable to include them in our measure of money. Personal checks are also widely accepted as payment, suggesting that balances in checking accounts (often called *demand deposits*) should be included when measuring money. There is little dispute about whether or not the above three items—cash, traveler's checks, and balances in checkable accounts—should be included in our economy's measure of money. Adding these together produces the monetary aggregate M1, the narrow definition of money.

Money plays four main roles in our society: as a medium of exchange, as a unit of account, as a store of value, and as a standard of deferred payment. The key feature of money, as far as macroeconomics is concerned, is its use as a medium of exchange because it is through this role that control over the money supply is connected to spending and to overall economic activity. M1 captures this dimension of money because it includes those items most widely used as media of exchange.

Other items exist, however, that can be used as media of exchange (transactions balances), although they are not as close substitutes for cash as are traveler's checks and checking account deposits. Savings accounts at banks, for example, can be turned quickly into cash without incurring major cost, as can term deposits. Subject to some restrictions, checks can be written on accounts

**Table 8.1**   M1 and M2 monetary aggregates ($ billions; seasonally adjusted averages of daily figures)

|  | Value, May 1996 |
| --- | --- |
| M1 = Currency | 377.0 |
| +Traveler's checks | 8.7 |
| +Demand deposits[a] | 409.7 |
| +Other checkable deposits[b] | 322.1 |
| Total M1 | 1,117.5 |
| M2 = M1 |  |
| +Small-denomination time deposits[c] | 928.5 |
| +Savings deposits and money market deposit accounts[d] | 1,197.7 |
| +Noninstitutional money market mutual fund shares[d] | 487.4 |
| Total M2 | 3,731.1 |

Source: *Federal Reserve Bulletin*, August 1996.
a. Demand deposits are checking accounts that pay no interest.
b. Other checkable deposits are accounts that pay interest, such as ATS (automatic transfer from saving) accounts and NOW accounts (see curiosity 8.2).
c. Time deposits, sometimes called term deposits, are deposits that are locked in for a specified length of time. An owner can access these funds earlier only by paying a penalty.
d. Money market deposit accounts and mutual fund shares are accounts on which checks can be written, but with some restrictions, such as that the check be for at least $500.

at brokerage firms and on balances in money mutual fund accounts. If we want a measure of money closely connected with spending, therefore, we should augment M1 to include all items that can quickly be used for spending. This is the rationale behind M2, the broad definition of money, thought by many to be more closely related to economic activity than is M1. It adds to M1 other assets with check-writing features, such as money market deposit accounts, and other assets that can quickly be turned into cash with very little cost, such as savings deposits. Such assets are described as being very "liquid." Table 8.1 documents the difference between M1 and M2.

The official Fed aggregates, M1, M2, and M3 (M2 plus some less-liquid assets) are reported regularly in the business sections of many newspapers. Each Friday, for example, the *Wall Street Journal* publishes these data in a "Federal Reserve Data" column in its "Money and Investing" section. It must be noted that these measures are often revised substantially; short-run movements in monetary aggregates should not be taken too seriously.

The distinction between M1 and M2 has important policy implications. As discussed in the next chapter, monetary authorities sometimes use one of these measures to monitor monetary policy. An inappropriate choice of money supply measure can lead to policy errors, which usually arise from using M1 because M1 is not as closely related to economic activity as is M2. One reason for this is that changes in interest rates entice people to switch balances in checking

**Curiosity 8.1:  What Is the Fed?**

The United States does not have a single central bank like other countries. Instead, its central banking activities are carried out by a group of twelve regional central banks called district Federal Reserve Banks. Collectively, they are known as the Federal Reserve System. This system nonetheless acts just like a single central bank because of its centralized power structure. The power lies with the Federal Reserve Board of Governors and the Federal Open-Market Committee (FOMC). The former consists of seven members appointed by the president for fourteen-year terms (with a new term beginning every two years so that no one president can control the board). One of these members is appointed by the president to be chairman of this committee for a four-year period. He is called the "chairman of the Fed" (a female has not yet filled this position, so it is not known by what name she would be called) and is generally regarded as the most powerful person in the Federal Reserve System, if not the most powerful civil servant in the country. The FOMC consists of the seven governors plus five of the district Reserve Bank presidents. In practice, monetary policy decisions are made by the Federal Reserve Board of Governors or by the Federal Open-Market Committee, which is dominated by the governors. This makes the Federal Reserve System act as though it were a single central bank.

accounts, which pay no interest, into savings accounts, which do pay interest. This causes M1 to shrink, but does not affect M2 because both these deposits are included in M2.

M1 is also misleading because of ongoing financial innovations occurring in the banking industry, in part due to the computer revolution. It used to be the case, for example, that the Fed prohibited interest payments on checking accounts, so that interest-bearing accounts were counted in M2 but not M1, but banks found clever ways of getting around this regulation. For example, they created savings accounts that earned interest but whose balances were transferred automatically into checking accounts when needed. This meant that such savings accounts—called automatic transfer from savings (ATS) accounts—should have been counted in M1. As the use of such savings accounts grew, M1 balances became more and more misleading as a measure of transactions balances. Finally, the Fed recognized the existence of such accounts and included them in the M1 measure category "other checkable deposits."

Financial deregulation is a third reason why M1 became misleading. Nonbank financial institutions—mutual savings banks, credit unions, and savings-and-loan associations—were at one time not allowed to have checking accounts, so their deposits were not included in M1. As these institutions circumvented this regulation in imaginative ways, M1—which measured only checkable deposits in commercial banks—became misleading as a measure of the nation's transactions balances. Current monetary aggregate measures include deposits at all financial institutions.

---

**Curiosity 8.2:   What Is a NOW Account?**

In 1970, a mutual savings bank in Massachusetts discovered a loophole in Fed regulations that prohibited payment of interest on checking accounts. It created a special kind of check called a *negotiable order of withdrawal* (NOW). Accounts on which NOWs could be written were not legally checking accounts, so they could pay interest.

This is an example of a financial innovation that caused trouble for the M1 money-supply measure. Growth in NOW accounts caused M1 to omit a significant amount of transactions money. Eventually, NOW accounts were included in M1, as they should be, in the category "other checkable deposits."

---

## 8.2   Fractional-Reserve Banking

Regardless of what measure of the money supply is employed, we must first understand how our banking system operates to understand how the central bank controls the money supply. The key thing to recognize is that banks can create money by extending loans. If a bank loans you $1,000, you sign a legal agreement with the bank, and it simply opens an account in your name with a balance of $1,000. This $1,000 is now counted as part of the economy's money supply: it has been created by this bank out of thin air!

When a bank creates money out of thin air like this, it is taking a chance, hoping that you and other depositors will conduct financial transactions by using checks rather than cash. If you wanted to withdraw the $1,000 in cash, it could be embarrassing for the bank. Because it created the $1,000 deposit out of thin air, it may not have $1,000 in cash to give you!

To guard against this kind of embarrassment, banks refrain from creating money (loans) in unlimited quantities. Most customers make transactions by writing checks, so that banks are continually experiencing increases and decreases in deposit balances as checks clear, as well as increases and decreases in their vault cash as cash is deposited or withdrawn. They know from experience, however, that the amount of cash they must have on hand to deal with withdrawals of cash is a small fraction of total deposits, so they limit the money they create (loans they make) to ensure that their reserves of cash are at least this fraction of total deposits.

The implication of all this for the money supply is best explained via an example. Suppose banks figure that their cash requirements should be 5 percent of total deposits. If the banking system's cash holdings are $40 billion, then the banks will increase loans until the amount of deposits, and thus the money supply, is $800 billion. (5 percent of $800 billion is $40 billion.) Because the central bank (the Fed) creates cash, any balances in the commercial banks' accounts with the Fed are just as good as cash. This implies that the reserves

---

**Curiosity 8.3:   What Are the Legal Reserve Requirements?**

The Fed imposes reserve requirements for all depository institutions of 10 percent on all checkable deposits and has the power to vary this rate between 8 percent and 14 percent. There are no reserve requirements on other deposits (such as term deposits). By changing the reserve requirements, the Fed can affect the money supply. Decreasing the required reserve ratio causes commercial banks suddenly to find themselves with excess reserves, so they can increase loans, thereby expanding the money supply. Increasing reserve requirements causes a contraction in the money supply. Changing the required reserve ratio is a very blunt way of affecting the money supply, however, so it is rarely used.

Many countries—such as Canada, Switzerland, New Zealand, and Australia—have no reserve requirements at all. Banks in these countries still hold reserves to deal with their everyday cash requirements and are immediately loaned extra reserves by their central bank (at a very high price) should they experience an embarrassing shortfall of cash, so there is no danger of banking disasters. By eliminating reserve requirements, these countries strengthen their banks' ability to compete in a multinational banking environment.

---

held by banks to handle possible cash disbursements can be either cash or balances in their accounts at the central bank (such balances are called "claims on the central bank"). The money supply is thus a multiple of these reserves, which are controlled by the central bank. Because such reserves are a fraction of the total money supply, this banking system is called a *fractional-reserve banking system*.

There is an obvious danger inherent in such a banking system. Because a smaller percentage of reserves means a greater quantity of loans and therefore more profits, there is a temptation for banks to underestimate the fraction of reserves they should hold. This increases the chances of an inability to meet requests for cash, with the consequent financial ruin of the bank should depositors panic and create a run on that bank. Government regulation of banks, including deposit insurance and the setting of a *reserve requirement*, arose because of such banking disasters and because the government wanted to be able to control the total amount of money circulating in the economy to affect the pace of economic activity.

## 8.3   Controlling the Money Supply

The central bank influences the money supply by controlling the *money base*—cash plus commercial banks' deposits with the central bank (claims on the central bank)—and thereby controlling the quantity of reserves in the banking system. Commercial banks can use as reserves any part of the money base in their hands. By increasing the money base, the Fed increases commercial banks' reserves, enabling them to increase their loans (and thus the money supply) while continuing to meet their reserve requirement. Note that this does not guarantee that the money supply will increase; for this to happen commercial banks must react by increasing loans. The central bank's control over the money supply is thus subject to some uncertainty.

The main way in which the central bank controls the money base is by buying and selling bonds, a process referred to as *open-market operations.* Suppose the central bank buys a $1,000 bond from you, paying you with a check drawn on itself. When you deposit this check in your bank account, your bank credits your account and ends up in possession of this $1,000 check, a claim on the central bank. This check could be taken to the central bank and exchanged for cash, so it is treated as cash for the purposes of satisfying the legal reserve requirement. It ends up increasing your bank's deposits with the central bank and thus your bank's reserves.

Therefore, any bond purchase by the central bank increases reserves in the banking system, directly increasing the money supply and indirectly inducing banks to increase the money supply further by making it possible for them legally to make more loans. The ultimate increase in the money supply is therefore more than the original purchase of bonds.

## 8.4   The Money Multiplier

It is instructive to trace through the process whereby an open-market bond purchase by the Fed increases the money supply. Suppose the Fed buys a government bond from you for $4,000, paying you with a check for $4,000. When you deposit this check in your checking account the money supply increases by $4,000 because your account balance has increased by $4,000 and nobody else's has decreased. When your bank (bank AAA) increases the balance in your checking account by $4,000, it now possesses a $4,000 claim on the central bank. Its balance with the central bank increases by $4,000, so its reserves increase by $4,000.

Now view this situation through the eyes of bank AAA. Its deposits are $4,000 higher, and it has $4,000 extra reserves. Suppose the reserve requirement is 5 percent. Bank AAA must keep an extra $200 (five percent of $4,000) on hand as extra cash holdings because of its higher deposits, leaving it with $3,800 *excess* reserve holdings. It can increase its profits by loaning out this $3,800, so it does so to stranger X, thereby increasing the money supply by $3,800. (Note that at this stage the total money-supply increase is $4,000 + $3800 = $7800.) Stranger X may write a check for $3,800 to firm W, which has an account in bank BBB. When this happens, firm W's account in bank BBB increases by $3,800, and bank BBB has a claim of $3,800 on bank AAA. Bank BBB asks bank AAA to send it $3,800, accomplished when bank AAA transfers $3,800

| Money multiplier process | Total money supply increase |
|---|---|
| Fed buys $4,000 bonds | |
| ⇒ ↑ bank AAA reserves by $4,000 | |
| and ↑ money supply by $4,000 | $4,000 |
| ⇒ $3,800 excess reserves in bank AAA | |
| ⇒ ↑ loans by bank AAA by $3,800 | |
| ⇒ ↑ money supply by $3,800 | $7,800 |
| ⇒ check for $3,800 to account in bank BBB | |
| ⇒ $3,610 excess reserves in bank BBB | |
| ⇒ ↑ loans by bank BBB by $3,610 | |
| ⇒ ↑ money supply by $3,610 | $11,410 |
| ⇒ check for $3,610 to account in bank CCC | |
| ⇒ $3,429.50 excess reserves in bank CCC | |
| ⇒ ↑ loans by bank BBB by $3,429.50 | |
| ⇒ ↑ money supply by $3,429.50 | $14,840 |
| ⇒ and so on until ultimately ↑ money supply by $80,000 | |

**Figure 8.1** The money multiplier process
In the numerical example the reserve requirement is 5 percent. In this example because the initial increase in reserves is $4,000 and the ultimate increase in the money supply is $80,000, the money multiplier is 20.

from its account at the Fed to bank BBB's account at the Fed, increasing bank BBB's reserves.

Now look at the situation through the eyes of bank BBB. It has an extra $3,800 in reserves and a corresponding extra $3,800 in deposits. It needs $190 extra cash (five percent of $3800) and so has $3610 in excess reserves. It loans this out, the money supply increases by $3610, and the procedure described above is repeated over and over, with the money supply growing by progressively smaller amounts at each stage. This process is illustrated in figure 8.1.

The process of increasing the money supply continues until ultimately it increases by $80,000, deduced by noting that $4,000—the original increase in the money base—is 5 percent of $80,000. This phenomenon—that the money supply increases by a multiple of the increase in the money base—is formalized by the concept of the *money multiplier: the ultimate increase in the money supply per dollar increase in the money base.* In this example, the money multiplier is 20. In formal terms it is written as

$$\text{money multiplier} = \frac{\Delta\,\text{money supply}}{\Delta\,\text{money base}}.$$

The calculation of 20 for the money multiplier is misleading, however. As deposits increase, you and others may wish to hold some fraction of the increased deposits in cash, draining reserves from the banking system. This lowers the amount of extra loans the banking system can make, thus decreasing the magnitude of the money multiplier.

---

**Curiosity 8.4:   How Big Is the Money Multiplier?**

The actual magnitude of the money multiplier is determined by both legal and behavioral factors. For M1 it is about 3 and for M2 it is about 8. Because the money multiplier is defined as

$$\text{money multiplier} = \frac{\Delta \text{ money supply}}{\Delta \text{ money base}},$$

the change in the money supply can be calculated as

$$\Delta \text{ money supply} = \text{money multiplier} \times \Delta \text{ money base}.$$

Consequently, if the Fed bought $5 million of bonds, M1 would increase ultimately by $15 million, and M2 would increase ultimately by $40 million.

Why is the M2 money multiplier larger? As loans are made and account balances rise, people have a tendency to keep most of those balances in term deposits to earn a higher rate of interest. Banks encourage this by offering higher interest rates on term deposits because required reserves on term deposits are zero; banks can make more loans, and thus more profit, if extra deposits are in term deposits rather than demand deposits. As a result, M2, which includes term deposits, increases much more than M1, making the M2 multiplier larger.

---

Other complications are also possible. There may be different legal reserve requirements for different types of deposits—10 percent for checking accounts, perhaps, and 0 percent for time deposits—so that the value of the money multiplier may depend on the mix of accounts into which the money-supply increase goes. Another possible complication is that banks may wish to hold reserves in excess of those they are legally required to hold as a safety precaution against having to pay a penalty should their reserves inadvertently fall below their legal requirement. In general, the magnitude of the money multiplier is determined by the interaction of various legal requirements and behavioral reactions on the part of the public and commercial banks.

## Media Illustrations

### Example 1
**M1 can be a slippery commodity. The central bank admits to having significantly underestimated the transactions money flying around the system. One reason is that banks' bigger corporate customers cottoned onto the advantage of so managing their moneys as to achieve, at a consolidated, central checking account, practically zero balances. For the banks promoting this switch of idle money to easily accessible interest-bearing deposits, there were similar economies: reserve requirements on such deposits are much lower.**

*What is meant by "transactions" money, as opposed to what other kind of money?*
Transactions money is money used to pay for purchases (monetary transactions) as opposed to money used purely as a store of value.

*What is the significance of underestimating transactions money?*
Transactions money is thought to be connected to spending, so if it is underestimated, monetary policy will promote more spending than is suitable, thus creating inflation.

*Why would corporations want to achieve zero balances?*
Checking accounts pay little or no interest. By keeping most of their transactions money in savings (interest-bearing) accounts, which are easily switched into checking accounts, they can earn interest on most of their transactions money.

*Explain how the banks gain from this corporate behavior.*
Because the legal reserve requirement on interest-bearing accounts is lower (it is now zero, but when this clipping was written it may not have been zero), the banks are able to make more loans and thus more profits.

**Example 2**
**In the process, the money multiplies, because the banks are allowed to lend more money than they actually have, within limits set by the Federal Reserve Board. The Board tries to anticipate how much the money will multiply as this process unfolds. If its calculations are right, just enough money will be created to accommodate the growth it desires for the economy. If the calculations are wrong, the Board would make them right by pumping some money into the economy or pumping some out.**

*What money is being multiplied here?*
The Fed has increased the money base, which is being multiplied.

*What are the limits set by the board?*
The board has a legal reserve requirement that must be met by the banks. This limits the amount of extra loans that banks can make.

*What name do economists use to refer to "how much the money will multiply as this process unfolds"?*
The money multiplier.

*How does the board pump money into or out of the economy?*
Money is pumped into the economy by buying bonds and is pumped out of the economy by selling bonds.

**Example 3**
**The deficit will mainly be financed by selling bonds to the general public and not to the central bank.**

*What happens to the money supply if a deficit is financed by selling bonds to the general public?*

The money supply decreases when bonds are sold to the public, but when the government spends the proceeds, this money is injected back into the economy, so the net effect is zero change in the money supply.

*What happens to the money supply if a deficit is financed by selling bonds to the central bank?*

The money supply increases if bonds are sold to the central bank. Whenever the central bank buys bonds, the money supply increases.

## Chapter Summary

- Measuring an economy's money stock is challenging because so many different things can be used as a medium of exchange. The two most popular monetary aggregates are M1 and M2. Financial innovations and other changes have disrupted the connection between economic activity and these aggregates, especially M1.

- In a fractional-reserve banking system, an economy's central bank can create a multiplied increase in the money supply by increasing the monetary reserves in the banking system. By buying a bond, for example, the central bank writes a check on itself, which a commercial bank comes to possess whenever the person who sold the bond deposits this check. This bank's account balance with the central bank therefore increases, giving it immediate access to cash if required. The increase in this bank's holdings of legal reserves permits it to increase loans and thereby to increase the money supply.

- The main way in which the central bank influences the money supply is by controlling monetary reserves (the money base) through buying or selling bonds, a process known as open-market operations.

- The money multiplier tells us by how much the money supply ultimately increases whenever the central bank increases reserves by a dollar (by buying a bond worth a dollar, for example).

## Formula Definition

- $$\text{money multiplier} = \frac{\Delta \text{ money supply}}{\Delta \text{ money base}}.$$

## Media Exercises

1. **Bank reserves are created in the process because the Fed can "pay" simply by crediting the amount of its purchases to the account of the bank involved in the transaction. As a result, ...**

a. What kind of a transaction is being discussed here?

b. Complete this statement.

2. **The annual growth rate in what had once been the officially watched aggregate, M1, was 4 percent last year, but for M2, the rate was 12 percent.**

Why might M2 be growing so much faster than M1?

3. **Money deposited for a term is not left in bank vaults but is loaned out by the banks (subject to minimum cash reserve requirements). This means that a dollar on deposit can flow back into the banking system one or more times, and that dollar can expand the money supply.**

a. What is meant by the minimum cash reserve requirements referred to in this clip?

b. What terminology do economists use to refer to the process described in this clip?

4. **During May, the rate of growth in the narrowly defined money supply, M1, moved below its current target range of between 5 and 9 percent annual growth. Two main causes were identified: the delayed impact of rising interest rates earlier this year and the increasing use of daily-interest savings accounts by bank customers.**

Explain how each of these two main causes contribute to a lowering of growth in M1.

5. **The impact on the monetary aggregate of extensive financial innovation—the changes in the kinds of deposits and services offered by banks—led the central bank to drop M1 as an intermediate target. With the changes in the way the public was holding payments balances, the M1 aggregate no longer had the same reliable link to ...**

a. What impact would these financial innovations have on M1?

b. Complete this clipping.

6. **Because it is broader in coverage than M1, M2 is less prone to the shifts resulting from financial innovation that caused difficulties in the interpretation of M1.**

What are the "shifts resulting from financial innovation," and why do they cause difficulties in the interpretation of M1?

7. **Although he didn't say so, this may ultimately compel him to resort increasingly to managing the money supply by managing banks' excess cash reserves—the stuff from which the banks create loans.**

a. What are excess cash reserves?

b. Why are they called "the stuff from which the banks create loans"?

c. How would the central bank manage these excess reserves?

8. **Another potential thorn in the flesh of central bank money-measurers is the daily-interest savings account.**

Why would daily-interest savings accounts be a thorn in the flesh of central bank money-measurers?

9. **U.S. broad money, M2—the Federal Reserve's preferred measure—rose by only 1.7 percent in the year to August, whereas U.S. narrow money, M1, jumped by 12.3 percent. The money supply is a useful guide for policymakers only if it has a predictable relationship with GDP. In practice, the link is fickle. The biggest problem is that the various measures are sensitive to shifts within portfolios. The recent sharp drop in short-term interest rates in the United States has made bank deposits unattractive compared to bonds and equity mutual funds.**

Explain how this phenomenon could explain the disparate rates of growth of M1 and M2.

10. **In Russia, if I ask a worker to get me a spare part for my car, he'll refuse to do it for money, but will do it for vodka.**

What must be happening in Russia to cause this phenomenon to occur?

11. **Monetizing the debt means that the Federal Reserve is not seeking buyers for all the government bonds, but is _____. This, essentially, means that the presses are ...**

Fill in the blank and complete this clipping. Hint: "Monetizing the debt" means printing money to finance the debt.

## Numerical Exercises

N1. Suppose that the central bank buys $4 billion of bonds on the open market.

a. If banks wish to hold reserves of 6 percent, by how much can the money supply ultimately increase?

b. What would the money multiplier be in this case?

c. If, when extra deposits are created, customers increase their holdings of cash by some fraction of those extra deposits, does the money multiplier become larger, smaller, or stay the same?

N2. Suppose the money multiplier is 6. What happens to the money supply if the Fed buys $3 billion of bonds?

N3. Suppose you sell a bond to the Fed for $10,000 and deposit the proceeds in your checking account. As a direct result of this,

     a. what has happened to *M1?*

     b. what has happened to *M2?*

Now suppose you withdraw $500 in cash and use the rest to buy a term deposit. As a direct result of this,

     c. what has happened to *M1?*

     d. what has happened to *M2?*

N4. Suppose you switch $1,000 from your checking account to your savings account. As a direct result of this,

     a. what happens to *M1?*

     b. what happens to *M2?*

     c. are your answers to (a) and (b) different if you allow for indirect effects? Explain.

# 9     The Monetarist Rule

By the early 1960s, the Keynesian view of the macroeconomy had become the status quo, evidence of which was its explicit use as the rationale for the Kennedy tax cut. Just as the Keynesian view was reaching the peak of its popularity, however, in 1963 Milton Friedman and Anna Schwarz published their book *A Monetary History of the United States, 1867–1960*, heralding the arrival of a competing view of the macroeconomy that has since come to be known as *monetarism*.

Monetarists deplored the way in which disciples of Keynes neglected the role of money, something that Keynes himself had stressed, and placed money at center stage of the macroeconomy, the position it had held in the classical view (see appendix 4.1 at the end of chapter 4), which was the status quo before the Keynesian revolution. In the late 1960s and early 1970s, the monetarist view gained considerable popularity, primarily because during this time the money supply increased dramatically, causing monetarist predictions to be more accurate than those of the Keynesians. Monetarists claim that crowding out forces are so strong that fiscal actions are completely ineffective, and that only money matters in determining the level of economic activity. Keynesians soon came to agree that money matters and modified their thinking to develop a more eclectic approach. Monetarists, however, insisted that *only* money matters. This dogmatism, at first very effective as an attention-getting debate tactic, has ultimately been a main reason for the decline of monetarism, as it became evident that several factors in addition to money play roles in the operation of the macroeconomy.

The purpose of this chapter is to examine the monetarist approach and to exposit a major legacy of monetarism: the monetarist rule that the money supply should grow at a rate equal to the real rate of growth of the economy.

---

**Upon completion of this chapter you should**

- be conversant with the quantity theory of money;
- know what is meant by velocity; and
- understand the rationale behind the monetarist rule.

---

## 9.1  The Quantity Theory

In the classical school of thought, supplanted eventually by Keynesianism, a prominent role was played by the *quantity theory of money*, represented by the mechanical formula

$$Mv = PQ.$$

Here, $P$ is the overall price level, and $Q$ is the physical quantity of output produced, so that the right-hand side of this formula is the money value of output or, equivalently, nominal GDP. $M$ is the money supply and $v$ is the *velocity of money*, interpreted as the number of times in a year each dollar of money supply is used to buy a final good or service. This is usually expressed as the number of times the money supply "turns over" in financially supporting the production of output.

According to this formula, if velocity is constant, a rise in $M$ causes a rise in either $P$ or $Q$, depending on whether or not the economy is at full employment. This result is easily seen from looking at the formula $Mv = PQ$. Clearly, the role of money is center stage in determining the level of economic activity. What is not so easily seen is what is going on in the economy to cause this result to hold, the greatest drawback of the quantity theory: it offers no explanation of how an increase in the money supply causes an increase in economic activity. The quantity theory formula seems to appear as gospel without any theoretical justification. Indeed, velocity is merely defined as the ratio of income to the money supply, thus making the quantity theory formula a mere tautology. (Take the equation above and solve it for $v$, obtaining $v = PQ/M$. If this is how $v$ is defined, then the quantity equation becomes true by definition—a tautology!)

The monetarists reinterpreted the quantity theory as representing an economy's demand for money, and with this reinterpretation they were able to structure an explanation for how an increase in the money supply caused an increase in economic activity. The result is referred to as the *modern quantity theory of money* and is a cornerstone of monetarism.

## 9.2  The Modern Quantity Theory

The original quantity theory formula is rewritten as $M = (1/v)Y$, where $Y$ is the nominal level of income. This formula is interpreted as a behavioral equation that reflects the economy's demand for money. Individuals and firms demand money for the convenience it provides as a medium of exchange and a store of value. Individuals' money holdings increase and decrease as their bank accounts are augmented by paychecks and as they spend money between paychecks. Firms' money holdings increase and decrease as they receive payment for goods and services and as they pay out wages. How much money (cash and balances in bank accounts) do we collectively want to hold on average? This average is the economy's demand for money.

Essentially, the modern interpretation of the quantity of money equation says that the demand for money is higher when the level of income is higher. Higher consumption spending associated with a higher level of income should cause individuals to hold more cash in their pockets and larger bank balances to facilitate this higher consumption spending. A person earning $30,000 per year may on average hold about $1,000 in money balances, for example, but a person earning $60,000 per year will on average hold considerably more, probably about $2,000. In general, as income/output increases, producers require more money to support financially the higher level of production, and consumers require more money to facilitate their higher level of consumption. In this new interpretation, the parameter $1/v$ is not determined tautologically from the definition of velocity, but rather reflects the economy's money-demand behavior. Economists consider velocity $v$ to be a function of other forces in the economy, such as the interest rate, but it is thought nonetheless to be quite stable.

How is this new interpretation of the quantity theory used to explain the reaction of the economy to an increase in the money supply? People end up holding more of their wealth in the form of money than they really want to hold in the form of money: the supply of money exceeds the demand for money. People are assumed to react by spending these excess cash balances in an effort to draw them down. This increases aggregate demand for goods and services and sets in motion the traditional Keynesian multiplier process. Initially, people's efforts to rid themselves of excess cash balances are unsuccessful because by spending these balances they are simply giving the excess balances to others, not eliminating them. As this process continues, however, the level of income rises, which causes an increase in the demand for money. This reduces the excess cash balances and slows down the multiplier process. Eventually, income increases to the point at which the rise in demand for money exactly equals the original increase in the supply of money, stopping this multiplier process.

This story is sometimes told via the hot potato analogy. Suppose the extra money takes the form of a hot potato, which nobody wants to hold because everyone currently has all the potato (money) they want to hold. Whoever has

| General process | Numerical example |
|---|---|
| Open-market operations | Open-market operations |
| ⇒ Fed buys bonds | ⇒ Fed buys $2b bonds |
| ⇒ people trade bonds for money | ⇒ people trade bonds for money |
| ⇒ money multiplier operates | ⇒ money multiplier (=3) operates |
| ⇒ ↑money supply | ⇒ $6b ↑ money supply |
| ⇒ excess money holdings | ⇒ $6b excess money |
| ⇒ spend excess money | ⇒ people spend excess money |
| ⇒ ↑ agg D for g&s | ⇒ $6b ↑ agg D for g & s |
| ⇒ Keynesian multiplier process | ⇒ Keynesian multiplier (=2) process |
| ⇒ ↑ income | ⇒ $12b ↑ **income** |
| ⇒ ↑ money demand | ⇒ $2.4b ↑ money demand |
| ⇒ smaller excess money holdings | ⇒ ↓ **excess money supply** by $2.4b |
| | ⇒ $3.6b excess money |
| | ⇒ people spend excess money |
| | ⇒ $3.6b ↑ agg D for g & s |
| | ⇒ Keynesian multiplier (=2) process |
| | ⇒ $7.2b ↑ **income** (so cumulative ↑ income is $19.2b) |
| | ⇒ $1.44b ↑ money demand (so cumulative ↑ money demand is $3.84b) |
| | ⇒ ↓ **excess money supply** by $1.44b |
| | ⇒ $2.16b excess money |
| | ⇒ people spend excess money |
| | ⇒ and so on until cumulative ↑ income reaches $30b to cause $6b ↑ money demand and thus to eliminate completely the original $6b excess money supply |

**Figure 9.1**  The impact of monetary policy
In the numerical example the money multiplier is 3, "the" multiplier is 2, and a dollar increase in income increases money demand by 0.2 dollars. The multiplier process stops when money demand increases by enough to equal the new money supply.

the hot potato wants to get rid of it and does so by using it to buy something from a neighboring merchant. This merchant now has the hot potato, but doesn't want it, so does the same thing—namely, gets rid of it by buying something from another merchant. This second merchant does the same thing, and so on. As this process continues, the merchants notice that business has improved and that their income is higher. They require more money to lubricate a larger business and to facilitate their own higher consumption spending, so they say to themselves, "The next time that hot potato comes around, I will slice a bit off to augment my potato (money) holdings," which is what happens. Over time, the hot potato (excess money supply) gets whittled away to nothing.

---

**Curiosity 9.1:   Does Excess Money Really Affect Spending?**

Excess money can affect spending either *directly*, as we have claimed in this chapter, or *indirectly*, as will be explained in the next chapter when we examine the role of the interest rate. The following example of how an excess demand for money can directly decrease spending is informative. In the early 1970s in Washington, D.C., a babysitting co-op club was formed in which parents babysat for club members and in turn could call on club members to babysit for them. The club began by giving each member several units of scrip, each worth one hour of babysitting time. This scrip served as the medium of exchange for babysitting services, thus playing the role of money in this babysitting economy.

The club was successful and grew, but then began to experience a mysterious decline in babysitting activity, but not because club members were unwilling to babysit. On the contrary, members very much wanted to babysit to obtain scrip to use to buy babysitting from other club members. The problem was that although everyone claimed to want to buy babysitting services, very few were actually buying. All of the available scrip was being held by club members for emergency babysitting needs, with no extra scrip left over for members to use to buy normal babysitting services. Everyone wanted to babysit to earn scrip to buy babysitting services, but no one could collect any scrip to spend because everyone else was also trying to accumulate scrip by not buying.

This babysitting economy was in a recession caused by a low demand for babysitting services, which was in turn caused by an inadequate supply of scrip. The club's growth had increased the demand for scrip, and without an equal increase in scrip supply, an excess demand for scrip developed. To accumulate scrip, members cut down on babysitting demand, creating the problem described above. To an economist, the obvious solution is to increase the supply of scrip (money). This was done and the babysitting club revived.

---

This process is illustrated in figure 9.1. In the numerical example, there is a money-supply increase of $6 billion, brought about by open-market bond purchases of $2 billion. We have assumed that the money multiplier is 3, that "the" multiplier is 2, and that a dollar increase in income increases money demand by $0.2.

The multiplier process causes the original increase in the money supply ultimately to lead to a "multiplied" increase in the level of income. The strength of monetary policy is usually measured by the *income multiplier with respect to the money supply: the increase in equilibrium income due to a unit increase in the money supply*. In the numerical example in figure 9.1, the $6 billion increase in the money supply leads eventually to an increase in income of $30 billion, so the income multiplier with respect to the money supply is $30/6 = 5$. This multiplier should not be confused with the money multiplier, described in the preceding chapter (and assumed to be 3 in this example), or with "the" multiplier (the income multiplier with respect to government spending, assumed to be 2 in this example).

## 9.3   The Monetarist Rule

The essence of the story presented in figure 9.1 is that an increase in the money supply causes changes in the economy so that the demand for money increases to equal the now higher supply of money. In the new equilibrium, the change in the demand for money must equal the change in the supply of money. In modern quantity theory, the demand for money is given by $(1/v)PQ$, so there are three possible sources of change in demand for money—namely, changes in $v$, $P$, and $Q$. The exposition above assumed that $v$ and $P$ were constant, so that a change in $M$ elicited an equal percentage change in real income $Q$.

If the economy is at full employment, real income does not change; instead, the extra money supply causes an increase in the price level. To be specific, if the money supply increases by 8 percent when the economy is at full employment, prices increase by 8 percent to increase the demand for money to its higher supply. If the monetary authorities adopt a policy of increasing the money supply at a rate of 8 percent per year, an inflation of 8 percent per year develops, reflecting the adage that inflation is caused by too much money chasing too few goods.

This result is too crude, however, because it does not recognize that the full-employment level of income in the economy is growing due to population changes and investment that augments the nation's capital stock. Suppose the economy's real growth rate is 2 percent per year. This 2 percent real growth in income causes the demand for money to increase by 2 percent per year. If the money supply is growing at 8 percent per year, then prices will increase by only 6 percent per year because 2 percent of the extra money supply is needed by the increasing real income. Only money-supply growth rates in excess of the rate of real growth of the economy should create inflation.

The thinking articulated above gives rise to the following rule of thumb for predicting the economy's long-run annual rate of inflation:

long-run inflation = rate of growth of the money supply – real rate of
                          growth in income.

The long-run qualification attached to this rule of thumb is important. In the short run, we could be in a recession, so that money-supply increases can elicit output increases rather than price increases. Several other short-run factors can play a role in influencing price increases, most notably aggregate demand shocks, energy price increases, and generous wage settlements. The rule of thumb says that although these other factors can influence prices, they will not create sustained price increases unless they are supplemented with money-supply increases. This is the basis for the monetarists claim that, in the long run, inflation is always and everywhere a monetary phenomenon.

Figure 9.2 presents evidence of this relationship for selected low-inflation countries. Data from 1971 to 1985, a period of relatively high money-supply

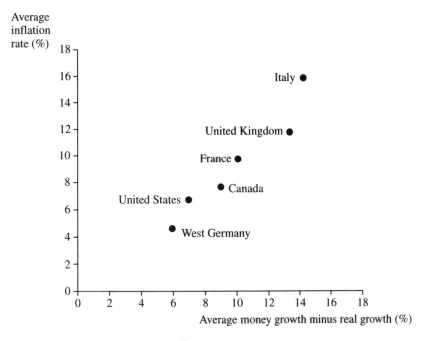

**Figure 9.2**  Money growth and inflation
To reflect the long-run nature of this relationship, data have been averaged for the 1971–1985 period.
Source: *International Financial Statistics*, 1974–1986.

growth worldwide, were averaged to produce the points plotted. Averaging should dilute the influence of short-run phenomena affecting inflation and allow the long-run relationship to be more apparent. This graph suggests that the monetarist equation is a good guide to long-run inflation behavior. Had we plotted figures for high-inflation (*hyperinflation*) countries, the graph would be even more convincing. Brazil had money growth of 83 percent and inflation of 81 percent; Chile had money growth of 133 percent and inflation of 144 percent; and Argentina had money growth of 234 percent and inflation of 251 percent.

Two implications of the inflation equation are that (1) an economy does not experience inflation if its money supply increases at a rate equal to the real rate of growth of the economy, and (2) an economy will experience a low, steady inflation in the long run if its money supply grows at a low, steady rate. These implications form part of the rationale behind the monetarists' belief that monetary authorities should be replaced by a robot programmed to increase the money supply at a low, constant rate—a controversial prescription known as the *monetarist rule*.

**Curiosity 9.2:   What If Velocity Isn't Constant?**

Implicit in our derivation of the formula for inflation is an assumption that velocity is constant, but financial innovations are steadily increasing velocity. For example, the growing use of credit cards has made it possible for people to coordinate more closely their consumption payments and income receipts, reducing their need to hold money. They are able to make a smaller amount of money holdings support the same amount of spending. This influence of financial innovations could be called a decrease in the demand for money or, equivalently, an increase in velocity.

Suppose, as was the case during the 1960s and 1970s, that financial innovations are decreasing the demand for money, and thus increasing velocity, at an annual rate of about 3 percent per year. If long-run growth is 2 percent, then there is a net decrease in money demand of 1 percent per year. If the supply of money is increasing at 8 percent per year, a gap of 9 percent between money supply and money demand opens up, causing prices to rise by 9 percent. As a result, we must modify our equation for inflation:

inflation = money growth rate − real growth rate + velocity growth rate.

From 1950 to 1980, M1 velocity climbed steadily from about 3 to about 7, but then fell dramatically (by about 7 percent) in the early 1980s and behaved irregularly thereafter. During this same period, M2 velocity held constant at about 1.7, but also fell markedly (by about 10 percent) in the early 1980s and has recently behaved irregularly. These velocity changes are illustrated in figure 9.3. A steadily growing velocity can be accommodated, as shown in the new equation for inflation above, but an irregularly changing velocity implies that this equation is of less value as a summary of long-run economic behavior.

For the mathematically minded, the modified inflation equation can be derived by using the quantity equation $Mv = PQ$ to obtain the approximate result that

$$\%\Delta M + \%\Delta v = \%\Delta P + \%\Delta Q,$$

implying that

$$\%\Delta P = \%\Delta M - \%\Delta Q + \%\Delta v.$$

## 9.4   The Rules-versus-Discretion Debate

Monetarists advocate their rule for several reasons:

1. *It guarantees a low long-run rate of inflation.*   This creates a stable economic environment conducive to long-term investment projects, a necessary ingredient in the promotion of long-term growth.

2. *It creates automatic stabilizing forces.*   As the economy moves into recession, income and thus the demand for money grow more slowly. If money-supply growth is kept steady, the slowdown in money-demand growth causes an excess money supply that begins to stimulate the economy and pushes it

out of recession. If the economy overheats and begins to experience high inflation, the higher prices increase the demand for money, and an excess demand for money develops. This cuts back aggregate demand (as people stop spending to accumulate more money), which puts a damper on the inflationary forces.

3. *It insulates monetary policy from politics.* Just before an election, politicians are tempted to pump up the money supply, letting the later fallout of higher inflation appear after the election.

4. *It prevents the Fed from making mistakes.* History has shown that the Fed makes many mistakes in its efforts to use discretionary monetary policy to improve the economy. Although major mistakes—such as its failure to serve as a lender of last resort during the Great Depression and its overly expansionary monetary policy during the Vietnam War—have become less and less frequent over time as the Fed has learned, monetarists argue that even a clever and well-intentioned Fed is doomed to make mistakes continually because of the extreme complexity of the economy. For example, the magnitude of the income multiplier with respect to the money supply is uncertain and changing; the lags of monetary policy in affecting the economy are long, variable, and unpredictable; and forecasting the economy's behavior is difficult.

---

**Curiosity 9.3:   Should the Fed Be Independent?**

Although not as independent as the Swiss National Bank or the Bundesbank of Germany, relative to most other central banks the Federal Reserve System is quite independent from political influence, mainly because its board members are appointed for long, nonrenewable terms and because it is financially independent. It does not have complete autonomy, however. Congress has the power to affect the Fed through legislation.

The strongest argument in favor of an independent Fed is that subjecting the Fed to political pressures would impart an inflationary bias to monetary policy as politicians use monetary policy to enhance their reelections. Indeed, in countries with relatively independent central banks, such as the United States and Germany, inflation is relatively low, whereas in countries with less independent central banks, such as Italy and Spain, inflation is much higher. A related argument is that an independent Fed can resist financing large government budget deficits, which would also lead to excessive inflation. Many believe that politicians do not have the ability to make hard decisions on issues of great economic importance, such as reducing the budget deficit or reforming the banking system. An independent Fed can pursue policies that are politically unpopular yet in the public interest.

Those opposed to Fed independence claim that it is undemocratic to allow important economic decisions to be made by an elite group responsible to no one. Further, effective policy requires coordination from all policymakers. With an independent Fed, fiscal policy may be undone by contrary monetary policy.

The independence issue will never be settled. Those who like the Fed's policies will support its independence, but those who do not like its policies, will not.

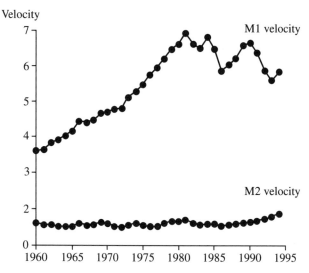

**Figure 9.3** Velocity over time
M1 velocity steadily grows, then dramatically becomes irregular. M2 velocity seems much steadier, but this is misleading because small changes are substantial percentage changes due to the low value of M2 velocity.
Source: *Economic Report of the President*, 1995.

However, those who believe in the use of discretionary monetary policy offer cogent criticisms of this monetarist prescription:

1. *Unstable velocity.* Although most economists concur with the general logic of the inflation equation, they note that to make it operational, a specific measure of the money supply must be chosen—in particular, one for which velocity is constant, or at least growing at a constant rate. M1 velocity and, to a lesser extent, M2 velocity have behaved irregularly at times, due to banking innovations and financial deregulations, as illustrated in figure 9.3. This objection is summarized in amusing fashion by Goodhart's Law: whatever measure of the money supply is chosen for application of the monetarist rule, it will soon begin to misbehave. It will no longer bear a stable relationship with income or inflation. One suggestion for overcoming this drawback is to change the rule to target a nominal GDP growth rate approximately equal to the historical real GDP growth rate. When nominal GDP grows faster than the chosen target rate, cut back on money-supply growth; when nominal GDP grows more slowly than the target rate, increase money-supply growth. Changes in velocity cause changes in nominal GDP, so they are automatically offset by this rule.

2. *Lack of Fed control over the money supply.* Even if velocity were constant, the Fed cannot maintain close enough control over the money supply to effect the monetarist rule. This lack of control arises from several sources: the public's holdings of currency fluctuate irregularly; banks and the public

shift deposits from one measure of the money supply to another; financial innovations are continually rendering money measures obsolete; banks can choose to hold excess reserves; and banks can obtain extra reserves if needed by borrowing cheaply from the Fed. Unstable velocity and the lack of control over monetary aggregates have prompted suggestions that it is better to target monetary policy directly on the inflation rate, rather than on a monetary aggregate.

3. *Short-run monetary shocks.* The economy is often hit with short-run increases in money demand that cry out for a temporary increase in the money supply. Turning the central bank into a preprogrammed robot would prevent the application of any such obviously correct policy. Examples of such situations are the Penn Central bankruptcy in 1970, the Franklin National Bank collapse in 1974, the Hunt brothers silver speculation crisis in the 1980s, the stock market crash of 19 October 1987, and postal strikes in Canada. An example easily built into a monetarist rule, however, is the seasonal increase in the demand for money that occurs every year before Christmas.

## Media Illustrations

### Example 1

**The central bank claims that "there are no aggregate measures or indicators of the rate of monetary expansion that are sufficiently reliable at present to be used as targets for policy, or that are uniquely helpful in the task of explaining the impact of monetary policy." Accordingly, judgment about financial and economic conditions—rather than following a monetary rule—will continue to be the guiding force behind monetary policy. Thus, it appears that monetary targeting isn't in the cards.**

*What are the most popular "aggregate measures or indicators of the rate of monetary expansion"?*
M1 and M2 are the most popular measures of the money supply.

*What is the monetary rule referred to here?*
The monetary rule requires that the money supply be increased at a steady, pre-announced rate, usually low enough to deliver an acceptable rate of inflation.

*What does "monetary targeting" mean?*
Monetary targeting means devoting monetary policy to achieving a specific rate of growth of a monetary aggregate.

*What argument is being used to defend the decision not to adopt such a rule?*
For this rule to work, the definition of the money supply used to measure the rate of money growth must be reliably connected to the level of economic activity. In more formal terms, its velocity must be roughly constant. It is claimed that no existing money-supply measure qualifies in this respect.

**Example 2**

**How can this be? How can the economy show just as much inflation with money growing only half as fast? After all, the growth of M1 has been cut to about 6 percent, which is close to the 4 percent that we were told five years ago would produce a stable price level.**

*How would one calculate the money-supply growth rate that would "produce a stable price level"?*
This rate would be equal to the long-run real rate of growth of the economy.

*What answer would you give to the two questions in this clipping?*
Although the growth of M1 has been cut to 6 percent, it is probably the case that an alternative measure of the money supply—perhaps M2, which is more closely related to spending—is growing at a much higher rate.

**Example 3**

**The rapid expansion of M2 occurred as inflation rates were at historically high levels. Instead of saving, people spent and turned money over quickly in the banking system.**

*This clip suggests that the historically high inflation rate has caused the rapid expansion of M2. Do you agree? Explain.*
No. It is more likely that the rapid expansion of the money supply, as measured by M2, has caused the historically high inflation. (It is possible, however, that some other factor, such a surge in consumption demand, has caused a temporary increase in inflation, which the monetary authorities have accommodated by increasing the rate of growth of the money supply to avoid constricting the economy.)

*What terminology do economists use to refer to "turning money over quickly in the banking system"?*
This would be called a *high velocity.*

*Why would velocity tend to be higher during an inflation?*
When inflation is high, money holdings lose their value more quickly. To avoid this loss, people try to get by with fewer cash balances, making this smaller level of cash balances work harder (i.e., turn over more frequently) to support their spending.

**Example 4**

**The central bank has got it right. Its job is to take the punch bowl away just as the party gets roaring. And if you have 6 percent real growth a quarter like we did last year, it's quite a party you've got going.**

*What is the "party" referred to in the clipping?*
A recovery from a recession.

*What is the "punch bowl" in this context, and what role does it play at this party?*
The punch bowl is money-supply growth. It has served to stimulate, or at least to accommodate, the economy's recovery from the recession.

*Why is it necessary to remove this punch bowl?*
Once the recovery is well under way, capacity output will soon be reached, implying that price increases rather than output increases will result from continued stimulation. To prevent this, the central bank must lower the money-supply growth to a level consistent with full-capacity real growth.

## Chapter Summary

- The original quantity theory, represented by $Mv = PQ$, was a tautology because velocity $v$ was defined to be the ratio of $PQ$ to $M$. If $v$ is constant, an increase in the money supply $M$ causes an equal percentage increase in the price level $P$ if the economy is at full employment and an equal percentage increase in real output $Q$ if the economy is below full employment.

- The modern quantity theory rewrites the quantity equation as $M = (1/v)PQ$ and interprets it as a money-demand equation, reflecting the fact that money demand increases as nominal income $PQ$ increases. This behavioral relationship is used to develop an explanation of how the economy reacts to an increase in the money supply to move to a higher income level. The magnitude of this reaction is captured formally by the income multiplier with respect to the money supply.

- By equating growth in supply of and demand for money, monetarists developed a rule of thumb for predicting long-run inflation: money growth less real growth. In the short run, many things affect inflation, but in the long run, inflation is always and everywhere a monetary phenomenon because price increases, through demand or cost increases, can be sustained only if supplemented with money-supply increases.

- The monetarist rule—that the central bank be replaced by a robot designed to increase the money supply at a rate approximately equal to the real rate of growth in the economy—is designed to keep long-run inflation low. This proposal has spawned the very active rules-versus-discretion debate between those who believe that policy authorities should be replaced by policy rules and those who believe that policy authorities should be permitted to take discretionary policy action as they see fit.

## Formula Definitions

- $\text{velocity} = \dfrac{PQ}{M} = \dfrac{\text{nominal GDP}}{\text{money supply}}$.

- $\text{income multiplier with respect to the money supply} = \dfrac{\Delta\text{GDP}}{\Delta M}$.

## Rule of Thumb

$$\text{long-run inflation} = \text{money growth rate} - \text{real income growth rate} + \text{velocity growth rate}.$$

## Media Exercises

1. **Of course, many economists now believe that if the 1970s taught us anything, it's that macroeconomic fine-tuning is more trouble than it's worth. In effect, the economy's steering gears are so loose that unless you hit a very sharp curve, fiddling with the wheel is just as likely to do harm as good.**

   a. What is macroeconomic "fine-tuning"?

   b. What kind of monetary policy is this an argument for? Explain.

2. **Followers of Milton Friedman of the University of Chicago were convinced that business cycles could be smoothed away simply by requiring that the Federal Reserve ...**

   a. Complete this sentence.

   b. Explain the logic behind the claim that business cycles can be smoothed away.

3. **The introduction of daily-interest saving accounts attracted a growing portion of funds away from checking accounts. The upshot was that a given amount of M1 supported a higher level of total spending or, in other words, its _____ increased.**

   a. Fill in the blank in this clip.

   b. Explain in your own words exactly why it increased.

4. **Monetarism's recognition of the usefulness of monitoring the money supply was an important contribution to economics, they say. They also accept the principal that, eventually, an economy that goes on producing more money than noninflationary growth requires will turn inflationary. "In the long run, monetarism has to be correct," said Richard Darman, the deputy secretary to the Treasury. Excessive money growth has to lead to inflation. "The problem with monetarism," he said, "is that its advocates have seen it as infallible over short periods of time and wish it to be rigid in its application over all periods of time."**

   a. What level of money-supply growth does "noninflationary growth" require?

b. Why do the advocates of monetarism "wish it to be rigid in its application over all periods of time"?

c. Why do others view this as a problem?

**5. Most economists look for the Fed to adopt a more restrictive policy once the recovery _____ and the presidential election _____ .**

a. What is meant here by "a more restrictive policy"?

b. Fill in the blanks.

**6. I really don't believe monetary policy is a very useful tool for fine-tuning the business cycle or for directly fighting unemployment. I do believe that what monetary policy can do is control the inflation rate.**

a. Why might one believe that monetary policy is not useful for fine-tuning the business cycle?

b. How can monetary policy be used to control inflation?

**7. Because the broader measure M2 encompasses most significant forms of money individuals may hold, it resolves the problem. The shifts in asset holdings take place *within* the broader measure. That doesn't make it impervious to distortion, but M2 velocity has shown substantial predictability for several years.**

a. What is M2 velocity?

b. Explain why M2 velocity may be more predictable than M1 velocity.

c. What is the problem referred to at the very end of the first sentence, and exactly how does M2 solve this problem?

**8. The experience of M1 still unnerves: innovations in the banking system, especially interest-bearing checking accounts, which at that time were not counted in M1, allowed the public to shift money holdings into and out of different instruments in such as way as to make the relationship between M1 and total spending in the economy unstable.**

a. Explain what must have been the unnerving experience with M1.

b. What technical terminology would economists use to describe "the relationship between M1 and total spending"?

**9. A monetary rule need not mean a single, bald number. If the central bank fears velocity shifts, rules could be adopted for adjusting the target in the face of a trend change in velocity.**

a. What might cause a velocity shift?

b. What is the "target" referred to in this clip?

c. By means of a numerical example, explain how this target would be adjusted for "a trend change in velocity."

10. **If the Fed's sole objective is to fight inflation, it may as well be run by a computer, say critics of a proposal to change its mandate. The proposal to strip the Fed of its other economic jobs, such as supporting the value of the dollar and promoting economic growth and employment, brings to wider public attention a debate that has quietly gone on among economists for the past few years.**

a. Explain how a computer could be used to run the Fed's inflation-fighting policy.

b. What is the debate referred to in this clipping?

11. **A growing number of economists view the Fed's new willingness to take on more of the nation's debt as inflationary in the long run.**

a. Explain the reason for the inflation worry.

b. Why is the "long-run" qualification added?

12. **Far better for central bankers to get out of the fine-tuning business. Instead, they should try to keep ...**

Complete this clip.

13. **In a study of ten European and North American countries, it was found that democratically controlled central banks pursue less-restrictive policies than do independent central banks and thus are less likely to try to veto the expansionary policies of left-wing governments.**

a. Do you think the authors of this study would have classified the Fed as democratically controlled or independent? Explain.

b. How would a central bank try to veto expansionary policies? Why would it want to do this?

c. Why do you think democratically controlled banks would in general pursue less-restrictive policies?

14. **With financial deregulation changing the meaning of money, the Fed finally abandoned the monetarist prescription of targeting the money supply.**

a. How did financial deregulation change the meaning of money?

b. Exactly what is the "monetarist prescription of targeting the money supply"?

c. Why would this monetarist prescription need to be abandoned?

15. **It is very difficult for politicians to take action—especially unpleasant action—against a problem until the problem seems compelling. By that time, though, action tends to be tardy. The point of economic management is to stabilize the economy, but a political system that requires signs of instability before it can act makes the process self-defeating.**

    In terms of classic debates over economic policy, what does this argument support?

16. **Inflationary policies can spur growth for a time, which is why politicians have often found them so tempting. This is the best argument for making central banks ...**

    Complete this clipping.

## Numerical Exercises

N1.  Suppose the income multiplier with respect to the money supply is 4, the money multiplier is 3, and "the" multiplier is 2.5.

   a. If the central bank buys $2 billion bonds, what increase in income should ultimately result?

   b. If the economy is at full employment when this policy is undertaken, what fraction of this increase in GDP is an increase in real GDP?

N2.  Suppose income is $800 billion, the price index is 120 (base year 1987), inflation is 10 percent, the long-run real rate of growth is 2 percent, and the current money supply is $200 billion.

   a. What is the level of real (1987 dollars) income?

   b. What is the velocity of money?

   c. What is the rate of growth of the money supply?

N3.  Suppose "the" multiplier is 3, the money multiplier is 6, and the income multiplier with respect to the money supply is 4. The government increases spending by $12 billion, but because the economy is operating at full capacity, it wants to use monetary policy to offset the impact this will have on income.

   a. Does the central bank need to buy or sell bonds to offset this fiscal policy?

   b. How many bonds must the monetary authorities buy or sell to accomplish this end?

N4.   Suppose that due to financial innovations the demand for money is decreasing by 1 percent per year, with all other factors unchanged.

a. What does this do to velocity?

b. What adjustment, if any, would you make to the inflation equation?

c. What adjustment, if any, would you make to the monetarist rule?

N5.   Suppose the current level of income is $600 billion, the long-run real rate of growth is 2 percent, the current money supply is $200 billion, and the rate of money-supply growth is 10 percent.

a. What is the velocity of money?

b. What long-run level of inflation is this economy experiencing?

N6.   Suppose "the" multiplier is 3, the money multiplier is 4, and the income multiplier with respect to the money supply is 5. If the government increases its spending by $10 billion at the same time that the central bank sells $2 billion of bonds on the open market (beyond the bond sales involved in financing the government spending), what will happen to the equilibrium level of income?

N7.   If the money supply is growing at 8 percent, the real rate of growth of GDP is 2 percent, and financial innovations are reducing the demand for money by 0.5 percent per year, what should be the long-run inflation rate?

N8.   Suppose "the" multiplier is 3.5, the money multiplier is 4.5, the income multiplier with respect to the money supply is 2.5, and the marginal tax rate is 20 percent. What ultimate change in the government's budget deficit would result if government spending increased by $10 billion and at the same time the central bank sold bonds (beyond those sold to finance government spending) worth $8 billion?

N9.   Suppose "the" multiplier is 4, the income multiplier with respect to the money supply is 2, the money multiplier is 3, and the government is obliged by an election promise to increase government spending by $5 billion, but wants the level of income to grow by only $8 billion to avoid inflation. What open-market operation will accomplish this?

N10.  Suppose that the income elasticity of the demand for money (the percent rise in the demand for money due to a 1 percent rise in income) is less than one. Does this imply that the inflation equation overestimates, underestimates, or remains an accurate estimate of inflation? Explain your reasoning.

N11.  If "the" multiplier is 6, the income multiplier with respect to the money supply is 4, and the money multiplier is 5, then which of the following policies will increase income by $50 billion dollars?

   a. Increase the money supply by $2.5 billion

   b. Increase government spending by $10 billion

   c. Have the Fed purchase $12.5 billion in bonds

   d. Increase government spending by $3 billion and the money supply by $8 billion

   e. Have the Fed sell $2 billion in bonds, and the government increase spending by $15 billion

   f. Have the Fed purchase $1 billion in bonds, and the government increase spending by $5 billion

N12. Suppose the aggregate supply curve is vertical, velocity is 4, and the money supply increases by 3 percent. According to the quantity theory of money, what will be the percentage change in (1) real income, (2) the price level, and (3) nominal income?

N13. Suppose the economy is at full employment with a real rate of growth of 3 percent. If innovations in the banking system are decreasing the need for money at 1 percent per year, what rate of growth of the money supply would you recommend to achieve a long-run inflation rate of 4 percent?

# 10　Monetary Policy and Interest Rates

It may be surprising that we have completed two chapters dealing with money and the role of the central bank but have only peripherally mentioned interest rates. This was deliberate. The fundamental role of the central bank is to control the supply of money in the economy. Effects on interest rates are a product of this control, so a prerequisite to any discussion of interest rates is a knowledge of the role of money creation.

Monetary policy influences interest rates in two distinct ways, depending on whether or not the monetary policy affects inflation. The purpose of this chapter is to discuss how monetary policy affects the interest rate in a noninflationary environment and how the interest rate in turn affects the operation of the economy. Chapter 11 examines interest rates in an inflationary environment.

---

**Upon completion of this chapter you should**

- be able to explain the crucial role played by the inverse relationship between the interest rate and the price of bonds; and
- understand how monetary policy affects the economy through interest rates.

---

## 10.1   A Multitude of Interest Rates

Macroeconomists talk of "the" interest rate, but in fact a myriad of interest rates exist, depending on such variables as time to maturity of the financial asset, how the interest is taxed, how liquid the financial asset is, and what is known about the borrower (in particular, the risk of default). Short-term debt instruments, of maturity less than a year, are traded in what is called the *money market*. Longer-term instruments are traded in the *capital market*.

Typical interest rates in the money market are T-bill rates (on U.S. government treasury bills); commercial paper rates (on loans by financial institutions to large banks and corporations); the federal funds rate (on very short-term loans between banks of their deposits at the Fed); and the Eurodollar rate (on U.S. dollars deposited outside the United States). Typical interest rates in the capital market are the mortgage rate, the corporate bond rate, the Treasury bond rate, and the municipal bond rate.

All these interest rates tend to move together, however, so little harm is done by analyzing the economy in terms of a single representative interest rate, as we do throughout the rest of this book.

---

## 10.2   Interest Rates and the Price of Bonds

The inverse relationship between the interest rate and the price of bonds is fundamental to understanding how monetary policy affects interest rates and why people in the financial world are always so worried about the future course of the interest rate. This inverse relationship is illustrated for the two main types of bonds—coupon bonds and discount bonds.

A *coupon bond* pays the owner of the bond a fixed interest payment each year until the bond matures when the face value (or par value) of the bond is repaid. The name "coupon bond" comes from the fact that, until recently, this fixed interest payment involved the bond owner clipping a coupon off the bottom of the bond each year.

Suppose you own a coupon bond due to mature in five years, with face value $1,000 and coupon $100. If the interest rate is 10 percent, the current price of this bond should be $1,000 because the $100 interest coupon payment is 10 percent of the price of the bond. Now suppose the interest rate rises to 12 percent. Seeing this, you decide to sell your bond and use the proceeds to buy a new bond that pays 12 percent. Unfortunately for you, however, nobody is willing to pay $1,000 for your bond because everyone knows he or she can earn a 12 percent return elsewhere. To sell your bond you will have to lower its price, in this case to $833.33, because at this price the $100 interest payment is a return of 12 percent.

Actually, the price will not fall quite this far. Because the bond will pay off at $1,000 in five years, the total return to investing in this bond is the stream of five $100 interest payments, plus a capital gain due to the rise in bond price to $1,000 over these five years. The yield to maturity, which is what economists mean by an interest rate, would be higher than 12 percent. For the yield to maturity to be 12 percent, the price need fall to only $927.90. For those interested, this calculation is explained in curiosity 10.1.

An opposite result would occur if the interest rate were to fall to 8 percent. Everyone would want to buy your bond if it were priced at $1,000 because the 10 percent return on your bond would be higher than the 8 percent return available elsewhere. As a result, potential buyers would bid up the price of your bond in their efforts to obtain it, in this case to $1,250 because the $100 return is 8 percent of $1,250. Once again, this is not quite correct. In five years this bond will pay off at $1,000, so holders will experience a capital loss if they buy it for a higher price, implying that the yield to maturity is lower than 8 percent. The price will be bid up to only $1,079.85.

A *discount bond* is a bond without a coupon (and is therefore sometimes called a zero-coupon bond). The return to holding such a bond comes entirely from buying it at a price below its face value. The most common example is a U.S. government Treasury bill, called a T-bill, sold originally at weekly auctions for maturity periods of three months, six months, and one year (and then, like all other bonds, available for resale on the regular money market). If the interest rate is 10 percent, the price for a one-year $10,000 T-bill will be $9,090.91 because the return of $10,000 − $9,090.91 = $909.09 is 10 percent of the $9,090.91 price paid.

If the interest rate were higher, say 12 percent, the price of the T-bill would be lower—in this case $8,928.57—to make the return of $10,000 − $8,928.57 = $1071.43 be 12 percent of the $8,928.57 purchase price. If the interest rate were lower, say 8 percent, the price of the T-bill would be higher, in this case $9,259.26.

Regardless of the type of bond, there is an inverse relationship between interest rates and bond prices. This relationship is as close to a true economic law that it can get: interest rates and bond prices are instantly connected, with the causal force going in either direction. If someone decides to sell a bond, for whatever

---

**Curiosity 10.1:   How Is Yield to Maturity Calculated?**

If the interest rate were $i$, then \$40 today would be worth $\$40(1 + i)$ next year, $\$40(1 + i)^2$ in two years, and $\$40(1 + i)^n$ in $n$ years. This logic can be worked in reverse to find out how much a future payment would be worth today, called its *present value*. Calculating a present value is done by *discounting* a future payment. If you were to receive \$100 in one year's time, it would be worth $\$100/(1 + i)$ today because this sum today would be worth \$100 in one year. Similarly, the present value of \$100 paid $n$ years from now would be $\$100/(1 + i)^n$.

A yield to maturity of a coupon bond is calculated by discounting the stream of future payments to the bondholder to find their present value, which should be equal to the current price of the bond. Thus for a bond maturing in $n$ years

$$\text{current bond price} = \frac{\text{coupon}}{(1 + i)} + \frac{\text{coupon}}{(1 + i)^2} + \cdots + \frac{\text{coupon}}{(1 + i)^n} + \frac{\text{face value}}{(1 + i)^n}.$$

This equation can be used to solve for the interest rate $i$—the yield to maturity—if the price of the bond is known, or to solve for the price of the bond if $i$ is known. Note that solving this equation to find yield to maturity is not easy without a computer. For the case of exactly one year to maturity, however, calculation of the interest rate is straightforward:

$$i = \frac{\text{coupon} + \text{capital gain}}{\text{current price}} = \frac{\text{coupon} + \text{face value} - \text{current price}}{\text{current price}}.$$

The annualized yield to maturity of a discount bond is calculated as

$$i = \frac{\text{face value} - \text{current price}}{\text{current price}} \times \frac{365}{N}.$$

where $N$ is the number of days until maturity.

All yields on financial assets should be reported as yields to maturity, but curiously some are not, perhaps because of tradition attached to simpler calculations done before the advent of the computer. One alternative, called the *current yield*, expresses the coupon as a percentage of its current price, ignoring the capital gain/loss. By tradition, newspapers usually report current yields for corporate bonds, but yield to maturity for most other bonds.

---

reason, and drops the bond price to sell it, the interest rate instantly rises. And if the interest rate rises, for whatever reason, the market reacts instantly to push down bond prices.

It should now be evident why this relationship between interest rates and bond prices is so important. A change in the interest rate can create substantial capital gains or losses for those holding bonds, particularly for those holding long-term bonds. This is why the financial pages of newspapers provide so much commentary on the future course of the interest rate.

Why are the capital gains and losses greater for longer-maturity bonds? Let's look at the earlier example of a \$1,000 face-value coupon bond with coupon \$100 and time to maturity five years. A rise in the interest rate to 12 percent dropped the bond price to $927.90. Suppose there had been only one year to maturity; then the price would have fallen to $982.14. Someone buying this bond would, during the remaining year of its life, receive the $100 coupon plus that year's capital gain, $17.86, generating a 12 percent return on outlay. If there had been five years to maturity, however, there would have to be five such annual capital gains as the bond price crawls up to its face value over the five years. Consequently, the price must fall further for a longer maturity bond. Capital losses and gains are much larger on long-term bonds than on short-term bonds.

## 10.3   Monetary Policy and Interest Rates

The central bank controls the money supply through open-market operations—buying and selling bonds. If it wishes to increase the money supply, it buys bonds on the open market, but to buy these bonds it must induce us to sell them by bidding up their price. This rise in the price of bonds means that the interest coupon on a bond is now a lower percentage payment—that is, the interest rate falls. Similarly, if the central bank wishes to decrease the money supply, it sells bonds on the open market. To sell bonds it must make them attractive to potential buyers by offering a higher interest rate, accomplished by selling the bonds at a lower price.

The main result here is that by changing the money supply, the central bank also changes the interest rate by affecting the price of bonds: an increase in the money supply lowers the interest rate by bidding up the price of bonds, and a decrease in the money supply raises the interest rate by lowering the price of bonds. This explains why the role of the central bank is often exposited in terms of its interest rate policy rather than in terms of its money-supply policy. The one is a mirror image of the other.

The explanation of the determination of the interest rate given above focuses on what is happening in the bond market. For convenience, economists often view the determination of the interest rate in another, equivalent way—by interpreting the interest rate as the "price" of money and by looking at what is happening to the supply of and demand for money. The rationale for this is that individuals are thought to hold wealth in one of only two forms, money and bonds, so an increase in the demand for one implies a decrease in the demand for the other.

Consequently, because buying bonds increases the supply of money, it should lower its "price," the interest rate. An increase in the demand for money, due, for example, to an increase in the level of income, should increase its "price," so the interest rate should rise. In terms of the bond market, the increased demand for money means people want to sell bonds to get cash. This lowers the price of bonds, raising the interest rate. This could be exposited via some graphical

Open-market operations

 ⇒ Fed buys bonds to ↑ money supply
 ⇒ ↑ price of bonds
 ⇒ ↓ i rate
 ⇒ ↑ consumption, investment, and government spending
 ⇒ ↑ aggregate demand for goods and services
 ⇒ Keynesian multiplier process
 ⇒ ↑ income

**Figure 10.1**   The transmission mechanism
Monetary policy lowers the interest rate, which increases aggregate demand for goods
and services and sets the Keynesian multiplier process in motion.

curve-shifting, but is an instance in which the common sense of supply-and-
demand forces are all that is necessary; the curves themselves are superfluous.
Don't confuse supply and demand for money with the "money market," which
refers to the market for short-term bonds.

## 10.4   The Transmission Mechanism

Introducing the interest rate means that we must change the story we had told
earlier about how monetary policy affects economic activity. In our earlier
story—the explanation of modern quantity theory—an increase in the money
supply caused people to find themselves holding more of their wealth in the
form of money than they wished to hold in the form of money. We assumed
that they spent these excess money holdings to try to get rid of them. Now we
note that increasing the money supply causes the interest rate to fall, which (as
described in our discussion of crowding out, chapter 7) stimulates spending by
consumers, firms, and local governments. The increase in spending leads to the
familiar Keynesian multiplier process, moving the economy to a higher level of
income, as illustrated in figure 10.1.

In this new story, the impact of monetary policy is transmitted to economic
activity through the intermediary of the interest rate. Most economists feel that
this *transmission mechanism* is the one that describes the way in which monetary policy operates to influence economic activity, and the one we will adopt
henceforth in this book. How, then, does the monetarist view of the transmission mechanism, as described by the modern quantity theory, fit in?

Monetarists feel that a rise in the money supply transmits itself to an increase
in spending through a variety of channels that cannot adequately be captured
by a single interest rate measured on a market. The simple assumption that
people spend to rid themselves of excess cash balances is a crude summary of
a much more complicated story. An increase in the money supply upsets the
balance of an individual's wealth portfolio. This portfolio is now comprised of

---

**Curiosity 10.2:   What Are the Discount and Federal Funds Rates?**

Although most interest rates are determined by the forces of supply and demand in the money or capital markets, one important interest rate—the *discount rate*—is not. This rate is an administratively determined rate charged by the Fed to banks when they borrow reserves from the Fed. This borrowing is supposed to be for seasonal and emergency needs, but because the discount rate is usually below going market rates, banks find it profitable to borrow at the discount window even when they are not in need of reserves. The Fed discourages such borrowing, however, because it dilutes Fed control over the money supply.

Although a higher discount rate should discourage bank borrowing from the Fed and thus decrease the money supply, it is a very inefficient way of affecting the money supply and is not used for this purpose. The Fed changes the discount rate from time to time mainly to give a signal or "announcement" to markets concerning the Fed's intentions regarding interest rates. Such changes usually follow changes in market rates and serve to indicate that the Fed views these market rate changes as permanent.

When the Fed focuses on an interest rate rather than on a monetary aggregate to conduct monetary policy, it uses the *federal funds rate* instead of the discount rate. The federal funds rate is the rate charged by one bank to another for borrowing (usually overnight) some of its excess reserves at the Fed. Commercial banks that are unable to meet their legal reserve requirement borrow other banks' excess reserves, paying the federal funds rate, what is determined by the forces of supply and demand in this market.

The advantage to the Fed of focusing on the federal funds rate is that it is determined by supply-and-demand forces and thus is a good indicator of the "tightness" of current monetary policy insofar as market interest rates in general are concerned. Suppose the Fed buys bonds on the open market and thereby increases reserves in the banking system. As a result, few commerical banks will be unable to meet their reserve requirement, and many banks will have excess reserves. Demand for excess reserves will be low and supply high, so the federal funds rate—the "price" in this market—will be low. Furthermore, we can expect this low federal funds rate to spread quickly to the economy at large: the excess reserves that have created the low federal funds rate will cause banks to increase loans and thereby to lower interest rates in general.

---

more cash, less bonds, and the same quantity of such things as consumer durables and capital goods. The individual reacts to this imbalance by shifting the excess cash into other components of this portfolio, in the process bidding up the prices of these other components. The consequent rise in the price of capital goods and consumer durables stimulates the production of new capital goods and consumer durables.

Each of the alternative components of the individual's wealth portfolio have an implicit rate of return (an interest rate) associated with them. Consumer durables, for example, return a stream of services to their owner, which determines how much of the excess money holdings are shifted to each category of the wealth portfolio. Money holdings also have an implicit return to them associated with the convenience they provide us in undertaking our everyday financial transactions. Consequently, a multitude of interest rates transmit the impact of monetary policy, some of them (such as that associated with consumer durables) being implicit rather than measured rates. Thus, the transmission mechanism of the modern quantity theory can be viewed as a subtle version of the story in which monetary policy works through affecting interest rates.

## 10.5   Using Monetary Policy

The view of discretionary monetary policy that has emerged in this chapter and the preceding two chapters is that through open-market operations the central bank can stimulate the economy by increasing the money supply, alternatively viewed as pushing down the interest rate. In a longer-run context, an eye must be kept on the rate of growth of the money supply to ensure that inflation is not allowed to escalate, but in a noninflationary environment, discretionary use of monetary policy is a useful alternative or supplement to fiscal policy.

Both fiscal and monetary policy shift the AD curve in the aggregate supply/ aggregate demand diagram. Fiscal policy changes aggregate demand directly; monetary policy changes aggregate demand by changing the interest rate. Some marked differences between monetary and fiscal policy, however, should be noted. Monetary policy can be implemented much more quickly than fiscal policy because it does not require congressional approval. Once implemented, however, it affects the economy more slowly than fiscal policy because it takes time for decision makers to react to lower interest rates. It has been estimated, for example, that only about one-third of the impact of an interest-rate change on aggregate demand occurs within one year, and only about one-half within two years. Furthermore, these lags are variable as well as long, making it quite difficult for monetary authorities to deduce the correct timing for monetary policy. Therefore, any temporary, discretionary diversion from the monetarist rule must be undertaken with great care.

Monetary policy affects the economy very broadly, allowing the impersonal forces of supply and demand to distribute efficiently its impact across the economy. This happens with fiscal policy when it takes the form of tax changes, but not when it takes the form of government spending changes, which could be either an advantage in that government spending could be directed at a depressed region or a disadvantage in that government spending may be directed by political whims. Despite the impersonality of monetary policy, however, it is discriminatory. The components of aggregate demand that are more sensitive to interest rate changes bear the costs of adjustment. The sector most strongly affected in this regard is the housing sector, which is notoriously sensitive to interest rate changes. A fall in the mortgage rate from 10 percent to 8 percent, for example, decreases the monthly payment on a thirty-year mortgage by over

16 percent. This markedly increases the demand for residential construction. The export and import-competing sectors are also strongly affected. Interest rate changes cause foreigners to adjust their demand for our currency to invest in our financial assets, which alters the exchange rate and affects the profitability of business in the international sector.

Our discussion of monetary policy is not yet complete. The next chapter examines its role in an inflationary environment, providing further insight into the relationship between monetary policy and interest rates. Chapter 16 looks at how monetary policy is affected by international influences.

## Media Illustrations

### Example 1

**The average yield at this week's auction of $17.8 billion of ninety-one-day Treasury bills was 11.17 percent, up from 10.95 percent last week. Accepted bids for the bills ranged from a high of $97.300 for an 11.13 percent yield to a low of $97.288 for an 11.18 percent yield. The average bid price was $97.290.**

*Has the average bid price risen or fallen from what it was last week?*
The yield, or interest rate, has risen from last week to this week. The price must have fallen to produce this rise in yield.

*How would one calculate that a bid of $97.300 corresponds to a yield of 11.13 percent?*
A 91-day T-bill bought now for $97.30 will be worth $100.00 in 91 days when it matures, so its return over 91 days is $(100 - 97.30)/97.30$. To find the corresponding annual yield, we must convert the return over 91 days to a return over 365 days by multiplying by 365/91, obtaining 11.13.

### Example 2

**Some economists criticized the central bank for not moving in the face of the waning recovery. One, who prefers anonymity, stated: "The failure to move today leaves us with low inflation, a weak economy, and climbing jobless claims; these are classic signs of an impending downturn. The Fed fiddles while the economy burns."**

*What kind of Fed movement would this economist want to see?*
He must feel that there is little danger of an expansionary monetary policy creating inflation and would argue that a discretionary increase in the money supply or, equivalently, a fall in interest rates, is in order.

*Why might the Fed not move?*
The Fed may not yet feel that the economy is definitely entering a recession. Often, early numbers are revised, and what appears to be the beginning of a recession is no more than a temporary downturn. If the Fed is too quick to react, it could overstimulate and spark inflationary forces.

### Example 3

**Several Treasury bond issues will raise $40 billion, with the Federal Reserve Board picking up at least $20 billion. The Fed can also be counted on to take down more of the bonds than the planned $20 billion it has announced if they seem to be selling badly.**

*What is the main implication of the Fed picking up $20 billion of these bonds?*
The money supply will increase by $20 billion times the money multiplier.

*What does the second sentence imply about the Fed's monetary policy?*
If the bonds are selling badly, the interest rate is not high enough to attract buyers. If the Fed does not step in, the price of these bonds will fall and the interest rate will rise. The fact that the Fed can be counted on not to let this happen suggests that the Fed's monetary policy is targeting the interest rate, with little concern about money-supply growth.

### Example 4

**The eagerly awaited weekly money stock figures measure more than just the supply of money. The weekly number measures money demand as much as it does supply. The evidence now suggests that the alarming growth rate of the money stock mainly reflects an upsurge in money demand, rather than an overly expansive money-supply policy.**

*What would happen to the interest rate if there was an upsurge in money demand with no corresponding increase in money supply?*
There would be a rise in the interest rate. The higher demand for money would bid up its price, the interest rate. Alternatively, those wanting more cash balances would sell bonds to obtain money. This would lower the price of bonds, thus raising the interest rate.

*What monetary policy does the central bank appear to be following here?*
The central bank appears to be matching changes in the demand for money with changes in the supply of money in order to keep the interest rate constant.

*Comment on the conclusion that the money-supply policy is not "overly expansive."*
This is an erroneous conclusion. By targeting the interest rate, the central bank has lost control over the rate of growth of the money supply, so it can easily become overly expansive, as it has in the situation described in this clipping. For example, if inflation temporarily becomes higher, demand for money increases accordingly, and this policy produces a concomitant increase in the money supply. The rise in money-supply growth causes this temporary increase in inflation to be maintained: the economy moves permanently to a higher money-supply growth and inflation.

### Example 5

**On Friday the market withstood what bond investors ought to have viewed as a rather bearish jobless report. The number of employed U.S. workers rose by**

**125,000 in April, higher than the 75,000 expected. The unemployment rate dropped to 7.2 percent from 7.3 percent the previous month.**

*This jobless report looks "bullish"—that is, job creation is up and unemployment is down. Why is it called "bearish"?*

This is a bullish report for the economy, but not for the bond market. The upswing in economic activity should lead people to expect that the Fed will fear that the economy will overheat and so will act to raise interest rates, causing bond prices to fall.

## Chapter Summary

- The inverse relationship between the interest rate and the price of bonds is important because interest rate changes can create sizeable capital gains or losses for those holding bonds, particularly long-term bonds.

- Open-market operations affect the interest rate, thereby changing aggregate demand for goods and services and setting in motion the traditional Keynesian multiplier process. Because of this, monetary policy is often viewed as operating through interest rates.

- Both monetary and fiscal policies shift the AD curve to the right, but they differ in other respects, such as in lag structures and discriminatory impacts.

## Formula Definitions

- current bond price $= \dfrac{\text{coupon}}{(1+i)} + \dfrac{\text{coupon}}{(1+i)^2} + \cdots + \dfrac{\text{coupon}}{(1+i)^n} + \dfrac{\text{face value}}{(1+i)^n}.$

- for one year to maturity $i = \dfrac{\text{coupon} + \text{capital gain}}{\text{current price}}.$

- annualized $i$ of $N$-day discount bond $= \dfrac{\text{face value} - \text{current price}}{\text{current price}} \times \dfrac{365}{N}.$

## Media Exercises

1. **Falling interest rates have triggered a rally in the bond market that has many investors rejoicing.**

   Why would falling interest rates trigger a rally in the bond market?

2. **Lenders would be wise to move their short-term holdings into longer-term assets to take advantage of the capital gains generated by declining interest rates.**

a. What are the capital gains mentioned in this clip, and how do they come about?

b. Why aren't these capital gains associated with short-term as well as long-term assets?

3. **Yields on Treasury bills started to rise early in the week as dealers began to unload the bills because of higher-than-anticipated carrying costs.**

How does unloading bills cause their yields to rise?

4. **Basically, investors profit in two ways from putting their money into bonds: through the coupon rate or interest rate attached to each bond, providing a steady income, and through potential ...**

Complete this clip.

5. **A twenty-year government bond paying 10.25 percent was selling for $1,007.10, priced above its par value of $1,000 to yield 10.15 percent.**

The quoted yield of 10.15 percent is slightly lower than $102.50 expressed as a percentage of $1007.10. Why?

6. **In the financial markets, red ink is flowing as some investment dealers continue to lose money on the Treasury bills they buy from the federal government. Since last September, the biggest buyers of the bills, the banks, have been steadily reducing their holdings in order to meet rising loan demand.**

a. Why are investment dealers losing money?

b. Is the information conveyed in the second sentence consistent with the fact that dealers are losing money? Explain your reasoning.

7. **It is now evident that loan demand has dropped sufficiently since the beginning of the year to allow the money supply to grow at a rate of less than 10 percent at current levels of interest rates.**

This clip suggests that the demand for money controls its supply. How can this be?

8. **Earlier in the week, the Fed's traders aggressively intervened in the money market to push the yield on last week's bills sharply higher.**

Exactly what kind of intervention is being referred to?

9. **Bonds rallied sharply yesterday, cheered on by the news that the recession isn't over yet. Prices climbed by as much as $8.75 for each $1,000 face amount in the U.S. government securities market after the Commerce Department reported that GDP fell by 0.1 percent in the second quarter.**

Why would bad news rally bonds?

10. **There are difficulties in having the central bank present growth rate targets in advance. Central banks find it much easier to explain events after the fact if they are allowed to operate from a position of secrecy, with little communication with the public. Politically unpopular increases in interest rates might also have to be tolerated at embarrassing times under a policy of published target growth rates.**

    a. What is a target growth rate policy, and how would this target rate be chosen?

    b. Why would such a policy imply that increases in interest rates might have to be tolerated?

11. **The decline in the number of both payroll jobs and hours worked surprised many analysts, who said the report put new pressure on the Fed to ...**

    Complete this sentence.

12. **The wiser course would be to avoid switching monetary policy and keep the money-supply growth stable. This will automatically bring interest rates down during the recession when demand for funds is weak.**

    a. What would be a switching monetary policy?

    b. Explain the logic that lies behind the second sentence.

13. **The Fed pumped more money into the nation's banking system to reduce the federal funds rate—the rate at which banks lend each other money overnight—to 3.75 percent from 4 percent.**

    a. How would the Fed pump more money into the banking system?

    b. Explain how doing so would lower the federal funds rate.

14. **Although the official unemployment rate stayed at 7.1 percent, other figures showed the local jobless rate reaching its highest level in nine years, and analysts predicted the Federal Reserve would come under renewed pressure to cut interest rates once more in hopes of kindling a recovery.**

    a. How would the Federal Reserve go about cutting the interest rate?

    b. How would this kindle a recovery?

    c. What technical economic term does the word "kindle" bring to mind in this context?

15. **The economy surprised the bond market again Friday, with a report on explosive job growth in February sending prices plunging in volatile trading, a day after higher-than-expected jobless claims sparked an early rally Thursday.**

    Explain why news on the job front affects bond prices this way.

16. **With the sharp fall in interest rates, central bank officials expect a pick-up in economic activity that will bring about an upsurge in monetary growth.**

    a. Why would a sharp fall in interest rates be expected to cause a pick-up in economic activity?

    b. Why would a pick-up in economic activity bring about an upsurge in monetary growth?

17. **The proper lines of action for controlling inflation are not too difficult to envisage. First, we must stop relying on monetary policy to do the job. The monetary tool has been easiest and most convenient for all governments to use because it requires no legislation. It's a matter of men speaking in well-modulated voices around a polished table with charts on the wall. It has been given a good trial, but it hasn't worked, and its ecomomic impact has been discriminatory.**

    a. What would be the monetarists' "proper lines of action for controlling inflation?"

    b. How has monetary policy been discriminatory?

18. **Monetary policy is a peculiar tool in that it does not seem to have an inter-mediate switch. It is either completely ineffective or it is too effective. In the past few months, it has been too effective, almost destroying our housing industry.**

    How would monetary policy destroy the housing industry?

19. **The release of U.S. housing starts in April—down 17 percent to their lowest level in eight years—drove North American bond markets higher yesterday.**

    Why would this bad news drive bond prices higher?

20. **Thanks to a sharp cut in interest rates engineered by the Fed, many economists expect the economy to be growing again, albeit slowly, by spring, which is the soonest any of President Bush's legislative proposals are likely to be enacted.**

    a. What major advantage of monetary policy over fiscal policy does this clipping underline?

    b. How would the Fed have engineered the cut in interest rates?

    c. If this policy is so good, why isn't it done more vigorously, more often?

21. **According to Ibbotson Associates, twenty-year government bonds are on track to post annual returns of 30 percent by the end of 1995, lagging only the 40 percent returns of 1982 and the 31 percent returns of 1985.**

    In 1995, the interest rate was far, far below 30 percent. How could 1995 returns on bonds be as high as 30 percent?

**22.** **"The thrust of the central bank's policy has been to reduce demand for loans on the basis of price—not by limiting the amount of money that is available." "It isn't the function of the commercial banks to be self-appointed rationers of credit. We are in a very competitive business. If my bank won't lend to you, another one will." These two comments summarize the responses of senior bankers who were asked whether their present lending policies—particularly on consumer loans—are consistent with the central bank's objective of lowering the inflation rate by cutting back on credit demand.**

a. What does "reduce demand for loans on the basis of price" mean?

b. In what way is this policy identical to a policy of "limiting the amount of money that is available," and in what way is it different?

c. Do banks ration credit? Explain how or why not.

d. Explain how a policy of "cutting back on credit demand" is accomplished, and how it will lower inflation, as claimed in the last sentence.

## Numerical Exercises

N1. Suppose a discount bond with par value $10,000 will mature in exactly one year.

a. If its current price is $9,500, what is its yield?

b. If its current price is $9,000, what is its yield?

c. Are your answers to the first two questions consistent with the inverse relationship between interest rates and the price of bonds?

N2. Suppose the current interest rate is 6 percent.

a. What price should one expect to pay for a new three-month Treasury bill with face value $10,000?

b. What price should one expect to pay for a one-month-old, three-month Treasury bill with face value $10,000?

N3. A bond due to mature and pay $1,000 in one year's time has a coupon of $85 and a current price of $1,025. What is the interest rate?

N4. Suppose the interest rate is 8 percent, and a bond with an annual coupon of $75 matures in one year's time, paying its face value of $1,000. What is this bond's current price?

N5. Suppose the current interest rate is 6 percent. What price should one expect to pay for a $1,000 Treasury bill, due to mature in six months, that had originally been sold when the interest rate was 7 percent?

N6. Consider a bond with a face value of $1,000, due to mature in one year's time. Its current price is $1,035, and the current interest rate is 5.8 percent. What must its coupon be?

N7. Suppose "the" multiplier is 3, the income multiplier with respect to the money supply is 4, the money multiplier is 5, and a $20 billion increase in the money supply during a recession drops the interest rate by one percentage point. Suppose that to fight a recession, monetary policy is undertaken to lower the interest rate by one-half a percentage point. What should happen to the income level?

N8. Suppose the impact on the interest rate of a $3 increase in government spending can be eliminated by a $2 increase in the money supply. If the income multiplier with respect to government spending is 4, and the income multiplier with respect to the money supply is 3, what mix of monetary and fiscal policy is required to increase income by $9,000 without changing the interest rate?

# 11    Real versus Nominal Interest Rates

Our analysis of interest rates has heretofore been in the context of a noninflationary economy. The interest rate that we read about in the paper, pay on our mortgages, and earn on our bank deposits, however, contains a premium for expected inflation. Consequently, a major determinant of this interest rate is the expected rate of inflation, which in an inflationary economy usually swamps the effects of the factors discussed in the preceding chapter. Forecasting interest rates in an inflationary economy hinges on forecasting inflation. All other forces affecting interest rates are of secondary importance.

Economists draw a distinction between the interest rate with and without this premium for expected inflation; the former is called the *nominal interest rate*, and the latter the *real interest rate*. The most common error students make when analyzing the interest rate is to overlook the difference between the real and nominal interest rates. The purpose of this chapter is to spell out this difference and to explain its importance in a variety of contexts.

---

**Upon completion of this chapter you should**

- understand the difference between nominal and real interest rates;
- appreciate that monetary policy is much more complicated than the previous chapter would have us believe; and
- recognize that anything affecting the expected rate of inflation, such as money-supply growth, influences the bond market through its impact on the nominal interest rate.

---

## 11.1 Expected Inflation

Suppose the interest rate is 5 percent and that suddenly everyone expects prices to rise by 3 percent (instead of 0 percent) during the next year. Those loaning money for a year at 5 percent will expect to receive, at the end of the year, dollars worth 3 percent less in terms of their purchasing power, so their expected net return in real terms is only 2 percent. To obtain a return of 5 percent, they will want to charge 8 percent. Those willing to borrow earlier at 5 percent should now be willing to pay 8 percent because they expect to be able to save 3 percent by buying their car (for example) now rather than next year. Consequently, the interest rate increases by 3 percent, the expected rate of inflation.

This example reflects a fundamental economic result: built into the interest rate is a premium for expected inflation. Lenders require this premium to prevent inflation from eroding the real value of their wealth, and borrowers pay this premium to be able to buy now before prices go up. We thus expect the interest rate to be affected by the expected rate of inflation, as illustrated in figure 11.1a. Economists have captured this phenomenon by distinguishing between the real and the nominal interest rates.

The *nominal interest rate* includes the inflation premium; it is the interest rate observed on the markets, discussed in the media, paid on mortgages, and earned on savings accounts. The *real interest rate* is the nominal rate less the expected rate of inflation:

real rate = nominal rate − expected inflation.

---

## 11.2 The Real Rate

Although the real interest rate cannot be measured directly, measurements of it do appear in the media. Any such measurement may have two possible origins.

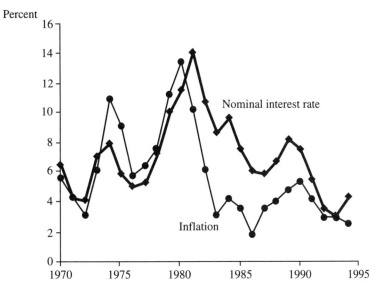

**Figure 11.1a**   Inflation and the nominal interest rate
Changes in inflation are closely matched by changes in the nominal interest rate as our theory would predict if inflation changes cause changes in inflation expectations.
Source: *Economic Report of the President*, 1995.

First, it could be an *ex post* measurement, perhaps calculating last year's real interest rate as last year's nominal rate less last year's actual rate of inflation. Note that this does not tell us what the current real interest rate is, nor does it tell us what the real interest rate was at the beginning of last year. Such an *ex post* measurement is shown in figure 11.1b, calculated by subtracting the two curves in figure 11.1a. Second, it could be an *estimate* of the current real interest rate (the *ex ante* real interest rate), obtained by subtracting an estimate of the expected rate of inflation from the nominal rate of interest. A popular (but usually unjustified) estimate of the expected rate of inflation in this context is the previous period's actual rate of inflation. A more realistic estimate of the expected rate of inflation would incorporate knowledge of variables known to affect inflation, such as the money-supply growth rate.

Despite these measurement difficulties, the real rate of interest is a useful concept because it is the real rather than the nominal interest rate that affects aggregate demand for goods and services. This is best explained via an example.

Suppose there is zero expected inflation, and a firm calculates that at an interest rate of 5 percent (in this case both the real and the nominal interest rate), it is profitable to build a new plant. Now suppose that expected inflation jumps from 0 to 7 percent, raising the nominal interest rate to 12 percent. Because the firm must now pay 12 percent interest to borrow the funds to build the plant, it seems that the investment project is no longer profitable, but this is not so. Paying the extra 7 percent to cover expected inflation should not affect the firm's decision. The firm's future costs should rise by 7 percent, but so also

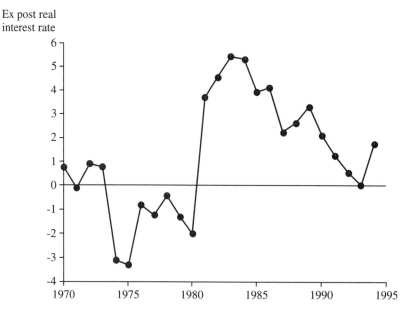

**Figure 11.1b**   Ex post real interest rate
Subtracting actual inflation from the nominal interest rate yields the ex post real interest rate. In the mid-1970s, inflation exceeded the nominal interest rate, so the ex post real interest rate was negative, due probably to the unexpected nature of the inflation. In the 1980s, the nominal interest rate was quite a bit higher than inflation, making the *ex post* real interest rate very high, perhaps due to very high expectations of inflation or to the high real interest rate policies of the time.
Source: *Economic Report of the President*, 1995.

should its receipts, so that its profits should grow, in nominal terms, by 7 percent. This provides just enough extra return to pay for the extra 7 percent interest costs. The relevant interest rate is thus the real rate of interest, not the nominal rate of interest.

This example suggests that firms should use the real rate of interest to evaluate investment projects, and economists should use the real rate of interest to analyze the influence of the interest rate on aggregate demand in the economy. What role does the nominal interest play?

## 11.3   The Nominal Rate

It would be a mistake to conclude from the discussion above that the nominal interest rate is unimportant either to individuals or to government. It is the nominal rate that makes headlines in newspapers, determines homeowners' monthly mortgage payments, and influences voters. But most important, because the nominal rate is determined in the bond market, changes in this rate create capital gains or losses in the bond market, and predictions of it can make or lose fortunes for speculators.

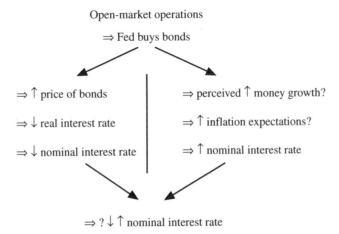

Open-market operations

⇒ Fed buys bonds

⇒ ↑ price of bonds        ⇒ perceived ↑ money growth?

⇒ ↓ real interest rate     ⇒ ↑ inflation expectations?

⇒ ↓ nominal interest rate  ⇒ ↑ nominal interest rate

⇒ ? ↓ ↑ nominal interest rate

**Figure 11.2**  The impact of monetary policy on the interest rate in an inflationary environment
Expansionary monetary policy can raise or lower the nominal interest rate, depending on the policy's impact on inflation expectations.

The influence of open-market operations on the interest rate become complicated and equivocal once one recognizes that it is the nominal interest rate that is determined on the bond market. Suppose the central bank increases the money supply. It does this by buying bonds, in the process bidding up their price and thereby lowering the interest rate. This was the main point in the preceding chapter.

The increase in the money supply, however, may be interpreted as an increase in the rate of growth of the money supply, causing the expected rate of inflation to increase, especially if the economy were at full employment. The increase in expected inflation pushes up the nominal rate of interest, and although the real rate of interest falls, it is not clear what the net effect on the nominal interest rate will be. This is illustrated in figure 11.2.

If in due course it becomes clear that the increased money supply does not represent an increase in the rate of money-supply growth, expectations of higher inflation should disappear, leaving us with an unequivocal fall in the interest rate.

This suggests that the central bank's short-run control over the interest rate is not so clear-cut as the previous chapter indicated. In particular, it suggests that in an inflationary environment, the most effective way for the central bank to decrease the interest rate is to lower the inflation rate. This should lower *expected* inflation (perhaps with a lag, depending on the credibility of the central bank), which should lower the nominal interest rate directly. To accomplish this, the central bank will have to lower the money-supply growth rate, which in the short run will raise, not lower, the interest rate. In other words, to lower the interest rate in an inflationary environment, the central bank must lower money-supply growth (the opposite of what the previous chapter suggested) in

---

**Curiosity 11.1:   What Is the Term Structure of Interest Rates?**

Bonds with identical risk, liquidity, and tax characteristics usually have different interest rates because of different times remaining to maturity. A graph of interest rates against times to maturity for identical bonds is called a *yield curve*; it describes the *term structure of interest rates*. Yield curves almost always slope upward, showing that usually bonds with longer time to maturity pay higher interest rates (i.e., have higher yields to maturity). Why is this?

One reason may be that investors require a liquidity premium for taking on a longer maturity bond. A long-term bond involves more risk from interest rate fluctuations, which change its price much more than the price of a short-term bond. A second reason may be that people fear a resurgence of inflation at any time and require a premium for locking in their money at an interest rate that does not protect them from future unexpected inflation. A third reason may be that long-term interest rates embody expectations of what short-term interest rates will be between now and when the long-term bond matures. An upward-sloping curve therefore simply reflects expectations of higher short-term interest rates in the near future, perhaps because of higher expected inflation. Of course, people may expect that future inflation will be lower than current inflation, in which case the yield curve will be downward-sloping.

The yield curve is closely watched in financial sections of newspapers because of information it may provide regarding the direction in which the market expects short-term interest rates to move. A sharply upward-sloping curve, for example, often occurs after inflation has been brought down because people do not yet believe inflation's fall is permanent.

---

order to create a short-run increase in the interest rate (the opposite of the ultimate goal). This helps lower inflation, which ultimately allows the interest rate to fall.

Another complication faced by the monetary authorities is that the interest rate is no longer a reliable indicator of monetary policy. The preceding chapter suggested that a high interest rate corresponded to a restrictive monetary policy and a low interest rate corresponded to an easy monetary policy. A high interest rate can arise, however, because of high inflation, which can by no stretch of the imagination be due to a restrictive monetary policy. This creates problems for central banks that want to use the interest rate as a target of monetary policy.

## 11.4   Policy Implications

Using the interest rate as a target of monetary policy is an important issue, mainly because the Fed has gotten into trouble in the past for doing so (e.g., its use of the federal funds rate as a target during the 1970s). There are two major problems with using an interest rate as a target:

1. *The Fed may lose control of the money supply.* Suppose for some reason the inflation rate bumps up, which soon raises expectations of inflation, thus increasing the nominal interest rate. If the Fed is targeting on an interest rate, it will increase the money supply to push the interest rate back down. This stimulus to the economy will exacerbate the inflation, and the increase in the money supply will reinforce people's expectations of a higher inflation. Expected inflation rises again, pushing up the nominal interest rate, this time by more than before. The Fed now needs a bigger increase in the money supply to push the interest rate back down, and the process is repeated. Targeting on an interest rate can create a vicious circle, leading the Fed to increase the money supply at an undesirably high rate and creating a high inflation.

2. *The approach may destabilize the economy.* Suppose the economy is hit with an increase in aggregate demand—say, an increase in export demand. The multiplier begins to operate and income increases. This increases the demand for money, so the interest rate increases, serving as an automatic stabilizer by somewhat decreasing aggregate demand. If the Fed is targeting on the interest rate, it will increase the money supply to prevent the interest rate from increasing, thus preventing the automatic stabilizer from operating.

Do these problems with an interest rate target mean that the Fed should use a monetary aggregate growth rate as a target? No. Using a monetary aggregate as a target also has its own serious problems:

1. *Measurement problems.* With the exception of the money base, monetary aggregates are not reliably measured. Both M1 and M2 measures experience substantial revisions over time.

2. *Uncontrollability.* With the exception of the money base, monetary aggregates are not tightly enough under the control of the Fed. M1 and M2 are affected by bank discount borrowing, public cash demands, banking innovations, and shifts among deposit types, for example.

3. *Velocity changes.* All monetary aggregates are not reliably linked to economic activity because of velocity fluctuations caused by financial innovations and deregulations.

4. *Money-demand shocks.* Shocks to money demand, such as failure of a large bank, a postal strike or a stock market crash, destabilize the economy under a monetary aggregate growth target because the central bank won't react by matching the demand for money shock with a money supply change.

Problems with both types of policy targets create a dilemma: how should monetary policy be conducted? The Fed appears to have solved this dilemma by adopting the following principles:

1. Quickly adjust the money supply to meet shocks to money demand. Adopt stability of the financial system as a priority goal.

**Curiosity 11.2:   Was the Fed Ever Monetarist?**

For a variety of reasons, in the 1970s the Fed lost control over the money supply and a high inflation developed. Paul Volcker was brought in as chairman of the Fed in late 1979, and shortly thereafter the Fed announced that it was following a new policy—restricting M1 growth to fight inflation. The predicted happened: low money-supply growth due to Fed policy collided with high money-demand growth due to inflation; and real interest rates shot up, causing a severe recession that, after a long adjustment period in the early 1980s, squeezed inflation out of the economy.

This period is often thought of as a monetarist period in the Fed's history because of its announced policy of targeting on a monetary aggregate. Some economists claim that this characterization is inaccurate, however. They note that during this period the Fed did not appear to be serious about its alleged targets because it consistently missed its target range. A more reasonable explanation of Fed behavior, they argue, is that the Fed was focusing on interest rates, moving them high enough to create a severe recession needed to kill inflation, but claiming, as a smokescreen, to be using monetary targets so that it would not be blamed directly for the high interest rates.

Currently, the Fed is definitely not monetarist, having abandoned in frustration any use of monetary aggregates because of their erratic velocities.

2. Never use an interest rate target in an inflationary environment.

3. Use a monetary aggregate target only in cases of strong inflation.

4. In a noninflationary environment, be pragmatic and eclectic; use the deliberately vague concept "credit conditions" as a target that may or may not, depending on circumstances, involve what is happening to interest rates or to monetary aggregates.

5. Adopt low inflation as a priority goal, and only use discretionary policy to deal with other goals, such as smoothing the business cycle, if (*a*) action is definitely warranted, and (*b*) doing so will not jeopardize the inflation goal.

These points summarize much of what the Fed has learned, often the hard way, since its creation in 1913.

■ *Be pragmatic:*   do what works; use interest rates (or monetary aggregates) as an indicator of monetary policy only when circumstances warrant.

■ *Be eclectic:*   do not pay undue attention to any one polar view of the economy, such as that of the monetarists, the Keynesians, or the supply-siders.

■ *Be flexible:*   do not commit yourself publicly to a specific policy in case it becomes necessary to alter course; criticism is more easily deflected this way.

■ *Be careful:*   move only when the right move is unequivocally clear. Never try to "fine-tune" the economy.

■ *Exploit strengths:* because inflation is always and everywhere a monetary phenomenon, make inflation a top priority.

The growth in Fed wisdom has come at a good time. Many believe that because the huge government deficit has made fiscal policy inflexible, and because political paralysis has prevented rectification of this problem, monetary policy has become the main macroeconomic policy tool.

## Media Illustrations

### Example 1

**The bond markets were stunned by the shock of Thursday's flash second-quarter news that the economy has grown *three whole percentage points*. You and I would say that's good news, but the bond markets' terrified interpretation last Thursday was that it might encourage the private sector to borrow, nudging up interest rates. Add this discomforting prospect to the other horrifying disclosure that, at last reading, our money supply had climbed by a mammoth $4.8 billion, and you'll know why people were heading for the bond market exits.**

*Why are people heading for the bond market exits?*
Nominal interest rates are expected to rise because of higher private borrowing and higher expected inflation due to the large growth in the money supply. People are selling bonds to avoid the capital loss that the rise in the interest rate will cause.

### Example 2

**Many borrowers fear that if U.S. inflation can't be whipped, U.S. bond markets may evolve into replicas of Europe's capital markets—surrendering their status as providers of long-term, fixed-cost funds to government and industry. Of course, some economists see long-term bonds returning to favor with a vengeance as inflation finally succumbs to slowing money-supply growth. Others, though, envisage inflation and interest rates peaking higher and higher each business cycle, as sound money management succumbs to electoral politics, so that investors progressively shorten their commitments.**

*Why will long-term bond markets lose favor if inflation is not whipped?*
If inflation continues to rise, the nominal interest rate will also rise, decreasing the price of long-term bonds. People will be reluctant to invest in long-term bonds if there is a high probability that they will suffer a fall in their value. Only a very high expected real rate of return would convince people to take on this risk of capital loss. Rising inflation would make the long-term bond market a prohibitively expensive way to raise funds.

*What does "as sound money management succumbs to electoral politics" mean?*

Monetary authorities will cave in to politicians' demands to increase the money supply prior to elections in order to produce a temporary decrease in the interest rate and a brief lowering of unemployment below the NRU.

*How does increasing the money supply raise interest rates to higher and higher levels?*

Before each election, this temporarily pushes interest rates down, but after a while, when higher inflation becomes expected, nominal interest rates rise.

*Why would investors progressively shorten their commitments?*

When the interest rate rises, capital losses on short-term bonds are much less than on long-term bonds.

**Example 3**

**The Fed chairman added that the principal misunderstanding about the Fed's role in the present situation is that the Fed could achieve a low level of interest rates more or less immediately if it wanted to.**

*Doesn't the Fed control interest rates? Why can't it immediately achieve a low interest rate if it wanted to?*

The Fed's main control over interest rates comes from its control over inflation. To lower interest rates, it could decrease the rate of growth of the money supply, which would in time lower the rate of inflation, causing the interest rate to fall. In the short run, though, this would involve an increase in the interest rate. An immediate decrease in the interest rate could be achieved by an increase in the money supply, but this would last only so long as expectations of inflation do not rise.

**Example 4**

**Although interest rates were for many years the main policy indicator used by most central banks, the experience with severe inflation beginning in the 1970s made it clear that interest rates were fickle guides for ensuring that monetary policy was directed toward price stability.**

*How would interest rates be used to indicate whether monetary policy was restrictive or easy?*

High interest rates may indicate that monetary policy is restrictive because high interest rates may be created when the central bank decreases the money supply. Similarly, low interest rates may indicate an easy monetary policy.

*How would a central bank ensure that monetary policy was directed toward price stability?*

For price stability, the money supply should be increased at a rate approximately equal to the real rate of growth of the economy.

*Why would severe inflation show that interest rates are fickle guides for monetary policy?*

Severe inflation raises expectations of inflation, which bumps up nominal interest rates, making it appear—using the interest rate indicator—that monetary policy is restrictive. This would lead the monetary authorities to increase the money supply, exactly the wrong policy to deal with high inflation.

### Example 5

**The idea of investing in debt securities was a gamble on the government's good intentions to fight inflation. The budget makes it clear that the government has taken this task to heart. It stresses the fact that the deficit will be covered by sales of bonds to the general public and not to the central bank—a sign that the government has recognized the need to manage its cash requirements within the limitations of a capital market regulated by a well-determined monetary policy.**

*What is the nature of the gamble?*

Buying debt securities, or bonds, would be a profitable move if the interest rate were to fall, increasing the price of these bonds. This is what will happen if the government is successful in reducing inflation.

*Of what relevance to this gamble is the fact that security sales will be to the general public rather than to the central bank?*

If the bonds were sold to the central bank, the money supply would be increased, thus aggravating the inflation.

*What is a "well-determined monetary policy"? What limitations does it impose in this context?*

A well-determined monetary policy is one in which the central bank increases the money supply at a low, steady rate. This implies that there is a limit to the quantity of government bonds the central bank can buy each year.

### Example 6

**It had been feared that more good economic readings would trigger a sell-off in the bond market, which typically responds negatively to such news because ...**

*Complete this clipping.*

... good economic news means either that inflationary pressures are mounting, which would raise the nominal interest rate and lower the price of bonds, or that the Fed may put on the brakes, decreasing the money supply and raising interest rates, which would also lower bond prices.

## Chapter Summary

- A premium for expected inflation is built into the interest rate. This phenomenon is formalized by distinguishing the *nominal* from the *real* interest rate. The former is what is observed and discussed in the media. The latter is what affects spending behavior.

- Open-market operations designed to affect the interest rate may move the nominal interest rate in a direction opposite to that intended if inflation expectations are affected. One important policy lesson is that in an inflationary environment the most effective way to lower interest rates is to lower the rate of growth of the money supply, which in the short run will probably increase the interest rate.

- Targeting the interest rate as a policy goal can create major problems, such as an accelerating money-supply growth rate. Targeting a monetary aggregate growth rate can be difficult because of measurement problems, lack of full control, and velocity changes. Several Fed guidelines for effective monetary policy have emerged from years of experience.

## Formula Definition

nominal interest rate = real interest rate + expected inflation.

## Media Exercises

1. **A smaller-than-expected decrease in the U.S. money supply dealt the North American capital market a hard blow as bond prices sagged across a broad front.**

   Explain why bond prices sagged.

2. **Swings in the price of bonds reflected a high degree of uncertainty about inflation and changing perceptions in the market. The release of figures that showed the economy to be stronger than expected tended to push prices _____ and yields _____.**

   Fill in the two blanks, and explain your reasoning.

3. **One view in the market has been that because the economy seemed weaker than it should be, the Federal Reserve Board would cut its discount rate from 7.5 percent. This, of course, would be positive for bonds. On the other hand, some think that rising money-supply growth would rule out such a discount rate reduction.**

   a. Why would a cut in the discount rate be positive for bonds?

   b. Why might rising money-supply growth rule out a discount rate reduction?

4. **Analysts say that the three-month rally in bonds has been fueled by Washington's promise to balance its budget by 1991 and by OPEC's decision to abandon support for world oil prices in the short run.**

   Explain the logic behind these two explanations for the bond rally.

5. **Corporate treasurers should not be frightened by the recent rise in interest rates on bonds. Rates of even 13 percent will look like bargains if inflation heats up over the next eighteen months. Investors should continue to shun the market for long-term securities.**

   a. Why will rates of even 13 percent look like bargains?

   b. Why should long-term securities be shunned?

6. **News of economic weakness last week cleared the way for higher bond prices. Traders went on a buying spree after Friday's announcement by the Labor Department of a lower-than-expected increase in nonfarm payrolls. The New York market moved quickly to capitalize on this good bad news: prices shot up more than a point ($10 on every $1,000 of face value) in minutes.**

   a. Why is this referred to as "good bad news"?

   b. Explain why bond prices rose.

7. **The Fed is scrambling hard to keep interest rates from increasing in the face of renewed inflationary pressures, but the banking industry is a lot less interested in cooperating with the Fed because of the rising loan demand they are facing.**

   a. Why would loan demand be rising?

   b. What policy would you recommend to the Fed?

8. **Producer prices crept up a modest 0.2 percent in April, the government said yesterday in a report that could give the Federal Reserve room to cut interest rates again in a bid to boost the slowly recovering economy.**

   How does the modest rise in prices give the Fed room to cut interest rates?

9. **The Franklin Savings bonds will carry a 3 percentage-point premium over inflation. The yield of every fixed-income instrument is determined by two things: expectations of the inflation rate and expectations of real return. This deal takes the uncertainty out of the inflation component.**

   a. What real rate of return will an investor get if he or she buys this inflation-indexed bond?

   b. Will an investor be better off buying this bond (rather than a regular bond) if the current market expectation of inflation is too high, or if it is too low? Explain your reasoning.

10. **As a result, interest rates—which particularly affect certain sectors (capital spending, houses, and cars)—are raised to levels previously viewed as impossible, but clearly they aren't out of line with what the central bank views as appropriate.**

a. How might interest rates rise to such high levels?

b. Why might they nonetheless be viewed as appropriate?

11. **Contrary to the central bank's pronouncements, higher interest rates have not caused everyone to borrow less. Most people are borrowing as much as ever—or more than ever—to buy goods now.**

Why have higher interest rates not led to a decrease in borrowing, as standard economic theory suggests should happen?

12. **When you look at real interest rates, they're way too high, probably because most people are still determining whether low inflation is a long-term reality.**

Explain the logic of this claim.

13. **A decline in the rate of inflation is the one sure route to lower interest rates, the central bank told us two years ago. Inflation is now only about one-third of what it was two years ago, but interest rates are higher. How come? We've paid the price, a fearsome price in slow growth and high unemployment, for this one sure route to lower interest rates. Why haven't we had the promised results?**

a. What is the rationale behind this "one sure route" to lower interest rates?

b. What could have prevented the promised results from materializing?

14. **Amid all the evidence of a budding recovery, however, there lurks a spoiler: long-term interest rates. Bond traders, worried about inflation and a massive supply of Treasury debt, have bid long rates up above 8 percent, raising real interest rates to about 5 percent.**

a. How would bond traders go about bidding rates up?

b. Why would worries about inflation cause them to do this?

c. Why would a massive supply of Treasury debt cause them to do this?

d. How do you suppose the 5 percent real interest rate figure was obtained?

15. **The battle is between the rate-lowering effect of the recession and the high rate of inflation. That sums up the problem now facing the interest rate forecasters.**

Explain how these two effects operate on interest rates in different directions.

16. **In one camp are those who think interest rates will either stabilize or move up because the economic outlook is improving, and will thus rebound from the paltry 0.7 percent real growth in the gross domestic product in the first**

**quarter. Moreover, they argue, growth in money supply has been way above the Fed's target.**

Explain the rationale behind the two reasons given for expecting a higher interest rate.

17. **In economic theory, money is a commodity that responds to the law of supply and demand. When the supply of money rises, the price—the interest rate—should drop. The market for money is perverse, however. When lenders see the money supply increasing, they think ...**

Complete the argument about to be developed here.

18. **Capacity utilization at 82.4 percent was unchanged in January for U.S. mines, factories, and utilities. Economists are worried that demand on industry may soon outstrip capacity, thereby encouraging producers to raise prices. Inflation, the undisputed Achilles' heel of bonds, would result.**

Why is inflation the "Achilles' heel" (great weakness) of bonds?

19. **The past few years have been, in effect, a crash course in basic economics for investors and others with a hand in the game. They're much harder to fool now with actions that seem to improve the situation in the short run, but make it worse in the long run.**

Give an example of a policy action that improves the situation for investors in the short run, but makes it worse in the long run.

20. **The Canadian bond is structured so that the coupon payments are low, in this case 4.25 percent, and the principal is adjusted as inflation changes over the life of the bond. The issue met stiff opposition, mainly because of the size of the coupon.**

   a. What name would you give to this bond? (Take a guess!)

   b. From the information given, what can you say about the current Canadian real interest rate? Explain your reasoning.

21. **The principal power of the central bank to lower interest rates lies in its ability to contribute to a lower rate of inflation, and that takes time.**

   a. How would the central bank contribute to a lower rate of inflation?

   b. How would this action lower interest rates?

   c. Why does all this take time?

22. **For some months now, the central bank has reduced the attention it pays to the levels of interest rates and has kept a close eye on expansion of the money supply, a policy change that has made market interest rates more responsive to the high rate of inflation.**

a. Why would this policy change cause interest rates to become more responsive to the high rate of inflation?

b. Is this a good or a bad thing?

23. **Bond prices soared and yields plunged after the Labor Department said
that the producer price index rose by 0.4 percent in March. Although Wall
Street had been expecting a rise of only 0.3 percent, the core index—
excluding the volatile food and energy sector—rose a slight 0.1 percent
against expectations of a 0.3 percent rise.**

Explain why bond prices would soar and yields would plunge because of
this news.

24. **If the real interest rate is expected to remain unchanged, the upward-
sloping term structure suggests that the market expects inflation to . . .**

Complete this clipping, and explain your rationale.

25. **The thirty-year Treasury bond, usually called the long bond on Wall Street,
is far more volatile than other fixed-income securities. However, although
the Fed has been successful in pushing down short-term interest rates
to 4 percent, the long bond yield has fallen very little and is still up at 7.5
percent.**

a. Why would the price of the long bond be so volatile relative to other bonds?

b. Why would the yield on the long bond be so much higher than on short-
term bonds?

26. **I think the bond market has room on the upside. With real rates so high and
inflation looking as if it's not coming back, there's room for further rally.**

Explain the logic of this thinking.

27. **Continued relief that the slowly growing economy is not producing significant levels of inflation moved the thirty-year benchmark treasury bond
19/32 for the week to $103.28 to yield 7.30 percent versus 7.35 percent a
week earlier.**

a. Are these numbers consistent with the fact that the economy is not
producing significant levels of inflation? Explain why or why not.

b. What was the price of this bond "a week earlier"?

## Numerical Exercises

N1. The current price of a Treasury bill due to pay $1,000 in one year's time
is $930. Suppose it suddenly becomes apparent that the money-supply
growth rate has jumped from 6 percent to 8 percent.

a. What should the interest rate become?

b. What should the price of this T-bill become?

N2. Suppose the economy is at full employment with expected inflation rate 7 percent and nominal interest rate 11 percent. Suppose, though, that the expected inflation rate rises to 9 percent. After this change,

a. what is the nominal interest rate?

b. what is the real interest rate?

N3. If the money supply is growing at 9 percent, the real interest rate is 3 percent, the real rate of growth of GDP is 2 percent, and financial innovations are reducing the demand for money by 1 percent per year, what should be the nominal interest rate?

N4. Suppose the real interest rate and the real growth rate are both 3 percent, the money multiplier is 4, banking innovations are decreasing the demand for money by 1 percent per year and the money supply is growing at 10 percent per year. What should be the price of a T-bill due to mature in one year at its face value of $1,000?

# 12    Stagflation

For a decade, ending in the late 1960s, economists believed a trade-off existed between inflation and unemployment. This trade-off was represented graphically by the Phillips curve (shown in figure 12.1), a part of economic folklore so prominent that it has actually appeared on the front pages of newspapers. This curve was thought to be downward sloping because a rise in unemployment should dampen forces that influence inflation, and a fall in unemployment should strengthen these forces.

The existence of this trade-off implied that the economy could "buy" a reduction in unemployment with an increase in inflation or "buy" a reduction in inflation with an increase in unemployment. All a policymaker needed to do was determine the character of the economy's Phillips curve, choose the point on that curve considered the least undesirable, and then adopt monetary or fiscal policy to move the economy to that chosen position. Throughout the 1960s, this theory was regarded with some respect. Policymakers subscribed to it and undertook policies accordingly.

These policies did not lead to the expected results, however; if anything, the economic situation seemed to become worse. The economy began to experience *stagflation* (high or rising levels of both inflation and unemployment), a phenomenon the Phillips curve theory claimed could not exist. The 1975–1985 data points shown in figure 12.1 illustrate this and hint that perhaps the Phillips curve shifted upwards during this period of high inflation. In response to this problem, economists have modified considerably their conception of the Phillips curve—developing a distinction between the long and short runs, incorporating the economy's natural rate of unemployment, and recognizing the role of expectations in determining economic activity.

The purpose of this chapter is to explain the modern interpretation of the Phillips curve and, in doing so, to offer an explanation for stagflation and a look at several related policy problems. Although at first glance this purpose appears to involve learning a different curve-shifting apparatus, it turns out that the Phillips curve is merely a convenient way to express and analyze aggregate supply. The Phillips curve and the story it helps us tell about macroeconomic reactions are remarkably similar to the aggregate supply curve and to the discussion in chapter 5.

**Upon completion of this chapter you should**

- know the distinction between the short- and long-run Phillips curves, as well as the implication this distinction has for a trade-off between inflation and unemployment;

- understand the rationale behind wage-price controls as a policy to deal with stagflation; and

- be able to explain how stagflation can come about.

## 12.1    The Phillips Curve

The modern interpretation of the Phillips curve rests heavily on the concept of the natural rate of unemployment, described in chapter 3. This rate, currently thought to be about 6 percent in the United States, is determined by the amount of frictional and structural unemployment and by institutional phenomena such as minimum-wage legislation and unemployment insurance programs. It is the "full-employment" rate of unemployment to which the forces of supply and demand push the economy in the long run.

In the long run, the rate of inflation is determined by the rate of growth of the money supply, so once the economy adjusts to this money-supply growth, it should settle at its natural rate of unemployment. Consequently, in the long run the natural rate of unemployment can coexist with any rate of inflation: there is no trade-off between inflation and unemployment. Reflecting this, the long-run Phillips curve is a vertical line located at the natural rate of unemployment NRU, as shown by LRPC in figure 12.2.

A trade-off is thought to exist in the short run, however—represented by a traditional downward-sloping Phillips curve, shown by SRPC in figure 12.2. Let us begin with the economy in equilibrium at position A, at the NRU, and with an inflation of 3 percent. Now suppose the central bank increases the rate of growth of the money supply by two percentage points, with the idea of moving the economy to position B, where inflation is 5 percent and unemployment is lower. The reaction of the economy to this shock can be explained in a fashion virtually identical to our explanation of a movement along the short-run aggregate supply curve as exposited in chapter 5. There are two main differences: (1) now we measure unemployment instead of GDP on the horizontal axis, so that the upward-sloping, short-run aggregate supply curve is represented by a downward-sloping, short-run Phillips curve; and (2) now we measure inflation instead of the price level on the vertical axis. The following paragraphs present a shortened version of the chapter 5 explanation, with only a slight modification changing "price increases" to "price increases in excess of the 3 percent expected inflation."

**Figure 12.1**  The Phillips curve
From the 1960–1970 period to the 1975–1985 period, the Phillips curve has shifted upwards.
Source: *Economic Report of the President*, 1995.

The jump in money-supply growth creates an excess supply of money and stimulates aggregate demand. Inventories fall and business in the service industry is turned away, indicating to firms that demand for their good or service has risen. Two basic reactions are possible:

1. *Perfect competition.*  In industries where perfect competition prevails, at the current rate of price increase of 3 percent, no one is willing to increase output because it is not profitable to do so. Consequently, the extra demand bids up price by perhaps 5 percent, in which case established firms are induced to increase output, new firms are prompted to enter the market, and the demand for workers increases.

2. *Imperfect competition.*  Firms that are not in perfectly competitive industries have the option of meeting this extra demand by increasing output and may find this option attractive for two reasons. First, there are the costs of adjusting prices, so-called menu costs such as printing new catalogues and annoying loyal customers. And second, there is a danger that competitors may not follow this extra price increase, creating considerable loss of demand for the firm that initiates the price increase. Consequently, firms may react initially by adjusting quantity to meet extra demand. Many firms can do this by getting workers to work overtime, but some may find it necessary to hire extra workers. Once this extra demand is seen to be permanent, most firms will want to hire extra workers, and extra price increases should occur. Price increases beyond 3 percent may entice new firms to enter this industry, and they too will need to hire new workers.

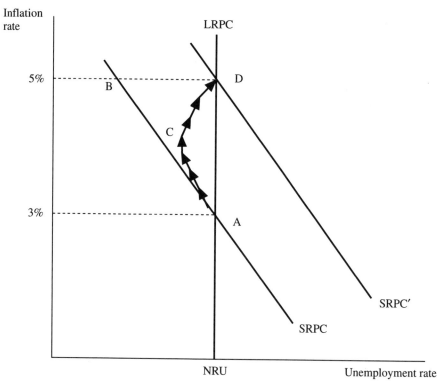

**Figure 12.2**  Phillips curve reaction to increase in money-supply growth
The higher rate of money-supply growth stimulates the economy, creating an unexpect-
edly higher inflation rate and, consequently, a lower unemployment rate: the economy
moves towards point C. Once this inflation becomes expected, however, SRPC shifts
upward to SRPC′, and unemployment returns to the NRU: the economy moves to
point D.

At this stage, the reader should see two important things happening: (1)
although some prices may not immediately rise beyond 3 percent, prices rise
overall and so does output (in figure 12.2 the economy starts to move out
towards point B); and (2) although some firms may not want to hire extra
workers right away, overall firms will want to hire extra labor. When they try to
hire these extra workers, however, they discover to their surprise that workers
are hard to come by. Because the economy is at its natural rate of unemployment, a pool of unemployed people eager to work at the going wage does not
exist. To solve this problem, firms bid up the wage rate slightly more than the
3 percent that everyone expects, by perhaps 4 percent, which induces some
students to quit school, some homemakers to leave home, and some job
searchers to find more quickly a job with the wage they feel they deserve. This
strengthens the move out toward point B in figure 12.2.

In essence, firms are willing to employ the extra workers because it is profitable for them to do so. The extra rise in price (5 percent) has more than com-

pensated firms for the extra wage (4 percent) that they are now paying. The real wage has fallen. Ordinarily, workers would not put up with this. At a real wage lower than that corresponding to the natural rate of unemployment, some workers would withdraw their services, choosing instead to become students or homemakers or to search the job market for a better job. Consequently, for the movement out towards point B in figure 12.2 to be maintained, workers must for some reason be willing to supply more labor at a lower real wage. Economists offer two main explanations for this:

1. *Information problems.* Workers may not realize what is happening, genuinely mistaking a 4 percent increase in the money wage for a 1 percent increase in the real wage. They know exactly what is happening with the money wage, but are slow to recognize what has happened to the overall price/inflation level.

2. *Contract obligations.* Workers may be obliged by a formal or informal contract to supply labor at a money wage that increases at a 3 percent annual rate until the expiration of that contract. Some contracts are renegotiated sooner than others, implying that overall wages do not keep up with overall price increases beyond 3 percent.

What is notable about both of these explanations is that they explain only a temporary fall in real wages. Workers eventually realize that their real wage has fallen and demand a rise in the money wage to compensate them fully for unexpected higher prices. Eventually, all contracts are renegotiated, bringing the real wage back to its original level and *building into new contracts the higher expected inflation*. Consequently, the economy's movement toward point *B* is only temporary. People's expectations of inflation increase; in time, money wages rise to restore the original real wage and thereafter rise at a rate matching the new, higher inflation rate.

In figure 12.2, higher expected inflation shifts the SRPC curve upwards. The economy moves along the curved arrowed line from A out towards B, perhaps as far as point C, but eventually back to the NRU at point D, and the SRPC curve ends up eventually at SRPC'. Why does SRPC shift upwards with higher inflation expectations? If everyone expects inflation to be two percentage points higher, then—regardless of the unemployment rate—workers demand and firms grant wage increases two percentage points higher than usual, thus shifting up the SRPC by two percentage points.

A clear implication of this is that, in the long run, the economy moves along the long-run Phillips curve rather than the traditional downward-sloping, short-run Phillips curve, with no trade-off between inflation and unemployment. Persistent government action to move the economy to a lower level of unemployment only serves to push it to higher levels of inflation, with no long-run improvement in unemployment, thus contradicting the opinions of those who advocate the use of government policy action to influence the level of unemployment in an inflationary environment.

---

**Curiosity 12.1:    What Are New Classicals and New Keynesians?**

Several schools of macroeconomic thought have appeared in this book at one stage or another: the Keynesian school, which supplanted the classical school; monetarists, who critiqued the Keynesians; and supply-siders and real business-cycle theorists who focused on the supply side of the economy. Two recent schools are the *new classical school* and the *new Keynesian school*. Both schools place great emphasis on generating explanations based on individuals acting rationally in their self interest, which collectively causes macroeconomic phenomena such as excessive unemployment and business cycles. Like the Keynesian school, the new Keynesian school favors government intervention in the economy, whereas the new classicals—like the classicals and the monetarists—do not.

Oversimplifying somewhat, the difference between them is most sharply drawn on the issue of what gives the short-run aggregate supply curve its upward slope, or, equivalently, what causes the short-run Phillips curve to be downward-sloping. New classicals believe that wages and prices are flexible, that markets always clear, and that information problems cause short-run deviations from the NRU, thereby explaining business cycles.

In contrast, new Keynesians believe that wages and prices are not flexible, that markets do not always clear, and that information problems must be supplemented by the concept of sticky wages and prices. They have devoted their research energies to finding intellectually respectable ways of explaining wage and price rigidities as arising from efficient, rational microeconomic behavior on the part of labor and firms. They would note, for example, that firms find it easier in the short run to meet demand changes by adjusting quantity rather than price. Contractual labor markets and, in particular, implicit contracts play a major role in their explanations, causing some to distinguish between new classicals and new Keynesians on the basis of their belief in the invisible hand versus the invisible handshake.

---

## 12.2   Policy Implications

Several interesting policy considerations stem from the above theory that there is no long-run trade-off between inflation and unemployment.

1.  *Reducing the NRU.*   In the long run, unemployment can be reduced only by lowering the NRU. Government policy in this regard takes the form of alleviating imperfections in the labor market: labor retraining programs; programs to increase labor market information or to reduce the cost of obtaining such information; programs to increase labor mobility; elimination of minimum-wage legislation; restructuring of unemployment insurance programs; and fiscal policy to reduce demand in geographic or industry bottlenecks.

2.  *The accelerationist hypothesis.*   By accelerating the inflation rate, the government may continually fool labor and outstrip contracts, lowering unem-

ployment permanently below its natural rate. This reflects the *accelerationist hypothesis* that the relevant trade-off is between unemployment and accelerating inflation rather than between unemployment and inflation. In this context, the natural rate of unemployment is sometimes called the non-accelerating inflation rate of unemployment (NAIRU). This offers an explanation for how a central bank could be led to increase the money supply at an excessive rate.

3. *The policy ineffectiveness debate.* In our modern society information is communicated rapidly and interpreted sophisticatedly. An increase in the rate of growth of the money supply soon becomes widely known, and the new, higher rate of inflation that it implies quickly becomes anticipated. If people form their expectations of future values of economic variables by working through the appropriate economic theory in conjunction with the best available information, they are said to produce *rational expectations*. Such expectations should be much more accurate than expectations formed by ignoring current information on relevant economic variables and simply extrapolating past values of the variable to be forecast.

   In the example of figure 12.2, if people rationally form their expectations of inflation, when the higher money-supply growth rate becomes known, the inflation of position D is expected. This suggests that SRPC shifts immediately up to SRPC′ and the economy moves directly to D, without taking the path through C. It thus appears that if expectations are formed rationally, even the short-run trade-off disappears. According to this thinking, once we are at the NRU, any systematic policy is completely ineffective. Only erratic, unpredictable policies can have any effect, and even then only in the short run.

   This remarkable conclusion has sparked what is known as the *policy ineffectiveness debate*. Opponents of such a view make two arguments:

   a. *Policy credibility.* If a policy change is not thought to be credible—for example, if people do not believe that the Fed will maintain a change in the rate of growth of the money supply—then short-run reactions can be quite different from long-run reactions.

   b. *Wage and price inflexibility.* Even if expectations are formed rationally, the conclusions about policy ineffectiveness do not follow because prices and wages are not perfectly flexible (existing wage contracts may prevent wages from adjusting immediately, for example).

4. *Reducing inflation quickly.* Although the policy ineffectiveness conclusion does not hold exactly, it does suggest that movement up the long-run Phillips curve may occur much more rapidly than the exposition of figure 12.2 suggested. If people form their expectations in a sophisticated fashion, and if their past experience has led them to believe that increases in the inflation rate can occur quickly, inflation expectations adjust quickly in the upward direction when the money-supply growth rate rises. In figure 12.2

**Curiosity 12.2:   How Can the NRU Be Estimated?**

Analysis of the Phillips curve suggests that whenever the unemployment rate is below the NRU, or the NAIRU (nonaccelerating inflation rate of unemployment), inflation should be rising, and whenever the economy is at an unemployment rate higher than the NRU, inflation should be falling. This implication is evident in figure 12.3, which plots unemployment against changes in the inflation rate. The relationship drawn to fit this scatterplot suggests that the level of unemployment for which the rate of change of inflation is zero should be the NRU or NAIRU—in this diagram about 6.5 percent. This method works well if the NRU has remained constant during the years for which the data are plotted.

Recent experience in the United States—a steady inflation at an unemployment rate below 6 percent—suggests that the U.S. NRU has fallen. NRUs for other countries can be quite different, mainly because of differences in institutionally induced unemployment, as explained in chapter 3. Canadian and most European NRUs are much higher, whereas the Japanese NRU is much lower.

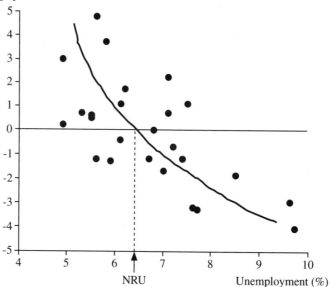

**Figure 12.3**   Estimating the NRU
Above/below the NRU, inflation should be falling/rising, so an estimate of the NRU can be obtained by seeing what unemployment rate corresponds to a zero inflation rate change. Data plotted are from 1970–1994.
Source: *Economic Report of the President*, 1995.

this is reflected by a relatively steep short-run Phillips curve. The short-run reduction in unemployment due to an increase in the inflation rate is small and of short duration.

Inflation can thus rise quickly. If this is true, shouldn't the process operate in reverse equally quickly? If expectations are formed rationally, a decrease in the rate of growth of money supply from 5 percent to 3 percent should cause the economy to move down quickly from point D to point A in figure 12.2, so that the cost of lowering inflation is only a modest increase in unemployment for a short period of time. Unfortunately, this is not so. An effort to decrease the rate of inflation by decreasing money-supply growth involves a prolonged period of high unemployment.

## 12.3   Fighting Inflation with Recession

The reasons why lowering inflation requires a major recession highlight the two arguments of those who oppose the policy ineffectiveness conclusion.

1. *Is the policy credible?*   When the Fed announces that it is decreasing the rate of growth of the money supply, people have reason not to believe that the central bank will stick to this policy; they accordingly do not revise inflation expectations downward. In the past, there have been too many instances in which such a policy was announced and then abandoned later when the resulting unemployment became politically too uncomfortable. This *credibility effect* inhibits the success of the policy.

2. *Are wage and price inflexible?*   Contract obligations slow down wage adjustments in the downward direction just as in the upward direction, but a more important factor affects wage stickiness in this context. In contrast to the case of increasing prices and wages, people are quite reluctant to lower their customary annual wage and price increases, for reasons exposited at some length in chapter 5. Money wages do not fall quickly because of implicit contracts, concern about relative wages, worker belief that recessions are temporary, and the payment of efficiency wages.

The upshot of all this is that when the central bank decreases the rate of money-supply growth from 5 percent to 3 percent, there is little immediate decrease in the rate of inflation. Because prices continue to increase at 5 percent while the money supply increases at 3 percent, the demand for money grows by more than the supply of money. The resulting excess demand for money decreases aggregate demand for goods and services, creating a major recession. (Recall our babysitting co-op example of this phenomenon in curiosity 9.1 in chapter 9.) In figure 12.4, the economy begins at position D and moves out towards point E. The SRPC is drawn relatively flat to the right of the natural rate of unemployment to reflect this stagflation phenomenon. The economy

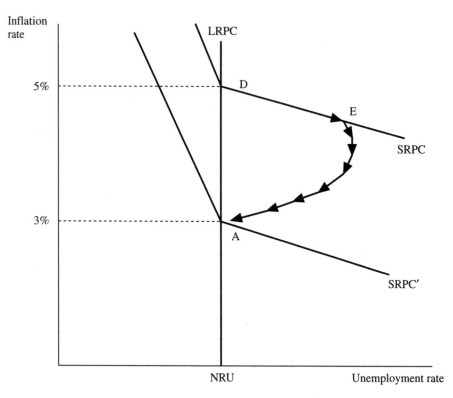

**Figure 12.4**  Phillips curve reaction to decrease in money-supply growth
The lower rate of money-supply growth, with inflation remaining at 5%, decreases the
real money supply, thereby creating a recession. The economy moves to point E and
remains there until expectations of inflation fall, shifting the SRPC downwards to SRPC′
and taking the economy to point A.

remains at point E until the natural economic pressures of the recession force
firms and labor to moderate price and wage increases and to lower inflation
expectations, eventually allowing the economy to move along the arrowed path
towards position A.

The path down towards postion A in figure 12.4 contrasts sharply with the
path up towards position D in figure 12.2, implying that the SRPC has a kink
because it is steeper below the NRU and flatter above the NRU. The movement from A up to D occurs quickly and has only a small short-term reduction
in unemployment, whereas moving from D down to A involves a prolonged
period of high unemployment. This asymmetry explains why inflation is fought
so fiercely. Inflation can quickly rise, with little benefit, but it is pushed back
down only at high cost.

It should by now be obvious why the Fed is so reluctant to intervene to
stimulate the economy during a recession. If the recession is a figment of measurement problems, or if the economy has already begun to climb out of recession, but that fact is not yet evident, action by the Fed could inadvertently

---

**Curiosity 12.3:   What Is the Sacrifice Ratio?**

What is the cost of reducing inflation by a percentage point? According to the 1995 *Economic Report of the President*, the cost is currently thought to be a cumulative total of two percentage points of lost output. For example, to decrease inflation by three percentage points we must sacrifice 2 percent of GDP for three years or 1 percent of GDP for six years, or some other combination of number of years and loss of annual output. This calculation is formalized through the concept of the sacrifice ratio, defined as

$$\text{sacrifice ratio} = \frac{\text{cumulative cost as \% of GDP}}{\text{percentage point} \downarrow \text{inflation}}.$$

The cost can be translated into unemployment using Okun's Law. As described in chapter 3, Okun's Law says that 2.5 percentage points of annual output are lost by each percentage point in unemployment above the NRU. This implies that 1 percentage point of output is lost when unemployment is 0.4 percentage points above the NRU. Losing 2 percentage points of output therefore involves $2 \times 0.4 = 0.8$ extra percentage points of unemployment lasting one year. This is the annual extra unemployment required to reduce inflation by 1 percentage point.

The sacrifice ratio can vary across countries and over time depending on the flexibility of wage-setting systems and the credibility of central bank policies. Estimates suggest that during the late 1970s it was about 5 or 6 and that during the later years of the Volcker era at the Fed it had fallen to 3 because Volcker had built up such high credibility. It's current estimated value of about 2, reflecting continued Fed credibility, may be optimistically low.

This description of the sacrifice ratio suggests that the total cost in terms of lost output is the same whether the central bank adopts the "cold turkey" approach to lowering inflation, in which there is an immediate large reduction in the rate of growth of the money supply, or the "gradualism" approach in which the rate of growth of the money supply is lowered gradually over an extended time period. Realistically, however, it would be advisable only to use the "cold turkey" approach if the central bank has high credibility and if the nation's wage and price setting systems are quite flexible. Otherwise, inflation would not fall quickly to match the lower growth in the money supply, the demand for money would increase by much more than the supply of money, aggregate demand would then fall, and the economy would enter a severe recession.

---

trigger higher inflation, which would be costly to eradicate. The main problem, it seems, is that the only way the Fed knows how to lower inflation is to create a recession. Wage-price controls are allegedly a means of avoiding this high cost.

---

## 12.4   Wage-Price Controls

A major reason why lowering inflation requires a prolonged recession is the *coordination problem*: people will not moderate wage and price increases until everyone else does. A wage-price control policy, such as that imposed by President Nixon in 1971, puts legal constraints on wage and price increases. Controls policies and their variants, such as wage-price guidelines with no formal legal penalties, or guidelines with a tax on excessive wage or price increases, are called *incomes policies*. An incomes policy imposes the missing coordination and, by doing so, allows the economy to move quickly down the long-run Phillips curve, thus avoiding the high cost of a prolonged recession. This is the benefit of a policy of wage-price controls.

Most economists do not look upon wage-price controls with favor, for two reasons.

1. *Complementary monetary and fiscal policy are required.* Most empirical evidence suggests that control policies do not work, even if, as was done by Diocletian during the Roman Empire, the death penalty is imposed for violation. This evidence, however, comes from situations in which the control policies could not have been expected to be successful. In figure 12.4, if the rate of growth of the money supply were not reduced from 5 percent to 3 percent, it is impossible for a policy of wage-price controls to be successful. Recent evidence, such as the 1975–78 Canadian experience, suggests that control policies can be of benefit if they are complemented by appropriate monetary and fiscal policies—a crucial proviso to the adoption of wage-price control policies.

2. *Costs and benefits should be compared.* There are high costs associated with controls. The most important of these result from the constraints they place upon the operation of the price system, hindering its job of allocating and distributing goods and services in an efficient fashion. These costs could be considerable, but can be alleviated somewhat by designing some flexibilities into the controls program. For example, the controls rules could permit extra wage or price increases in markets experiencing obvious shortages. In any event, a decision to adopt or reject a guidelines or controls program should be made by comparing both its costs and its benefits.

## 12.5 Explaining Stagflation

The Phillips curve can be used to create some explanations for stagflation, which can be defined as high inflation combined with high unemployment or as rising inflation in conjunction with rising unemployment. In the world of the original Phillips curve, both such phenomena were impossible.

Consider first stagflation defined as high inflation combined with high unemployment. High inflation can be created by a high money-supply growth rate. There are three basic ways in which high unemployment can accompany this high inflation.

1. *High NRU.*   The natural rate of unemployment may itself be high, due to factors that affect frictional or structural unemployment, or for institutional reasons such as generous unemployment insurance benefits.

2. *A current fight against inflation.*   The government may be in the process of fighting an inflation by creating a recession, so that the economy is temporarily lodged near a point like E in figure 12.4.

3. *Real wage overhang.*   A permanent negative supply shock may have occurred, and workers may refuse to allow their real wage to fall. If they have sufficient power or a wage indexation policy to hold their real wage up, unemployment beyond the natural rate will develop.

Consider now stagflation defined as rising inflation in conjunction with rising unemployment. There are several ways in which this can happen.

1. *An increase in money growth.*   The dynamic reaction of the economy to an increase in the rate of money-supply growth is such that, in its later stages, inflation and unemployment increase together, as illustrated by the path from point C to D in figure 12.2.

2. *A supply shock.*   A negative supply shock raises costs, causing producers to raise prices. The higher prices lower aggregate demand, so output and employment fall.

3. *Labor hoarding.*   As an economy moves into recession and unemployment rises, firms tend to keep on some redundant employees (in order to keep trained labor available for when the recession ends). This raises per-unit costs, requiring higher markups to maintain profitability. The lower output level also implies a loss of economies of scale, also raising per-unit costs.

4. *Participation rate changes.*   A rise in inflation often occurs when employment is rising. It is possible that discouraged workers may rejoin the labor force if they see employment rising, which causes the measured level of unemployment to rise.

5. *Inflation variability.*   When inflation is higher, its rate is more variable, increasing uncertainty in economic markets. Firms react by investing less, thus decreasing economic growth.

## Media Illustrations

### Example 1
**Just as in the 1930s when government intervened to save capitalism from itself, so again must it intervene massively now to save government capitalism from itself. Because government now protects individuals and corporations from the consequences of excessive wage and price increases, government must now prevent those excessive increases by permanent wage-price controls.**

*How did government intervene in the 1930s to save capitalism from itself?*
The author of this clipping views the Great Depression as a product of the capitalist system. The government intervened in the Depression by using fiscal policy to increase government spending.

*What are the consequences of excessive wage and price increases, and how does the government protect individuals and corporations from these consequences?*
Excessive wage and price increases, if not accommodated by money-supply increases, decrease sales and lead to unemployment. Government protection takes the form of monetary accommodation designed to maintain full employment.

*Under what circumstances would wage-price controls succeed in preventing these excessive increases?*
Controls would succeed only if complemented by a decrease in money-supply growth.

### Example 2
**The central bank was presumably trying to maintain very high interest rates and, I assume in the face of political reality and pressure from the economy, released the interest rate a few weeks ago. The monetarists will allow you to go ahead and ruin people and countries, but when eventually in good and common sense you say "enough is enough," the monetarists say, "Well, you spoiled the experiment."**

*How and why was the central bank maintaining high interest rates?*
The central bank was fighting inflation by employing a tight monetary policy—cutting back on the rate of money-supply growth, which would push up interest rates.

*What does "releasing the interest rate" imply about the central bank's monetary policy?*
Releasing the interest rate means that the money supply has been allowed to grow at a faster rate.

*What does "ruining people and countries" mean in this context?*
Ruining people and countries means that the economy is forced to endure a very high rate of unemployment for a prolonged period of time.

*What was "the experiment," and how and why was it spoiled?*
The experiment was the maintenance of a low rate of money-supply growth to see if and how long it would take to lower inflation. It was spoiled when the central bank allowed money-supply growth to rise before inflation had been lowered. This change in policy was prompted by the political unacceptability of the prolonged high rate of unemployment that the policy produced.

### Example 3
**This suggests that wages play a game of catch-up, then fall behind for a while, but on the average they advance about 3 percent a year in real terms. We are still not far off this pace. The only trouble is that the economy is no longer pro-**

ductive enough to yield 3 percent average wage gains in real terms. If the cycle now goes into the catch-up phase, the demands for real gains to make up for the real losses of the past three years will collide with an economy going into at least a temporary stall.

*Describe a scenario in which wages in real terms fall behind for a while, then go through a catch-up stage.*

An unexpected increase in inflation will cause the real wage to fall. Once labor realizes that this has happened, it will demand catch-up wage increases.

*Explain how catch-up wages in conjunction with a productivity slowdown could create a "stall" in the economy.*

Catch-up wages would restore the real wage to its original level, plus the traditional annual 3 percent for productivity gains. If actual productivity gains were less than 3 percent, however, the rise in the real wage would put it higher than what is consistent with the natural rate of unemployment. Firms could not afford as much labor and would lay off workers, creating a "stall."

*Why would this stall be temporary?*

Eventually, the higher unemployment would dampen real wages, thus restoring the real wage to a level consistent with the natural rate of unemployment.

### Example 4

He favors a slow recovery, for example, because the natural rate of unemployment may turn out to be higher than anyone thinks.

*Explain why underestimation of the natural rate implies that a recovery should be slow.*

Policymakers may feel free to engineer a recovery if inflation has fallen to an acceptable level. A stimulating policy may be undertaken to move the economy back to the natural rate of unemployment from its present, inflation-fighting rate. In doing this, however, it is important that the natural rate of unemployment be known. If it is underestimated, the recovery policy may push the economy below this rate and quickly accelerate the inflation, destroying the hard-won results of the fight against inflation. By engineering a slow recovery, policymakers may notice an underestimation before too much damage is done.

## Chapter Summary

- The Phillips curve can not be interpreted, as it once was, as a menu of choice offering policymakers an exploitable trade-off between inflation and unemployment. Instead, this relationship reflects supply forces, analyzed earlier in the short-run aggregate supply curve. An unexpected increase in inflation causes a temporary increase in aggregate supply because of worker misperceptions and contracts. In the long run, however, workers become fully aware of the new inflation rate, and contracts are renegotiated accordingly, causing unemployment to return to the NRU. Higher inflation expectations cause the Phillips curve to shift upward, explaining why the Phillips curve relationship appeared to break down after the 1960s.

■ Although movements up the long-run Phillips curve occur quite quickly, movements down this curve require a prolonged period of high unemployment to sqeeze down high inflation expectations, mainly because people do not at first find a Fed policy of fighting inflation fully credible, and because wages and prices are downward-sticky. These different reactions create an asymmetry in the Phillips curve, implying that benefits from accelerating inflation are small and short-lived, whereas costs associated with lowering inflation are substantial and long-lived—explaining why governments have become so concerned about inflation.

■ Wage-price control policies are designed to force coordination of deceleration of wage and price increases, thereby facilitating a movement down the long-run Phillips curve. Although this policy inhibits the operation of the price system, it has the benefit of avoiding the prolonged high unemployment that would otherwise characterize the movement to a lower inflation rate. Such a policy would succeed only if accompanied by complementary monetary and fiscal policies.

■ Several explanations were offered for *stagflation*, defined either as high unemployment in conjunction with high inflation or as unemployment and inflation increasing simultaneously.

## Definitional Formula

■ sacrifice ratio $= \dfrac{\text{cumulative cost as \% of GDP}}{\text{percentage point} \downarrow \text{inflation}}$.

## Media Exercises

1.  **The central bank warned about a possible "collision" in the future between rising wages and prices and its hold-the-line monetary policy.**

    What is the nature of this collision, and what results will it produce?

2.  **The damnable paradox is that we are also at "full employment," or at least at the "natural rate" of unemployment. This means only that we are at or near the lowest rate to which unemployment can be pushed by expanding demand without ...**

    Complete this clipping.

3.  **Unemployment rates in Canada and the United States are sufficiently low that employers are having difficulty filling many jobs. The point at which red**

flags go up, economists say, is 9 percent in Canada and 6 percent in the United States.

    a. What two names are given to the unemployment rates described in this clipping?

    b. What danger do the red flags signal?

4. **The traditional macroeconomic approach—flooding the entire economy with demand in hopes of floating any unemployed little boats—no longer applies. Unemployment today is more a matter of defective labor markets. So, make labor markets work better.**

    a. With whose name is the traditional macroeconomic approach usually associated?

    b. Why is this traditional approach no longer applicable?

    c. How does the policy prescribed in this clipping fit into modern macroeconomic theory?

5. **Nor will decrees of 1 percent cuts in interest rates bring anything but more inflation. Nor yet do grand spending programs "create" more jobs: they merely redistribute them, from industry to industry, from region to region, from private sector to public sector.**

Explain how the contents of this clipping fit with modern macroeconomic theorizing.

6. **The response of the monetary authorities to any hint of inflation is to dampen demand by raising interest rates and slowing economic activity—that is, *by causing a recession*. It always seems to me that one of the great failures of the economic profession is that the only thing it seems to be able to recommend to eliminate inflation is a recession, but that's the way it is.**

    a. What diagram is usually used to illustrate this phenomenon?

    b. What role does the recession play in the economy's movement to a lower inflation rate?

    c. What alternative policy could be recommended, and how would it work?

7. **In the 1980s, the United States has succeeded in lowering unemployment and inflation at the same time, and the council believes this can continue even though industry is now running at more than 80 percent of capacity.**

Explain how inflation and unemployment could have been lowered at the same time. Illustrate this movement on a Phillips curve diagram.

8. **We're not likely to see a really tight monetary policy. The governor of the central bank made clear that the central bank is following an "intentionally moderate" monetary policy in order to "minimize the strains involved in**

adjusting to a less inflationary economy." He points to the "awkward economic fact that in the short run anti-inflationary policies tend to restrain output more than prices."

This is a good example of the way in which bureaucrats disguise harsh facts in flowery language. What is being said here, in blunt terms?

9.  We cannot afford to take any major risks with inflation. If we let inflation get away from us again, even for just a while, the path back to price stability will be even more painful than it has been during the last few years.

    a.  What is meant by a painful path?

    b.  Why would letting inflation get away for only a while require a painful return?

10. "Walk, don't run" is the message from the monetary authorities. Clearly, their thinking is that what the economy needs now is not a speedy recovery from recession, but one that is slow, drawn out, and, in many respects, painful.

    What rationale could lie behind this thinking?

11. Those policies were predicated on 1930s Keynesian assumptions that economic recoveries always run out of steam and at certain points need artificial stimulation of demand and fine-tuning to keep them running at acceptable levels. The evidence of the 1970s and beyond is that whenever governments stepped in to administer stimulative medicine, they triggered runaway inflation that finally had to be stopped with strong, painful doses of recession.

    a.  What do Keynesians recommend for artificial stimulation of demand?

    b.  Describe how such stimulation could trigger runaway inflation.

    c.  Explain why stopping this inflation requires a recession.

    d.  What alternative policy might be possible?

12. He warned yesterday that economic recovery in the Western world could be short-lived if governments injected too much financial stimulus into their economies in an attempt to boost employment and output.

    a.  What is "too much financial stimulus" in this context?

    b.  Why would too much stimulus make the recovery short-lived?

13. If a policy is to be credible enough for workers, consumers, and investors to build their expectations upon it, then at the least it must appear feasible to them. Because the central bank has not achieved zero inflation in the postwar era, why should individuals believe in such a policy now? If a zero-

**inflation goal lacks credibility, then an attempt by the central bank to achieve it will ...**

Complete this clipping, and explain your reasoning.

14. **What it does mean is that overall financial policy must be—and must be seen by a skeptical public to be—consistent with a continuing movement towards cost and price stability.**

   a. What kind of monetary policy would be consistent with a continuing movement towards price stability?

   b. Why is it important that the public sees this consistency?

15. **He defended the slow, steady decline in interest rates beginning in the spring of 1989 as the best that could have been done, given the fear of future inflation—a fear that has, until recently, kept long-term interest rates high despite repeated cuts in short-term rates by the Fed.**

   a. Explain why a faster fall in interest rates was not advisable.

   b. How does fear of inflation prevent long-term interest rates from following short-term rates?

16. **As actual inflation increased, workers and businesses began to incorporate expectations of higher and higher inflation into their behavior. The Phillips curve consequently ...**

   Complete this sentence.

17. **Price control policies have been tried on several occasions and in a number of countries, including Canada and the United States. The U.S. program, which was adopted in the second half of 1971, partly suspended the market system, producing distortion and shortages while suppressing inflation instead of resolving it.**

   a. What is the difference between suppressing inflation and resolving it?

   b. What element of the U.S. policy probably caused the suppression phenomenon?

18. **The Fed has always acknowledged openly that disinflation involved employment costs. A key message in its officials' speeches during disinflation was that the employment consequences would be reduced once wage and price setters realized that it was absolutely committed to lowering inflation.**

   a. Explain why disinflation (a reduction in inflation) involves employment costs.

   b. Explain the role of wage and price setters in reducing these costs.

19. **Stockman told the U.S. Chamber of Commerce that "High interest rates, unacceptable levels of current unemployment, lost output, financial strains, and the rising bankruptcies in the economy are all unpleasant facts of life, but are all part of the cure, not the problem."**

   Explain how these developments could be part of the cure, not the problem.

20. **Some economists said that the declining unemployment rate partly explains why the central bank has been pursuing a restrictive monetary policy for more than a year.**

   Explain the logic behind this explanation.

21. **Most estimates suggest that the U.S. natural rate of unemployment is around 6 percent, only slightly higher than it was in the 1960s. Because the current jobless rate is 6.1 percent, this suggests that the Fed was right to push up interest rates this spring and that it may even have acted a bit too late.**

   Explain the rationale behind the claim that the Fed was right to push up interest rates.

22. **On the other hand, there was a singular economic success in the past decade: a rampant inflation was curbed, albeit at the cost of _____, and Federal Reserve actions to keep the flow of money into the economy at moderate levels have kept the lid on it since.**

   a. How do you think the inflation was curbed?

   b. Fill in the blank.

   c. Explain how keeping the flow of money into the economy at moderate levels keeps the lid on inflation.

   d. What would you guess this moderate level to be?

23. **The chairman of the Fed had come to represent what many liberals regard as a policy-induced recession.**

   What is a policy-induced recession?

24. **The civilian unemployment rate has declined nearly two percentage points in the past two years and now stands at 5.25 percent, the lowest rate in ten years. Many worry that because this rate is below the sustainable "natural" rate of unemployment ...**

   Complete this clipping.

25. **Many economists applaud increased unemployment and lower growth as a necessary evil.**

   Explain what is meant here by "a necessary evil."

26. **By tying the pay of the governor of the central bank to his success in keeping inflation below 2 percent, New Zealand has succeeded in keeping inflation low. Now there are calls to tie the pay of the minister of employment to his success in keeping unemployment below 2 percent.**

    Comment on the wisdom of this proposal.

## Numerical Exercises

N1. Suppose the short-run Phillips curve is such that a two percentage point increase in inflation decreases unemployment by one percentage point. Suppose the economy is in long-run equilibrium, with a real growth rate of 2 percent and an unemployment rate of 7 percent, and the central bank increases the rate of growth of the money supply from 5 percent to 8 percent. When the economy has reached its new long-run equilibrium, what will be the levels of inflation and unemployment?

N2. Suppose person A forms his inflation expectations as the average of this period's inflation and last period's inflation, whereas person B forms her expectations rationally (i.e., by using all information plus knowledge of how the macroecoomy operates). Suppose the economy is in equilibrium at its NRU, and the Fed surreptitiously increases the money-supply growth rate from 6 percent to 7.5 percent, increasing inflation during the year from 4 percent to 4.5 percent and lowering unemployment slightly. At the end of this year, it becomes clear what the Fed has done. At this point,

    a. what is A's expected inflation?

    b. what is B's expected inflation?

N3. Suppose the economy is at its natural rate of unemployment of 6 percent, but policymakers plan to reduce inflation from 7 percent to 4 percent gradually over a period of three years by creating a recession. If the sacrifice ratio is 5,

    a. relative to maintaining full employment, what is the cumulative loss in output that this recession will entail?

    b. what steady level of unemployment over these three years should accomplish this goal? (Hint: Use Okun's Law.)

N4. The Bank of Canada's battle to cut inflation to 2 percent from 5 percent cost the Canadian economy $105 billion in lost production, says a new study.

    If Canada's full employment level of output is $700 billion, what is its sacrifice ratio?

# 13    The Real Cause of Inflation

At one time, economists classified inflation into two types: (1) *demand-pull inflation* is generated by excess demand for goods and services pulling up prices; and (2) *cost-push inflation* is generated by higher costs—such as energy price increases due to an oil cartel or wage increases due to powerful labor unions being passed on in higher prices by monopoly firms. Currently, this classification is seldom used, except in classifying short-run forces affecting prices. In the long run, neither type of inflation can be sustained without an accommodating growth in the money supply.

If the central bank does not accommodate demand-pull and cost-push price increases with accompanying increases in the money supply, the demand for money grows faster than the supply of money. The resulting excess demand for money decreases aggregate demand for goods and services, killing the inflationary forces. Consequently, economists have come to view the cause of inflation as excessive money-supply growth, agreeing with the monetarist view that in the long run inflation is always and everywhere a monetary phenomenon.

Surely, though, the real cause of inflation is whatever is causing the central bank to increase the money supply at an excessive rate! The purpose of this chapter is to consolidate material from earlier chapters that lend insight to this issue.

---

**Upon completion of this chapter you should**

- be familiar with several circumstances in which a central bank could lose control of the money supply; and
- understand the concept of seigniorage.

---

## 13.1   Losing Control of the Money Supply

If we know that excessive money-supply growth causes inflation, and if the money supply is under the control of the central bank, why does inflation rise? Why would the monetary authorities allow the money supply to grow too quickly? Although it is true that monetary authorities have known for some time that in the long run inflation is due to excessive money growth, this fact was not always given the prominence it deserved. On occasion, central banks pursued a policy that at first appeared not to involve a loss of control of the money supply, but in retrospect clearly did. We have encountered several examples of such situations in earlier chapters of this book.

**Underestimating the NRU**

Suppose the central bank has chosen to target monetary policy on the NRU, so that whenever unemployment departs from its natural rate, monetary policy reacts by pushing it back. A problem with this approach is that the NRU is never known. It must be estimated, and it can easily be underestimated. One reason for this is that many politicians find it difficult to believe that the natural rate can be so high and, consequently, continually bring pressure to bear on the central bank to lower unemployment.

Suppose the economy is at the NRU, but the central bank does not realize this and thinks that the NRU is lower. An expansionary monetary policy will be undertaken to push down unemployment, creating some unexpected inflation. The unexpected inflation causes the real wage to fall, either because workers are slow to realize what has happened or because of contract obligations that prevent immediate adjustment of wages. The fall in the real wage induces firms to increase output. After a time, however, inflation expectations increase and contracts are renegotiated, restoring the real wage to its original level and moving the economy back to the true natural rate. This prompts the central bank to increase its stimulation in order to keep the economy below the NRU, which accelerates the inflationary forces and causes this process to be repeated. The economy is prevented from moving back to its actual NRU, but at a cost of an accelerating inflation. By targeting on an underestimate of the NRU, the central bank could lose control of the money supply.

---

**Curiosity 13.1:   What Is Hysterisis?**

The current level of unemployment may be a factor affecting the NRU. A high unemployment rate means a fall in overall worker experience and job skills, and it may also change people's attitudes toward working, increasing both structural and frictional unemployment. *Hysterisis* refers to this phenomenon. The historical path taken by the economy affects its NRU and creates a vicious or a virtuous cycle, depending on whether current unemployment is high or low. Hysterisis is a possible explanation for a rising NRU during recessions.

---

**Reacting to a Negative Supply Shock**

There are two ways in which a negative supply shock can lead to an inappropriate central bank policy.

1. A negative supply shock makes the economy less productive, causing the level of national output/income to fall, even if the level of unemployment does not change. If the government does not recognize this and thinks instead that the decrease in income reflects a cyclical downturn, it may use monetary policy to stimulate the economy. The policy of targeting on the income level would then create a situation very similar to that described above for targeting on the unemployment rate. Stimulation will be successful in the short run but not in the longer run because the situation will require further stimulation and an acceleration of inflation will take place. By targeting on the presupply-shock level of output, the central bank could lose control of the money supply.

2. A negative supply shock decreases the productivity of labor. Firms cannot afford to hire as many workers at the prevailing real wage, so unemployment develops unless the real wage falls to reflect the lower productivity of labor. If the real wage is prevented from falling—by strong labor unions, for example, or a national labor contract expressed in real terms—the economy will become stuck at a level of unemployment above the natural rate. The central bank could misread this as a cyclical phenomenon and adopt a stimulating dose of monetary policy. The result is similar to that given earlier for targeting on an underestimate of the NRU. As long as the real wage is artificially held too high, this policy will accelerate the inflation. By targeting on the presupply-shock unemployment rate, the central bank could lose control of the money supply.

**Fixing the Nominal Interest Rate**

It has been common for central banks to adopt a policy of targeting on or fixing the nominal interest rate. Under this policy, a shock to the monetary sector that causes a rise in the interest rate would prompt the central bank to increase the money supply to push the interest rate back down. The increase in the money supply may cause people to revise upwards expected inflation, a revision reinforced by any actual price increases created by the extra money, which is likely if the economy is near full employment. Higher expected inflation increases the nominal interest rate. Any success the central bank has in pushing down the nominal interest rate will be temporary and likely to be more than offset by a rise in expected inflation. The rise in the interest rate prompts the central bank to increase again the money supply to meet its target interest rate, thus leading to a vicious circle. By targeting on the interest rate, the central bank loses control of the money supply.

### Financing Government Spending

Countries with military dictatorships or with central banks that lack independence from politicians sometimes finance a large portion of government spending by printing money. This is a tempting option for any government faced with a budget deficit because printing money reduces interest costs and achieves the political end of avoiding higher taxes. Real growth causes an economy's demand for money to grow, so the money supply should increase to meet the extra demand for money. Buying government bonds on the open market is how this is done, so that some financing of government spending by money printing is acceptable. This is formalized by the concept of *seigniorage*, discussed in curiosity 13.2. Money printing beyond this amount, however, creates inflation. A central bank that promises to finance government budget deficits loses control of the money supply.

### Repeating the Political Business Cycle

When the central bank is not independent, politicians can and do pump up the money supply shortly before an election to buy votes with lower interest rates and a lower unemployment rate. After the election, these short-run effects wear off, however, returning the economy to its natural rate of unemployment but at a higher inflation rate and a higher nominal interest rate. Because of the asymmetry of the Phillips curve, it is often the case that by the time the next election rolls around the economy has not been squeezed back to its original inflation rate, so the next round of politically induced money-supply increases start from a higher base. As this cycle repeats itself, the central bank loses control of the money supply.

### Fixing the Exchange Rate

As explained more fully in chapter 16, fixing the exchange rate causes an economy's money supply to grow at whatever money-supply growth rate char-

---

**Curiosity 13.2:   What Is Seigniorage?**

The government, through its agent the central bank, has the legal right to print money. Whatever new money is printed each year is a source of funds for the government. *Seigniorage* is the amount of funding made available to the government through printing money, currently about 2 percent of total government revenue. The term stems from the right of the lord of the realm (in French, the *seigneur*) to coin money.

Printing money and spending it—or, equivalently, having the central bank finance spending by buying government bonds—increases the money base, which in turn increases the money supply by an amount determined by the money multiplier. To calculate seigniorage, therefore, first determine how much the money supply needs to increase during the year, and then divide by the money multiplier. To maintain the current inflation rate, the money supply must grow at a rate equal to the nominal rate of growth of income, matching higher demand for money with higher supply. This gives rise to the following formula for calculating seigniorage:

$$\text{seigniorage} = \frac{\text{nominal growth rate} \times \text{money supply}}{\text{money multiplier}}.$$

Seigniorage can be broken into two parts: that corresponding to money-supply increases matching real income increases, and that corresponding to money-supply increases maintaining current inflation. The latter dimension of seigniorage is called the *inflation tax*. Those holding money balances experience a "tax" on those balances equal to the rate of inflation because the purchasing power of money balances is eroded by inflation. Central banks that lack independence from politicians frequently finance spending through seigniorage and, by doing so, create high inflation.

---

acterizes its major trading partners. In effect, monetary policy must be devoted to fixing the exchange rate, so control over money growth is lost. Suppose, for example, our rate of inflation is 5 percent and that of our trading partners is 15 percent. If we fix the exchange rate, each year our goods become 10 percent less expensive to foreigners, and foreign goods become 10 percent more expensive to us. We soon experience a dramatic increase in our exports and a decrease in our imports, which produces a surplus of foreign currency in the hands of our citizens. When the central bank exchanges the foreign currency for dollars at the fixed rate, these dollars increase the domestic money supply. By targeting on the exchange rate, the central bank loses control over the money supply.

---

## Media Illustrations

### Example 1
**The Federal Reserve Bank Act of 1978 requires the Fed to pursue full employment as well as low inflation, but Mr. Greenspan has said that he favors legislation to make price stability the Fed's sole objective.**

*Why might the chairman of the Fed prefer to have price stability as his sole objective?*

Using monetary policy to achieve a specific unemployment rate could cause the Fed to lose control over the money supply, with consequent disaster for the inflation goal. The Fed would argue that monetary policy is capable of achieving only one objective, and because money growth is so strongly related to inflation, it seems reasonable to make inflation the primary goal of the monetary authority.

### Example 2

**Monetary policy cannot be tuned to real economic variables such as growth or employment, not only because policy takes effect with long and uncertain lags, but because any commitment to real growth targets simply invites workers and business to increase wages and prices at will, in the knowledge that the central bank will "ratify" their demands via the money supply.**

*What is meant by "commitment to a real growth target"?*

The government has promised to maintain the economy at a specified level of unemployment. This implies a steady real growth as the labor force grows.

*What is meant by the central bank ratifying demands for higher wages and prices?*

Higher prices and wages cause the demand for money to exceed the supply of money. The excess demand for money causes demand for goods and services to fall—decreasing the level of economic activity, cutting into business profits, and causing layoffs, so in general firms and workers will think twice about raising wages and prices. If the central bank increases the money supply to prevent this unemployment, however, it has effectively approved ("ratified") the price and wage hikes.

### Example 3

**The realistic alternative to high interest rates is not lower interest rates (except temporarily), but rather even higher interest rates and a monetary inflation that would make our heads spin.**

*What monetary policy scenario does the author of this clip have in mind?*

Suppose the monetary authorities decide to target on a lower nominal rate of interest and increase the money supply to attain that rate. The increase in the money supply could increase inflation expectations, which increases the nominal rate, causing the monetary authorities to renew their efforts to lower the interest rate to the target level. Accordingly, they increase the money supply by even more, accelerating the inflation and continuing this vicious cycle.

*How does the "except temporarily" fit in?*

Each increase in the money supply will decrease the interest rate in the short run. It is not until expectations of inflation increase that the interest rate rises.

*What policy would you recommend to achieve a lower interest rate?*

What is needed is a policy of cutting down on the rate of growth of the money supply to cut inflation and thereby to lower the nominal rate of interest. In the short run, this causes a rise in the real (and nominal) interest rate and slows economic activity. After a time, inflation should fall to a lower level, reducing inflation expectations and allowing the nominal interest rate to fall.

### Example 4

**We at the Fed are frequently pressed by people to do things that would involve giving up control over money creation without any apparent recognition on their part that this is what they are asking. We, of course, have to refuse.**

*Give four examples of such requests.*

A common request is for an immediate lowering of the interest rate. Doing this would require increasing the money supply in ever increasing quantities in order to outstrip people's expectations. A second common request is to produce a rate of unemployment lower than the NRU. Doing so would require an accelerating inflation. A third common request is to use monetary policy to fight a negative supply-side shock. Monetary policy is not able to undo the negative consequences of such a shock, so its use in this circumstance serves only to disrupt money-supply growth. A fourth common request is to finance government deficits to avoid the higher interest rates that they produce. Doing so would mean that the government deficit would determine the money-growth rate.

## Chapter Summary

- In the short run, inflation can be influenced by cost or demand pressures, but in the long run such pressures cannot sustain an inflation unless accommodated by money-supply increases. The real cause of inflation, therefore, is whatever is causing the central bank to increase the money supply at an excessive rate. Several scenarios were described in which a central bank, by targeting its monetary policy on something other than the rate of money-supply growth, could inadvertently be led to increase the money supply at an undesirably high rate.

## Formula Definition

- $$\text{seigniorage} = \frac{\text{nominal growth rate} \times \text{money supply}}{\text{money multiplier}}.$$

## Media Exercises

1. **There is little doubt that the key reason for this slide toward ever more inflation was an effort by public policy in most countries to achieve and**

maintain more output and employment from their economies than was consistent with price stability.

a. What level of output and employment would be consistent with price stability?

b. How would public policy be used to achieve more output and employment?

c. Explain how doing so would create a "slide toward ever more inflation."

2. The message from the central bank to the private sector is: do not give in to inflationary psychology; do not assume that you can easily accommodate cost pressures; and do not expect monetary accommodation of accelerating energy price increases.

a. What is meant by "assume that you can easily accommodate cost pressures"?

b. What is meant by "monetary accommodation of accelerating energy price increases"?

3. In the longer term, things will be different. It is worth recalling that seigniorage is no longer being exercised by all those seigneurs—emperors, kings, and imperial governments—who once possessed it. The reason is simple: seigniorage is such a tempting privilege that it always ends up being abused.

How is seigniorage abused, and what are the consequences?

4. As the election draws nearer, the prospect of an economy awash in money becomes likely. It is therefore reassuring that the central bank remains vigilant about the dangers of inflation.

Why would the proximity of an election affect money creation?

5. There's nothing wrong with any level of interest rates produced by the natural forces in the economy, but artificially lowered rates are dangerous because they are produced by artificial increases in the money supply. The extra money sluicing around in the system at a time when production is close to capacity is more likely to go into higher prices than anywhere else.

a. What is meant here by "artificial increases in the money supply?"

b. Explain how such artificially lowered rates may in fact end up creating higher interest rates.

6. I wouldn't say that a lower dollar is inflationary. A lower dollar means you're paying more for your imports. In other words, it adds to your cost of living, and it can become inflationary if . . .

Complete this statement to explain how a lower dollar can become inflationary.

7. **Governments increase the money supply too rapidly because it enables them to finance an expanding government sector without increasing taxes or borrowing from the economy's savings.**

   a. What is this means of financing usually called?

   b. What is its drawback?

   c. What is meant by "borrowing from the economy's savings"?

8. **What is important for inflationary expectations is how the bank has responded to such shocks in the past. A central bank that has shown it will not accommodate inflationary shocks will find it much easier to maintain a stable inflation rate—whatever its level—than one with a reputation for accommodation.**

   a. What does "accommodate inflationary shocks" mean?

   b. Explain why a central bank with a reputation for not accommodating inflationary shocks will find it easier to maintain a stable inflation rate.

9. **A second flaw in economic policy lay in the contradiction between price stability and the pledge to maintain full employment. Why? Because firms and workers took the full-employment pledge seriously.**

   Explain how this flaw ruined economic policy.

10. **According to one theory, the U.S. recession-inflation debate boils down to whether the natural unemployment rate is higher or lower than the current 5.7 percent level.**

    a. What theory is being referred to?

    b. The debate is about what policy is appropriate. Explain the role of the natural rate in this debate.

11. **The Fed, though one of the world's most independent central banks, also faces the dilemma of potentially conflicting objectives of low inflation and low unemployment. Having such dual objectives almost guarantees that inflation will be higher.**

    Why would dual objectives make more difficult the task of controlling inflation?

12. **"The Federal Reserve must be conscious of the limits of its capabilities. We can try to provide a backdrop for stable, sustainable growth, but we cannot iron out every fluctuation, and attempts to do so could be counterproductive," Alan Greenspan, the Fed chairman, said.**

a. How would the Fed provide a backdrop for stable, sustainable growth?

b. Give an example of how an attempt to iron out a fluctuation could be counterproductive.

13. **This brings us back to the fears of higher interest rates before the market break. These fears are still potent, especially if investors see through the temporary reduction in interest rates made possible by stepping up the rate of creation of the money supply.**

a. How does stepping up the rate of creation of the money supply reduce interest rates?

b. Why would the reduction be only temporary?

14. **Beset by low productivity growth, spiraling oil prices, and declining international competitiveness, Jimmy Carter adopted a policy of low interest rates, economic expansion, and dollar depreciation. It's problem was that this policy generated ...**

Complete this clipping.

15. **Many politicians say they favor low interest rates but believe in their hearts that higher rates are necessary to control ...**

Complete this clipping.

16. **The governor of the central bank responded by saying that there is nothing in the experience of any country that would suggest that monetary policy can produce sustainable decreases in unemployment beyond those that can be achieved by maintaining stable prices.**

Explain the rationale behind the governor's view.

17. **The government made the biggest blunder. Between 1985 and 1989, the Bank of Japan (Japan's Fed) kept interest rates too low.**

How could keeping interest rates too low be a mistake?

18. **From their perspective, the only other way to lower interest rates is for the Fed to increase the supply of funds by continuously pumping more money into the economy. They argue against such a loose monetary policy, however, claiming it would not be tolerated for long by the financial markets because it would lead to a further fall in the value of the dollar and to renewed ...**

Complete this clipping.

19. **The desire to see interest rates lower, or to avoid increases, is natural, but attempts to accomplish this desirable end by excessive monetary growth**

would soon be counterproductive. The implications for interest rates would in the end be perverse.

Explain why interest rate movements would in the end be perverse.

20. Increasingly, there does seem to be agreement on one point—namely, that government's advancing share (via big deficits) in the economy has been strongly inflationary, mainly because individuals and companies have not been prepared to pay (through taxes) for extra public services or income redistribution and have, instead, demanded bigger and bigger income increases to offset the tax and to keep real incomes growing.

   a. The argument presented here is not the usual argument claiming government deficits are inflationary. What is the usual argument?

   b. How would you exposit the argument in this clipping on a Phillips curve diagram?

## Numerical Exercise

N1. Suppose the current level of income is $800 billion, the income multiplier with respect to the money supply is 4, the money multiplier is 5, the long-run real rate of growth is 2 percent, the current money supply is $200 billion, and the rate of inflation is 8 percent.

What level of seigniorage is the government currently enjoying?

# 14    Budget Deficits and the National Debt

Before the great depression of the 1930s, government spending was less than 5 percent of GDP. Introduction of the "New Deal" during the depression doubled this percentage, and since then it has increased to between 20 and 25 percent of GDP, a range in which it has hovered since the mid-1970s. About 44 percent of the government's revenue comes from individual income taxes, about 36 percent from Social Security payroll taxes, and about 11 percent from corporate income taxes, accounting for over 90 percent of tax receipts. About 18 percent of the government budget is spent on defense, about 22 percent on Social Security, about 10 percent on Medicare, about 6 percent on Medicaid, and about 15 percent on interest payments on the national debt. Other areas of expenditure are much smaller: welfare and foreign aid, for example, are together less than 3 percent of total government spending.

When government spending exceeds tax revenues, there is a *government budget deficit*, which is financed by selling bonds. The sum of all outstanding government bonds is called the *national debt*, which grows each year by the amount of the budget deficit. (It could shrink if there were a budget surplus, but these days that doesn't seem to happen!) Some bonds are sold to the central bank, an agent of the government, so this part of the national debt the government owes to itself; consequently, nobody worries about it. The remaining bonds are sold to the public, augmenting the publicly held national debt. Recent growth in this debt has become of concern.

An important legacy of Keynes is that budget deficits became respectable side effects of efforts to keep an economy operating at full employment. Keynes's intention was that deficits required to stimulate the economy when it is in recession would be offset by budget surpluses in times of full employment—ensuring that in the long run the national debt would not continually grow.

History has not treated the Keynes legacy kindly. Once initial fears of budget deficits were overcome, politicians went overboard, producing deficits in both good times and bad. In the 1960s the federal budget deficit was less than 1 percent of GDP; in the 1970s this jumped to over 2 percent; and in the 1980s and 1990s it ballooned to over 4 percent. There are three main culprits responsible for the growing deficit.

1. *Tax decreases.*  The ratio of tax revenue to GDP is about 30 percent in the United States, the lowest of all OECD countries. Canada's ratio is about 40 percent, and Sweden's is about 52 percent.

2. *Growing entitlement expenditures.* Social Security and Medicare expenditures cannot easily be controlled because anyone eligible is entitled to coverage. As our population ages, spending in these two categories continually increases, with politicians refusing to increase taxes to pay for it.

3. *Higher interest payments.* Because of higher interest rates and a higher national debt, interest payments as a fraction of government spending have jumped from about 9 percent to about 15 percent in the past fifteen years.

Because each year a dollar of budget deficit increases the national debt by a dollar, deficits have caused growth in the national debt that has many worried about our future. The purpose of this chapter is to examine the issue of budget deficits and the national debt.

---

**Upon completion of this chapter you should**

- know what's involved in calculating the structural deficit, a deficit measure designed to provide a more accurate view of the extent to which we should worry about the size of the deficit; and

- recognize the circumstances in which an increase in the national debt can be viewed as a burden on future generations.

---

## 14.1   Implications of Budget Deficits

Budget deficits carry both costs and benefits for the economy. Any assessment of deficits' desirability must weigh carefully these costs and benefits.

1. *Lower unemployment.* Allowing budget deficits permits Keynesian fiscal policy (as described in chapter 4) to keep the economy closer to full employment than might otherwise be the case. Furthermore, movements into recession are automatically dampened if recession-induced decreases in tax revenues and increases in unemployment insurance payments are permitted to create a deficit. Output lost due to unemployment above its natural rate can be substantial and is output lost forever. Furthermore, the human cost of unemployment is considerable by any measure.

2. *Public investment.* Allowing budget deficits permits the government to borrow in order to invest in projects that have a high social payoff, such as education or infrastructure. This is similar to a private corporation borrowing to invest in a project whose payoff is expected to be high enough to pay back the loan with interest.

3. *Lower national saving.* A deficit requires that the government bid up the interest rate to obtain financing for its deficit, crowding out private financing needs, prominent among which are private investment projects. This decreases the long-run rate of growth of the economy and inhibits productivity growth. (Chapter 6 analyzed how budget deficits reduce national saving.)

4. *International implications.* Higher interest rates attract foreign investors. To buy our bonds foreigners must first obtain our dollars. This increase in the demand for our dollar increases its value, making our exports expensive to foreigners and their goods inexpensive to us, as well as making life difficult for exporters and for those competing against importers. Furthermore, the associated buildup of foreign ownership of our assets implies that more future income must be sent abroad in the form of interest and dividends. (The international dimension of the budget deficit issue is discussed further in chapter 15.)

---

**Curiosity 14.1:   What Is the Full-Employment Budget?**

When tax revenues fall as the economy enters a recession, the government budget moves automatically towards deficit. Two implications of this process are of note:

1. Many years ago, when politicians feared deficits, such a deficit triggered calls from politicians to decrease government spending or to raise taxes to eliminate the deficit. This contractionary fiscal policy would be inappropriate because it would make the recession worse.

2. The budget deficit is misleading as an indicator of government discretionary fiscal policy because it was not caused by a conscious government policy action of increasing spending or decreasing taxes. Consequently, any effort to measure the strength of fiscal policy by matching up budget deficits with economic activity would be inaccurate.

The full-employment budget is actual government spending minus tax revenues that would be generated by a fully employed economy. This concept was developed to deal with the two problems noted above:

1. Although a recession decreases tax revenues and pushes the actual budget toward deficit, it does not change the full-employment budget (because when calculating the full-employment budget, full-employment tax revenues are used). Consequently, politicians averse to budget deficits could be persuaded to permit an actual budget deficit on the grounds that the full-employment budget was in balance. This argument was used during the early 1960s when the Keynesian policy view reached the height of its popularity.

2. By eliminating automatic tax revenue changes caused by income changes, the full-employment budget allows fiscal policy initiatives to be measured accurately by changes in the full-employment budget. We can thus see more clearly what is happening with fiscal policy and more accurately measure the influence of fiscal policy.

---

5. *Debt monetization.*   Budget deficits create a danger that government will choose to finance them by monetizing them—by printing money—and thereby create inflation. This danger is not high in countries like the United States that have a central bank quite independent of politicians.

6. *Growing national debt.*   Continued budget deficits increase the national debt. A growing national debt has several important implications.

   a. A growing national debt means growing interest payments on that national debt. Over time, the interest payments may become a sufficiently large fraction of the government's financing needs that they render fiscal policy inflexible. Fiscal policy to attack unemployment, for example, may not be undertaken because financing is not available.

   b. A growing national debt inevitably means that tax rates rise as much as politicians dare to facilitate handling the high interest payments, creating disincentive effects, as emphasized by the supply-siders.

    c. A growing national debt means that we may be placing a burden on future generations who will inherit that debt. Many view this as morally wrong. (See section 14.3 for further discussion of this issue.)

    d. A national debt could grow to the point where it will become too large for the country to service, causing a major crisis in the economy, such as that experienced by New Zealand in the 1980s. One way of measuring whether an economy is headed in this direction is to calculate the structural deficit.

## 14.2   The Structural Deficit

One implication of financing a budget deficit by selling bonds to the public is that as the budget deficit continues, the national debt grows. How worried should we be about this? Although there is no unique answer to this question, there is some consensus that we should worry about a budget deficit only if its size is such as to cause a long-run rise in the ratio of the publicly held national debt to nominal GDP. This ratio is a crude measure of our capacity to service the national debt, and if it continues to grow, at some stage the economy will not have enough GDP to be able to service the debt, so a major crisis will ensue.

*The structural deficit* is the part of the current budget that in the long run increases the ratio of the publicly held national debt to nominal GDP. Three adjustments must be made to the current budget deficit to calculate the structural deficit:

1. A correction is needed for cyclical effects that hinder the current deficit's ability to reflect accurately any long-run trends. For example, if GDP drops below its long-run trend average by $100, it is estimated that tax receipts fall by $25 and government spending on transfers increases by $8, so that $33 of the deficit does not correspond to long-run behavior. It should be noted that there is not a universal definition of the structural deficit. Some textbooks claim that it involves only this cyclical adjustment.

2. A correction is needed for real growth and inflation because if nominal GDP is growing, the publicly held debt can grow without affecting their ratio.

3. A correction is needed for seigniorage. Each year, an increase in the money supply is required to accommodate money demand increases, allowing the government to finance some of its deficit by printing money. This financing does not affect the publicly held debt.

The best way to explain these corrections is by means of an explicit example. Consider an economy with a 2 percent real rate of growth, a 4 percent inflation rate, 9 percent unemployment, a money supply of $500 billion, a publicly held national debt of $400 billion, a current budget deficit of $43 billion, a money multiplier of 5, and a 7 percent long-run average unemployment rate. The economy's tax and unemployment compensation systems are such that a one percentage point change in unemployment changes the budget deficit position by $4 billion.

1. *Correction for cyclical effects.*   The economy is currently experiencing an unemployment rate greater than its long-run average, so part of the currrent deficit does not reflect the long-run contribution of the deficit to the national debt. In this case, the extra deficit is $8 billion, calculated as $4 billion times the two percentage points by which current unemployment exceeds its long-run average. Note that this long-run average is not the NRU. The economy spends more time above its NRU than below, so the long-run average un-employment rate for this calculation is greater than the NRU.

2. *Correction for nominal growth.*   Nominal GDP—the denominator of the ratio of the publicly held debt to GDP—is growing, so the numerator can grow at the same rate without increasing this ratio. In this case, GDP is growing in nominal terms by 6 percent, calculated by adding the real growth rate and the inflation rate. 6 percent of the numerator is $24 billion, so this much of the current deficit does not contribute to raising the debt/GDP ratio. Note that the calculation implicitly builds in a correction for inflation decreasing the real value of the debt.

3. *Correction for seigniorage.*   Each year the central bank increases the money supply to accommodate the economy's nominal growth. The deficit can then be financed by selling bonds to the central bank (printing money) rather than to the public. These bond sales do not affect the publicly held debt and thus do not affect the ratio of the publicly held debt to GDP. In this case, the central bank will be increasing the money supply by 6 percent (2 percent for the real growth, plus 4 percent to sustain the inflation), which equals $30 billion. Because the money multiplier is 5, the increase is accomplished by buying $6 billion of bonds. Note that there is a further correction for infla-tion inherent in this calculation.

What these numbers mean is that the current deficit would have to be more than $38 billion before it would cause the ratio of the publicly held debt to GDP to rise in the long run. Because the current deficit is $43 billion, the structural deficit, by this definition, is $5 billion, and the debt/GDP ratio is rising. (See figure 14.1.)

Other adjustments for calculating the structural deficit are possible. Unusual expenditures, for events such as the Iraqi war or the savings and loan bailout, do not reflect long-run spending, so they should be excluded. State and local budget surpluses should be accounted for when measuring national saving, but not when calculating the structural deficit because it refers to only federal debt.

A controversial proposal is to reduce the deficit by the amount spent on capital projects, on the grounds that they create higher income, but this sug-

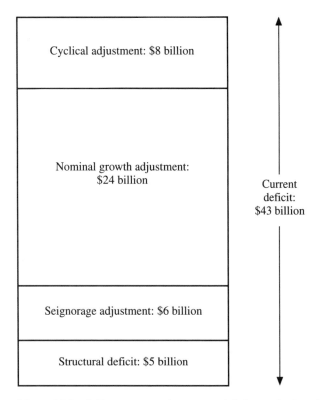

**Figure 14.1**   Adjustments to the current deficit to calculate the structural deficit

gested adjustment is already incorporated into the structural deficit calculation by using GDP in the denominator of the ratio that represents our ability to carry debt. At best, this argument can be used to justify a short-run structural deficit so that capital projects with big future payoffs can be undertaken.

It is clear that a continually rising debt/GDP ratio cannot be sustained forever. Eventually, the debt will rise to a level at which GDP will not be large enough to meet the interest payments; we can therefore conclude that, in the long run, a structural deficit is undesirable. As shown in figure 14.2, in recent years this ratio has been rising steadily, an unusual phenomenon except during wartime. Unfortunately, there is no economic prescription for determining an "optimal" debt/GDP ratio, so we cannot say that a structural deficit is necessarily a bad thing in the short run. A common argument in this context is that a rise in the ratio implies that a burden is being placed on future generations.

## 14.3   Burdening Future Generations

The question of whether a burden is being passed on to future generations is best addressed by examining what capital stock is being passed on at the same

Debt (% GDP)

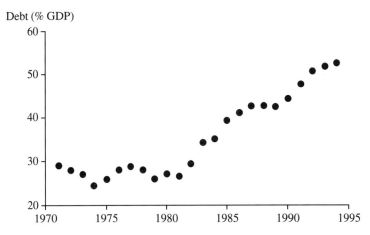

**Figure 14.2**   Publicly held national debt as a percent of GDP
Source: *Economic Report of the President*, 1995.

time. Let us examine this first by assuming only domestic borrowing and second by assuming borrowing from foreigners.

**Domestic Borrowing**

If the borrowing is domestic, then we owe the debt to ourselves, and it seems that overall there is no intergenerational burden. This reasoning is misleading, however. Domestic borrowing to finance a deficit crowds out some investment spending. If the deficit spending is on capital assets such as roads and airports, the capital stock passed on to the future generation may be of more value than the investment spending that is crowded out.

On the other hand, if the deficit spending is on things other than capital assets, such as medicare and unemployment insurance, then the future generation will receive a smaller capital stock. If the economy is at full employment, more crowding out occurs, increasing the likelihood that future generations will be made worse off. The key feature, however, is the nature of the deficit spending. If the deficit spending is on consumption items rather than investment items, the present generation is "living it up" at the expense of a future generation that will receive a smaller capital stock.

**Foreign Borrowing**

The great advantage of borrowing from foreigners is that crowding out can be avoided. The foreign exchange obtained by this borrowing can be used to import more goods and services, allowing the economy to have extra output to distribute to its citizens. In this case, however, future generations must pay interest and principal to foreigners, so it looks as though they are being burdened. Once again, though, this conclusion depends on the nature of the deficit

**Curiosity 14.2:  What Is Intergenerational Accounting?**

The size of our national debt is a misleading measure of possible burdens on future generations, mainly because the national debt measure does not incorporate financing obligations associated with promises that the government has made regarding future spending.

Most prominent among these promises are future expenditures on Social Security (i.e., pension payments) and Medicare (i.e., subsidies for medical costs). Such programs are financed on a pay-as-you-go basis, which means that the current working generation pays for benefits being enjoyed by older generations who have retired. (Since 1983, the working generation has through extra payroll taxes been building up a fund to help pay for its future benefits, but this fund is far too modest, so in effect we continue to operate on a pay-as-you-go basis.) The current generation has been promised that its benefits will be paid for by the following generation of workers. Notice that each generation is being taxed to pay for the preceding generation's benefits, rather than being taxed to pay for its own expected benefits. This system works well if the later generation can produce sufficient income to finance these promised benefits easily.

In the past it has been easy for later generations to meet this promise, primarily because later generations have always had more—and more productive—workers than earlier generations. But what if there is a slowdown in population and productivity growth so that a later generation finds itself unable to meet this promise easily? This might imply that the earlier generation is placing a burden on the later generation.

Intergenerational accounting is the name given to calculations designed to measure future taxes required to meet promised future government spending. These calculations suggest that the United States is facing a big problem. The demographics are such that when the current working generation (the baby boomer generation) retires, there will not be enough workers in the following generation to make the financing of this promise realistic. If the current generation continues to pay only about a third of its lifetime income in taxes, future generations will have to pay more than 80 percent of lifetime income in taxes to meet the intergenerational promises described above.

There is some justice in an intergenerational transfer if the higher productivity of the later generation is in part due to the higher capital stock passed on by the earlier generation. The above numbers are too extreme to be justified on these grounds, however, especially given the recent slowdown in productivity growth. Clearly, such high taxes are not collectable, implying that some change is necessary: (1) tax the current generation more heavily so that it is forced to pay for much more of its own future benefits; (2) increase immigration dramatically to increase the number of people working to produce the income required to meet these promises; and (3) do not meet the promises—the most likely change.

spending. If the government has borrowed to invest in social infrastructure that increases the economy's productivity by enough to create additional annual income sufficient to pay off the interest and principal of the debt, then the deficit cannot be said to burden future generations.

A good example of "investment borrowing" is when the United States used foreign borrowing to build railroads and steel mills during the nineteenth century. If the deficit arises because the government has borrowed to spend on overly generous social security or Medicare, or unnecessary military hardware, however, future generations will be asked to reduce their consumption to repay the principle and interest. In this case, a burden is placed on future generations.

## Media Illustrations

### Example 1

**Prices in all areas of the bond market traded in a narrow range for most of the week, but jumped sharply yesterday morning in reaction to the news that the U.S. Senate voted to approve specific deficit reduction measures.**

*Why would bond prices jump in reaction to this news?*
If the deficit is reduced, the government will not be selling so many bonds, implying that the interest rate should fall. A fall in the interest rate will push up the price of bonds. Anticipating this, bond traders buy bonds, thus bidding up their price.

### Example 2

**The damaging effect to the marketplace created by the persistence of heavy government borrowings is an ever present concern for bond investors. A fear is that the solution to the government's seemingly insatiable appetite for funds will be debt monetization. As a result, most observers expect interest rates to remain historically high.**

*What is debt monetization, and why is it feared?*
Debt monetization is printing money to finance a deficit (i.e., selling bonds to the central bank). Doing this would increase the money supply and lead to inflation, raising the nominal interest rate and lowering the price of bonds. The fall in bond prices is the reason why debt monetization is feared by bond investors.

*Why would most observers expect interest rates to remain high?*
Because debt monetization cannot be completely discounted, expected inflation is high, in turn causing a high nominal interest rate.

### Example 3

**A rise in the debt/GDP ratio means that the current generation is consuming goods and services at the expense of future generations. We are in effect stealing from the future by consuming more than we can produce.**

*How can we possibly consume more than we can produce?*

By borrowing from foreigners, we can pay for imports and thus augment the output we produce for distribution to our citizens. Borrowing domestically causes crowding out. The total output distributed to various ends within the economy remains constant, but some people get less (those crowded out) and others get more (those who have borrowed). If we look at consumption only, it may be that the present generation is consuming more by investing less, implying that a smaller capital stock will be passed on to future generations.

*Does this necessarily imply that we are stealing from future generations?*

If the borrowing is to finance consumption goods, then future generations will pay, but if the borrowing is to finance investment goods, it is possible that future generations will be better off. The investment goods may make future generations much more productive.

### Example 4

**As to how the federal deficit would be cut back, the economists rule out tax increases. Instead, the cuts must come on the expenditure side with the average growth of federal expenditures—including interest payments on the national debt—kept below average growth of GDP.**

*Why would economists favor cutting back government spending over raising taxes?*

This is purely a conservative value judgment on the part of these economists; they feel that the level of government spending is already too large. Liberal economists would favor more government involvement in the operation of the economy. Most economists are conservatives in this respect, however, because through studying economics, they have come to respect the efficiency of the free market. They do not believe that government-directed spending creates extra benefits as great as those that would be created by private spending.

## Chapter Summary

- Budget deficits augment the national debt, but this is of concern only if this debt becomes so big relative to GDP that we are unable to service it. A *structural deficit* indicates that the long-run ratio of the publicly held national debt to GDP is rising and, therefore, that the economy is heading for trouble.

- The structural deficit is calculated by adjusting the current deficit for cyclical effects, for nominal growth, and for seigniorage.

- An increase in the national debt may not be a burden on future generations if a larger capital stock is passed on to them. A key factor here is the purpose of the extra government spending—transfer payments or infrastructure, for example.

**Media Exercises**

1. **Another criticism of deficit budgets is that they hamper the private sector's ability to raise capital.**

   a. How do budget deficits hamper the private sector's ability to raise capital?

   b. How could the central bank avoid this, and at what cost?

2. **Ordinarily, an increase in the budget deficit raises interest rates, but this does not always happen.**

   Describe a scenario in which an increase in the budget deficit is accompanied by a lower interest rate.

3. **U.S. Federal Reserve Board chairman Paul Volcker told senators Thursday that the huge federal budget deficit is causing "disturbing pressures" on interest rates.**

   Explain in what direction and how pressure is placed on interest rates.

4. **The debt buildup is worrisome because it is not financing ...**

   Complete this sentence.

5. **A significant difference exists between the consequences of federal as opposed to state borrowing if the federal government borrows by selling bonds to the Federal Reserve. It alone can do so; the central bank buys only federal bonds.**

   What is the "significant difference" mentioned here?

6. **It is the rare consumer or investor who would not conclude that where government debt was growing faster than GDP, tax increases and/or accelerated inflation could not be far off.**

   How can accelerated inflation be an alternative to taxation?

7. **There is no direct connection between the deficit and inflation. If there were, why did inflation hit 14 percent in 1948, a year when the government had a spending surplus? And why has inflation continued to fall the past two years while the deficit has been rising?**

   a. What is the logic behind the view that there is a connection between the budget deficit and inflation?

   b. Do the facts cited in the clip contradict this view?

8. **The arithmetic is straightforward. If growth falls one percentage point below the government's 3 percent forecast, the deficit would widen by about $15 billion.**

   How does growth affect the budget deficit?

9. **Of course, if the government uses borrowed funds to invest in assets– hospitals, schools, roads, dams—that themselves have large future returns, then any costs of crowding out will be ...**

   a. What are the costs of crowding out?

   b. Complete this clipping.

10. **Both research groups said last week that the deficit has bottomed out and will begin to rise next year. They predicted economic growth would slow this year to 2.5 percent in real terms, from a robust 3.7 percent last year.**

    What connection, if any, is there between the predictions stated in the first and second sentences?

11. **Much more important than the size of the deficit is whether government resources are being used to ...**

    Complete this sentence.

12. **However, some important differences in the relative situations of the two countries suggest that the urgency of reducing the federal deficit right now is not as great in Canada as it is in the United States. This conclusion follows from the fact that Canada is currently much farther below its potential output than is the United States.**

    Explain the rationale behind this view.

13. **The government's deficit-reduction policies are "eerily reminiscent of the 1930s" and will only drive the economy deeper into recession and push up unemployment, says a report issued Monday by a private think tank.**

    Explain the rationale behind this opinion.

14. **The structural deficit is about $110 billion if the normal real growth of the economy is put at 3 percent, but the structural deficit is calculated at about $125 billion if this growth is 2.6 percent. A huge difference in the structural deficit results from a small change in what is considered normal growth.**

    Explain the connection between normal growth and the structural deficit, showing how a small change in the former can create a large change in the latter.

15. **Economists call the process debt monetization. Without it, rising federal deficits tend merely to shuffle spending to the government sector from the private sector.**

    a. What is the process called "debt monetization"?

    b. Without it, how would the spending merely get shuffled?

    c. Is there any disadvantage to debt monetization?

16. **High interest rates, not the deficit, are the country's major problem. It is high interest rates that have caused unemployment, which in turn has cut into government revenues and forced up spending, adding to the deficit.**

    a. How do high interest rates cause unemployment?

    b. How does unemployment add to the deficit?

    c. Evaluate the argument in this clip.

17. **One reason for raising interest rates was the prospect of a refinancing issue: a $12 billion issue matures April 1, and the government is expected to seek some new money in excess of its refinancing needs.**

    Why doesn't the government get the central bank to wait until after the refinancing before increasing interest rates in order to minimize its interest costs?

18. **The economists argued that a program focused on stimulating investment would be healthy for the economy, even if it increased the deficit in the short term, and that cutting income taxes would be exactly the wrong approach.**

    a. What healthy changes would higher investment engender?

    b. How might higher investment not increase the deficit in the long term?

    c. How does cutting income taxes differ?

## Numerical Exercises

N1. Suppose that seigniorage is $2 billion, the economy is at its long-run average level of unemployment, the publicly held national debt is $400 billion, real growth is 2 percent, and inflation is 3 percent. If the current budget deficit is $15 billion, what is the structural deficit/surplus?

N2. If "the" multiplier is 3, the marginal tax rate is 20 percent, and the money multiplier is 4, what impact will a $10 billion increase in government spending have on the government budget deficit?

N3. Suppose an economy is currently experiencing $3 billion of extra taxes and $2 billion lower unemployment insurance payments than would be the case at its long-run average rate of unemployment. There is a budget deficit of $40 billion, a publicly held national debt of $400 billion, a money supply of $600 billion, a nominal growth rate of 5 percent, and an annual seigniorage of $4 billion. What is the economy's structural deficit?

# 15    Balance of Payments

Economies in which foreign trade plays a prominent role are said to be "open." Macroeconomic analysis of such economies requires that considerable attention be paid to economic forces generated by the interaction of one economy with its major trading partners—for convenience usually referred to collectively as "the rest of the world." Individuals voluntarily engage in international trade because doing so allows them to enjoy a higher standard of living. How this comes about is explained in appendix 15.1 at the end of this chapter, where the principle of comparative advantage is discussed. The rest of this chapter, and the following three chapters, examine the macroeconomic implications of international economic interactions.

Thirty years ago, U.S. imports and exports were each only about 5 percent of GDP, so the United States was for many years considered a closed economy, the macroeconomic analysis of which could safely ignore forces arising from the international dimension. Now both imports and exports are about 11 percent of GDP, and although the United States is not nearly so strongly affected by international forces as is a small open economy such as Canada (in which imports and exports each comprise about 25 percent of GDP), U.S. worries about the value of the U.S. dollar and a persistent trade deficit are persuasive testimonies to the need to include the role of international forces in our macroeconomic analysis. The advent of the global economy, the rise of multinational corporations, and the growth of speculative trading in international currencies during the past decade underline this need. The most convincing factor from our perspective, however, is that it is currently impossible to analyze media commentary on the U.S. economy without a good understanding of the role played by international forces.

Integrating the international sector into macroeconomic analysis all at once can be overwhelming. To avoid this, our discussion of the international sector is divided into four short chapters. This chapter looks at the balance of payments, a summary measure of the foreign exchange market, which unifies analysis of the international sector of the economy.

---

**Upon completion of this chapter you should**

- view a country's balance of payments as a measure of disequilibrium in its international sector;
- know how the balance of payments, the balance of trade, the current account, and the capital account are interrelated; and
- understand the main reason for recent persistent U.S. trade deficits.

---

## 15.1   The Balance of Payments

An economy has two basic kinds of economic interactions with the rest of the world: buying/selling goods and services, and buying/selling assets, mainly financial assets. In the former category are imports and exports of physical goods, such as lumber and automobiles; imports and exports of services, such as transportation and tourism; and payments for capital services, such as interest and dividend payments. The main components of the latter category are purchases or sales of bonds and common stock, and direct investment through purchase of businesses or real estate.

Each of these activities gives rise to a situation in which either foreigners wish to obtain our dollars or we wish to obtain foreign currency. The former is viewed as a demand for our dollars on the *foreign exchange market*, and the latter is viewed as a supply of our dollars on this market (because we bring our dollars to this market to get foreign currency).

For example, exports of either goods or services creates a demand for our dollars as those buying the exports seek dollars to pay for them (or, if they pay with foreign currency, as we seek to convert that currency into our dollars). Imports, on the other hand, cause us to supply dollars to the foreign exchange market as we seek foreign currency to pay for these imports. If foreigners wish to buy our bonds, a demand for our dollar is created. If we wish to buy foreign bonds, we supply dollars to the foreign exchange market to obtain the foreign currency to pay for the bonds.

*The balance of payments is the difference between the sum of all the demands for and all the supplies of our dollar on the foreign exchange market.* Any purchases or sales of dollars on this market by a government, typically undertaken by its central bank, are not counted because they are thought to be artificial, rather than reflecting the true forces of supply and demand. If the total number of dollars supplied is equal to the total number of dollars demanded, the result is a zero balance of payments. In this case, the international sector of the economy is said to be in balance or in "equilibrium," and no economic forces for change arise from the international sector.

A *balance of payments surplus* occurs when the demand for our dollars on the foreign exchange market exceeds the supply. A *balance of payments deficit* is the opposite—a situation in which the supply of dollars exceeds its demand. Be careful here! In most supply-and-demand diagrams a surplus occurs when supply exceeds demand. If you wish, think of a balance of payments surplus as a surplus of foreign currency flowing into our country.

## 15.2  Determinants of Foreign Exchange Market Activity

Balance of payments surpluses and deficits arise from changes in the supply of and demand for our dollar on the foreign exchange market. Several variables affect supply and demand activity in this market.

1. *Exchange rate.* The price or value of our dollar in terms of foreign exchange, called the *exchange rate*, is determined in the foreign exchange market. If, for example, a dollar can buy five French francs, the exchange rate is five francs per dollar. A balance of payments surplus means that demand for our dollar on the foreign exchange market exceeds its supply, so the price of the dollar (the exchange rate) will be bid up to six francs per dollar. The dollar is now more valuable; it buys six instead of five francs. This makes imports cheaper for U.S. citizens, so imports increase—thus increasing the supply of dollars on the foreign exchange market. Similarly, our exports are more expensive to foreigners, so exports fall, decreasing the demand for dollars on the foreign exchange market. In this way, the rise in the exchange rate eliminates the balance of payments surplus. The opposite occurs when we have a balance of payments deficit: the exchange rate falls to eliminate the deficit.

2. *Income.* At a higher level of income, we import more. This increases our supply of dollars on the foreign exchange market, creating a balance of payments deficit and downward pressure on the exchange rate. Note that the result assumes that our rise in income is unique to us; it is not part of a worldwide boom. If other countries' incomes are increasing at the same time, then our exports should also increase, making uncertain the net effect on our balance of payments and exchange rate.

3. *Interest rate.* When our interest rate is higher, foreigners are more interested in buying our financial assets, so they demand more of our dollars on the foreign exchange market. This creates *capital inflows*, a balance of payments surplus and upward pressure on the exchange rate. Two caveats concerning capital inflows are important. First, the result depends on the interest rate increase not being part of a worldwide pattern. If interest rates throughout the world rise, the fact that our interest rate is higher should not entice foreigners to switch to our bonds. Second, the relevant difference in

---

**Curiosity 15.1:   Why Is There More Than One Exchange Rate?**

There are two ways of measuring the exchange rate between U.S. dollars and
French francs. Earlier, we defined it as the number of francs per dollar, five francs
per dollar. Alternatively, we could have defined it as the number of dollars per
franc, or 0.2 dollars per franc. They are equivalent ways of expressing the exchange rate; one is just the inverse of the other. Both measures appear in the
media. This book uses the former because when that measure of the exchange rate
increases—to six francs per dollar, for example—the dollar becomes more valuable. With the latter measure, however, an increase in the exchange rate corresponds to a fall in the value of the dollar.

If the exchange rate is five francs per dollar and also two marks per dollar, it
may appear that there is more than one exchange rate, but the exchange rate
between francs and marks should be two and one-half francs per mark, implying
that both measures of the value of the dollar are equivalent. Suppose this were not
the case, and the franc/mark exchange rate was three francs per mark. People
could make easy money by using 100 dollars to buy 200 marks, using the 200
marks to buy 600 francs, and then using the 600 francs to buy 120 dollars. This
"arbitrage" activity serves to make all exchange rates consistent with one another.

---

interest rates is the difference in real interest rates, not nominal interest rates.
Investors are concerned with real returns. For more on this, see chapter
18.

4. *Price level.*   A rise in our price level increases the price of our exports and
   the price of import-competing goods and services, so our exports fall and
   our imports rise. This decreases demand for our dollars and increases supply
   of our dollars, creating a balance of payments deficit and downward pressure on the exchange rate. Again, such effects occur only if there is no
   equivalent price increase in the rest of the world.

5. *Expectations.*   If foreigners expect the value of the dollar to rise, they can
   reap a capital gain by buying our bonds and then selling them again after
   the exchange rate has risen. This creates a speculative inflow of capital, a
   balance of payments surplus, and upward pressure on the exchange rate.
   Such speculative funds are currently available in large amounts and can
   be moved very quickly from one currency to another. Indeed, speculative
   activity is the primary determinant of exchange rates in the short run. Daily
   volume on the foreign exchange market is about $1 trillion, the bulk of
   which is speculative.

To summarize, several factors influence activity in the foreign exchange
market. The balance of payments summarizes this activity, telling us if the
market is in disequilibrium, in what direction and by how much, allowing us to
predict economic forces for change (see chapter 16).

**Table 15.1**   Balance of payments, 1994 ($ billions)

|  | Demand for $US | Supply of $US | Balance |
|---|---|---|---|
| **Current account** |  |  |  |
| Merchandise exports | 576 |  |  |
| Merchandise imports |  | −749 |  |
| Trade balance |  |  | (−173) |
| Service exports | 214 |  |  |
| Service imports |  | −145 |  |
| Investment receipts | 208 |  |  |
| Investment payments |  | −216 |  |
| Net transfer payments |  | −35 |  |
| Current account balance |  |  | −147 |
| **Capital account** |  |  |  |
| Capital inflows | 315 |  |  |
| Capital outflows |  | −298 |  |
| Statistical discrepancy | 31 |  |  |
| Capital account balance |  |  | 48 |
| Current account plus capital account (balance of payments) |  |  | −99 |
| **Official settlements balance** (negative of the balance of payments) |  |  | 99 |

Source: *Federal Reserve Bulletin*, August 1996.

## 15.3   The International Economic Accounts

Knowledge of the balance of payments is all that is needed for analysis of the economic forces that are automatically set in motion whenever there is a disequilibrium in the international sector of the economy. Often, however, analysts are more interested in the source of any disequilibrium in the international sector—that is, the relative contributions to an equilibrium position of the various components of the demand for and supply of dollars on the foreign exchange market. Consequently, the balance of payments is broken down into several subsidiary measures, which together are referred to as the *international accounts* or the balance of payments accounts.

At the most general level, the balance of payments is broken into two accounts, the current and capital accounts, as shown in table 15.1.

The *current account* measures the difference between the demand for and the supply of dollars arising from transactions that affect the current level of income here and abroad—including exports, imports, investment income payments (e.g., interest and dividend payments), and transfers (e.g., gifts and foreign aid). Within the current account, the difference between exports and imports of goods is called the *balance of merchandise trade* or simply the *balance of trade*.

The *capital account* measures the difference between the demand for and the supply of dollars arising from sales or purchases of assets to or from foreigners. The capital account measures *capital flows* between a country and the rest of the world. A capital account surplus measures a net capital inflow, and a capital account deficit measures a net capital outflow.

When added together, the current and capital accounts produce the balance of payments. In an accounting sense, because the demand for and supply of dollars on the foreign exchange market must balance, a nonzero balance of payments must be matched by changes in government holdings of foreign exchange reserves. In table 15.1 there is a $99 billion balance of payments deficit—that is, an excess supply of $99 billion on the foreign exchange market. This will be matched by a $99 billion excess demand for dollars by the central bank on the foreign exchange market. The central bank should pay out $99 billion in foreign exchange reserves to satisfy the excess demand for dollars, in the process accumulating $99 billion domestic dollars and losing $99 billion worth of foreign exchange reserves. The *official settlements account* measures the accumulation of domestic dollars in the foreign exchange reserve account of the Fed and the change in dollar holdings held by foreign central banks in the United States. Central banks' demands for dollars are not included in the balance of payments because they do not represent free market forces. The economist's concept of the balance of payments can be measured by the negative of the official settlements balance.

## 15.4   The Twin Deficits

An interesting aspect of the balance of payments accounts is that it is quite possible to have an economy in international equilibrium while simultaneously its subsidiary accounts are unbalanced, as long as they offset each other. The U.S. economy, for example, has for several years now had a current account deficit, offset by a surplus in its capital account.

How might this come about? A prominent explanation is that this situation is a side effect of large government budget deficits—hence, termed the *twin deficit problem*. A large government deficit increases the interest rate as the government sells bonds to finance its deficit. The rise in the interest rate makes U.S. bonds look very attractive to overseas investors, so capital flows into the United States, creating a balance of payments surplus. Under our flexible exchange rate system the surplus bids up the value of the dollar, which in turn decreases exports and increases imports, creating a balance of trade deficit.

Students with good memories might recall from chapter 6 that foreign financing can be used to supplement national saving. That is exactly what is happening here.

---

**Curiosity 15.2:   How Do We Know the Statistical Discrepancy?**

In table 15.1, the statistical discrepancy entry seems large. This is, in fact, quite common because the government is unable to monitor closely the movement of dollars across its borders. Cross-border shopping, for example, is not tracked accurately, and illegal cross-border activities can be of significant magnitude.

An interesting question here is how the international accounts statistician could possibly provide a measure of this statistical discrepancy. It is possible because *the final figure for the balance of payments is known.* The final figure is accurately measured by the net amount of buying or selling of foreign currency by the Fed, plus changes in foreign central bank dollar holdings in the United States. Thus, in order to measure the statistical discrepancy all that need be done is to subtract the sum of the current and capital accounts from total official transactions.

An unresolvable problem is that it cannot be known how much of the statistical discrepancy belongs to the current account and how much to the capital account. By tradition, it is included in the capital account on the belief that most hidden transactions take the form of capital flows.

---

## Media Illustrations

### Example 1
**Looking at the data, some people might say the balance of payments has "improved" radically, from a $7 billion current account deficit three years ago to surpluses of $4 billion and $2 billion in the last two years. It is this ongoing current account surplus that led the optimists to predict that the dollar should appreciate.**

*What is the logic behind predicting that the dollar should appreciate?*
The logic is that the improvement in the current account causes a balance of payments surplus (an excess demand for the dollar on the foreign exchange market), which under a flexible exchange rate system should lead to a rise in the value of the dollar.

*What problem is there with this logic?*
It is careless to identify a change in any subsidiary account of the balance of payments with a change in the balance of payments itself. It could be, for example, that there has been a fall in the capital account, offsetting the impact on the balance of payments of the improvement in the current account.

### Example 2
**The link between the current and capital accounts is often misunderstood. Leaving aside the relatively small influence of central bank intervention in foreign exchange markets, any deficit or surplus on capital account must be matched by an equal and opposite surplus or deficit on current account. It follows that, as long as the United States is to be a capital importer, it must have ...**

*To what does the "central bank intervention" refer?*
It refers to net purchases or sales of foreign currency by the central bank.

*What is the implication for the balance of payments of this central bank intervention being very small?*
The implication is that the balance of payments is essentially zero. The magnitude of the balance of payments is measured by the net government sales or purchases of foreign currency.

*Why* must *any deficit or surplus on the capital account be matched by an equal and opposite surplus or deficit on the current account?*
If the balance of payments is zero, then the sum of the current and capital accounts, which yields the balance of payments, must be zero.

*How would you complete the final sentence?*
... a current account deficit.

**Example 3**
**Although some economists in the United States put the trade deficit down to failing U.S. competitiveness or protectionist policies abroad, others claim that its genesis lies in the budget deficit and in the consequent shortfall in U.S. domestic savings relative to investment.**

*How would failing competitiveness or protectionist policies abroad lead to a trade deficit?*
Failing competitiveness means that foreign competitors are underpricing U.S. businesses both abroad and at home, decreasing U.S. exports and increasing U.S. imports, both of which create a trade deficit. Protectionist policies abroad are foreign tariffs or quotas that inhibit or prevent U.S. exports, creating a trade deficit.

*How would a budget deficit lead to a shortfall in domestic savings relative to investment?*
To finance the deficit, the government would sell bonds, diverting domestic savings from financing private investment.

*How could the budget deficit be responsible for the trade deficit?*
The budget deficit causes the interest rate to rise, making U.S. bonds attractive to foreign investors. To get U.S. dollars to buy U.S. bonds, foreigners bid up the value of the U.S. dollar. This causes U.S. exports to become more expensive to foreigners and imports to become cheaper to U.S. buyers, which in turn causes exports to fall and imports to rise, thus creating the trade deficit.

*What connection is there between this example and the preceding example?*
In this example, the budget deficit induces capital inflows, creating a surplus on the capital account, which must be offset by a deficit on the current account. This reflects the result illustrated in the preceding example, which demonstrated that a deficit or surplus on the capital account *must* be matched by an equal and opposite surplus or deficit on the current account.

*What conclusion can be drawn about U.S. competitiveness?*
The existence of the trade deficit in this context does not point to unproductive U.S. business. All it says is that the exchange rate is too high to allow U.S. business to sell abroad at historical levels.

## Chapter Summary

- The *balance of payments* is the difference between the demand for and supply of dollars on the foreign exchange market, so it measures disequilibrium in the international sector of the economy. Demand for dollars on the foreign exchange market arises from demand by foreigners for our exports or for our assets, particularly financial assets. Supply arises from our demand for imports or foreign assets.

- The *exchange rate* measures the price of our dollar in terms of foreign currency, determined by the forces of supply and demand in the *foreign exchange market*. The major variables influencing supply and demand in this market are income, the interest rate, the price level, and expectations of the future exchange rate.

- The balance of payments account is broken into two halves, the *current account* measuring transactions affecting our current income, and the *capital account* measuring purchases and sales of assets. The *balance of trade* is the component of the current account that measures the difference between exports and imports of goods.

- A popular explanation for the twin deficits is that the government budget deficit is responsible for the trade deficit. To finance a government deficit, the interest rate must rise. This creates capital inflows, bidding up the value of the dollar, which discourages exports and encourages imports, thus producing the trade deficit.

## Media Exercises

1.  **A strong dollar is a mixed blessing. It _____ the price of imports, thus _____ inflation, and it makes trips to foreign countries _____ for travelers from the United States. But it makes U.S. exports _____ .**

    Fill in the blanks.

2.  **According to the trade report, the U.S. trade surplus with western Europe more than quadrupled in 1991 to $16.13 billion from $4 billion in 1990. This partly reflected strong demand in Europe, combined with a _____ in the value of the dollar.**

    Fill in the blank.

3. **Analysts have warned for months that the trade gap would widen once consumer demand picks up.**

   Explain why this would happen. Will the trade gap become a bigger surplus or a bigger deficit?

4. **One by-product of the ballooning federal deficits of the early 1980s was a large rise in _____ and a concomitant loss of U.S. competitiveness on world markets. The resulting increase in the U.S. _____ was the counterpart of the _____ that kept domestic investment from falling as much as did national saving.**

   Fill in the blanks.

5. **Through the mid-1980s the policies followed by the Reagan administration, particularly tight monetary policy combined with large government deficits, made the value of the dollar very high.**

   How would these policies increase the value of the dollar?

6. **An overvalued dollar would be just another blow to an already fragile economy.**

   Explain how an overvalued dollar would be a blow to the economy.

7. **The rise of the dollar could batter the profits of some U.S. companies this year and slice into capital spending.**

   a. Which companies may have their profits battered, and why?

   b. Why would this slice into capital spending?

8. **Now it's the once-mighty German mark's turn to come under attack. Following Thursday's cuts in the Bundesbank's trend-setting interest rates, the mark slipped further against the pound and the U.S. dollar.**

   Explain why the mark is falling here.

9. **Normally, a weak trade figure would send the dollar into a tailspin, but market players could be judging that signs indicate a still-strong U.S. economy, implying continued upward pressure on interest rates. Currency traders may be working on the expectation that the Fed is going to have to push up short-term rates to choke off some domestic demand.**

   a. Why would a weak trade figure normally send the dollar into a tailspin?

   b. Explain why a strong economy suggests high interest rates.

   c. Why would the tailspin be avoided here?

10. **Historically, the winners on the foreign exchange market are the big banks. Citicorp, for example, typically earns about $600 million a year from its**

currency trading operation. The losers? Central banks, for one. Recently, the Bank of England bought pounds to _____, but the pound kept _____ and huge losses developed. Many small speculators are also losers. Of the 1,287 seats on the Chicago Mercantile's International Monetary Mart, about 25 percent change hands every year, most because unsustainable losses have been incurred.

a. Fill in the blanks.

b. What would a bank like Citicorp do to make money at the expense of the Bank of England in the scenario described in this clipping?

11. **The survey found that 28 percent of U.S. dollar trading in North America is in the mark, 23 percent in the yen, 13 percent in the British pound, and 9 percent in the Swiss franc. Rounding out the list of major trading currencies at 3 percent to 7 percent each are the Canadian and Australian dollars and the French franc.**

The U.S. trades more with Canada than with any other country. Why is the Canadian dollar so low in this survey?

12. **The statistical evidence is that there is a strong correlation between increases in current account surpluses and decreases in the value of the dollar. This is just the opposite of the conventional wisdom.**

a. What is the conventional wisdom and what logic lies behind it?

b. How can this statistical evidence be explained?

13. **With our unemployment rate so close to the natural rate, there is no room for interest rate cuts, but if unemployment should start to rise, Alan Blinder, vice chairman of the Federal Reserve Board, may want to make an early cut in rates. If he succeeds, bond yields and the dollar could both be in for a mauling.**

Why would the dollar fall in this circumstance? Would this be desirable?

14. **The large and persistent trade deficit has provoked concern among the general public and in the financial markets. The deficit resulted from the high-dollar policies of the Reagan administration in the early 1980s.**

What is a high-dollar policy, how does it work, and how would it create a trade deficit?

15. **The reports suggest that the United States is heading for a recession. Activity on the futures market for the U.S. dollar suggests that the market thinks the dollar will soon depreciate.**

What logic lies behind the market's thinking?

16. **In many Canadian export sectors the devaluation of the Canadian dollar will not greatly aid sales. Progress will be slow because any U.S. slowdown will overshadow the price effects of the devalued dollar.**

    a. How would the devaluation of the Canadian dollar normally aid Canadian sales?

    b. What is meant by the U.S. slowdown overshadowing the price effects of the devalued Canadian dollar?

17. **"The stronger yen is the best single thing that could have happened to the trade deficit," a senior administration official said last week.**

    Explain the logic behind this statement.

18. **A major negative influence on the U.S. economy has been the strong dollar. Its strength causes excessive imports. The excess of imports over exports—more than $120 billion (U.S.) a year—must be subtracted when calculating GDP.**

    a. How might a strong dollar be a negative influence on the economy?

    b. GDP measures the amount produced domestically. Imports are produced by foreigners and so should be irrelevant for measuring GDP. Explain why this clipping suggests that they be subtracted when calculating GDP.

19. **The U.S. trade deficit is not permanent. When the U.S. ceases to be a major importer of capital, ...**

    Complete this argument, explaining why the U.S. trade deficit will disappear.

20. **The April U.S. trade deficit narrowed by 41 percent from March. Investors greeted the news with gusto, in minutes driving bonds more than a point higher. It was a classic suckers' rally. Traders soon realized that the trade improvement was because of a 23 percent climb in exports. Fears of surging demand in an environment of near-full employment and capacity constraints were rekindled. Prices turned on a dime and wound up nearly two points off their highs by the end of the day.**

    a. Explain why the narrowing of the trade deficit would cause the price of bonds to rise.

    b. Explain in your own words why prices then fell, as reported in the second half of the clipping.

21. **Everyone loves the U.S. dollar these days, and the fall in the current account deficit just added to its popularity.**

    Why would a fall in the current account deficit make the dollar more popular?

22. **The degree of openness of the economy is sometimes measured by imports or exports expressed as a fraction of GDP. By this measure, Singapore probably wins the prize because both exports and imports are about 150 percent of GDP.**

How can imports or exports be more than 100 percent of GDP? (Hint: Imports can be inputs to the production of goods.)

23. **The report concludes that the recent strength in U.S. investment has been financed by domestic investors redirecting funds from foreign capital markets to U.S. capital markets. Thus, increased demand for U.S. dollars isn't the reason for the strength of the U.S. dollar, but rather a decreased U.S. demand for foreign currencies.**

What could have caused U.S. investors to redirect their funds?

24. **If domestic savings increases and domestic investment decreases, it is possible that a budget deficit may not lead to a deficit on current account.**

Is this so? Explain your reasoning.

## Numerical Exercises

N1. Suppose a U.S. Toyota dealer imports one hundred cars worth $10,000 each, and the Japanese manufacturer buys a U.S. bond with the $1 million proceeds. What happens to the U.S. balance of trade? The current account? The balance of payments?

N2. If the exchange rate is 4 francs per dollar and 1.5 marks per dollar, what should be the exchange rate between francs and marks?

N3. Suppose the central bank has intervened in the foreign exchange market to fix the exchange rate by selling $4 billion. If the current account deficit is $10 billion, what is the capital account balance?

## Appendix 15.1:   The Principle of Comparative Advantage

Economists believe that countries are better off specializing at what they do best: trading, rather than forbidding trade and trying to meet all their needs through domestic production. Some examples make this obvious. It would, for example, be very expensive for the United States to grow its own supply of bananas. It is much cheaper to grow extra wheat and trade it for bananas.

This banana example is easy to understand because banana-producing countries such as Ecuador are much more efficient at producing bananas than is the

United States, and the U.S. is much more efficient at producing wheat than Ecuador is. In such a case, specializing and trading is obviously to the advantage of both countries. What if, however, the United States were more productive than Ecuador in the production of both bananas and wheat? Suppose, for example, that the United States is six times as productive as Ecuador in producing wheat and twice as productive as Ecuador in producing bananas. The United States has an absolute advantage in the production of both wheat and bananas, but in relative terms, its *comparative* advantage lies in the production of wheat because its advantage is sixfold for wheat but only twofold for bananas. Similarly, Ecuador's comparative advantage is in bananas.

Now look at this situation from Ecuador's point of view. Ecuador is less productive than the United States in the production of both goods, and so is said to be at an absolute disadvantage in growing both wheat and bananas. Because Ecuador is one-sixth as productive as the United States in growing wheat, but only one-half as productive in growing bananas, it is said to have a comparative advantage in the production of bananas—when compared to the United States it is more productive in growing bananas than in growing wheat.

It turns out that under very general conditions both countries are better off if they specialize in production and then trade. In this example, the United States should specialize in wheat because it has a comparative advantage in its production, and Ecuador should specialize in bananas, the commodity in which it has a comparative advantage in production.

This result is referred to as the *principle of comparative advantage*: total output is maximized if countries specialize in the production of commodities in which they have a comparative advantage. A classic example used to illustrate this phenomenon is the case of a lawyer who can earn $100 per hour lawyering and $20 per hour typing, whereas her secretary's skills are such that he can earn only $5 per hour either lawyering or typing. Should the lawyer do her own typing? She would be foolish to do so. By doing her own typing, she would be foregoing lucrative lawyering. More work in total would be accomplished if the lawyer specialized in lawyering and the secretary specialized in typing, despite the lawyer being more productive at both.

A similar story explains why the United States is better off specializing in wheat and trading for bananas with Ecuador. Using the numbers given earlier, suppose that the United States foregoes 60 tons of wheat to produce 20 tons of bananas and that, using the same resources, Ecuador produces either 10 tons of wheat or 10 tons of bananas. Suppose both want equal amounts of each commodity. Without trade, Ecuador would enjoy 5 tons of wheat and 5 tons of bananas, whereas the U.S. would enjoy 15 tons of each. Now let us see what could happen if Ecuador specialized in bananas and traded. By producing 10 tons of bananas and trading 5 tons to the United States for 5 tons of wheat, Ecuador ends up even, but the United States can now devote 5 tons of banana production to wheat production, yielding an extra 15 tons of wheat, 5 tons of which is traded to Ecuador for 5 tons of bananas, leaving a bonus of 10 tons of wheat. It is this bonus that the law of comparative advantage is all about.

How is the bonus divided between the two countries? In the explanation above, Ecuador ends up even, so it has no motivation to specialize, unless the United States gives Ecuador some of the bonus. The U.S. will clearly be willing to share the bonus because if it doesn't, the bonus will never appear. To get a share of the bonus, Ecuador will demand a higher price for its bananas. The forces of supply and demand for bananas versus wheat will determine the relative price of bananas and wheat, in turn determining the share of the bonus going to each country. The relative price is called the *terms of trade*. For the macroeconomy, it is measured as the ratio of export prices to import prices.

# 16     Policy in an Open Economy

Balance of payments surpluses and deficits mean that the international sector of our economy is in disequilibrium. The importance of the balance of payments is that it measures imbalance in our international sector, thereby pointing to economic forces for change. One purpose of this chapter is to identify these forces and how they bring about change.

Monetary and fiscal policies are shocks to the economy that affect many economic variables, such as income, interest rates, and prices. Changes in these variables create imbalances in the international sector, which in turn set in motion forces that modify the impact of certain policies on the economy. A second purpose of this chapter is to examine how our earlier discussions of monetary and fiscal policies must be adjusted to recognize the influence of forces generated through the international sector of the economy. The recent increase in the openness of the U.S. economy requires that its macroeconomic analysis pay more attention to these forces.

> **Upon completion of this chapter you should**
>
> - be able to explain how a nonzero balance of payments affects the economy when the exchange rate is (*a*) flexible and (*b*) fixed;
> - understand how international forces affect the strength of monetary and fiscal policy, including the dramatic result that monetary policy is completely ineffective under fixed exchange rates; and
> - know how the government can influence the foreign exchange market and thus the exchange rate.

## 16.1   International Imbalance with a Flexible Exchange Rate

Exactly what forces for change are engendered by an imbalance in the balance of payments? This is a crucial question, the answer to which depends on whether the economy is operating on a flexible or a fixed exchange rate system. Let us first examine a flexible exchange rate system.

Under a flexible exchange rate system, the government allows the forces of supply and demand to determine the exchange rate. If there is a balance of payments surplus, demand for our dollar on the foreign exchange market exceeds its supply, so market forces create a rise in the value of our dollar. Those who want the extra, unavailable dollars try to obtain them by offering extra foreign currency for them, so our dollar becomes more valuable in terms of foreign currency. This *appreciation* of our dollar is often described by the statement, "The exchange rate has risen."

The process operates in reverse if there is a balance of payments deficit. In this case, the demand for our dollar on the foreign exchange market is less than its supply, so market forces cause a fall in its value. The *depreciation* of our dollar is often described by the statement, "The exchange rate has fallen."

Note that under a flexible exchange rate system, any tendency towards a balance of payments surplus or deficit is automatically and instantaneously eliminated by a flexing of the exchange rate, so that our measure of the imbalance (the balance of payments) is always zero. The balance of payments measure is nonzero only when the government engages in some net buying or selling of foreign currency. In the context of a flexible exchange rate, the terminology "balance of payments surplus or deficit" must be interpreted as reflecting a surplus or deficit that would appear if the exchange rate were not permitted to adjust instantaneously.

Under a flexible exchange rate, therefore, the initial reaction of the economy to an imbalance in the balance of payments is a change in the exchange rate, which in turn creates additional forces for change in the economy. If, with other

---

**Curiosity 16.1:   What Is the Effective Exchange Rate?**

Looking at the value of the U.S. dollar in terms of any other single currency can
be misleading. It is possible, for example, for the value of the U.S. dollar to rise
relative to one currency but at the same time fall relative to another currency. The
impact on the balance of payments is not clear. It would depend on how much
trade was conducted with each of these countries. A better measure of the U.S.
dollar exchange rate is the *trade-weighted* or *effective* exchange rate—an index
calculated as a weighted average of U.S. dollar exchange rates with all other
countries, where the weights reflect the proportion of total U.S. trade done with
each of these countries.

---

variables constant, the exchange rate rises, demand for our exports falls because
foreigners find our exports more expensive in terms of their currency. Furthermore, imports become cheaper to us (because our dollar now buys more foreign
exchange), so there is a fall in demand for domestically produced goods and
services that compete with imports. Both phenomena imply that aggregate
demand for domestically produced goods and services falls.

Similarly, if the exchange rate falls, demand for exports and import-competing goods and services should be stimulated, implying a rise in demand for
domestically produced goods and services.

To summarize, *if the economy has a flexible exchange rate, an imbalance in
the international sector of the economy, measured by the balance of payments,
automatically causes the exchange rate to change*, which in turn causes the
import-competing and export sectors of the economy to adjust, thus affecting
aggregate demand for goods and services.

## 16.2   International Imbalance with a Fixed Exchange Rate

Under a fixed exchange rate system, the government does not allow the forces
of supply and demand to determine the exchange rate. Instead, the government
fixes the exchange rate at what it believes is the "right" rate, and the central
bank, armed with a stockpile of *foreign exchange reserves*, stands ready to buy
or sell foreign currency at that rate. If there is a balance of payments surplus,
the demand for our dollar by foreigners is greater than the supply, so some of
these foreigners will seek extra, unavailable dollars. Under a flexible exchange
rate, they would have to get dollars by offering more foreign exchange, but
under a fixed exchange rate this higher cost can be avoided because the Fed will
exchange their foreign currency for dollars at the fixed rate. When the Fed does
so, it takes the extra foreign exchange (currency) and in return provides dollars.
The most important implication of this is that *the domestic money supply
increases* by the increase in dollars times the money multiplier. The increase in

the money supply in turn affects economic activity as described in chapters 8, 9, and 10.

When there is a balance of payments deficit, the opposite occurs. We are supplying more dollars on the foreign exchange market (seeking foreign currency to take vacations abroad, for example) than there is foreign demand for dollars, so those of us unable to obtain foreign currency from foreigners go to the Fed to buy foreign exchange at the fixed rate. To buy the foreign currency we give the Fed dollars, removing them from public circulation and thereby decreasing the domestic money supply.

To summarize, *if the economy has a fixed exchange rate, an imbalance in the international sector of the economy, measured by the balance of payments, automatically causes the money supply to change*, which in turn affects economic activity.

Armed with these two general results—that international imbalance causes exchange rate changes under a flexible exchange rate system and money-supply changes under a fixed exchange rate system—we can examine how monetary and fiscal policy are affected by repercussions from the international sector. To maintain simplicity, all analysis ignores price-level changes and inflation. Incorporating them would not change the general results, only the breakdown of nominal income changes into real changes and price changes.

## 16.3   Fiscal Policy under Flexible Exchange Rates

An increase in government spending leads to an increase in income and an accompanying increase in the interest rate, causing some crowding out. The increase in income increases imports, creating a balance of payments deficit, but the increase in the interest rate causes capital inflows, creating a balance of payments surplus. Which will dominate? The consensus among economists on this empirical question is that the latter will outweigh the former. Because of the high mobility of international capital, a slight increase in our interest rate causes a substantial capital inflow, outweighing the impact on the balance of payments of the accompanying rise in imports.

Once this empirical question is settled, it is easy to see how international forces modify the impact of fiscal policy. Under a flexible exchange rate system, the balance of payments surplus created by a stimulating dose of fiscal policy causes the exchange rate to appreciate. This decreases exports—directly decreasing demand for domestically produced goods and services. It also increases imports, which decreases demand for domestically produced goods and services that compete against imports. The decrease in aggregate demand for domestically produced goods and services partially offsets the impact on the economy of the stimulating dose of fiscal policy, decreasing the strength of fiscal policy in affecting the income level. All this is summarized in figure 16.1, where the

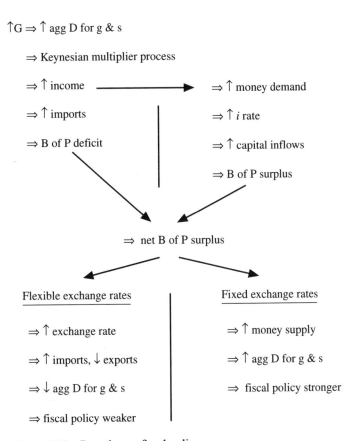

↑G ⇒ ↑ agg D for g & s

⇒ Keynesian multiplier process

⇒ ↑ income  ⟶  ⇒ ↑ money demand

⇒ ↑ imports  ⇒ ↑ *i* rate

⇒ B of P deficit  ⇒ ↑ capital inflows

⇒ B of P surplus

⇒ net B of P surplus

Flexible exchange rates  Fixed exchange rates

⇒ ↑ exchange rate  ⇒ ↑ money supply

⇒ ↑ imports, ↓ exports  ⇒ ↑ agg D for g & s

⇒ ↓ agg D for g & s  ⇒ fiscal policy stronger

⇒ fiscal policy weaker

**Figure 16.1**  Reaction to fiscal policy
This flowchart shows the economy's reaction to an increase in government spending under both flexible and fixed exchange rate systems.

terminology—such as B of P stands for balance of payments and agg D for g & s stands for aggregate demand for domestically produced goods and services—should be obvious.

## 16.4  Fiscal Policy under Fixed Exchange Rates

When the exchange rate is fixed, the balance of payments surplus created by a stimulating dose of fiscal policy does not cause the exchange rate to rise. Instead, it causes an increase in the money supply as the Fed buys foreign currency (the balance of payments surplus) with dollars. The increase in the money supply augments the stimulating effect of the policy dose, making fiscal policy stronger in affecting the income level. This too is shown in figure 16.1.

## 16.5   Monetary Policy under Flexible Exchange Rates

An increase in the money supply lowers the interest rate, which stimulates aggregate demand and moves the economy to a higher level of income. The rise in income increases imports, creating a balance of payments deficit, and the fall in the interest rate reduces capital inflows, thus augmenting the balance of payments deficit.

Under a flexible exchange rate system, the balance of payments deficit causes the exchange rate to depreciate. This increases exports—directly increasing demand for domestically produced goods and services. It also decreases imports—increasing demand for domestically produced goods and services that compete against imports. The rise in aggregate demand for domestically produced goods and services augments the impact on the economy of the stimulating dose of monetary policy, thus giving greater strength to monetary policy in affecting the income level. This is shown in figure 16.2.

## 16.6   Monetary Policy under Fixed Exchange Rates

When the exchange rate is fixed, the balance of payments deficit created by a stimulating dose of monetary policy does not cause the exchange rate to fall. Instead, it causes a decrease in the money supply as the Fed buys dollars with foreign exchange to prevent the balance of payments deficit from lowering the exchange rate. The decrease in the money supply diminishes the stimulating effect of the policy dose, making monetary policy weaker in affecting the income level. This also is shown in figure 16.2.

There is more to this story, however. An increase in the money supply created the balance of payments deficit, and an automatic decrease in the money supply is used to decrease the deficit. Consequently, only when the original money-supply increase has been completely wiped out will the deficit be eliminated. The economy will regain equilibrium back where it started, so the end result of this monetary policy is no change. This process reflects an extremely important general result: *under a fixed exchange rate, monetary policy is completely ineffective as a policy tool.* Monetary policy is being implicitly used to fix the exchange rate, so it is not available for other purposes.

## 16.7   Sterilization Policy

Monetary policy in the context of a fixed exchange rate is ineffective because an expansionary monetary policy creates a balance of payments deficit, which automatically decreases the money supply, which offsets and eventually eliminates the original increase in the money supply. What if, however, the monetary

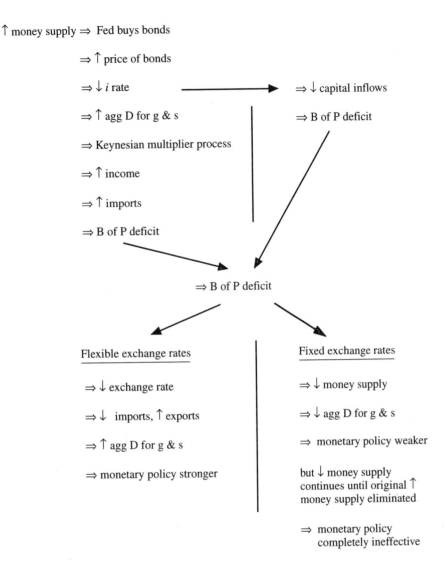

↑ money supply ⇒ Fed buys bonds

⇒ ↑ price of bonds

⇒ ↓ *i* rate                                        ⇒ ↓ capital inflows

⇒ ↑ agg D for g & s                          ⇒ B of P deficit

⇒ Keynesian multiplier process

⇒ ↑ income

⇒ ↑ imports

⇒ B of P deficit

⇒ B of P deficit

Flexible exchange rates                              Fixed exchange rates

⇒ ↓ exchange rate                              ⇒ ↓ money supply

⇒ ↓ imports, ↑ exports                        ⇒ ↓ agg D for g & s

⇒ ↑ agg D for g & s                            ⇒ monetary policy weaker

⇒ monetary policy stronger                    but ↓ money supply
                                               continues until original ↑
                                               money supply eliminated

                                               ⇒ monetary policy
                                                 completely ineffective

**Figure 16.2**   Reaction to monetary policy
This flowchart shows the economy's reaction to an increase in the money supply under
both flexible and fixed exchange rate systems.

**Curiosity 16.2:   What Is the J Curve?**

Demand is always less sensitive to price changes in the short run as compared to the long run, when there is sufficient time for people to acquire information, change habits, and renegotiate contracts. Consequently, when the exchange rate falls, although imports are more expensive and exports less expensive, in the short run (six months to a year) the volume of imports and exports won't change much. If the volume of imports doesn't change much, but they are more expensive, the value of imports increases. If the volume of exports doesn't change much, but they are less expensive, the value of exports falls. This pushes the economy to a balance of trade deficit, not the surplus we had claimed. In the short run, instead of improving the balance of payments, a devaluation worsens it.

Fortunately, in the long run volumes do change by enough to improve the balance of trade. A graph of the balance of trade over time would show an initial fall towards a deficit, but eventually a rise towards a surplus. This traces out a path that looks like the letter J and is accordingly called the *J curve*. The changes revealed in the J curve are very frustrating for policymakers because the economy initially goes in the wrong direction, creating great uncertainty.

authorities take monetary action to counteract the automatic change in the money supply, allowing the original monetary dose to be maintained? As the money supply decreases automatically in the example above, the monetary authorities could annually increase the money supply by exactly the same amount.

This policy is called a *sterilization* policy because it "sterilizes" the automatic money-supply change that results from an imbalance in international payments under fixed exchange rates. Pursuing this policy maintains the original monetary policy dose and allows monetary policy to retain its effectiveness.

Unfortunately, there is a catch: the sterililzation policy maintains the imbalance in international payments. In the example above, the balance of payments deficit, which would normally disappear as it automatically decreased the money supply, now persists as this automatic mechanism is "sterilized." What are the implications of a persistent balance of payments deficit, though?

Consider how the government, through its agent the central bank, deals with the balance of payments deficit. The deficit means that the supply of dollars on the foreign exchange market exceeds the demand, so those unable to obtain foreign currency for their dollars go to the government to exchange them at the fixed rate. The government sells foreign currency to them at the fixed rate, as it has promised to do, and in return obtains domestic dollars, which normally would thereby be removed from public circulation, thus decreasing the money supply. (Under a policy of sterilization, of course, the central bank arranges to have these dollars put back into circulation.) The key point here is that during this process the government is selling off its holdings of foreign exchange. As long as the balance of payments deficit continues, the government's stock of foreign exchange—its foreign exchange reserves—steadily falls.

The major problem with sterilization policy should now be evident. By maintaining the balance of payments deficit, the sterilization policy causes the government's foreign exchange reserves to run low, threatening its ability to continue this policy and, worse, alerting foreign exchange speculators that the dollar may soon have to be allowed to fall. The resulting foreign exchange crisis usually produces a devaluation (a substantive fall in the fixed exchange rate value), creating embarrassment for the government and profits for speculators. If a balance of payments surplus is being maintained by a sterilization policy, however, opposite results are obtained. Foreign exchange reserves cumulate to embarrassingly high levels, ultimately creating an upward revaluation of the currency and, once again, profits for speculators.

## 16.8   Government Influence on the Exchange Rate

It is rare to find an exchange rate system that is fully flexible. Usually, government intervenes in the operation of the foreign exchange market to "modify" the natural forces of supply and demand. Sometimes this is done to prop up an exchange rate for reasons of prestige, and at other times it is done to push down the exchange rate in order to produce jobs through stimulation of demand for exports and import-competing goods and services. Neither of these interventions can be viewed with favor because they attempt to set the exchange rate at an unnatural level. A more convincing rationale for government interference in this market is that without such interference the exchange rate may be volatile, so volatile that it is disruptive to international business activity. Government action designed to cushion temporary shocks to the exchange rate, rather than to influence its long-run level, is thought to be a legitimate policy.

The government employs two main mechanisms to influence the exchange rate. First, it can intervene directly in the foreign exchange market, buying or selling dollars. This intervention is viable as long as the government's stock of foreign exchange reserves is not threatened, as it would be, for example, if it tried to keep the exchange rate above its long-run level through continual purchases of dollars with its foreign exchange reserves. Second, government can influence the exchange rate by using monetary policy to change the real interest rate, which in turn affects capital inflows/outflows and, ultimately, the exchange rate. Most governments, through their central banks, adopt a combination of these two policies.

## Media Illustrations

### *Example 1*
**Then there's the state of the dollar, which has been bleeding steadily despite transfusions from borrowings and foreign reserves. Will the higher interest rates stop the hemorrhage?**

*What does "bleeding steadily" mean in this context?*
It means that the value of the dollar has been falling.

*What does "transfusions from borrowings" mean, and how do borrowings tend to stop the bleeding?*
The borrowings are bond sales to foreigners. Such sales mean either that foreigners buy dollars to buy the bonds or that we convert the foreign currency proceeds of these sales into dollars, both of which increase the demand for dollars on the foreign exchange market, putting upward pressure on the dollar.

*What does "transfusions from foreign reserves" mean, and how do foreign reserves tend to stop the bleeding?*
The government uses some of its foreign exchange reserves to buy dollars on the foreign exchange market. This extra demand for the dollar puts upward pressure on its price.

*What will happen if the "transfusions from foreign reserves" method is employed over a long period of time?*
The government will run out of foreign reserves, a currency crisis will develop, and the dollar will be devalued.

*What logic lies behind the idea that higher interest rates might "stop the hemorrhage"?*
The higher interest rates should induce capital inflows, thus increasing the demand for U.S. dollars and putting upward pressure on its price.

### Example 2
**Current monetary policy appears to be conducted as if we were on a fixed exchange rate. Policy is effectively geared to maintaining the exchange rate at the expense of a domestic recovery.**

*How would monetary policy be conducted if we were on a fixed exchange rate?*
Any change in the exchange rate would call forth a change in the money supply to push the exchange rate back to its original level. For example, suppose a balance of payments surplus develops, causing the exchange rate to rise. To offset this, the monetary authorities could increase the money supply, thus decreasing the interest rate, reducing capital inflows, and eliminating the balance of payments surplus. Note that this explanation is in essence just another way of telling our earlier story, in which the increase in the money supply happens automatically.

*How can policy be conducted at the expense of a domestic recovery?*
A domestic recovery involves an increase in income, which increases imports and creates a balance of payments deficit, putting downward pressure on the dollar. To prevent any change in the exchange rate, the monetary authorities would decrease the money supply, increasing interest rates to attract capital inflows which would eliminate the balance of payments deficit. This policy action dampens the domestic recovery in two ways. First, it prevents a fall in the exchange rate, which would stimulate the economy by increasing exports

and the demand for import-competing goods and services. And second, it involves a contractionary monetary policy, which works against any stimulus to recovery that the economy is experiencing.

### Example 3

**The government may be tempted to increase official currency reserves in order to reduce the pressure on the dollar and the consequent threat to manufacturing industries, but such a move would be difficult. It would need to borrow large sums on the market because its cash balances are not strong, especially considering its large cash requirements for the coming year.**

*What kind of pressure is the dollar under, and why would such pressure be a threat to manufacturing industries?*
The dollar is experiencing upward pressure. An increase in the value of the dollar makes it more difficult for manufacturing industries to sell abroad and to compete against imports in its domestic market. This difficulty may be overcome to some extent by reductions in the cost of imported inputs.

*How would increasing official currency reserves reduce the pressure on the dollar?*
To increase official currency reserves, the government would have to buy foreign currency on the foreign exchange market by selling domestic dollars, which puts downward pressure on the price of domestic dollars.

*Why would increasing official currency reserves be difficult? Can't the government have its central bank accomplish this by writing checks for the foreign currency?*
If the central bank wrote checks to buy the foreign currency, it would be creating new money. Because of other cash needs, the prudent (i.e., noninflationary) annual increase in the money supply may already have been reached. Thus, the extra dollars to pay for the purchases of foreign currency may have to come from bond sales. Other cash needs may already be requiring large bond sales, so in order to sell even more bonds the government may have to raise the interest rate.

### Example 4

**The response has been to search out the middle ground. The central bank has a simple operating formula: some of the adjustment will be taken through the exchange rate, some through interest rates, and the rest through a loss of international reserves.**

*To what is the central bank adjusting here?*
Because the economy is experiencing a loss of international reserves, it must be adjusting to a balance of payments deficit.

*In what direction will the exchange rate be adjusted?*
The balance of payments deficit will cause the exchange rate to fall.

*How will interest rates be adjusted?*
The central bank will sell bonds to raise interest rates in order to increase capital inflows or to decrease capital outflows, thus helping to eliminate the balance of payments deficit.

## Chapter Summary

■ In a flexible exchange rate system, a nonzero balance of payments causes the exchange rate automatically to change, but in a fixed exchange rate system, it causes the money supply automatically to change.

■ Recognizing the international sector of the economy modifies the impact of fiscal and monetary policy by an amount that depends on the exchange rate system. The most dramatic result is the complete ineffectiveness of monetary policy under a fixed exchange rate. By fixing the exchange rate, an economy has in effect opted to employ monetary policy to fix the exchange rate, rendering it unavailable for any other purpose.

■ Sterilization policy can be used to regain the use of monetary policy, but at the cost of continued disequilibrium in the international sector. The disequilibrium causes foreign exchange reserves continually to rise if there is a balance of payments surplus or to fall if there is a balance of payments deficit.

■ Governments may wish to influence the foreign exchange market to make it less volatile. They can do so either by buying or selling in this market or by using monetary policy to influence the interest rate and thereby to change capital inflows.

## Media Exercises

1. **The central bank, which handles the reserve fund for the government, sells reserves and buys dollars when it wants to ...**

   Complete this clipping, explaining your rationale.

2. **By keeping interest rates _____, the bank has attracted offshore investment and created a demand for dollars. In turn, this has pushed _____ the dollar, taking millions of dollars off the bottom lines of exporting companies. To curb the dollar's _____, the bank has periodically entered the foreign exchange market ...**

   a. Fill in the blanks and explain your reasoning.

   b. Explain why the bottom lines of exporting companies were affected.

   c. Complete the final sentence, explaining your reasoning.

3. **When the government wants to strengthen the dollar, it _____ foreign reserves and _____ domestic dollars. It does the opposite when it wants to keep the dollar from rising too sharply.**

   Fill in these blanks, and explain your reasoning.

4. **The central bank turned to _____ to stop the Canadian dollar's _____ when it became apparent it was using up reserves to little avail.**

   Fill in the blanks.

5. **The U.S. government launched a major effort yesterday to rescue the value of the dollar after the greenback took a beating in foreign exchange trading to fall to a new post–Second World War low against the Japanese yen. The _____ intervened repeatedly in currency markets, _____ more than one billion dollars in an unusually aggressive and successful attempt to stave off speculators.**

   Fill in the blanks.

6. **As interest rates rose by record leaps this week, the dollar continued its slide.**

   What is going on here? Isn't the value of the dollar supposed to rise when interest rates increase?

7. **The central bank, fearing inflation, has kept interest rates up. However, to offset the upward pressure that those rates are putting on the currency, it has also been ...**

   a. Why would fear of inflation cause the central bank to keep interest rates up?

   b. How do high interest rates put upward pressure on the currency?

   c. Complete this clipping to describe what other activity the central bank has been pursuing.

8. **Our international reserves fell by $330 million to $3.2 billion last month—not much ammunition if the going gets tough.**

   a. What must have been happening to cause the reserves to fall?

   b. What is meant by "not much ammunition if the going gets tough?"

9. **The two-pronged attack—raising interest rates to attract liquid capital into the country and using foreign currency holdings to sop up unwanted dollars—has been designed to cushion the fall of the dollar.**

   a. Explain how these two actions cushion the fall of the dollar.

   b. Which action is only of short-run validity? Why?

10. **The minutes also reveal that stemming the rise of the dollar forced the government to borrow heavily on domestic financial markets.**

    a. What is the government doing to stem the rise of the dollar?

b. Why does this action imply that the government needs to borrow on domestic financial markets? (That is, what alternative to borrowing is possible, and what are its implications?)

11. **These are the extreme positions. The Bank of Canada's actual path is somewhere in the middle. Some of the brunt of higher U.S. interest rates is taken in higher domestic rates, some through a lower-valued Canadian dollar, and some through a loss of international reserves.**

   a. What are the extreme positions to which the first sentence refers?

   b. What are the long-run implications of the middle-road policy?

12. **The floating exchange rate system has served us well. In recent years, currency flexibility has facilitated adjustment, first to higher inflation and then to sharp declines in export prices and volumes.**

   a. Explain how currency flexibility would facilitate adjustment to higher inflation. Would the exchange rate flex up or down?

   b. Explain how currency flexibility would facilitate adjustment to declines in export prices and volumes. Would the exchange rate flex up or down?

13. **It is surprising that, with the dollar trading so high, the central bank has not allowed some easing of interest rates at the expense of a weaker dollar. Insofar as North America has entered into recession and exports are falling off, clearly the capacity constraints argument with respect to export industries carries less weight.**

   a. Explain the rationale for easing interest rates.

   b. What is the "capacity constraints argument," and why is it relevant here?

14. **Official intervention in the foreign exchange market does appear to be a useful policy when overshoots take place in fragile circumstances.**

   a. What is an "overshoot"?

   b. Explain the exact form of official intervention to counteract a specific overshoot.

   c. What does official intervention do that makes it useful?

15. **Reagan's own Council of Economic Advisors put the case for a muscular dollar with surprising force: the strong dollar has stimulated production and investment in sectors less involved in international trade. In other industries, competition from imports has prompted more expenditure in plant and equipment as well as greater attention to controlling wages and other costs. Prices of traded goods and close substitutes have been kept lower**

than they would have been otherwise, thereby benefiting both U.S. consumers and U.S. producers who use imported inputs.

    a. What is the basic argument against a muscular dollar?

    b. Briefly summarize the case for a muscular dollar.

16. **Bennett is on a high horse about economists ignoring the supply-side effects of exchange rate changes. He thinks the supply-side effects make the impact of a devaluation much less palatable.**

    a. How would exchange rate changes affect the supply side?

    b. Why might these effects make a devaluation less palatable?

17. **By avoiding policies to slow the growth of domestic demand and instead forcing the U.S. dollar to serve as the adjustment vehicle in narrowing the trade deficit, the United States will ensure that the global economic landscape during the next five years will be turned upside down.**

    a. How would slowing the growth of domestic demand narrow the trade deficit?

    b. What is meant by "forcing the U.S. dollar to serve as the adjustment vehicle"?

18. **The problem is that it has taken longer than usual for the exchange rate to affect trade. It generally takes six months to a year before the J-curve effect takes hold, but this time it has taken a year and a half.**

    a. What is meant by the J-curve effect taking hold?

    b. What point on the J curve is probably being referred to?

19. **When the Bank of Canada's foreign exchange traders go into the market to support the Canadian dollar, they trade U.S. dollars from Canada's reserves for Canadian dollars that other people are trying to sell. The Canadian cash resulting from this transaction goes into the government's ordinary account, reducing the finance minister's need to borrow from other sources to cover the deficit. Since the beginning of the fiscal year, about $2 billion in Canadian funds has appeared from this source.**

    a. In the absence of the intervention, was the Canadian dollar trying to rise or fall during the period referred to in this clipping?

    b. What are the "other sources" from which the finance minister would ordinarily borrow?

    c. If this transaction is such a good way of supplementing tax revenues, why not do more of it, more often?

20. **The dollar has been falling largely because it was overvalued during the first half of the 1980s. The Fed's tight monetary policy drove up interest rates in an attempt to smother inflation and to hold wages down. The Reagan administration now sings the praises of the lower dollar.**

    a. Explain how the dollar was overvalued.

    b. How does tight money smother inflation?

    c. What are the "praises of the lower dollar"?

21. **Japanese officials and many private economists say that the stronger yen will initially cause Japan's trade surplus to rise because it inflates the U.S. dollar value of Japanese exports even though volume may be falling.**

    What technical terminology do economists use to refer to this phenomenon?

22. **Speculators are clearly betting that a French franc will soon buy fewer German marks. Although France and Germany apparently have had the financial muscle to fend off the speculators so far, it is not clear whether they are prepared to pay the price of a disrupted economy for a prolonged period.**

    a. What are the French and German central banks doing during this speculative attack?

    b. What is the disruption to the French economy?

    c. What is the disruption to the German economy?

23. **Canada's official international reserves rose to an all-time high in October as the Bank of Canada acquired close to US$600 million trying to ...**

    Complete this clipping.

24. **Aggravating the perils of an expansionary fiscal and monetary policy is its effect on our trade deficit, which has reached unprecedented heights in recent years. Expansion worsens the trade deficit in two ways.**

    What are these two ways?

25. **Indeed, the yen may have to stay strong for two years or more, many experts say, to have much impact on U.S.-Japanese trade.**

    a. What is the rationale behind this statement?

    b. What technical terminology do economists use to describe this phenomenon?

# 17     **Purchasing Power Parity**

Earlier discussions of the international sector were conducted in the context of a noninflationary environment, both here and in the rest of the world. Although relaxing this simplifying assumption does not undo the lessons we learned, it does allow us to modify them to explain some anomolies. The purpose of this chapter is to exposit a general rule, called purchasing power parity, which can provide a guide to the behavior of an economy's exchange rate over the long run in an inflationary environment.

> **Upon completion of this chapter you should**
>
> - understand why under a fixed exchange rate system a country's monetary policy and thus inflation rate are forced to be the same as that of the rest of the world;
>
> - know how to use the purchasing power parity theorem to predict what will be happening to the exchange rate in the long run in an inflationary environment under a flexible exchange rate system; and
>
> - be able to calculate the purchasing power parity exchange rate and to explain why it is used to calculate standard-of-living comparisons between countries.

## 17.1   Inflation with a Fixed Exchange Rate

In chapter 15 we saw that a rise in our price level, with no corresponding rise in foreign prices, leads to a balance of payments deficit, which under a fixed exchange rate system in turn leads to an automatic contraction of our money supply. The same will also happen if the rate of inflation in our economy is greater than the rate of inflation in the rest of the world.

Suppose U.S. inflation is 8 percent, but it is only 5 percent in the rest of the world, due to differing money-supply growth rates. With a fixed exchange rate, during the first year U.S. prices rise by 3 percent more than foreign prices. If nothing changes, during the following year the gap between U.S. and foreign prices widens by another 3 percent, and so on, year after year. It is not true, however, that nothing changes.

U.S. prices are rising relative to foreign prices, so U.S. exports should fall and imports should rise. As a result, the United States should develop a balance of payments deficit, and the rest of the world should develop a balance of payments surplus. Under fixed exchange rates, these developments should automatically decrease the U.S. money supply and automatically increase the foreign money supply. The fall in money-supply growth in the U.S. lowers its rate of inflation over the long run, and the increase in money-supply growth in the rest of the world increases foreign inflation over the long run. The pressure on both inflation rates continues as long as the U.S. inflation rate exceeds that of the rest of the world. Eventually, inflation and money-supply growth in the rest of the world should match those of the United States.

Does inflation in the rest of the world rise to match U.S. inflation? Does American inflation fall to match foreign inflation? Or do they both move to an intermediate rate? From 1945 to 1971, when most countries were on a fixed exchange rate system, the Bretton Woods system, all countries fixed their exchange rates relative to the U.S. dollar so that in essence everything was mea-

---

**Curiosity 17.1:    What Was the Bretton Woods System?**

In 1944, when an Allied victory was certain, the Allies held a conference at Bretton Woods, New Hampshire to discuss what kind of currency exchange rate system the world should adopt after the war. Influenced heavily by its most prominent participant, John Maynard Keynes, countries decided to have all central banks buy and sell their own currencies in order to fix their currency in terms of U.S. dollars, with gold or U.S. dollars serving as reserves. This decision imposed an automatic discipline and thus a balance of payments deficit on any country experiencing high inflation. The country would be forced to shrink its money supply, lowering its inflation and restoring equilibrium in its international sector. The only exception was the United States, which could ignore its balance of payments deficits because it, and it alone, could print reserves—U.S. dollars—to cover any loss of reserves.

The conference also established the International Monetary Fund (IMF) to provide loans to countries having temporary difficulties dealing with balance of payments problems. It also created the International Bank for Reconstruction and Development, commonly called the World Bank, to make long-term loans to assist developing countries in building infrastructure such as dams and roads.

---

sured in U.S. dollars. This meant that the United States could simply print U.S. dollars to cover its balance of payments deficit, eliminating any automatic contraction of the money supply. As a result, the rest of the world was forced to experience U.S. monetary policy and inflation rate.

The bottom line here is that under a fixed exchange rate, a small, open economy loses control of its monetary policy, which is forced to be identical to that of the larger country to whose currency its exchange rate is fixed. Note that this analysis corroborates the result of the preceding chapter: monetary policy is ineffective under a fixed exchange rate.

---

## 17.2   Inflation with a Flexible Exchange Rate

The fixed exchange rate system described above was attractive to the United States because it could do what it wanted and other countries had to adjust. Of course, if the United States created a big inflation, other countries could decide to abandon the fixed exchange rate system and no longer tie their currency to the U.S. dollar, thereby escaping the high U.S. inflation. This is exactly what happened during the Vietnam War, causing the world to move to a flexible exchange rate system.

Consider the same example: 8 percent inflation in the United States and 5 percent inflation in the rest of the world, but with a flexible exchange rate. Now the balance of payments deficit in the United States automatically causes the dollar to depreciate (or, viewed differently, foreign currencies to appreciate) rather than causing money supplies to change. If the depreciation is 3 percent

---

**Curiosity 17.2:   What Is the Real Exchange Rate?**

In the example in which U.S. inflation was 8 percent and rest-of-the-world inflation 5 percent, we saw that under a flexible exchange rate system the U.S. dollar
would depreciate by 3 percent per year. This 3 percent annual depreciation just
offsets the annual relative increase in U.S. prices of 3 percent, so there should be
no incentive for anyone to change demand for imports or exports. Although there
has been a change in the *nominal* exchange rate, there has been no change in the
*real* exchange rate.

The nominal exchange rate is the one we read about in the newspaper. It tells us
the rate at which our currency exchanges for foreign currencies. The real exchange
rate, sometimes called the *terms of trade*, tells us the rate at which our goods and
services exchange for foreign goods and services; it is therefore the exchange rate
that influences imports and exports. The real exchange rate can be calculated from
the nominal exchange rate as

$$\text{real exchange rate} = \text{nominal exchange rate} \times \frac{\text{domestic price level}}{\text{foreign price level}}$$

The foreign to domestic price ratio in this formula is calculated as the cost of a
typical basket of traded goods and services in the United States in U.S. dollars
divided by the cost of that same basket in the foreign country in its currency.

From this formula, if U.S. prices increase by 8 percent per year, and foreign
prices increase by 5 percent per year, then each year the ratio of their price levels
increases by about 3 percent, canceled out by the 3 percent fall in the nominal
exchange rate. The real exchange rate is unchanged, as it should be in this example.
A crucial assumption in the PPP theorem is that the real exchange rate is constant,
something we know is not true. Figure 17.1 shows how the real exchange rate can
change dramatically in response to factors such as real interest rate differentials.

---

per year, then the 3 percent inflation difference causing U.S. goods and services
to become 3 percent more expensive annually is exactly offset, and the international sector remains in balance. The *real* exchange rate is unchanged.

Automatic forces cause the rate of change of the exchange rate to equal the
difference between foreign and U.S. inflation rates. Notice that the change in
the exchange rate is ongoing. Each year, the exchange rate must change by an
amount equal to the difference in inflation rates. This result is often referred to
as *purchasing power parity* or PPP:

rate of change of exchange rate = foreign inflation − domestic inflation.

---

## 17.3   Purchasing Power Parity

Like the formula for inflation from chapter 9, the PPP relationship is best described as a rule of thumb for predicting long-run behavior. In the short run,

Real effective
exchange rate
index

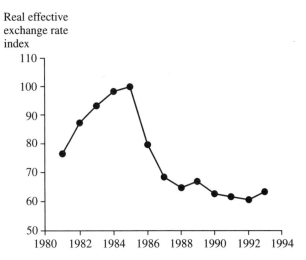

**Figure 17.1**   Real effective exchange rate
This graph shows how dramatically the real exchange rate can change. The high interest rate policies of the 1980s caused capital inflows, pushing up the real value of the U.S. dollar.
Source: *International Financial Statistics*, 1988–1994.

exchange rate changes are very volatile, affected by political events, business cycles, speculator activity, monetary policies, and rumors, among many other things. Consequently, PPP is unlikely in the short run to be a good guide to exchange rate behavior.

Even in the long run, PPP can be a poor guide because it ignores a variety of factors that permanently influence our ability to compete on international markets:

1.  Natural resource discoveries such as Alaska or North Sea oil

2.  Inventions of new products such as VCRs

3.  Changes in barriers to trade such as tariff reductions associated with free trade agreements

4.  Changes in consumers' tastes for imported versus domestic goods

5.  Permanent changes in countries' relative real interest rates

6.  Differing rates of productivity growth across countries

7.  Overall inflation rates not accurately reflecting price changes in traded goods and services

All the factors described above can permanently affect the exchange rate in the long run in the absence of inflation, thus invalidating the PPP result and marking a difference between the real and nominal exchange rates. This difference is illustrated in figure 17.1. A large swing in the real U.S. exchange rate occurred during the 1980s due to a high relative U.S. real interest rate. Despite the failures of the PPP theorem, it is still of value, mainly because predicting inflation differentials is sometimes easier than predicting changes in other factors that affect the exchange rate, so that PPP is a useful guide in predicting future exchange rates.

The PPP theorem is often described as stating that the cost of a tradeable good must be the same in dollars whether purchased abroad (after exchanging the dollars for local currency) or at home. If this were not the case, arbitrageurs would buy the product in the cheaper country and send it to the expensive country for sale. On a grand scale, such practices would cause a balance of payments deficit in the expensive country—causing its exchange rate to fall and eliminating the cost advantage of the cheaper country. Exactly the same logic was used earlier to derive the PPP result in terms of inflation differentials.

Anyone who has traveled to foreign countries can confirm that many tradeable goods do not cost the same in dollars at home as abroad. Transportation costs, taxes, imperfect product substitutes, and interest rate differences affecting exchange rates are some of the reasons for the differences, but whatever the reasons, PPP does not work well when defined in terms of absolute price levels.

Defining PPP in terms of inflation differentials circumvents this problem. Suppose that because of differentials such as taxes or transportation costs, the absolute dollar price of a particular tradeable good tends to be 10 percent higher in one country than in another. Defined in terms of absolute prices, PPP says something should change, but there are no forces to do so. If there are inflation differentials, however, the 10 percent difference grows or shrinks, eventually by enough to cause forces for change to arise. Thus, by looking at inflation differences, more confidence can be placed in the PPP prediction, at least insofar as the long-run picture is concerned.

## 17.4   The PPP Exchange Rate

A traveller also might notice that prices of nontradeables—such as haircuts and hotel rooms—can differ markedly from country to country, at times by amounts dramatically different from what PPP would imply. Because PPP applies only to tradeables, this phenomenon is not anomalous, but it does suggest that the exchange rate can be misleading if used to calculate cost-of-living comparisons.

Suppose you have been offered a job in France paying 160,000 francs per year. You check the newspaper, find that the exchange rate is 5 francs per dollar, and quickly calculate that this is US$32,000. It would be a mistake to compare this to your current salary in the United States because it may be that the cost of living in France differs markedly from the cost of living in the United States. To make a fair comparison, you would have to find out how much it would cost you to live your current lifestyle in France.

The real problem here is that the exchange rate does not reflect cost-of-living differences between countries. Instead, it reflects the forces of supply and demand for the dollar in the foreign exchange market, determined by the relative costs of tradeables and by a variety of other factors (such as interest rate differences). To make cross-country cost-of-living comparisons, we need a different exchange rate, one explicitly designed to tell us the purchasing power of a franc in France compared to the purchasing power of a dollar in the United States.

The *PPP exchange rate* does just that. It is calculated by taking the ratio of the cost of a typical bundle of goods and services in francs in France to the cost of that same bundle in dollars in the United States. Formally, it is calculated as

$$\text{PPP exchange rate} = \frac{\text{foreign cost of typical bundle}}{\text{domestic cost of typical bundle}}.$$

If the ratio is four, then the PPP exchange rate is 4 francs per dollar, so the 160,000 franc salary, in terms of its purchasing power in France, is equivalent to US$40,000.

Using this alternative exchange rate to make cross-country comparisons can make a big difference. Recently, the International Monetary Fund calculated world income shares using purchasing power parity exchange rates instead of current exchange rates. The result vastly boosts developing countries' share of the world's GDP—to 34.4 percent from 17.7 percent.

## Media Illustrations

### Example 1

**This is the reason why the fixed exchange rate system was scrapped in 1971. The United States had been pursuing an inflationary monetary policy to help pay for the Vietnam War and new social programs, but its trading partners did not all want to participate in such a policy.**

*What is an inflationary monetary policy?*
Inflation results from increasing the money supply at a rate greater than the real rate of growth of the economy.

*What are the three basic ways of paying for the Vietnam War and new social programs? To which does the "inflationary monetary policy" refer?*
This government spending must be financed by raising taxes, selling bonds to the public, or printing money (selling bonds to the central bank). The last of these is most directly tied to inflation.

*How can U.S. trading partners be forced to participate in the inflationary monetary policy?*
Under a fixed exchange rate, a small open country is forced to experience the same monetary policy as the country to which its exchange rate is fixed. In this example, the trading partners had fixed their exchange rates to the U.S. dollar.

*If the fixed exchange rate system were scrapped, what exactly would the trading partners have to do to opt out of participation in the inflationary monetary policy?* They would have to reduce their money-supply growth rate to produce the long-run inflation rate that they desire, and allow their exchange rate with the U.S. dollar to rise continually at a rate equal to the difference between the U.S. rate and their own rate of inflation.

### Example 2

**Although critics have suggested that the central bank could lower rates and, in so doing, let the dollar fall on international exchange markets, the report said that the dollar has already fallen in the last half-dozen years and raises the question of why things have not gone better if exchange rate depreciation is so good for the economy.**

*What rate is it suggested be lowered, and why would this action cause the dollar to fall?*
If the interest rate is lowered, capital inflows will fall—decreasing the demand for our dollar and causing its price in terms of foreign currency to fall.

*What is the rationale behind the belief that exchange rate depreciation is good for the economy?*
A fall in our exchange rate makes our exports cheaper to foreigners and imports more expensive to us, so demand for domestic production—in the form of exports and import-competing goods and services—should increase, thus stimulating our economy.

*How would you explain why the fall in the dollar over the last half-dozen years has not caused "things to go better"?*
Perhaps the reason why the dollar has fallen over the past half-dozen years is that, during this time, our inflation was greater than that of our trading partners, so the fall in the exchange rate served merely to keep the real exchange rate steady.

### Example 3

**In three to five years, the U.S. dollar will presumably resume its long-term slide unless Washington reverses its economic policies of the post–Second World War period and takes a tough stand against inflation. Observers believe a Reagan administration may take that tougher stand.**

*What would an administration need to do to take a tough stand against inflation?*
To cut inflation in the long run, the rate of growth of the money supply would have to be cut back to a level more in line with the real rate of growth of the economy.

*What is the logic of the first sentence of this clipping?*
According to purchasing power parity, if the rate of inflation in the United States is higher than that of its trading partners, in the long run the exchange rate will fall (the dollar will continue to slide) at a rate equal to the difference between U.S. and its trading partners' inflations.

**Example 4**
**News that U.S. job creation in January was more robust than anticipated sent a signal to currency markets to expect a stepped-up fight against inflation, unleashing a bout of buying fervor for the U.S. dollar.**

*Why would this news cause people to expect a "stepped-up fight against inflation"?*
Unexpected job creation may signal that the economy is moving into a boom, pushing unemployment below the NRU and thus threatening inflation.

*Why would "a bout of buying fervor for the U.S. dollar" result?*
A stepped-up fight against inflation would involve a rise in the real interest rate to dampen aggregate demand. The rise in the interest rate would increase capital inflows, bidding up the value of the U.S. dollar. In addition, if the stepped-up fight against inflation succeeds, inflation in the United States would fall below foreign inflation, which by PPP also leads to a rise in the U.S. dollar. Currency speculators anticipate these effects and buy U.S. dollars to reap the resulting capital gain.

## Chapter Summary

- With a fixed exchange rate, a small open economy is forced to experience the money-supply growth and inflation of its major trading partners. A lower inflation rate, for example, causes exports to become cheap and imports expensive, inducing a balance of payments surplus that automatically increases the money supply and pushes up inflation.

- With a flexible exchange rate, a country with a lower inflation rate will experience a rise in its exchange rate, offsetting any price difference created by differing inflation rates. Its real exchange rate remains unchanged, reflecting *purchasing power parity*: the rate of change of a country's exchange rate equals the difference between foreign and domestic inflation.

- Purchasing power parity is a rule of thumb for predicting long-run nominal exchange rate behavior. There are many reasons why PPP is unlikely to hold in the short run, and even in the long run several factors can cause the real exchange rate to change and thus purchasing power parity not to hold.

- The purchasing power parity exchange rate measures cost-of-living differences across countries.

## Definitional Formulas

- real exchange rate = nominal exchange rate $\times \dfrac{\text{domestic price level}}{\text{foreign price level}}$.

- PPP exchange rate = $\dfrac{\text{foreign cost of typical bundle}}{\text{domestic cost of typical bundle}}$.

## Rule of Thumb

■ PPP: rate of change of exchange rate = foreign inflation – domestic inflation.

## Media Exercises

1.  **Tourists form the United States who are pleased to get $1.35 or so Canadian for their U.S. dollars only to find that most purchases cost _____ are learning a simple lesson in the _____ theory of exchange rates.**

    Fill in the blanks.

2.  **If Ukrainian prices hadn't risen in line with Russia's, market forces would have sucked Ukraine dry of food and consumer goods as Russians sought cheaper goods than they could get at home.**

    How would this result have been different if both areas had their own currencies?

3.  **All countries that consistently run lower inflation rates than their trading partners over a long period of time have an upward trend in ...**

    Complete this statement.

4.  **How does the average Chinese person survive on just enough money each month for seventeen Big Macs—which is what official Chinese per capita income implies? The answer is, of course, that he or she doesn't because converting incomes at current exchange rates doesn't reflect _____.**

    Fill in the blank.

5.  **A second issue concerns how long the fixed exchange rate could be maintained. This, of course, depends on an uncertain future, but if the initial value chosen was appropriate and if domestic costs remained in line with foreign costs, then the rate may be sustainable for some time.**

    a. What is meant by "if domestic costs remained in line with foreign costs"?

    b. What would happen if domestic costs exceeded foreign costs?

6.  **To be sure, the central bank said that the broad money aggregates have merely been upgraded to "indicative policy guides," rather than formal targets, but it did make plain its rejection of the former unspoken policy of targeting the exchange rate.**

    Why would adoption of the new policy require rejection of the old?

7. **Although the table shows that there are more countries against which the U.S. dollar has appreciated rather than depreciated over the past twelve months, the extra local currency that a fixed U.S. dollar outlay will buy is not necessarily a great windfall to the U.S. traveler.**

   Explain why the U.S. traveler may not find the dollar appreciation to be a windfall.

8. **Word that growth in the cost of living was slower in the United States than in Germany last year attracted buyers for the U.S. dollar.**

   Explain why this report on cost of living should attract buyers for the U.S. dollar.

9. **The conventional wisdom has been that inflation is bad for the economy. If our inflation is running higher than our trading partners' inflation, according to this argument, our growth slows and jobs are lost.**

   a. Explain how the mechanism described here works.

   b. How could the growth problem be avoided without curbing our inflation?

10. **Monday's trade figures—twice as bad as analysts were generally expecting them to be—reinforced fears that the economy was overheating, with imports outstripping exports and inflationary pressures surging. The government is now expected to raise interest rates almost immediately.**

    a. Would you expect imports to outstrip exports in the presence of surging inflation? Explain why or why not.

    b. Why would the government be expected to raise interest rates?

11. **Foreign countries are now free to pursue an independent course of monetary policy, and old conflicts about the U.S. role in exporting inflation, and about the adjustment responsibilities of surplus (or deficit) nations, suddenly seem to have lost their relevance.**

    a. What major change do you think has led to the remarks in this clipping?

    b. How might the U.S. export inflation?

    c. What are the "adjustment responsibilities" mentioned in this clipping?

12. **The record has not been good. Our past experience with exchange rate depreciation has been that all too often it has led, not to a sustained improvement in our competitiveness, but to . . .**

    Complete this statement and explain your reasoning.

13. **Why has he argued for a stable dollar and a zero inflation? Aren't these inconsistent goals?**

    Explain how these goals could be inconsistent.

14. **Although acknowledging that a weaker dollar initially favors exports, he said this advantage will last only as long as ...**

    Complete this statement and explain your reasoning.

15. **Finally, there is the question of monetary policy and imported inflation. Under a fixed exchange rate, Canada's inflation would be more closely tied to that of the United States. Given the experience of the past few years, that may not be a bad thing.**

    a. Explain how Canada's inflation would be more closely tied to that of the United States under a fixed exchange rate.

    b. In light of the final sentence, what change in monetary policy would come about in Canada if the exchange rate were fixed? Explain why.

16. **Big Mac watchers rely on the theory of purchasing power parity (PPP) for currencies. This argues that an exchange rate between two currencies is in equilibrium (at PPP) when it leaves hamburgers costing the same in each country. Comparing actual exchange rates with PPPs is one indication of whether a currency is under- or overvalued.**

    a. What meaning would be attached to a statement that a currency is undervalued by a PPP measure?

    b. By means of an explicit example, explain how you would use the price of hamburgers to find the PPP exchange rate.

    c. How would you use this calculation to claim a currency is under- or overvalued?

    d. What objection might you have to using this method to calculate the PPP rate?

17. **Tying the Canadian dollar to the U.S. dollar may eliminate some worries, but it will create others, among them concern that the United States might not be as dedicated as Canada is to fighting inflation.**

    Explain why this concern is created when a fixed exchange rate is adopted.

18. **The surest way to sustain the exchange value of our currency is to maintain its purchasing power at home.**

    Explain the rationale behind this statement.

19. **Switzerland used to boast one of the lowest inflation rates and one of the strongest currencies in the world, thanks to sound monetary policies and prudent public finances.**

    a. What kind of monetary policy is being referred to here?

    b. After achieving a low inflation, what more would the policy authorities need to do to ensure a strong currency?

**20. The cheapest Big Mac—at \$1.03—is in China, and the most expensive—at \$3.96—is in Switzerland. These figures imply that the yuan is the most undervalued currency and the Swiss franc the most overvalued.**

What economic theory gives rise to this conclusion? What is its logic?

**21. Economic theory and our own experience tell us that using monetary policy to drive down the exchange rate will be successful only until ...**

Complete this statement.

**22. Exporters and some economists have argued that the central bank should drive down the value of the dollar to boost economic activity. The Fed claims, however, that its ability to influence the real exchange rate is severely limited.**

    a. How would the central bank drive down the value of the dollar?

    b. Why does the second sentence refer to the "real" exchange rate? What alternative exchange rate might be considered here?

**23. If inflation exists in the rest of the world, but not in Canada, our merchandise trade surplus should soar, with exports becoming cheap and imports expensive. Of course, that would stimulate economic activity in Canada and, pretty soon, the inflation rate would begin to rise. How would the authorities counter that undesirable development? By keeping money growth low and interest rates much higher than U.S. interest rates—the same way that the Bank of Canada has fought inflation in the past and still does today.**

    a. What exchange rate system must this author be assuming? How can you tell?

    b. Comment on the suitability of the monetary policy that this author claims the Bank of Canada would employ to fight inflation.

**24. An even better case study is Singapore. The Singapore Monetary Authority deliberately targets a trend appreciation in the Singapore dollar versus the U.S. dollar in order to maintain price stability.**

    a. Why would this policy achieve price stability?

    b. What trend rate would be appropriate?

**Numerical Exercises**

N1. Suppose that both the U.S. and Canadian economies, on a flexible exchange rate, are experiencing a real growth rate of 3 percent, but that the Canadian money-supply growth rate is 10 percent compared to only 6 percent in the U.S. Currently, 1.0 U.S. dollar buys 1.2 Canadian dollars. How many Canadian dollars would you guess 1.0 U.S. dollar will buy two years from now?

N2. In 1975, the U.S./Canada exchange rate was 1.02 (i.e., 1.00 U.S. dollar bought 1.02 Canadian dollars). The Canadian price level rose by 52 percent between 1975 and 1980, whereas the U.S. price level rose by 41 percent. From this information, what do you predict the 1980 exchange rate to be?

N3. Suppose the real rates of growth in the United States and Canada are both 2 percent, inflation in Canada is 9 percent, and the U.S. dollar is appreciating against the Canadian dollar by 4 percent per year. What is the U.S. money-growth rate?

N4. Suppose that in mid-1990 1.0 U.S. dollar bought 1.1 Canadian dollars, and in mid-1992 it bought 1.2 Canadian dollars. During this period, the annual rate of inflation in the United States was 5 percent and in Canada 8 percent.

   a. By how much does PPP predict the U.S. dollar nominal exchange rate should change during this period?

   b. Has the U.S. dollar real exchange rate risen or fallen during this period? By how much?

N5. Suppose a typical basket of goods and services consists of four units of housing and seven units of food. In the United States, a unit of housing costs 2 U.S. dollars and a unit of food costs 1 U.S. dollar; in Canada, these prices are 3 Canadian dollars and 2 Canadian dollars, respectively. If the current exchange rate is 1.5 Canadian dollars per U.S. dollar, what is the purchasing power parity exchange rate?

N6. Suppose the U.S. and Canadian economies are in equilibrium, with an exchange rate of 1.0 U.S. dollar per 1.3 Canadian dollars and a common inflation rate of 5 percent. If the United States increases the rate of growth of its money supply by two percentage points, what do you expect to happen to the real exchange rate:

   a. under a fixed exchange rate?

   b. under a flexible exchange rate?

# 18    Interest Rate Parity

The previous chapter explained how differing rates of inflation in trading countries affected the international balance between those countries and thereby influenced the exchange rate between their currencies. However, an important dimension of this international relationship was not addressed. One might expect differing inflation rates to give rise to different nominal interest rates, which could in turn influence the balance of payments and thus the exchange rate. The foregoing statement is misleading, however, because the exchange rate is affected by real, not nominal, interest rate differences, and the purpose of this chapter is to explain why this is so.

The central theme of this chapter is that real interest rates are approximately the same across countries, a result known as the *interest rate parity theorem*. Three questions should immediately come to mind: what causes interest rate parity? why is it only approximate? and why does it relate to the real interest rate rather than to the nominal interest rate?

---

**Upon completion of this chapter you should**

- understand why real interest rates should be approximately the same in all countries, a result known as interest rate parity;
- be able to explain why a nominal interest rate difference between countries should have no impact on the exchange rate except insofar as it reflects a real interest rate difference; and
- appreciate the relative merits of fixed and flexible exchange rate systems.

---

## 18.1   Why Are Real Interest Rates Similar in Different Countries?

In chapter 15 we saw that a rise in a country's real interest rate, with no change in other countries' real interest rates, causes a net capital inflow. We discussed how this would affect the balance of payments and consequently influence other economic variables of interest. One impact of the net capital inflow that we did not discuss, however, was its effect on the real interest rate itself.

Suppose, for example, that the real interest rate in a small country such as Canada rises, creating a net capital inflow into Canada. This puts downward pressure on the Canadian real interest rate. This happens for two reasons. First, foreigners will want to invest in Canadian bonds to obtain the higher return, so the demand for Canadian bonds increases, bidding up Canadian bond prices and thereby lowering the Canadian real interest rate. Second, Canadian firms selling bonds will find it cheaper to raise capital in other countries, so they will remove their bonds from the Canadian market and take them to foreign bond markets. The fall in the supply of bonds on the Canadian market also causes the price of Canadian bonds to rise, thus lowering the Canadian real interest rate.

The bottom line here is that a rise in the Canadian real interest rate sets in motion forces that push this interest rate back toward the "world" real rate of interest. In general, however, these forces will not succeed in pushing the Canadian interest rate all the way to the "world" real rate because the relationship between the "world" real rate and a specific country's real rate is only approximate.

---

## 18.2   Why "Approximately"?

The "world" real rate is a ficticious rate, thought to be determined by activity in a few large, stable financial markets such as those in the United States, Germany, Great Britain, and Japan. For expositional convenience, however, we consider

**Curiosity 18.1:   Can Monetary Policy Change Real Interest Rates?**

Interest rate parity suggests that the world real interest rate is determined by major countries such as the United States and that smaller countries such as Canada are forced to have a real interest rate equal to the world real interest rate, plus a risk premium. An implication of this is that Canadian monetary policy should not be able to affect the gap between the Canadian and U.S. real rates and thus unilaterally change the Canadian real interest rate. However, central banks do raise and lower their real interest rates to affect their exchange rate, at least temporarily—once again confirming the maxim that interest rate parity should be interpreted as an approximate relationship holding over the long run.

Suppose that the real interest rate in Canada rises to make the difference between Canadian and U.S. real interest rates greater than the Canada/U.S. risk premium. Investors hold diversified wealth portfolios consisting of optimal fractions of assets with different risk/yield combinations. When the Canadian yield moves higher, the optimal fraction of Canadian bonds in investor portfolios rises slightly, so investors adjust their portfolios to hold more Canadian bonds. The operative word here is "slightly": they are not willing to buy massive quantities of the Canadian bonds because that would raise the overall risk of their portfolio beyond what the higher yield on Canadian bonds warrants. Consequently, although the rise in the Canadian real interest rate is curtailed by extra foreign purchases of Canadian bonds, it is not eliminated.

In addition, the activity of buying these bonds creates a demand for Canadian dollars that bids up the value of the Canadian dollar beyond the level that many would consider to be normal. Because of this, investors may think the Canadian dollar is more likely to fall in the future and thus may consider Canadian bonds as riskier than they were before the interest rate rose. The rise in the value of the Canadian dollar also limits the quantity of extra bonds bought by foreigners, preventing the Canadian real rate from falling back to its original level.

A determined central bank can modestly increase its real interest rate above that of the world real rate, beyond the risk premium, thereby creating a continuing capital inflow. The capital inflow will initially be quite large, as investors readjust their portfolios, but then will fall off to a modest level that reflects a higher fraction of the flow of new saving. The U.S. policy of keeping the real interest rate above the world rate, such as that followed during the 1980s because of budget deficits and low savings rates, causes U.S. foreign debt to increase, something that cannot go on forever. Interest rate parity is consequently a better guide to long-run than short-run behavior.

the world real rate to be the rate prevailing in the United States, keeping in mind that the U.S. real rate can in reality be affected by financial activity in these other large countries. The forces described in the Canadian example above come about because the Canadian financial market is so small relative to the U.S. market. If the Canadian and other small markets were microcosms of the U.S. market, the rate prevailing in the U.S. market would undoubtedly also prevail in these smaller markets. They are not exactly the same as the U.S. market, however, if for no other reason than that they are located in another country, with bonds denominated in another currency. The U.S. market sets a standard, not just in terms of a numerical rate, but also in terms of the institutional structure associated with its financial transactions. Investing in a U.S. bond carries with it an implicit degree of riskiness, associated with the political stability, market liquidity, degree of business risk, and legal system characterizing the United States. The implicit degree of riskiness associated with, say, Canadian bonds (because of uncertainty caused by the possibility of Quebec separation or by the very large size of the Canadian national debt) may be greater than with U.S. bonds, implying that the real rate in Canada must incorporate a *risk premium* and therefore be higher than the real rate in the United States to compensate for the difference in risk.

A major dimension of the risk factor is the possibility of changes in currency values, and for this reason the risk premium is sometimes called a *currency premium*. A U.S. investor buying Canadian bonds, for example, will be paid Canadian dollars when the bonds mature, so the investor is running the risk that the value of the Canadian dollar may be lower at maturity than it was when he or she bought the bonds. Offsetting this is the possibility that the value of the Canadian dollar may be higher, but the point is that there is a risk. An investor will accept this risk only if a higher real rate of return is offered. He or she can purchase insurance to protect against this type of risk (called *hedging*), but at a cost that is of course higher, the higher the risk. To cover this cost, the real interest rate on the Canadian bond must be higher to make it comparable to U.S. bonds in the eyes of U.S. investors.

## 18.3   Why Not Nominal Interest Rates?

The best way to explain why nominal interest rate differences are not relevant, except insofar as they reflect differences in real interest rates, is to look at a specific example.

Suppose that the United States and Canada are in equilibrium with a flexible exchange rate, that both countries have a real growth rate of 2 percent per year, that their money supplies are both growing at 7 percent per year, and that their real rates of interest are 4 percent and 3 percent, respectively, implying a risk premium of one percentage point in favor of the United States.

What are the inflation rates in the United States and Canada? Using our rule of thumb from chapter 9, the rate of inflation in both countries should be 5 percent, calculated in each case as 7 percent − 2 percent.

What are the nominal interest rates in the United States and Canada? Using the relationship between the real and nominal interest rates, the nominal interest rate in the United States should be 3 percent + 5 percent = 8 percent, and in Canada if should be 4 percent + 5 percent = 9 percent.

What is happening to the exchange rate? Because the rates of inflation in these two economies are the same, the purchasing power parity theorem implies that the exchange rate is constant.

Will there be capital flows? Because the one-percentage-point higher real interest rate in Canada just compensates U.S. lenders for the higher risk of investing in Canadian bonds, there should be no capital flows.

Now suppose that the rate of growth of the money supply in Canada jumps to 13 percent per year. When a new equilibrium is eventually attained, what should have happened to Canada's inflation rate, nominal interest rate, and the exchange rate? Inflation should jump to 11 percent, calculated as 13 percent − 2 percent. The nominal interest rate should jump to 11 percent + 4 percent = 15 percent. Because the difference between the Canadian and U.S. inflation rates is now six percentage points, the exchange rate—from Canada's point of view—should be depreciating at a rate of 6 percent per year.

Suppose you are a U.S. investor who, before the change in the Canadian money-supply growth rate, was indifferent about buying bonds in Canada versus in the United States. There has been no change in the difference between the U.S. and Canadian real interest rates, so the interest rate parity theorem implies that there should be no change in the rate of capital flows. There has been, however, a dramatic change in the difference between the U.S. and Canadian nominal interest rates, with the Canadian rate now much higher. Why won't you and other U.S. investors rush to buy Canadian bonds to reap the higher nominal return?

The Canadian nominal interest rate has jumped by six percentage points relative to its U.S. counterpart, but a U.S. investor will discover that this extra 6 percent is illusory. While his or her funds are invested in the Canadian bond, the value of the Canadian dollar should fall by 6 percent, so when he or she cashes in the bond and repatriates the proceeds, the extra 6 percent return is needed to offset the loss on the currency exchange.

Can't the investor buy insurance against such a currency devaluation and thereby avoid this loss? Buying such insurance is possible (doing so is called hedging), but how much do you think the insurance premium will cost? It should be more than 6 percent. The insurance agent will go through the same arithmetic outlined above, concluding that the Canadian dollar should depreciate by 6 percent, and will charge a premium of 6 percent plus a commission.

This example can be summarized as follows: a difference in nominal interest rates that reflects only a difference in inflation rates (and thus does not

**Curiosity 18.2:   What Is a Forward Exchange Rate?**

A firm closes a big deal with a Mexican buyer who will pay five million pesos when the product is delivered in six months time. This firm is not in the business of speculating on the future value of pesos, so it may understandably be nervous about how many U.S. dollars this foreign currency will buy in six months. To avoid this problem, the firm can "hedge" the transaction by entering a contract to sell five million pesos in six months at the six-month *forward exchange rate*. In this way, the firm guarantees how many U.S. dollars the five million pesos will buy in six months.

If the current or *spot* Mexican peso exchange rate is 4 U.S. cents per peso, then the 5 million pesos would today be worth US$200,000. The person agreeing to buy the 5 million pesos from the firm in six months will want some reward for taking on the risk of an unexpected change in the value of the peso during this six-month period. The reward, which could be called an insurance premium paid by the firm, takes the form of a percentage "discount" of the spot rate to produce the forward rate.

The spot rate of 4.0 cents per peso could, for example, be discounted to produce a forward rate of 3.95 cents per peso. This implies that the 5 million pesos will in six months provide the firm with US$197,500 instead of the US$200,000 that the firm would have received if the forward contract was not signed and the exchange rate did not change. The magnitude of the discount depends on what the Mexican peso is expected to do during these six months. If inflation in Mexico exceeds inflation in the United States, everyone would expect the Mexican peso to fall, so the forces of supply and demand in this market should cause the discount to be greater.

The "Currency Trading" column of the *Wall Street Journal* reports daily the 30-, 90-, and 180-day forward rates for major currencies. The discounts embodied in these forward rates are sometimes used to measure the market's expectations of future relative inflations across countries.

correspond to a difference in real rates) generates no capital flows because the difference in nominal rates is offset by anticipated changes in currency values. Consequently, the *interest rate parity* result must be written in terms of real interest rates:

(foreign − U.S.) real *i* rates = risk premium.

The risk premium could be positive if investment in the foreign country is thought to be riskier than it is the United States, such as is the case with Canada. It could be negative if investment in the foreign country is thought to be less risky than it is in the United States, such as may be the case with Japan or Switzerland.

By exploiting what we know about the difference between real and nominal interest rates, however, we can formalize this relationship in terms of nominal interest rates as follows:

(foreign − U.S.) nominal *i* rates

= (foreign − U.S.) expected inflation rates + risk premium.

Furthermore, using the PPP result, we can write this in an alternative form:

(foreign − U.S.) nominal *i* rates

= expected rate of change of U.S. exchange rate + risk premium.

For example, suppose that investing in Canada is considered to carry a 1 percent risk premium and that inflation in Canada is four percentage points lower than inflation in the United States. Then the U.S. nominal interest rate should be three percentage points higher than the Canadian nominal interest rate.

None of these formulas is exact. Real interest rates can depart from the world real interest rate, as was explained in curiosity 18.1, and the latter two variants above rest on relationships that we know at best are rules of thumb suitable for predicting long-run behavior. These forms of expressing interest rate parity should be viewed from this perspective.

## 18.4   Fixed versus Flexible Exchange Rates

With our discussion of the international sector of the economy coming to a close, it seems appropriate to address briefly the question of which exchange rate system—fixed or flexible—is better. Both exchange rate systems have advantages and disadvantages, so that an answer to this question depends on the particular situation.

If every city in the United States had its own currency, economic activity and productivity in the United States would be severely curtailed. Commercial transactions involving firms in different cities would have currency exchange rate risks to contend with, people would have to bear the costs of changing currencies every time they visited a different city, and long-term investment would be inhibited by exchange rate uncertainty, for example. The same would be so, but to a lesser degree, if every state had its own currency, so tremendous benefits are associated with having a common currency (a fixed exchange rate) among all U.S. cities and all U.S. states. This is the main advantage of fixed exchange rates, and it is the rationale behind the proposal for a common currency in Europe.

Suppose, however, a fall in oil prices caused a major recession in Texas. Adjustment in Texas may take the form of an eventual fall in the wage of Texans, but primarily it takes the form of labor and capital moving out of Texas to other states. If Texas had its own currency, the adjustment could be facilitated by a fall in the value of the Texas currency, plus adoption of an appropriate Texas monetary policy. This is the advantage of flexible exchange rates. Flexing of the exchange rate and adoption of suitable monetary policy—

not possible under a fixed exchange rate—can facilitate adjustment to recessions and booms.

There is a major difference between the Texas example and a world consisting of different countries, however. With different countries, labor and capital are usually not allowed freely to move across borders, suggesting that the main mechanism whereby Texas adjusts to its recession does not work across countries. This difference markedly increases the importance of having a flexible exchange rate across separate countries, and explains why within a single country it is advantageous to have a fixed exchange rate and a common currency, but across countries it is better to have a flexible exchange rate.

Unfortunately, exchange rates can flex for reasons other than the need to facilitate adjustment to recession or boom. History has shown exchange rates to be much more volatile than experts had predicted when the Bretton Woods system broke down. As activity in financial assets markets has come to dominate the short-run determination of exchange rates, we have discovered that speculators can affect exchange rates dramatically, turning them from a stabilizing force into a destabilizing force. This possibility has caused central banks to modify the flexible exchange rate system by using monetary policy or direct intervention to stabilize exchange rates. In doing so, they must be careful to allow exchange rates to change to reflect fundamental forces—such as inflation rate differences, productivity growth rate differences, and natural resource discoveries. Preventing exchange rates from changing in such situations is why fixed exchange rates lead inevitably to exchange rate crises.

## Media Illustrations

### Example 1

**At the same time that Secretary Blumenthal was testifying to Congress, the Treasury borrowed $1.6 billion in Germany in the form of securities denominated in marks. It offered to pay an interest rate of roughly 6 percent per year on mark-denominated three- and four-year securities. On comparable securities denominated in dollars, the Treasury is currently paying about 9 percent—or three percentage points per year more.**

*Why is the rate of interest offered on mark-denominated securities less than that offered on dollar-denominated securities?*
The value of the U.S. dollar, relative to the German mark, must be expected to decline during the next three or four years.

*Assuming that mark- and dollar-denominated securities are risk equivalent, what would you guess is the difference between U.S. and German inflation?*
If these securities are risk equivalent, the difference in nominal interest rates should be due mainly to expected inflation differences, so a good guess would be 3 percent.

*What does the U.S. Treasury believe about the future value of the U.S. dollar in terms of marks? What do German investors who are buying these securities believe?*

If the value of the U.S. dollar fell by 3 percent per year over the life of these bonds, the cost to the U.S. Treasury would be the 6 percent interest plus the 3 percent fall in the exchange rate, for a total cost of 9 percent, equivalent to the cost of selling bonds denominated in dollars. Consequently, the U.S. Treasury must believe that, over the life of these bonds, the value of the U.S. dollar will fall by less than 3 percent per year. The German investors could have bought bonds denominated in dollars and earned 9 percent less the exchange loss, but instead opted for the guaranteed 6 percent. Consequently, they must believe that the U.S. dollar will fall by more than 3 percent per year over the life of these bonds.

### Example 2

**The Fed has made occasional attempts to lower interest rates and to accept some lowering of the dollar as a trade-off. Sometimes it works, and sometimes, like last summer, we end up with the worst of all possible worlds—higher interest rates and a lower dollar.**

*What causes the trade-off mentioned at the end of the first sentence?*

If interest rates are lowered, foreigners will decrease their purchases of U.S. bonds. This decrease in capital inflows creates a balance of payments deficit, leading to a fall in the value of the U.S. dollar.

*How would the Fed lower interest rates?*

The Fed could buy bonds, bidding up their price and thereby lowering the interest rate.

*What implication would this action have for the money supply and expected inflation?*

Buying bonds involves an increase in the money supply, which could create an increase in expected inflation.

*Explain how the "worst of all possible worlds" could occur.*

The Fed's efforts to reduce the interest rate could increase inflation expectations by causing the nominal interest rate actually to increase. The higher expected inflation rate would cause foreign exchange speculators, through the logic of purchasing power parity, to expect a fall in the U.S. dollar. To exploit this, they sell dollars, thus causing its value to fall.

### Example 3

**This does not mean there is a massive flow of U.S. funds into Canada because the differentials are mitigated by other factors. The discount on the forward Canadian dollar has kept step with the interest rate differential, and it is only on an unhedged basis that the full advantage of the differential can be gained.**

*What terminology do economists usually employ to describe a "flow of U.S. funds into Canada"?*

It would usually be referred to as *capital flows* from the United States to Canada.

*What must have happened to raise the possibility of a massive flow of U.S. funds into Canada?*

The difference between the Canadian and U.S. nominal interest rates must have widened considerably.

*What is the "discount on the forward Canadian dollar"?*

This discount is the difference between the Canadian spot and forward exchange rates. It reflects an anticipated fall in the Canadian dollar over the time horizon in question, plus a return for taking on the risk of holding Canadian dollars over this period.

*Why would the discount keep step with the interest rate differential?*

Suppose the interest rate differential increased by two percentage points, probably because of an increase in expected inflation in Canada of 2 percent (or a decrease of 2 percent in expected inflation in the United States, or some combination thereof). Purchasing power parity then predicts a 2 percent increase in the rate at which the Canadian dollar is depreciating. Because everyone can figure this out, the natural forces of supply and demand increase the discount by two percentage points.

*What is an "unhedged basis," and why does it imply that "the full advantage of the differential can be gained"?*

Contracting on the forward exchange market to avoid the risk of currency fluctuations is called "hedging." If this is not done, the full difference between the Canadian and U.S. interest rates is pocketed (but not necessarily kept because losses from an unfavorable movement in the exchange rate may be incurred).

## Chapter Summary

- Real interest rates are equal across countries except for a risk premium—a result known as interest rate parity.

- A nominal interest rate difference that only reflects a difference in expected inflation causes no capital flows because the purchasing power parity theorem causes people to expect an exchange rate change that will exactly offset the nominal interest rate difference.

- Fixed exchange rates reduce exchange rate risks and transactions costs, but inhibit adjustment to shocks. Modern exchange rate management tries to stabilize the exchange rate while permitting it to flex in response to changes in economic fundamentals.

## Rules of Thumb

- IRP: (foreign – U.S.) real $i$ rates = risk premium

- IRP: (foreign – U.S.) nominal $i$ rates
  = (foreign – U.S.) expected inflation rates + risk premium

- IRP: (foreign – U.S.) nominal $i$ rates
  = expected rate of change of U.S. exchange rate + risk premium

## Media Exercises

1. **He can't understand why we would put our money in domestic bonds at 9 percent, when we could get double-A rated New Zealand bonds at 19 percent.**

   Offer an explanation for this.

2. **Before the advent of modern international financial markets in the mid-1970s, domestic financial markets placed a serious constraint on the ability of governments to borrow their way to popularity or prosperity. Historically, domestic financial markets were largely closed systems in which excessive borrowing by governments led quickly to ...**

   Complete this clipping and explain how the advent of modern international financial markets has changed government's borrowing ability.

3. **The global trend toward higher short-term interest rates is a reflection of worldwide increases in _____. The 4.8 percent yield on Japanese short-term securities is due to a strong yen; Australia's 16.1 percent yield is a product of its weak dollar.**

   a. Fill in the blank.

   b. Why is the low interest rate associated with the strong currency and the high interest rate associated with the weak currency?

4. **An investor can sidestep the risk of _____ by obtaining a forward contract. In a forward contract, the bank guarantees the exchange rate for the investor when the issue is bought, so the investor is protected against _____. But there's a catch: _____. This catch usually renders the actual yield on the foreign bonds _____ the yield on domestic bonds.**

   Fill in the blanks.

5. **Higher inflation in both Germany and Japan has pushed up their interest rates. What he doesn't understand is why the U.S. interest rate hasn't**

followed suit. He claims that international financial markets are so closely integrated these days that the U.S. interest rate reaction should have been apparent by now.

Comment on this observation.

6. **What are the factors behind the recent decline in the value of the dollar? A speculative blip can be ruled out as the reason because the currency was selling at a forward premium for most of the period.**

   a. What is a forward premium?

   b. Why would a speculative blip be ruled out?

7. **He believes that Canada's lower inflation rate could lead to tighter spreads between the Canadian and U.S. interest rates.**

   What logic lies behind this thinking?

8. **Canadians must convince investors and speculators that the Canadian dollar will hold its value. For the moment, that means Canada must decisively match U.S. interest rates. Paradoxically, in the past Canada has usually ended up with the worst of both worlds: higher interest rates and a devalued dollar.**

   a. Construct a scenario in which the recommended policy of matching U.S. interest rates could lead to exactly the paradox cited.

   b. Why would the author have called the situation a paradox?

9. **Prior to 1989 it was widely believed that New Zealand ten-year government bond interest rates could not fall below those of Australia. Once New Zealand rates fell below those of Australia, the view on relative rates changed to one in which New Zealand rates could not fall below those of the United States due to the high liquidity of the U.S. bond market. But this also has been proved wrong.**

   What must be happening to cause New Zealand rates to fall below those of Australia and the United States?

10. **Few people are recommending a devaluation of the dollar. Rather, they are saying, "lower interest rates and accept the falling dollar that follows." Some might claim that this isn't possible because the interest rate is set by the market, but the central bank can certainly add money to the system (by purchasing bonds, for example) and that should drive rates down.**

    a. Explain why lowering interest rates should cause the dollar to fall.

    b. How does the central bank's bond purchase add money to the market?

    c. Will this purchase drive interest rates down? Explain why or why not.

11. **Although they may think they have little in common, the conservative corporate treasurer and the brash, high-flying currency trader are alike in one important respect: they both speculate on the value of the dollar.**

   a. How could a corporate treasurer be a speculator on the value of the dollar?

   b. How can he or she avoid undertaking such speculation?

12. **By narrowing the spread between short-term interest rates in Canada and the United States in line with the Canadian dollar forward rate, the Bank of Canada stopped the arbitrage activity that was pushing up the Canadian dollar.**

   a. What is the Canadian dollar forward rate, and why is it relevant here?

   b. Explain the arbitrage activity and how it would work in this case to push up the Canadian dollar.

13. **Although the chartered banks have so far refrained from raising their rates, the finance minister warned reporters that this situation cannot last. The Canadian and U.S. economies are so interrelated, he said, that it will be impossible for Canadian interest rates to remain much lower than U.S. rates for an extended period of time.**

   Contradict this Canadian politician's comment by constructing a scenario in which Canadian rates are persistently lower than U.S. rates.

14. **Last week's movement was largely triggered by Bank of Canada concerns about the drop in the Canadian dollar in the face of higher U.S. interest rates.**

   What is the "movement" referred to in this clip? Explain your reasoning.

15. **The governor of the Bank of Canada urged Canadians today to continue the fight against inflation, but warned that they cannot expect any significant drop in interest rates until the United States takes convincing action to reduce its budget deficit.**

   a. Explain the connection between the U.S. budget deficit and the Canadian interest rate.

   b. Under what circumstances is it true that Canadians cannot expect a drop in interest rates until the United States reduces its budget?

   c. Are these circumstances such that Canadians should be urged to fight against inflation, as the governor urges them?

   d. Under what circumstances could Canadians expect a fall in interest rates, in contradiction to the governor's claim?

**16. West Germany's decision to spend $85 billion on reunification probably pushed up interest rates in the United States by half a percentage point.**

How would West Germany's decision push up U.S. interest rates?

**17. A recent study claims that Japanese households are likely to decrease their saving rate in the 1990s, but it doesn't say what implication this will have for interest rates in the United States.**

What do you think this will do to U.S. interest rates? Why?

**18. Because the forward rate is currently higher than the spot rate, the market must be anticipating that the dollar will _____.**

Fill in the blank and explain your reasoning.

## Numerical Exercises

N1.   Suppose the current exchange rate is 200 yen per dollar, the U.S. interest rate is 6 percent, the Japanese interest rate is 4 percent, and there is no risk premium. What do you expect the exchange rate to be a year from now?

N2.   Suppose the current exchange rate is 4 francs per dollar, but is expected during the next year to rise to 4.4 francs per dollar. If the current U.S. interest rate is 6 percent, what should be the French interest rate on a comparable security, assuming a zero-risk premium?

N3.   Suppose the Canadian economy, on a fixed exchange rate, has a real growth rate of 2 percent and is in equilibrium with an inflation rate of 10 percent and a risk premium of 1 percent. Suppose changes in the United States cause the U.S. real rate of interest to increase from 3 percent to 4 percent and the U.S. inflation rate to increase by two percentage points. When the Canadian economy has settled to a new equilibrium after this change, what will be the Canadian nominal interest rate?

N4.   Suppose inflation in the United States is 8 percent, its real interest rate is 3 percent, and the real interest rate in Canada is 4 percent. Assuming a fixed exchange rate, what is the Canadian nominal interest rate?

N5.   Suppose the U.S. and Canadian economies are in mutual equilibrium with a flexible exchange rate, both with long-run real growth of 2 percent. The U.S. money-supply growth rate is 8 percent and its real interest rate is 3 percent. If the risk premium (Canada is riskier) is 1 percent, and the value of the U.S. dollar is appreciating by 4 percent per year, what is Canada's nominal interest rate?

N6.  If the Canadian risk premium is 1 percent, the Canadian interest rate is 10 percent, the U.S. interest rate is 15 percent, and the two economies are in mutual equilibrium, what should be happening to the U.S. exchange rate?

N7.  Suppose Canada and the United States are in equilibrium with a flexible exchange rate and a risk premium (Canada is riskier) of 1 percent. The real rates of growth in Canada and in the United States are both 3 percent, but the U.S. interest rate is 10 percent, and the Canadian interest rate is only 7 percent. What is happening to the U.S. exchange rate?

N8.  Suppose firm A signs a contract to buy some hardware from a Japanese company for 600 million yen, delivery and payment to take place one year hence. The current exchange rate is 200 yen per dollar, the U.S. interest rate is 6 percent, the Japanese interest rate is 4 percent, and there is no currency risk premium. Which of the following strategies would you recommend the firm adopt?

   a.  Firm A trades dollars for yen today and invests in Japanese bonds for a year.

   b.  Firm A invests in U.S. bonds for a year and enters a futures contract, agreeing to buy 600 million yen in one year at an exchange rate of 195 yen per dollar.

N9.  Suppose the Canadian economy, on a flexible exchange rate, has a real growth rate of 3 percent and is increasing its money supply by 10 percent per year. Suppose changes in the United States cause the U.S. real interest rate to rise from 4 percent to 5 percent and the U.S. inflation rate to increase by two percentage points. Assuming a risk differential premium of one percentage point (Canada is riskier), after the Canadian economy has settled to a new equilibrium, what is the Canadian nominal interest rate?

N10. Suppose that under a flexible exchange rate system the current exchange rate is 4 francs per dollar, inflation in France is 5 percent, and inflation in the United States is 8 percent. Suppose that you are a U.S. investor expecting to pay 10,000 francs in a year's time and wish to hedge against an unfavorable exchange rate movement. Approximately what forward exchange rate do you expect to pay?

N11. Under a fixed exchange rate, if U.S. real growth is 2 percent and money-supply growth is 8 percent, and if Canada's real interest rate is 4 percent, what should Canada's nominal interest rate be?

# Appendix A:   Supply and Demand

It has been claimed that even a parrot can become an economist. Teach a parrot to say "supply and demand," and it can answer any question on economics! Throughout this book, analyses of the forces of supply and demand are used to produce explanations of economic phenomena, but for the most part are not formalized via graphical representations. The purpose of this appendix is to allow interested readers to see how the forces of supply and demand are illustrated diagrammatically, and, in particular, to provide some perspective on how a traditional microeconomic diagram is employed in a macroeconomic context.

To this end, we begin by explaining the three fundamentals of microeconomic supply-and-demand analysis via a supply/demand diagram: the concept of an equilibrium; how the forces of supply and demand push a market to an equilibrium position; and the difference between a movement along a supply or demand curve and a shift in such a curve. Readers already conversant with microeconomic supply-and-demand curves may wish to skip this exposition and move directly to the section entitled "Macroeconomic Markets."

Then, we explain supply/demand diagrams representing each of the four major macroeconomic submarkets that interact to determine the character of the macroeconomy. Finally, we explain how activity in the four markets can be consolidated into a single diagram that summarizes and thereby avoids much curve-shifting associated with these markets' interaction. This final diagram—the aggregate supply/aggregate demand diagram—offers a summary picture of overall macroeconomic activity and is, for this reason, adopted in this book to aid exposition of macroeconomic behavior.

## Supply/Demand Diagrams

Supply/demand diagrams list a quantity of some good or service on the horizontal axis and its price on the vertical axis. As price varies, the demand curve traces out the quantity of the good or service people want to buy in a particular market, other things remaining the same (*ceteris paribus*). The supply curve

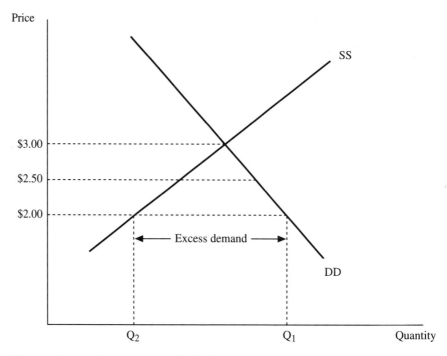

**Figure A.1**   Supply and demand for beef
At price $2.00 there is an excess demand of $Q_1 - Q_2$; excess demand continues to push
price up until equilibrium is attained at price $3.00.

traces out the quantity of the good or service that people/firms want to supply
to this market as the price changes, *ceteris paribus*.

To introduce the concept of supply and demand, let us look at the market for
beef. Figure A.1 is a supply/demand diagram for this market. On the vertical
axis the price of beef is measured, and on the horizontal axis the quantity of
beef is measured—either the quantity demanded, in the case of the demand
curve, or the quantity supplied, in the case of the supply curve.

The demand curve DD in figure A.1 portrays the amount of beef demanded
for each price. With all other things remaining the same, especially the price of
other meats, when the price of beef falls (as we move to a lower position on the
vertical axis), people find it more attractive to buy beef instead of other goods,
particularly other meats, so demand for beef increases. Therefore, the demand
curve for beef is downward-sloping.

The supply curve SS in the diagram portrays the quantity of beef that producers want to sell for each price. This quantity is determined by profit maximizing on the part of beef producers. As the price rises, beef producers can
cover the higher unit costs associated with increasing beef production and thus
find it possible to make more profit by supplying more beef. In addition, the
higher price may entice new producers to enter this market. Therefore, the
supply curve for beef is upward-sloping.

## Equilibrium

The intersection of supply-and-demand curves is of particular interest to economists. To see why, let us conduct the following thought experiment. If the price of beef in figure A.1 is $2 per pound, a price below the intersection of the supply-and-demand curves, then the quantity of beef demanded, from the demand curve, would be $Q_1$, and the quantity of beef supplied, from the supply curve, would be a smaller quantity, $Q_2$. At the price $2, demand exceeds supply, represented by an *excess demand* of magnitude $Q_1 - Q_2$. At this price, beef producers will not be willing to satisfy the demand for beef. Two things will happen: (1) those unable to obtain beef will offer a higher price to beef producers to ensure that they, rather than someone else, gets the available beef, and (2) beef producers will quickly deduce that profits can be increased by increasing price. Both phenomena reflect a fundamental law of supply and demand: *excess demand causes price to rise*.

If the price is increased to $2.50, as shown in figure A.1, demand falls as we slide up the demand curve, and supply rises as we slide up the supply curve, shrinking the excess demand. Because excess demand remains, however, the price continues to rise. The excess demand pressure on price continues until the excess demand for beef disappears, which happens at a price of $3, given by the intersection of the supply-and-demand curves.

If we had begun our thought experiment at a price higher than $3, we would have found an *excess supply* of beef. Beef producers would not be able to sell all beef produced, and an unwanted beef inventory would accumulate. Recognizing this, customers may offer beef producers a lower price in the hopes of getting a bargain. To get rid of the excess inventory, beef producers would accept such offers and may also initiate cuts in beef price. The consequence is that *excess supply causes price to fall*. This force lowering price continues so long as excess supply exists, so in this example price ultimately falls to $3.

The forces of supply and demand operate automatically to push the economy to the intersection of relevant supply-and-demand curves, a position in which there is no further pressure for change. Such a position is called an *equilibrium position*. Economists analyze a market by describing its equilibrium position, examining how quickly the automatic forces of supply and demand push the market to this equilibrium and noting how the equilibrium position changes whenever the market is subjected to a shock of some kind. A favorite shock to analyze is a government policy. For example, they may ask whether a government policy—such as increased government spending—can change the economy's equilibrium position and thus cause the economy to move in a particular direction.

## Shifts in Curves versus Movements along Curves

The supply-and-demand curves drawn in figure A.1 reflect a ceteris paribus condition—namely, that other conditions remained the same, but supply and

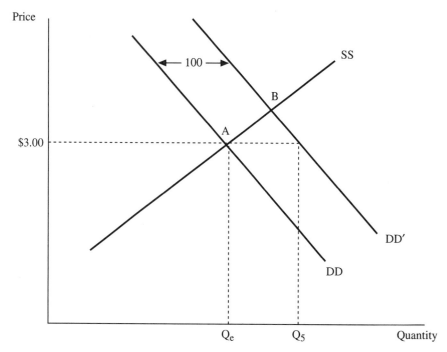

**Figure A.2**   Impact of an increase in income on the supply and demand for beef
The rise in income shifts DD to DD', causing excess demand of $Q_5 - Q_e$; this pushes the market from point A to point B.

demand are affected by more than just price. The level of income, for example, may also affect the amount demanded. Because of this, diagrams requiring all other things to remain the same could be misleading. Some way must be found to include other variables in the supply/demand diagram. Let us return to our beef example to illustrate how this is done.

Consider the market for beef illustrated in figure A.2, where the economy is currently in equilibrium at point A, the intersection of its supply-and-demand curves, at price \$3 and quantity $Q_e$. Now suppose that income level rises, causing a 100-ton increase in our demand for beef. At each price level, the demand is 100 tons higher, so the entire demand curve must shift right by 100, portrayed in figure A.2 as a rightward shift of DD to DD'. At the prevailing price of \$3, the shift creates an excess demand in the market of $Q_5 - Q_e = 100$. The excess demand causes upward pressure on price, moving the market to the new equilibrium at point B, the intersection of DD' and SS.

This example has introduced a new principle in using supply-and-demand curves. Movements along the supply-and-demand curves reflect changes in price and quantity, the variables measured on the two axes of the supply/demand diagram. However, a change in a variable not measured on these axes—in this example, a change in the income level—causes a shift in one or both of the supply-and-demand curves. This shift in turn creates a disequilibrium at the original price, which sets in motion automatic forces that push the economy along the supply-and-demand curves to a new equilibrium. Understanding the distinction between a *movement along a curve* and a *shift in a curve* should facilitate your understanding of supply/demand diagrams.

The distinction allows a supply/demand diagram to reflect the influence of changes that occur in other markets, thus permitting a more comprehensive analysis of the economy. For example, a change in the market for chicken may lower the price of chicken, which in turn should decrease the demand for beef, as people substitute the less-expensive chicken for beef, shifting the demand curve for beef to the left and thereby affecting the price of beef. Interaction between markets is particularly important in a macroeconomic context because we are looking at the behavior of the economy as a whole, rather than at the behavior of a single market.

## Media Examples

Let us complete this brief presentation of microeconomic supply and demand by looking at some examples of how supply-and-demand analysis can be used to interpret news clips.

### Example 1

**A freeze in southwestern U.S. and Mexican fields has resulted in damaged crops and inflated prices for produce such as lettuce, broccoli, and cauliflower.**

*How would this be interpreted on a supply/demand diagram?*
At every price, supply of produce is now less, so the supply curve shifts to the left. This causes excess demand at current produce prices, thus pushing them up.

### Example 2

**Smith opined that higher prices may make it possible for some producers who closed during the last two years to reopen.**

*How would this situation be interpreted on a supply/demand diagram?*
The higher price slides us along the supply curve to a higher output. Some of that higher output comes from new producers.

### Example 3

**There are still 2,500 vacant units in the city and just so many tenants to go around. Landlords will have to take measures to get people in their buildings.**

*What is the current status of this market?*
There is an excess supply of rental accommodation.

*What measures will the landlords have to take?*
They will be forced to lower rents.

### Example 4

**The economy is hot right now. People have higher incomes, so they want to borrow money to buy homes and big-ticket consumer durables. Imagine what this is doing to interest rates!**

*Use supply-and-demand analysis to explain what must be happening to interest rates.*

Higher incomes have shifted the demand for loans to the right, creating an excess demand for loans at the current interest rate, the "price" of loans. The excess demand for loans pushes up this price, the interest rate.

### Example 5

**Higher U.S. interest rates have caused foreigners to flock to the United States to buy our bonds. Surely, this is the main reason why our exchange rate is so high.**

*Use supply-and-demand analysis to explain how the high interest rate could cause a high value of the U.S. dollar.*

To buy our bonds, foreigners must first use their foreign currency to buy U.S. dollars. Thus, the high U.S. interest rate has shifted the demand for U.S. dollars to the right. The excess demand for U.S. dollars bids up their price, the exchange rate.

### Example 6

**The expected price drop for cherries due to the bumper crop this year won't be as much as we thought due to short supplies of pears and peaches.**

*Explain why the price of cherries is expected to drop.*

A bumper crop means that the supply of cherries is much higher than expected, shifting the cherry supply curve to the right. The excess supply at current cherry prices pushes cherry prices down.

*Why should short supplies of pears and peaches inhibit the fall in cherry prices?*

Short supplies of pears and peaches should bid up their prices, causing people to demand more of alternative fruits such as cherries. The extra demand for cherries should inhibit their price fall.

### Example 7

**Bumper grain crops this year will further encourage meat production.**

*Explain the rationale behind this statement.*

Bumper grain crops increase grain supply and push the price of grain down. The lower price of grain lowers the cost of producing meat, encouraging producers to increase meat production. Thus, the supply curve for meat shifts to the right.

---

## Macroeconomic Markets

Economists analyze the macroeconomy by visualizing four broad markets: the goods-and-services market, the labor market, the money/bond market, and the foreign exchange market. Each of these markets is represented by a supply/ demand diagram in which the values of the economy's important macroeconomic variables are determined. The *goods-and-services market* determines the price level/inflation rate and the amount of output/income produced annually by the economy. The *labor market* determines the wage rate and the employment/unemployment level. The *money market* determines the interest rate and the price of bonds. The *foreign exchange market* determines the balance of payments and the exchange rate. Collectively, these markets determine the values of the macroeconomic variables in which citizens and policymakers are most interested: inflation, unemployment, interest rates, and the exchange rate.

Market interaction makes macroeconomics challenging for students because analysis of one market cannot be undertaken in isolation from analysis of the other markets. The interest rate, for example, is determined in the money/bond market, but the interest rate affects demand in the goods-and-services market, which in turn affects the level of income, which in turn affects the demand for money/bonds in the money/bond market. Automatic forces of supply and demand serve to push each of these markets to equilibrium, with all four markets interacting. When all four markets are in equilibrium simultaneously, the economy as a whole is said to be in equilibrium.

Macroeconomics explains how the four markets interact—how and how quickly the automatic forces created by disequilibria serve to push the economy to an overall equilibrium, and how government intervention (via a macroeconomic policy) can influence equilibrium or speed the process of adjustment to equilibrium.

Unemployment, for example, reflects disequilibrium in the labor market. Automatic adjustment forces pushing the economy back to full employment may operate too slowly, so one might ask what government policy would speed up this adjustment. Because of the interconnections between the four markets, it is not obvious what government policy would be best. To influence the labor market, for example, it is not necessary to intervene directly in this market. The government could intervene in one of the other markets by using *fiscal policy* to affect demand in the goods-and-services market or *monetary policy* to affect supply in the money/bond market, for example.

The four macroeconomic markets have supply/demand diagrams similar to the supply/demand diagrams used to analyze a microeconomic market such as the market for beef, but there are some distinctive differences. The most prominent difference is that in a macroeconomic market quantity is an aggregate of quantities in different submarkets and price is an "average" or representative price of these submarkets. This should become clear in the following brief descriptions of these markets. Be warned that if you are just beginning your reading of this book, the details of these descriptions may be difficult to understand because some terminology may be unfamiliar and some concepts are not explained in detail. If you concentrate on seeing the big picture rather than the

Price index (P)

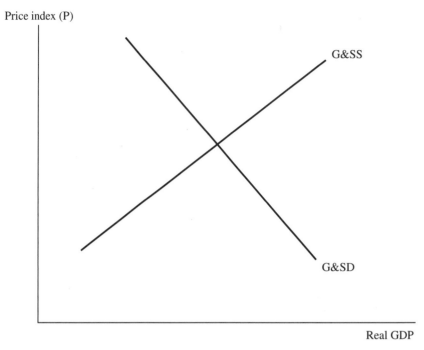

**Figure A.3**   Goods-and-services market supply-and-demand diagram

details, however, these descriptions will offer you an overview of macro-economics that should facilitate understanding the contents of this book. Read through the material looking for the overall perspective; the details you will master later.

## The Market for Goods and Services

The market for goods and services represents supply of and demand for the total output of goods and services in the economy and thus is an aggregation of all the economy's microeconomic markets for goods and services. The demand curve, G&SD in figure A.3, is consequently called the goods-and-services demand curve, and the supply curve G&SS is called the goods-and-services supply curve. The price on the vertical axis must now measure an overall or average price level of all goods and services, rather than the price of a specific product. Chapter 2 discusses how such a price index is measured. The vertical axis of figure A.3 measures P, the overall price index.

The horizontal axis now measures total output of the economy, rather than output of a specific product. As described in chapter 2, total output is the economy's income level, traditionally measured by gross domestic product (GDP). In order to remove the influence of price changes and to ensure that we focus on changes in physical outputs, GDP is measured in real terms. Consequently, the horizontal axis measures real GDP.

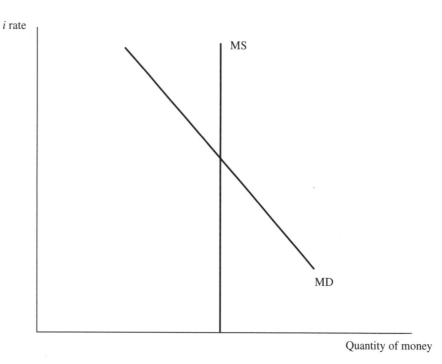

**Figure A.4**   Money market supply-and-demand diagram

Why is the G&SD curve downward-sloping? One explanation rests on the *wealth effect*. A rise in the overall price level causes people holding assets denominated in dollars to feel less wealthy, so they decrease their demand for goods and services. Other explanations are offered in chapter 5.

Why is the G&SS curve upward-sloping? A possible answer is that a higher price level makes it profitable for firms to increase output, so they do.

Important shifts of these curves come from government policy. Through fiscal policy, the government changes its spending, thus shifting the G&SD curve directly. Through monetary policy, the government intervenes in the money/bond market, affecting the interest rate, which in turn affects demand for goods and services and indirectly shifts the G&SD curve. Examples of other important shifts are wage increases, which raise firms' costs and shift the G&SS curve upward, and supply-side shocks, such as large increases in the price of energy, which do the same.

### The Money/Bond Market

The second of the four major macroeconomic markets is the "money" market, which represents the myriad of markets in the economy that deal with borrowing and lending and that thus affect and are affected by interest rates. The economy's many interest rates are represented by a single representative macroeconomic interest rate, which appears on the vertical axis in figure A.4. The horizontal axis measures the economy's supply of or demand for money, defined as the sum of cash in our pockets and balances in our bank accounts.

This diagram may seem peculiar: why doesn't the horizontal axis measure the aggregate of all funds borrowed and loaned? Macroeconomists believe that individuals hold their financial wealth in one of two forms: money (cash plus bank balances) or "other" financial assets, referred to generically as bonds. They also believe that any decision to hold more or less money is matched by a decision to hold fewer or more bonds, so an analysis of the financial market can be simplified by looking exclusively at the supply of and demand for money.

Why do people hold some of their wealth in the form of money (cash and balances in bank accounts), which earns little or no interest return? In a word, convenience: money facilitates day-to-day financial transactions. Consumers need it to buy things and firms need it to pay workers and to purchase raw materials. In general, our society uses money to facilitate the production and distribution of goods and services. People and firms demand money because of this very useful service it provides.

How much money is demanded? Several variables affect an economy's demand for money, one of which is the price of money—namely, the interest rate. At a high interest rate, the *opportunity cost* of money is high: wealth held in the form of money foregoes the high return that could be earned by investing that wealth in bonds. As the interest rate rises, people are induced to hold their wealth in bonds rather than in the form of money. The higher interest return on bonds compensates them for the inconveniences that a smaller money holding entails. Consequently, as the interest rate rises people decrease their demand for money, causing the demand-for-money curve, MD in figure A.4, to be downward-sloping. The supply-of-money curve, MS in figure A.4, is drawn vertically at a level determined by the economy's central bank.

What might cause these curves to shift? The most prominent factor causing the MS curve to shift is central bank monetary policy action. If the central bank increases the money supply, for example, the MS curve shifts to the right. Shifts of the MD curve result from changes in variables other than the interest rate that affect the demand for money—the most prominent of which is the income level. If an economy has a higher income level, for example, more money is demanded to facilitate its higher level of production and consumption, so the MD curve shifts to the right. Another prominent factor shifting the MD curve is financial innovation in the banking system, such as the increased use of credit cards, which make it easier for people to get by without large money holdings. Such factors shift the MD curve to the left.

**The Labor Market**

The third of the four major macroeconomic markets is the labor market. As with the other macroeconomic markets, this market should not be seen as a gathering of participants in a single physical location at a specific time. Buying

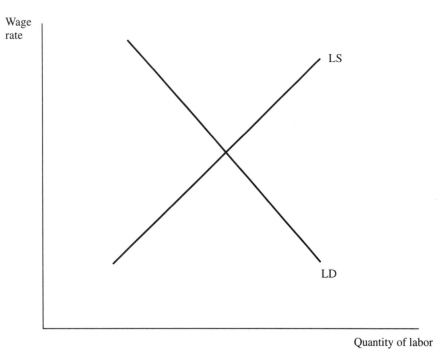

**Figure A.5**   Labor market supply-and-demand diagram

and selling of labor is ubiquitous, occurring in many different locations, at many different times of the day and year. Furthermore, labor is not homogeneous. Workers possess different skills, so in reality there is a large number of separate labor markets with different wage rates, each rate relating to specific skills and locations. Macroeconomists ignore all this and create a conceptual overall market for labor in which there is a single, representative wage rate—measured on the vertical axis in figure A.5—and a generic type of labor—measured on the horizontal axis.

In figure A.5, the demand curve LD portrays the quantity of labor that firms want on this market, an amount determined by profit-maximizing considerations. With all other things held constant, when the value of the wage rate falls (as we move to a lower position on the vertical axis), firms' costs fall, making it profitable to increase output, so the demand for labor rises. Thus, the demand curve for labor is downward-sloping.

The supply curve LS in figure A.5 reflects the quantity of labor that workers want to supply. As the wage rate rises, workers are induced to supply more labor. Existing workers are enticed to work longer hours, and many of those not currently working are prompted to enter the labor market, both of which increase the supply of labor. Thus, the supply curve for labor is upward-sloping.

What would cause these curves to shift? The most prominent variable causing these curves to shift is the price level. If prices rise, then for a given wage rate

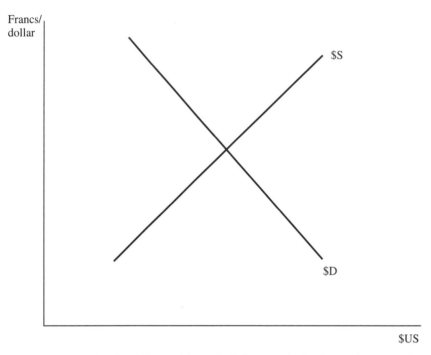

**Figure A.6**   Supply of and demand for U.S. dollars on the foreign exchange market

firms would find it profitable to increase output and would attempt to do so by increasing their demand for labor. The demand-for-labor curve would shift to the right. If the overall price level rose, however, workers would sooner or later discover that their real wage was lower and would accordingly be reluctant to work as much. The supply-of-labor curve would shift to the left.

**The Foreign Exchange Market**

The fourth major macroeconomic market is the foreign exchange market for the U.S. dollar. As with the other macroeconomic markets, this market should not be visualized as a gathering of participants in a single physical location at a specific time. Buying and selling of U.S. dollars is performed over the telephone and by electronic means around the world at all times of the day. In figure A.6, the vertical axis measures the value/price of the U.S. dollar in terms of foreign exchange—that is, the number of francs that a dollar can buy (francs/dollar) or, equivalently, the number of francs required to buy a dollar. This measure is known as the *exchange rate*. The horizontal axis measures quantity of U.S. dollars.

Of course, a very large number of different foreign currencies can be used to measure the price on the vertical axis. French currency was chosen merely for expositional convenience. Francs per dollar should be thought of as representing the value of the U.S. dollar, in much the same way that the prices measured on the vertical axes in the other macroeconomic markets represent several different prices.

In figure A.6, the demand curve $D portrays the number of U.S. dollars ($US) wanted on this market by foreigners, (for example, to buy U.S. goods and services or to invest in U.S. financial assets) as a function of the dollar's price—the exchange rate. With all other things held constant, when the value of the U.S. dollar falls (as we move to a lower position on the vertical axis) foreigners find that buying U.S. goods and services is cheaper (because they can get more dollars for a franc), so they buy more, thus increasing their demand for U.S. dollars. The demand curve for U.S. dollars on the foreign exchange market is downward-sloping.

The supply curve $S in figure A.6 reflects the quantity of U.S. dollars that U.S. residents bring to the foreign exchange market for the purpose of buying foreign currencies (in this example represented by francs). The U.S. supply of dollars reflects U.S. residents' wishes to purchase imports or to invest in foreign financial assets, both of which require them to obtain foreign currency. As the value of the U.S. dollar rises, they find it cheaper (in terms of dollars) to buy foreign goods and services, so they buy more, thus increasing the supply of U.S. dollars. The supply curve for U.S. dollars on the foreign exchange market is upward-sloping.

What could cause these curves to shift? A rise in U.S. income would cause U.S. consumers to increase their demand for imports because at a higher income level they will buy more goods in general, some of which will be imported or will have imported components. To pay for these imports, they will need foreign currency, so they take U.S. dollars to the foreign exchange market to obtain the foreign currency, thereby increasing the supply of U.S. dollars on the foreign currency market. Thus, an increase in U.S. income shifts the supply curve $S to the right. Suppose, on the other hand, that the U.S. interest rate rises so as to become higher relative to interest rates in foreign countries. Because of this higher interest rate, foreigners will wish to buy more U.S. bonds and, consequently, will demand more U.S. dollars to buy them. This action shifts the demand curve $D to the right.

## Macroeconomic Analysis Using Supply and Demand

This whirlwind tour of the supply/demand diagrams of the four macroeconomic markets may have left you with a headache because the markets themselves are complicated. Their supply-and-demand curves are subject to all kinds of shifts, and the markets interact in subtle ways. Because everything seems to affect everything else at the same time, it is not clear how an analysis of the macroeconomy can be structured in a logical fashion. Any analysis of what is happening in one market immediately gets tangled up with repercussions from activity in the other three markets.

What is needed here is some way of collapsing all four diagrams into a single diagram that incorporates implicitly all interactions that otherwise would give us headaches. Such a diagram would be of immense value because it would produce a summary picture of the macroeconomy—a picture that hides and therefore circumvents much curve shifting. Such a diagram is used in this text.

### The Aggregate Supply/Aggregate Demand Diagram

The diagram representing the goods-and-services market as described earlier is misleading. The G&SD and G&SS curves in figure A.3 were described as telling us how aggregate demand for and aggregate supply of goods and services varied as the overall price level varied, other things being constant. However, it is not legitimate to hold other things constant for these curves. As the price level changes and we slide along to a different income level, the G&SD curve shifts because the level of income is itself a determinant of aggregate demand for goods and services. Also, when the price level changes, workers may demand compensating wage increases that remove firms' incentive to increase output, thus shifting the GS&S curve. We cannot claim, therefore, that the intersection of the G&SD and G&SS curves in figure A.3 tells us the equilibrium level of income because that level of income may imply a different G&SD curve, and it may not be consistent with what is happening in the labor market.

To deal with this problem, economists have invented an entirely different diagram, one which continues to use price and income on the two axes and therefore unfortunately looks quite similar to the G&SS/G&SD diagram. In this new diagram, one curve represents equilibrium in the goods-and-services market, and the other curve represents equilibrium in the labor market. Their intersection, therefore, corresponds to simultaneous equilibrium in both markets. The former curve should have been called the G&SME or "goods-and-services market equilibrium" curve, but was instead called the AD or "aggregate demand" curve. The latter curve should have been called the LME or "labor market equilibrium" curve, but instead was called the AS or "aggregate supply" curve. Together, the two curves produce the aggregate supply/aggregate demand or AS/AD diagram shown in figure A.7.

The AD curve represents equilibrium in the goods-and-services market. *The aggregate demand curve consists of combinations of price and income that correspond to equilibrium in the goods-and-services market.* It builds into its derivation the fact that aggregate demand for goods and services is affected by the income level. For those interested, this derivation is illustrated in appendix 5.1 at the end of chapter 5.

The AS curve represents equilibrium in the labor market. *The aggregate supply curve consists of combinations of price and income that correspond to equilibrium in the labor market.* It builds into its derivation the fact that workers may demand wage increases when the price level increases. In the short run, workers may misjudge what is happening or be constrained by contracts, so

Price index (P)

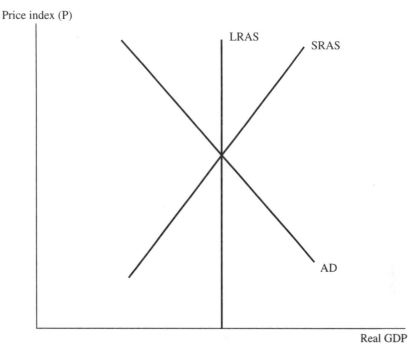

**Figure A.7**   AS/AD diagram

firms may be able to increase profit by increasing output; the AS curve will thus be upward-sloping, as shown by SRAS in figure A.7. In the long run, however, workers should be successful in increasing wages by enough to offset fully the original increase in prices, pushing the equilibrium level of employment back to its original level. This implies no change in income, so the AS curve is vertical, as shown by LRAS in figure A.7.

The intersection of AS and AD, then, is a combination of price and income that corresponds to simultaneous equilibrium in both the goods-and-services market and the labor market. Whenever the economy is not located on both of these curves, disequilibrium forces should act to push the economy in one direction or another. Much of the macroeconomic analysis in this book consists of stories about disequilibrium reactions, utilizing the AS/AD diagram to picture the equilibrium character of the economy.

What about the money/bond market and foreign exchange market? The influence of these markets can be built into the AD curve, so that in advanced analyses the AD curve actually is defined as combinations of price and income corresponding to simultaneous equilibrium in the goods-and-services, money/bond, and foreign exchange markets. As we slide along the AD curve, there is a lot of activity in the background, with interest rates and exchange rates adjusting quickly to maintain equilibrium in the money/bond and foreign exchange markets and with their influence on aggregate demand for goods and services being incorporated into the slope of the AD curve.

The AS/AD diagram simplifies things immensely because it can be used to portray equilibrium in the goods-and-services and labor markets without having to worry about interactions with the money/bond and foreign exchange markets. Activity in the money/bond and foreign exchange markets is incorporated into the diagram, but is hidden from view, thus allowing both a clear picture of disequilibria in the goods-and-services and labor markets and a clear outline of associated pressures on price, income, and unemployment. The AS/AD diagram is truly a picture worth more than a thousand words.

# Appendix B: Additional Media Exercises

1. **Alan Blinder, the Fed's newish vice chairman, insisted that central banks could use interest rates to reduce unemployment, at least for a few years. "Sell dollars," said a former European finance minister, summing up many economists' feelings.**

   a. Explain how the Fed could use interest rates to reduce unemployment.

   b. Under what circumstances would this action be appropriate, and under what circumstances would it not be appropriate?

   c. Why might the reaction of many economists be to "sell dollars"?

2. **Consumer prices rose just 0.1 percent in July from June. Although the increase from a year earlier is 2.8 percent, inflation in the last three months is a mere 0.8 percent annualized. As a result, the long bond plunged to a new low of 6.33 percent from 5.63 percent a week earlier.**

   Explain why the long bond plunged.

3. **The reason for Clinton's caution is obvious: the bond market sent him a signal a month ago that big spending is just not acceptable. In anticipation of Clinton's victory, coupled with talk from the Clinton camp about fresh spending, the sell-off of Treasury bonds boosted long-term interest rates to about 7.7 percent from 7.3 percent.**

   Explain why interest rates rose.

4. **Analysts are wondering if Canadian yields can fall while U.S. yields rise.**

   Can they? If so, how? If not, why not?

5. **The two-year-old recession appears to have deepened in the past two months, paving the way for steep cuts in interest rates and a steady depreciation of the dollar in coming months, economists say.**

   Explain the logic behind this prediction.

6. **Bonds were at the mercy of the dollar this week as a midweek currency slump sent ...**

Complete this clipping and explain your reasoning.

7. **That is why the jump in May's unemployment rate—from 7.2 percent to 7.5 percent, the highest during this business cycle—caused dismay. Yet, this may be missing the point. The number of people in the labor force in the month of May jumped by 330,000.**

Of what relevance is the jump in the labor force?

8. **Monetary policy, by winning on inflation, is about to confer to the federal government an enormous fiscal dividend.**

Explain what is meant here.

9. **Democratic presidential nominee Bill Clinton yesterday won the endorsement of nearly six hundred economists who said they like his plan to revitalize the economy through government spending and tax breaks for business investment.**

Explain how this policy would work to revitalize the economy.

10. **There is no evidence we are suffering from either high inventory stocks or a sharp inflationary spike, the two factors that typically cause a major recession.**

Explain how these two factors could cause a recession.

11. **Economists claim that a strong dollar is a result of the Fed's pitched battle against inflation.**

Explain the logic of this.

12. **One way to alleviate inflationary pressure is to engineer an upward valuation of your currency against that of your major trading partners. A higher dollar means that imports are cheaper and prices should move lower.**

How would a rise in the value of the dollar be engineered? Is this compatible with a move to a lower inflation rate?

13. **Nevertheless, the finance minister has taken a preemptive strike in recent weeks against any pressure on his currency by cutting government spending to slow domestic consumption. That should reduce the trade deficit, but will also slow the economy.**

a. How will cutting government spending slow domestic consumption?

b. How will this reduce the trade deficit?

14. **The dilemma facing the Fed is whether to cut the discount rate charged to commercial banks—now at 3 percent—to rejuvenate the stalled economy and risk undermining an already weak dollar.**

   a. How would cutting the discount rate rejuvenate the economy?

   b. How would it undermine the dollar?

   c. Would undermining the dollar be good or bad for this economy?

15. **Economists, who a week ago were talking about economic sluggishness, now fear a strong recovery that, coupled with an expansive fiscal package, will strengthen the dollar, hurt T-bills, and drive market yields _____.**

   a. Why will the dollar be strengthened?

   b. Why will T-bills be hurt?

   c. Fill in the blank and explain your reasoning.

16. **Any major attempt to reduce rates for the sole purpose of cutting the federal government's huge interest payments on the public debt would likely backfire and drive rates higher.**

   Explain what logic might lie behind the claim that the attempt to reduce rates will "backfire and drive rates higher."

17. **Economists and important figures in the U.S. government have been debating whether it is government spending deficits, restrictive monetary policy, capital inflows, or anticipated inflation that is the real culprit for interest-rate increases in the United States.**

   a. Which of the four possible economic factors could definitely *not* have caused high interest rates? Why?

   b. Explain how the other three factors could have led to higher interest rates.

18. **U.S. money supply in the October-to-March period grew at a 10 percent annual rate, compared with growth of less than 1 percent between June and October last year. This behavior tends to weaken the U.S. dollar, as it becomes progressively less profitable to invest in U.S. dollar–denominated, short-term investments.**

   a. Why does it become less profitable to invest in U.S. bonds?

   b. Why should this weaken the U.S. dollar?

19. **The central bank isn't ready to lay down its main weapon—high interest rates—in the fight against inflation despite signs that prices have stabilized and that exporters are being hurt by this policy.**

a. How are high interest rates a weapon in the fight against inflation?

b. Why are exporters hurt by this policy?

20. **Our trade account has remained in a deep deficit even though the dollar has fallen sharply over the past four years, a development that normally would have led to an improvement in trade figures. Now, economists and others say that only a cut in our growth rate will bring the trade deficit down.**

   a. Why would a fall in the dollar normally lead to an improvement in the trade deficit?

   b. What might be preventing this from happening?

   c. How would a cut in our growth rate influence the trade deficit?

21. **The central bank can defend the long-term external value of our currency only by defending its internal value.**

   Explain the rationale behind this statement.

22. **There is no historical evidence of countries finding enduring prosperity in a strategy of currency devaluation: we cannot devalue our way to the kind of competitive, high-performance economy we want.**

   What logic lies behind this view?

23. **Helping to spark yesterday's bond rally was a major drop in oil prices.**

   Explain what oil prices have to do with bond rallies.

24. **Most economists say that one crucial way to lift savings and investment would be to slash the federal budget deficit.**

   Explain how slashing the deficit would lift savings and investment.

25. **The drop in sales provided a boost to the credit market, where many analysts believe a slowing economy would relieve upward pressure on interest rates.**

   How would you explain why a slowing economy would lower interest rates?

26. **Estimates of multipliers tend to reach a peak after two or three years and decline thereafter, sometimes being negative.**

   Why might the change in estimates occur?

27. **Comments by Alan Greenspan, chairman of the Federal Reserve Board, have intensified speculation that inflation will remain subdued and have prompted some investment managers to predict even further declines in _____. Prices of some actively traded thirty-year Treasury bonds**

**wound up the day with** _____ **of about three-quarters of a point, or about $7.50 per $1,000 face amount.**

Fill in the blanks.

28. **The French economy took a nosedive after the Socialist government was elected in 1981. In reaction, Mr. Mitterand's government shortened the workweek, raised the minimum wage, and increased various social benefits—whereupon unemployment actually increased further.**

    Would you label the extra increase in unemployment an increase in the rate of cyclical or natural unemployment?

29. **He pays particular attention to the "yield curve"—the spread between long-term and short-term interest rates. Many economists believe that rising long term rates signal financial-market expectations that ...**

    Complete this clipping.

30. **Alan Greenspan stated that what we have seen in the past is that the willingness of foreigners to hold dollars is closely related to their sense of the soundness of our economic policies.**

    Just what is meant by "soundness" in this statement, and why?

31. **It will be impossible for monetary authorities to get long-term interest rates down unless they can convince lenders that they can hold down the rate of inflation.**

    Explain the logic of this claim.

32. **Bond prices sank on news that the unemployment rate fell to its lowest point in January in a year, to 7.1 percent, but then strengthened after the numbers proved too good to be true. On closer examination, most of the decline was caused by reductions in the labor force.**

    a. Why would bond prices sink on news of lower unemployment?

    b. How are reductions in the labor force relevant here?

    c. What name do economists often give such reductions?

33. **Fed chairman Alan Greenspan worries that new Treasury borrowings could cause some crowding out and keep long rates _____ and economic growth _____ than normal.**

    a. Why would new Treasury borrowings cause crowding out?

    b. Fill in the blanks.

34. **The recent surge in the money supply must be contained, and in very short order, if the hope for a viable long-term bond market is to be sustained.**

What does the money-supply surge have to do with the viability of the long-term bond market?

35. **Many countries, such as the United States, do not include mortgage rates in their CPI measure, but in those countries that do, such as New Zealand, monetary authorities must focus on the underlying inflation rate, not on the "headline" rate.**

How would the inclusion of mortgage rates in the CPI measure complicate monetary policy?

36. **Another criticism of defense spending is that it promotes inflation by adding to total demand in the economy without increasing the supply of new goods available to meet it because a soldier spends his pay on things he has not helped produce and the munitions worker does not go out and buy a tank.**

Comment on this argument.

37. **The evidence has been available for some time that real multipliers have fallen and may now be below one. This means that government deficits are no longer stimulative: an increased deficit of $1 billion will yield less than a $1 billion increase in real output and will accelerate inflation.**

a. What is the difference between a regular multiplier and a "real" multiplier?

b. Which would you expect to be larger? Why?

c. What does a multiplier less than one mean? Does it mean that the policy is not stimulative, as the clipping claims? Explain why or why not.

d. Is the inflation acceleration mentioned at the end of the clipping a long-run or short-run phenomenon? Explain why.

38. **Higher interest rates must boost the cost of all sorts of things for businessmen, whether because they may need loans to finance inventories or because the nature of their business entails time lags between delivering the goods and getting paid. How can higher interest rates be anti-inflationary?**

How would you answer this question?

39. **The Fed based its monetary policy in the 1980s on the assumption that velocity would continue its downward trend. Had they assumed a constant velocity, inflation would have been _____ than what we actually experienced.**

Fill in the blank and explain your reasoning.

40. **Indexing of personal income taxes was intended to take inflationary gains out of tax revenues. It was also intended to be a discipline on governments.**

Explain how indexing was supposed to act as a discipline on governments.

41. **A $10 billion tax cut to ease the bite of inflation was urged yesterday by the Democratic majority of the Congressional Joint Economic Committee. Senator William Proxmire (D-Wis.), the committee's vice chairman, said in a separate statement that he thinks austerity, not stimulation, is the correct economic prescription.**

    With which opinion do you agree? Why?

42. **Inflation results when the quantity of money and credit is increased, on a sustained basis, at a rate that is ...**

    Complete this statement.

43. **Don't expect any easing of interest rates yet, said analysts, adding that rates will probably remain at their current levels or possibly rise somewhat until there is clear evidence of an easing of inflation.**

    Why would "clear evidence of an easing of inflation" lead to a fall in interest rates?

44. **As someone who has been a proponent of low inflation, I am often asked how I can support a policy that seems to penalize those, such as seniors, who live off the interest from their savings. Low inflation means lower interest rates, the argument goes, so seniors lucky enough to have savings have to live on less. The person posing the question often illustrates it with the plight of a parent, uncle, or aunt now forced to draw on capital to make ends meet.**

    a. Does low inflation mean lower interest rates? Why or why not?

    b. How would you respond to the criticism aimed at the speaker?

45. **Not only were both sets of headline data stronger than analysts had expected, but the "core" measures of producer and consumer price inflation—which exclude the volatile food and energy components—were also above Wall Street's estimates. The figures sparked heavy selling in the bond market, where the thirty-year bond yield jumped from 6.81 percent to 6.97 percent in just two days.**

    a. Explain why the figures sparked bond selling.

    b. Is the yield jump consistent with this selling? Explain why or why not.

46. **There aren't a lot of advantages to high inflation, but there is one. High inflation reduces the value of debts, making them easier to pay off.**

    Evaluate this advantage of high inflation.

47. **The Bank of Canada began easing monetary conditions during the summer of 1990 in response to the recession and the resulting substantial reduction**

in inflationary pressures. The prime rate fell from 14.7 percent to the current 9.5 percent. Although the U.S. Federal Reserve was also easing, the pace of easing in Canada exceeded that in the United States, resulting in a three hundred basis-point narrowing in the Canada-U.S. short-term interest rate spread. Surprisingly, this did not result in a decline in the value of the Canadian dollar; in fact, it strengthened.

a. Why might one normally expect a decline in the value of the Canadian dollar when the interest rate spread narrows by three percentage points?

b. Explain why such a decline did not happen in this case.

48. Lawson, the British Chancellor of the Exchequer, made the logical mistake of trying to track the Deutschmark without also tracking German monetary policy. The British money supply was allowed to increase three times as fast as the German money supply. That difference doomed the policy of aligning the pound to the Deutschmark.

Explain the logic of the claim made in the last sentence.

49. Because Canadian inflation will continue to accelerate while United States inflation starts to decline, the Canadian dollar will probably come under pressure this year, forcing the Bank of Canada to keep interest rates up. With inflation accelerating, you have to be very careful about bonds.

a. What kind of pressure will the Canadian dollar experience? Explain why.

b. Would it be appropriate for the Bank of Canada to raise the Canadian interest rate? Explain why or why not.

c. Why do you "have to be careful about bonds," as suggested at the end of this clipping?

50. What would happen, for example, if Canada adopted a deliberate policy of reducing the budget deficit and lowering interest rates? Listen to the market through the voice of Richard Kapsche, a futures floor manager at Chicago's International Monetary Market: we would read that as an inflationary policy and start selling off Canadian dollars.

a. Would the adopted policy be inflationary? Why or why not?

b. Why would the market start selling Canadian dollars if it thought Canada was adopting an inflationary policy?

51. While reiterating that there is no target for the Canadian dollar, Bank of Canada governor John Crow said demands for it to be devalued to help the trade sector amounted to asking the bank "to print more money." A devaluation seen as deliberate and inflationary would probably force up interest rates, he said.

a. How would a devalued dollar help the trade sector?

b. Why would devaluation involve printing more money?

c. What is the main drawback of printing more money?

d. Why would interest rates be forced up?

52. **Winning the battle but losing the war? That seems to be the situation of the central bank in its fifth year of trying to apply the monetarist prescription for defeating inflation by squeezing the money supply.**

a. What exactly is the monetarist prescription?

b. What is the "battle" here, and what is the "war"?

c. What could be causing the central bank to be winning the battle but losing the war?

53. **When assessing the effect of the U.S. growth slowdown on Canadian exports, it is important to bear in mind that much of the U.S. slowdown is due to the diversion of U.S. demand abroad.**

a. What would cause a diversion of U.S. demand abroad?

b. Why would the diversion cause a U.S. growth slowdown?

c. What impact would a U.S. growth slowdown have on the Canadian economy, and how?

54. **If we can't borrow from abroad all of the funds we need to finance expenditures that we are going to make in any event, we should at least look at the advisability of the central bank itself financing some of those expenditures simply by creating the money. That might be no more inflationary than borrowing the same amount of money abroad to finance the same expenditures.**

Comment on this view.

55. **Is the Fed tightening or easing? Analysts approach it in different ways. Some focus on interest rates while others focus on the growth in reserves. And, as is so often the case in economics, these two approaches can give different answers.**

Explain a circumstance in which these two approaches could give different answers.

56. **However, Friedman said, if politicians and the Fed overreact to the current recession, the roller-coaster pattern of the past twenty years could continue, with ever-greater inflation-deflation peaks and troughs.**

a. Explain how this roller-coaster pattern would come about, and why the peaks and troughs would become ever greater.

b. What kind of policy does this argument support?

57. **These politicians talk as though they expect a Third World nation to be able to attract large inflows of capital and at the same time have large trade surpluses.**

Comment on the feasibility of a country having large capital inflows in conjunction with trade surpluses.

58. **People widely believe that there is a correlation between higher interest rates and capital inflows, but this belief is as false as the once accepted belief that there is a correlation between unemployment and inflation, causing the one to go up when the other goes down. These correlations don't stand up to scientific research.**

Explain why both these correlations will not stand up to scientific research.

59. **High interest rates are unquestionably anti-inflationary. Despite this, people no longer believe an increase in interest rates is a sign that inflation is about to be beaten—quite the opposite. People now take a jump in interest rates as a sign that inflation is about to get worse.**

a. How are high interest rates anti-inflationary?

b. Why would people view a rise in interest rates as a sign that inflation is about to get worse?

60. **It was claimed that the extent to which we can get them down and keep them down depends mainly on getting the inflation rate down.**

What does "them" refer to in this clipping?

# Appendix C: Suggested Answers to Even-Numbered Exercises

## Chapter 2: Measuring GDP and Inflation

### Media Exercises

2. The work of homemakers is not included in the GDP measure unless it is explicitly paid for, such as the salary of a butler, maid, or housecleaner.

4a. Consumer Price Index

4b. ... the prices of all domestically produced goods and services, not just those paid by consumers.

6. They do not get counted into GDP because they were not purchased by final consumers; their loss becomes a cost to producers. Although they could be viewed as an inventory demand, this view is misleading because their loss after rotting reduces inventory holdings by the same amount.

8. Subtract from GDP the pollution costs of production unless the pollution is cleaned up, and do not add cleanup costs into GDP.

10. If the Turkish national accounts measure GDP, then income earned by Turks abroad is properly neglected because the accounts try to measure what is produced inside Turkey's geographic boundaries. But if one wishes to measure the income Turks have at their disposal to spend, then all sources of income, including internal as well as external sources of transfer payments, should be included.

12. GDP would increase by $200 billion because variables previously not counted as final expenditure are now counted as such. The $980 billion is just a switch from one category of final expenditure to another.

14. Ecological damage is not deducted from GDP, and expenditures to clean up damage are added to GDP.

16a. The cost of living reflects the cost of buying what one buys. The CPI reflects the cost of buying a fixed bundle of goods and services, ignoring the fact that individuals change this bundle as relative prices change, buying more of the relatively cheaper items and less of the relatively expensive items.

16b. The CPI increases by more because it neglects the fact that people switch expenditures to cheaper items.

18. Indirect taxes such as sales taxes are included in the price of an item; consequently, an increase in indirect taxes increases prices and so is directly incorporated into price indices.

20. Residential construction is a consumer purchase that is thought to be more like an investment good than a consumption good because it yields a flow of housing services over a long period of time, and is often financed by borrowing.

**Numerical Exercises**

N2a. No, this steel is an intermediate product.

N2b. Yes, government services are valued at the cost of their production.

N2c. If the value of the cars sold by GM is not affected (i.e., if GM does not increase prices by enough to increase sales by $200), then there is no increase in GDP. The service of the paper shuffler is an intermediate product, not a final product, so it is not counted in GDP. In terms of income payments, the $200 salary increase is offset by a $200 profit decrease.

N2d. The antique dealer's $200 commission is a currently rendered final service, so it is included in GDP.

N2e. No, transfer payments are not included in GDP.

N2f. No, this would mean that part of this year's demand bought items produced last year, not this year, so $200 would have to be subtracted, not added when calculating GDP.

N2g. No, capital gains are not included in GDP.

N4. $(180/150) \times 100 = 120$.

N6. Real GDP = nominal GDP/price index, so $500 = (600/P) \times 100$, implying that $P = 120$.

N8. Inflation = rate of change of CPI = $(120 - 110)/110 = 9.1\%$.

N10a. Inflation = rate of change of CPI = $8/112 = 7.1\%$.

N10b. Real consumption = nominal consumption/CPI = $(300/120) \times 100 = \$250$ billion.

N10c. Because inflation in 1995 was 10 percent, then the CPI must have increased by 10 percent during 1995, to $120 \times 1.1 = 132$.

N12. Overstate, because the CPI calculation does not account for consumers shifting expenditure from the relatively more expensive items to the relatively cheaper items. No need to do any calculations to deduce this!

N14a. $(950/123) \times 100 = \$772.4$ billion

N14b. $(123 - 119)/119 = 3.36\%$

N14c. Real income this year is $772.4 billion; real income last year was $(900/119) \times 100 = \$756.3$. Growth is $(772.4 - 756.3)/756.3 = 2.1\%$.

## Chapter 3:   Unemployment

### Media Exercises

2a.  When the labor force grows, if the extra people seeking employment do not find jobs, the unemployment rate increases.

2b.  If people don't bother looking for a job, they are not considered part of the labor force and are not counted as unemployed, so the unemployment rate is lower than otherwise. If people look harder for jobs, the opposite occurs.

4.  ... the rise in the unemployment rate was dampened. This happens because many unemployed leave the labor force, perhaps as discouraged workers.

6a.  Recent increases in employment may cause people not in the labor force to feel that their chances of obtaining a job are better, so they begin job hunting.

6b.  This will increase the unemployment rate because now these people are counted as unemployed.

6c.  The encouraged worker effect.

8.  Higher. A higher participation rate means that more people are looking for jobs and thus more are unemployed. Second blank is "lower."

10.  The low unemployment rate could be due to discouraged workers.

12a.  Some people may deliberately become unemployed to live a life of leisure on unemployment insurance.

12b. The people looking for jobs may take longer to accept a job because with unemployment insurance to support them they can be fussier about what job they take.

14a. Without unemployment insurance, firms prone to laying off employees would have to pay a higher wage to entice workers to take such a job; with unemployment insurance, workers should find such a job more palatable, so would accept it without as high a wage.

14b. Less sensitive because firms would think twice before laying off employees: doing so would increase their future unemployment insurance premiums.

16. A much smaller fraction of the jobless are the sole breadwinners in their families.

18a. A slowdown in the growth of the labor force will imply a slowdown in the long-run growth of the economy. In the short run, it can mean a fall in the unemployment rate.

18b. rising

20. ... the labor force will grow just as quickly.

22. The unemployment rate is affected by labor-force growth, whereas job creation reflects more accurately the state of the economy.

24. An increase in employment may cause discouraged workers to become encouraged workers, thus increasing the unemployment rate.

**Numerical Exercises**

N2. Labor force is 70% of 150 million = 105 million. Unemployed is 10% of 105 = 10.5 million.

N4. If the unemployment rate is 10 percent, then the 90 million employed must be 90 percent of the labor force. Thus, labor force is 100 million, so participation rate is $100/150 = 66.7\%$.

N6. Labor force is 80% of 25 million = 20 million. Employment is $16 + 2 = 18$ million, so unemployment is $20 - 18 = 2$ million. Unemployment rate = $2/20 = 10\%$.

N8. Labor force is 60% of 150 million = 90 million. Number of unemployed is 10% of 90 million = 9 million, so number of employed is 81 million. Labor force grows by 3% of 90 million = 2.7 million to 92.7 million. Employment grows by 2% of 81 million = 1.62 million to 82.62 million. Unemployed is thus $92.7 - 82.62 = 10.08$ million, so unemployment rate = $10.08/92.7 = 10.87\%$.

## Chapter 4: The Keynesian Approach

### Media Exercises

2a.   A fiscal policy, either an increase in government spending or a decrease in taxes, would increase aggregate demand and, through the multiplier process, stimulate the economy. A large deficit could inhibit politicians from voting for a policy that would make the deficit even larger.

2b.   A decrease in the savings rate means higher consumption, which increases aggregate demand and stimulates the economy.

4.   They imply higher consumption spending, which increases aggregate demand and stimulates the economy.

6a.   Keynesians believe that the economy's automatic back-to-full-employment forces often do not work quickly, implying a need for government discretionary policy actions to keep the economy at full employment.

6b.   Fiscal policy is the government policy most identified with Keynesians.

8a.   An increase in consumer spending increases aggregate demand, thus stimulating the economy.

8b.   In this case, the reduced rate of inventory liquidation is because higher production is meeting some of the demand. This implies higher income, which leads to higher consumer spending and thus stimulates the economy.

10a.   Fiscal stimulus could be an increase in government spending or a decrease in the tax rate.

10b.   ... inflation.

12.   The large addition to inventories implies that aggregate demand has fallen below aggregate supply. This means that producers must cut back on production, which pushes the economy towards recession.

14a.   An inventory correction is an addition to or a reduction of inventories to adjust them to their desired level.

14b.   GDP will fall because, in this case, inventories are being reduced by cutting back production.

16a.   The folly is deficit spending—spending more than your income.

16b.   Deficit spending may be a wise policy for a government because it can keep an economy at full employment.

18.    ... the deficit was caused by the recession reducing tax revenues, not by increases in government spending designed to stimulate the economy.

20.    the multiplier process

22.    Reducing the deficit means a reduction in government spending or an increase in taxes, both of which decrease aggregate demand.

24.    Firms are liquidating inventories by decreasing production, which lowers income and sets a negative multiplier process in motion.

26.    An inventory buildup can be a source of strength if firms undertake it deliberately. It can be a source of weakness if it is undesired because then it indicates that aggregate demand is lower than aggregate supply, so firms will soon have to cut back on production.

28.    recession; boom

**Numerical Exercises**

N2a.   Increasing government spending by $4 billion will increase income by $4 \times 3 = \$12$ billion.

N2b.   The increase in government spending must have been $63/3 = \$21$ billion.

N4.    The $8 billion increase in government spending increases income by $2.5 \times 8 = \$20$ billion, which increases tax receipts by $20 \times .25 = \$5$ billion, so the budget deficit increases by $8 - 5 = \$3$ billion.

N6a.   Income should increase by $4 \times 5 = \$20$ billion, so nominal income increases to $620 billion, a percentage increase of $20/600 = 3.3\%$. Because all of this is a price increase, the price level must have increased by 3.3 percent.

N6b.   Nominal income increases by 3.3 percent.

N6c.   Real income stays constant.

N8.    Equilibrium income is $250 billion because at that level of income aggregate demand is also $250 billion.

N10a.  Disposable income last year was $(900 - 240) = \$660$ billion and this year it was $(950 - 250) = \$700$ billion, so disposable income increased during the year by $(700 - 600) = \$40$ billion. Consumption increased by $(600 - 570) = \$30$ billion, so the MPC is $30/40 = 0.75$.

N10b.  Income increased by $(950 - 900) = \$50$, causing tax receipts to increase by $(250 - 240) = \$10$ billion. The marginal tax rate is $10/50 = 20\%$.

## Chapter 5: The Supply Side

### Media Exercises

2a. He must believe the economy is to the right of the peak of the Laffer curve.

2b. The tax cut could stimulate work effort, increasing aggregate supply by enough to meet the extra aggregate demand that is bidding up prices.

4. ... natural rate of unemployment.

6a. If the real wage refuses to fall, firms will not hire as many workers as the natural rate of unemployment would otherwise imply. The economy could become stuck at a level of unemployment higher than the natural rate—at a point on the AS/AD diagram to the left of the NRU.

6b. efficiency wages

8. Tax revenues will be overestimated because higher tax rates create incentives to work less, to make a move to the underground economy, and to evade taxes.

10. ... tax revenues.

12. The answer is provided in the chapter section entitled "Analyzing Supply Shocks."

## Chapter 6:  Growth

### Media Exercises

2. ... saving. Lower saving leads to lower investment, which slows growth of the capital stock, more slowly replaces obsolete capital stock with modern capital stock, and lowers the rate at which we come up with productivity-enhancing inventions through research and development.

4a. slowdown in productivity growth

4b. Higher saving promotes higher investment, which increases the capital stock, hastens the replacement of obsolete capital stock with modern capital stock, and raises the rate at which research and development produces new inventions—all of which raise productivity.

6. productivity growth; keeping the economy at full employment

8. ... the short run.

10. ... financing investment in research and development and in the installation of new capital equipment.

12. By protecting jobs, the United States may be inhibiting the changes necessary to make the economy more productive and directed toward producing the goods and services that the population wants.

14. The budget deficits increased the interest rate, lowering private investment and decreasing the productivity of the economy over the long run.

16. ... foreign financing helped finance domestic investment.

## Chapter 7:  Crowding Out

### Media Exercises

2.   higher interest rates

4.   An extra dollar of government spending increases aggregate demand by one dollar, but a tax reduction of one dollar increases aggregate demand by only the marginal propensity to consume (MPC) times that dollar; some of it is saved.

6.   The Keynesian view rests heavily on the multiplier effect: an increase in government spending can have a greater impact on income. If the effect of higher government spending is crowded out, higher government spending cannot push the economy out of recession.

8a.  The reduction in income reduces the demand for money, causing its price—the interest rate—to fall.

8b.  The lower interest rate increases aggregate demand, which offsets the original decrease in aggregate demand, perhaps causing the net change in aggregate demand to be zero, implying a multiplier of zero.

10.  Government borrowing raises the interest rate, which makes many private borrowers decide to abandon or postpone their borrowing.

12a. raising the interest rate

12b. ... foreign financing.

14.  interest rates

### Numerical Exercises

N2. Both a decrease in taxes and an increase in transfer payments increase aggregate demand by less than $200 because some of the extra income is saved. The balanced-budget increase in government spending is largely offset by the higher taxes, so increasing government spending by $200 should increase income by more than the alternatives.

## Chapter 8:   The Money Supply

2.  People may be putting their money holdings into savings accounts to benefit from a high interest rate. This adds to M2 but is not included in M1.

4.  Higher interest rates mean that people will want to take extra care to have their funds in savings accounts (not included in M1), which earn the higher interest rate, rather than in checking accounts (included in M1), which do not. Daily interest savings accounts allow people to earn interest on daily balances rather than on minimum monthly balances, so it is worthwhile to make an extra effort to hold money balances in savings accounts for short periods, thus reducing on average holdings in checking accounts.

6.  Financial innovation opens up many alternative means of holding cash balances, which are just as liquid and just as quickly accessed as traditional checking accounts, but bear a higher interest return. These alternatives are not included in M1, however, so looking at growth in M1 no longer gives an accurate picture of what is happening to the quantity of easily accessed spending funds.

8.  Daily-interest saving accounts allow people to earn high interest rates on daily balances rather than on minimum monthly balances, so they will on average hold more of their readily spendable balances in this form. Because these balances are not included in M1, money-measurers find that their usual measure of readily spendable balances is unrepresentative.

10. There must be a huge inflation, making people unwilling to be paid in currency, which quickly loses its value.

### Numerical Exercises

N2.  Buying $3 billion of bonds increases the money base by $3 billion, so the money supply increases by $3 \times 6 = \$18$ billion.

N4a. M1 decreases by $1,000.

N4b. No change in M2 because M2 encompasses both types of accounts.

N4c. If the required reserve ratio is lower for saving accounts than for checking accounts, banks will increase both M1 and M2 by extending more loans.

## Chapter 9:   The Monetarist Rule

### Media Exercises

2a.    ... increase the money supply at a low, steady rate.

2b.    When we move into recession, the slowdown in income growth also slows growth in the demand for money, causing the fixed money-supply growth to produce excess money supply and thus stimulate the economy. When we move into boom, the high income growth raises growth in money demand, which with a fixed money-supply growth leads to excess demand for money and thus dampens the boom.

4a.    Noninflationary growth requires a money-supply growth equal to the real rate of growth of the economy.

4b.    They wish it to be rigid because they believe that discretionary changes in money supply are likely to do more harm than good (due, for example, to long and variable lags).

4c.    Others believe that situations (such as the savings and loan crisis) arise in which the appropriate monetary policy is obvious, so by refusing to allow discretionary use of monetary policy, we are foregoing benefits.

6a.    Monetary policy is not useful for fine-tuning the business cycle because the money supply is too difficult to control precisely, its connection with aggregate spending is too fickle, and the lags associated with its impact on the economy are too long and variable.

6b.    By setting the rate of growth of the money supply at a low, fixed rate, inflation will be controlled in the long run.

8a.    M1 was increasing at a modest rate, but inflation was proceeding at a much higher rate.

8b.    velocity

10a.   Program the computer to increase the money supply at a low, fixed rate.

10b.   the rules-versus-discretion debate

12.    ... the rate of money-supply growth at a low, fixed rate, approximately equal to the real rate of growth of the economy.

14a.   Financial deregulation caused financial instruments previously not closely connected with spending to become easily used as media of exchange.

14b.   Set the rate of growth of the money supply equal to a low, fixed rate approximately equal to the real rate of growth of the economy.

14c. Confusion/uncertainty regarding the appropriate definition of money makes it impossible to use this rule.

16.    ... independent, so that they cannot be influenced by politicians.

**Numerical Exercises**

N2a. Real income $= 800/120 \times 100 = \$667$ billion.

N2b. Velocity $= 800/200 = 4$.

N2c. Money-growth rate $= 10\% + 2\% = 12\%$.

N4a. Velocity increases because smaller money holdings are able to maintain current income and spending.

N4b. Money-demand growth, due to real income increases or to inflation, equals money-supply growth. If money demand shrinks by 1 percent per year, an extra 1 percent of inflation is required to make money demand increase by as much as the money supply increases.

N4c. Adjust the monetarist rule to increase the money supply at a low, fixed rate equal approximately to the real rate of growth less the rate of decrease in money demand due to financial innovations.

N6.   Higher government spending increases income by $3 \times 10 = \$30$ billion. Selling \$2 billion bonds decreases the money supply by $2 \times 4 = \$8$ billion, which decreases income by $8 \times 5 = \$40$ billion. The net change in income is a fall of \$10 billion.

N8.   Higher government spending increases income by $3.5 \times 10 = \$35$ billion. Selling \$8 billion bonds decreases the money supply by $8 \times 4.5 = \$36$ billion, which decreases income by $36 \times 2.5 = \$90$ billion. Thus, income falls by $90 - 35 = \$55$ billion, causing tax revenue to fall by 20% of $55 = \$11$ billion. Adding in the \$10 billion higher government spending implies that the budget deficit increases by \$21 billion.

N10.  In the derivation of the inflation equation, when real income increased by $x$ percent, money demand also increased by $x$ percent, and the resulting gap between this annual money-demand increase and the annual money-supply increase created inflation. If the income elasticity is less than one, then real growth does not increase money demand by as much, making the gap bigger and thus inflation greater. Thus, the original inflation equation underestimates inflation in this circumstance.

N12.  Zero change in real income (because the supply curve is vertical), 3 percent change in prices and in nominal income.

## Chapter 10:   Monetary Policy and Interest Rates

### Media Exercises

2a.   When interest rates fall, the prices of bonds rise, thus creating capital gains.

2b.   Short-term financial assets shortly pay off at their face value, so their price will not depart much from their face value.

4.    ... capital gains.

6a.   The interest rate must be rising, causing the price of these bonds to fall.

6b.   Yes. Rising loan demand is probably pushing up interest rates.

8.    The Fed is selling T-bills, depressing their prices and causing yields to rise.

10a.  A target growth rate policy is a policy of increasing the money supply at some fixed, target rate of growth, usually chosen to be a low rate approximately equal to the real rate of growth of the economy.

10b.  If you target on the money supply, changes in interest rates cannot be offset by manipulating the money supply.

12a.  Switching would involve increasing or decreasing the money supply as economic conditions demand rather than fixing the rate of growth of the money supply.

12b.  During a recession, the growth of income slows. This lower growth in income implies a lower growth in money demand, causing it to fall short of the annual growth in money supply. The resulting excess money supply lowers the interest rate.

14a.  The interest rate would be cut by the Fed buying bonds on the open market.

14b.  The lower interest rate would increase aggregate demand and move the economy to a higher income level.

14c.  The multiplier process. "Kindling a fire" means doing something to start it going.

16a.  A fall in interest rates increases aggregate demand, which stimulates the economy.

16b.  A higher growth rate for the economy means that the Fed will probably increase the money supply in order to sustain this higher growth. Only when the economy grows out of the recession, returning to full employment, will the Fed cut back on the money-supply growth.

18. A restrictive monetary policy raises interest rates, which markedly cuts demand in the housing industry.

20a. Monetary policy can be enacted very quickly compared to fiscal policy, which must be approved by Congress.

20b. by increasing the money supply through open market operations—by buying bonds

20c. If undertaken at the wrong time in too strong doses, such a policy could create inflation.

22a. Lowering demand on the basis of price means raising the interest rate in order to discourage some borrowers.

22b. This is identical to a policy of limiting the amount of available money and letting the forces of supply and demand allocate the funds. It is different from a policy of rationing a limited quantity of money on the basis of criteria other than price.

22c. The banks ration credit by not making loans to people or firms that are not creditworthy. They also ration credit by setting interest rates. They do not ration credit in the sense that they extend loans at interest rates below the market rate of interest.

22d. Credit is cut back by raising interest rates, squeezing some borrowers out of the market. The higher interest rate dampens aggregate demand and thus slows inflation.

**Numerical Exercises**

N2a. The annualized interest rate for a discount bond is given by

$$i = (\text{capital gain}/p_b) \times 365/\text{N}$$

where $p_b$ is the price of the bond and N is the number of days to maturity. In this case, we have

$$.06 = [(10,000 - p_b)/p_b] \times 4,$$

which when solved gives $p_b = \$9,852.22$.

N2b. If it is one month old, and so has two rather than three months to maturity, the $\times 4$ above should be $\times 6$. This produces $p_b = \$9,900.99$.

N4. The current interest rate should be given by

$$i = (\text{coupon} + \text{capital gain})/p_b,$$

which for this case becomes

$$.08 = (75 + 1000 - p_b)/p_b,$$

which when solved gives $p_b = \$995.37$.

N6.   The current interest rate should be given by

$$i = (\text{coupon} + \text{capital gain})/p_b,$$

which for this case becomes

$$.058 = (\text{coupon} + 1,000 - 1,035)/1,035,$$

which when solved gives coupon $= \$95$.

N8.   If we increase government spending by \$3 and increase the money supply by \$2, the interest rate does not change. Income increases by $3 \times 4 = \$12$ plus $2 \times 3 = \$6$ equals \$18, but we need an income increase of \$9,000. If this package is applied 500 times, income will increase by $500 \times 18 = \$9,000$. This implies an increase in government spending of $3 \times 500 = \$1,500$ and an increase in the money supply of $2 \times 500 = \$1,000$. An alternative way of finding this solution is to set up two equations in the two unknowns $\Delta G$ and $\Delta Ms$. To keep the interest rate constant we must have

$$\Delta G/\Delta Ms = 3/2,$$

and to increase income by \$9,000 we must have

$$4\Delta G + 3\Delta Ms = 9,000.$$

---

## Chapter 11:   Real versus Nominal Interest Rates

### Media Exercises

2.   … prices lower and yields higher. The unexpected strength in the economy may increase demand for money or raise expectations of future inflation—both of which raise interest rates; it may also prompt the Fed to raise interest rates to cool off the economy.

4.   A balanced federal budget means the government has less need for financing, which lowers the interest rate. The OPEC action means less fear of oil price increases, thus lowering expected inflation, which lowers the interest rate. Lower interest rates mean higher bond prices.

6a.   It is bad news on the employment front, but good news for those invested in bonds because they experience a capital gain.

6b.   Economic weakness means (1) less demand for money, so interest rates should fall; (2) less fear of inflation, so interest rates fall; and (3) the possibility of Fed action to decrease the interest rate to stimulate the economy. Falling interest rates mean rising bond prices.

8.  The modest increase in prices can serve to lower expectations of inflation, permitting the interest rate to fall. The Fed can lower interest rates because the nominal interest rate should fall in any event (due to lower inflation expectations) and because a fall in the real interest rate should not create inflationary increases in aggregate demand (due to the economic weakness).

10a. A high inflation may have raised inflation expectations to a high level, thus raising the nominal interest rate.

10b. In light of the existing inflation, these high interest rates correspond to a normal real interest rate, so they are appropriate.

12. Actual inflation is low, so when it is subtracted from the high nominal interest rate, we see a very high real interest rate. Expected not actual inflation determines the nominal interest rate, however; inflation expectations are still high, despite the low actual inflation, so they are keeping nominal interest rates high.

14a. Bond yields would be bid up by traders selling bonds, causing their price to fall and consequently their yields to rise.

14b. If traders believe inflation will rise, they will want to get rid of bonds to avoid the capital loss caused by a fall in the price of bonds when people begin to expect higher inflation.

14c. To obtain financing for the massive supply of Treasury debt the government will have to offer a high interest rate. Higher interest rates will lower bond prices, so to avoid a capital loss, bond holders should sell bonds.

14d. They probably subtracted the current inflation from 8 percent.

16. Higher growth should increase the demand for money, causing interest rates to rise. Further, if growth rebounds, the Fed may raise interest rates to guard against inflation. The very high rate of money-supply growth means inflation in the long run, according to our inflation equation. This raises expected inflation, which increases interest rates. The high money growth may also imply that the Fed may cut back sharply on the money supply in order to contain this long-run money-supply growth. Such a cutback on the money supply should increase interest rates in the short run.

18. Higher inflation causes expected inflation to rise, which increases interest rates and thus lowers bond prices, causing those holding bonds to suffer a capital loss.

20a. A real interest rate bond or a real return bond are good guesses for a name here. In reality, it is probably called an indexed bond.

20b. The current Canadian real interest rate must be greater than 4.25 percent, explaining why investors are not keen on buying this bond.

22a. Higher inflation should increase the interest rate. If the Fed is targeting on the interest rate, it will try to prevent this, but if it is targeting on money-supply growth it cannot act to prevent this.

22b. This is a good thing. By trying to prevent a rise in the interest rate caused by higher inflation, a short-sighted Fed may increase the money supply to lower the interest rate. This action could create higher inflation by raising inflation expectations, which would push the interest rate even higher.

24. ... increase. If inflation is expected to increase, future interest rates should be higher, so those buying long-term bonds need to be protected from this.

26. Expectations of inflation should fall, implying that interest rates should fall and bond prices should rise.

**Numerical Exercises**

N2a. Nominal interest rate becomes 13 percent.

N2b. Real interest rate remains unchanged at 4 percent.

N4. Inflation should be $10 - 3 + 1 = 8\%$, so the nominal interest rate should be $8 + 3 = 11\%$. The T-bill price $Tp$ can be deduced from $0.11 = (1,000 - Tp)/Tp$. So $Tp = 1,000/1.11 = \$900.90$.

## Chapter 12:  Stagflation

**Media Exercises**

2. ... accelerating inflation.

4a. Keynes

4b. It is now recognized that there is a natural rate of unemployment below which the economy cannot be pushed without accelerating inflation.

4c. This policy is designed to decrease the natural rate of unemployment.

6a. the Phillips curve diagram

6b. Unemployment serves to decrease aggregate demand and thereby to slow inflation, eventually killing inflation expectations.

6c.  Wage/price controls could be used to circumvent the prolonged period of high unemployment. If supplemented with appropriate monetary and fiscal policy, it can quickly lower inflation expectations and force coordination of slowdowns of the wage and price increase.

8.  Inflation fighting by decreasing aggregate demand causes firms to cut back on production rather than to lower price increases, which causes a recession. The governor of the central bank believes that by lowering the rate of growth of money supply gradually, firms will be more likely to adjust by lowering price increases than by cutting output.

10.  A slow recovery avoids running the risk of activating inflation expectations. Furthermore, it avoids the danger of inadvertently stimulating the economy too much, which would move it below the natural rate of unemployment and accelerate inflation.

12a.  Too much financial stimulus would be enough to activate inflationary forces.

12b.  If inflation were reactivated, governments would have to kill it off by pushing the economy back into recession.

14a.  A policy of holding the money-supply growth rate to a low level, approximately equal to the real rate of growth of the economy, would be consistent with a continuing movement towards price stability. An alternative here might be a credible policy of steadily reducing the money growth rate to the real rate.

14b.  A decrease in the public's expectations of inflation is a key ingredient in reducing inflation without a prolonged period of high unemployment.

16.  ... shifted upwards.

18a.  To lower inflation, the rate of growth of the money supply must be lowered; also, people must change their expectations of inflation and reduce the rate at which prices and wages are rising. Because expectations change slowly and because contracts prolong wage and price increases in the short term, inflation usually continues, despite lower money-supply growth. The continuation of inflation causes money demand to exceed money supply, which decreases aggregate demand for goods and services and pushes the economy into recession.

18b.  If wage and price setters quickly lower their expectations of inflation and, because of this, settle for lower wage and price increases, the time spent in recession will be shorter.

20.  As the unemployment rate declines, it increases the danger of falling below the unknown NRU and creating inflationary forces. To ensure that

these inflationary forces do not get started, the monetary authorities are adopting a restrictive monetary policy.

22a. The inflation was probably cured by reducing the money-supply growth rate and thus creating a major recession until inflation fell.

22b. high unemployment or a major recession

22c. In the long run, inflation is equal to the money-supply growth rate less the economy's real rate of growth.

22d. approximately equal to the real rate of growth of the economy

24. ... inflation will accelerate.

26. If New Zealand's natural rate of unemployment is above 2 percent, this proposal would conflict with the policy of the central bank governor. It could only succeed if inflation were allowed to accelerate.

**Numerical Exercises**

N2a. A's expected inflation is the average of this year's and last year's inflations, 4.25 percent.

N2b. B's expected inflation is the rational expectation—the inflation rate implied by the money-growth rate of 7.5 percent. Raising the money-growth rate by 1.5 percentage points increases inflation by 1.5 percentage points, to 5.5 percent.

N4. Dropping inflation by three percentage points cost $105 billion, which is a cost of $35 billion per percentage point. The sacrifice ratio is the cumulative cost of reducing inflation by one percentage point expressed as a percent of GDP. $35 billion is 5 percent of $700 billion, so the sacrifice ratio is 5.

---

## Chapter 13:   The Real Cause of Inflation

### Media Exercises

2a. Accommodating cost pressures means passing higher costs on in higher prices.

2b. Monetary accommodation of accelerating energy price increases means increasing the money supply, which will prevent overall price increases caused by higher energy prices from creating unemployment. Without monetary accommodation, these higher prices increase the demand for money by more than current money-supply growth. The resulting excess demand for money decreases aggregate demand for goods and services, consequently pushing the economy into a recession.

4.   If politicians have some control over the central bank, they are likely to buy votes by pumping up the money supply before an election, which will lower interest rates and stimulate the economy.

6.   ... the central bank accommodates the increase in cost by increasing the money supply.

8a.  Accommodating inflationary shocks means increasing the money supply to prevent those shocks from decreasing economic activity.

8b.  If a central bank has a reputation for not accommodating inflationary shocks, business and labor will try not to increase prices and wages during these shocks because to do so will risk losing sales and jobs. Price and wage increases without corresponding money-supply increases will create excess money demand, which decreases aggregate demand for goods and services.

10a. The Phillips curve theory, or the accelerationists' theory

10b. If the NRU is lower than 5.7 percent, there is some room for expansionary policy. If it is higher than 5.7 percent, expansionary policy would be a serious mistake because it would exacerbate an inflation that is sure to develop.

12a. by increasing the money supply at a low, fixed rate equal approximately to the economy's real rate of growth.

12b. A movement into recession could prompt Fed action to stimulate the economy, but when this stimulus finally occurs after a long and uncertain lag, the economy may have moved on to a boom, so that the stimulus would make things worse. A jump in the interest rate might prompt the Fed to iron it out. This action would involve adjusting the money supply, which may trigger inflation expectations and lead to a need for more adjustments, causing the Fed to lose control over the money supply.

14.  ... inflation.

16.  There is a natural rate of unemployment below which it is impossible to lower unemployment permanently, regardless of the inflation rate.

18.  ... inflation.

20a. The usual argument is that the government will resort to the printing press to finance its deficit: increasing the money supply and thus causing inflation.

20b. By preventing the real wage from falling, the economy will be stuck at an unemployment level to the right of the long-run Phillips curve.

## Chapter 14:   Budget Deficits and the National Debt

### Media Exercises

2.      Suppose the economy moves into a recession. This lowers income, which lowers tax revenues, creating a budget deficit. The lower income level also lowers the demand for money and thus causes the interest rate to fall.

4.      ... productive investment.

6.      As an alternative to taxation in order to finance the deficit, the government may print money, which will create inflation.

8.      Lower growth means lower tax revenues, directly affecting the deficit.

10.     The lower growth means a lower growth in tax revenues. If spending growth continues unchanged, a larger budget deficit will result.

12.     Canada has a greater need for expansionary fiscal policy to push the economy back to full employment. Furthermore, because it is in a bigger recession, more of Canada's deficit is due to cyclical factors, which renders the deficit of less concern.

14.     Suppose the publicly held national debt is $4 trillion. If growth were 3 percent, the growth adjustment for calculating the structural deficit would be $4 \times 0.03 = \$120$ billion, but if growth were 2.6 percent, the adjustment would be only $4 \times 0.026 = \$104$ billion, a difference of $16 billion. The key here is that a small change in growth is multiplied by a very large publicly held national debt, so it produces a large change in the structural deficit adjustment.

16a.    High interest rates decrease aggregate demand, which through the traditional multiplier process lowers income.

16b.    Higher unemployment means less income produced and less taxes paid, thus increasing the budget deficit.

16c.    This argument is not very convincing because it is likely that the high interest rates were caused by the deficit.

18a.    Higher investment would increase the economy's capital stock, thereby enhancing growth and productivity.

18b.    The favorable supply-side impact may raise income enough to generate extra taxes sufficient to decrease the deficit.

18c.    Lower income taxes would increase consumer spending rather than investment spending.

**Numerical Exercises**

N2. Income increases by $10 \times 3 = \$30$ billion, so tax revenue increases by $.2 \times 30 = \$6$ billion. Thus, the budget deficit increases by $10 - 6 = \$4$ billion.

---

## Chapter 15:   Balance of Payments

**Media Exercises**

2.    a fall in the value of the dollar

4.    value of the U.S. dollar; balance of trade deficit; capital account surplus or capital inflows

6.    A high value for the dollar would make our exports very expensive to foreigners, so demand for our exports falls, beginning a multiplier process that decreases our income level.

8.    The fall in the German interest rate makes it less attractive to invest in German bonds, so foreign investors send their funds elsewhere, which decreases the demand for German marks and causes a fall in their value.

10a.  push up the value of the British pound, or cushion its fall; falling

10b.  Citicorp would sell British pounds for future delivery, buying these pounds when the value of the pound fell. For example, Citicorp could contract to sell GM a million British pounds in six months time, at a price of $2 per pound. If within six months the price of pounds falls to $1.90, as Citicorp expects, it buys the pounds it needs to deliver to GM, making a profit of ten cents per pound.

12a.  The conventional wisdom is that a current account surplus corresponds to a balance of payments surplus, which should lead to a rise in the value of the dollar.

12b.  Decreases in the value of the dollar are causing the current account surpluses. Large capital account deficits are outweighing the current account surpluses, causing a balance of payments deficit which drops the value of our dollar.

14.   A high-dollar policy is one that creates a high interest rate, which induces capital inflows, bidding up the value of the dollar. This increases imports and decreases exports, thereby creating a balance of trade deficit.

16a. A devaluation of the Canadian dollar makes Canadian exports cheaper to U.S. consumers because they can buy more units of Canadian currency with a U.S. dollar.

16b. The devalued dollar makes Canadian goods and services cheaper, so Canadian sales to the United States should improve, but the U.S. recession decreases U.S. income and decreases U.S. imports by far more.

18a. The strong dollar makes our exports expensive to foreigners, so exports fall. The fall in demand for domestically produced goods and services sets a negative multiplier effect in motion.

18b. GDP is calculated by adding up all sales of final products, some of which are imports and some of which have imported components. To calculate only what has been produced domestically, therefore, imports must be subtracted out.

20a. When the U.S. trade deficit narrows, fewer capital inflows are required for balance in the international sector, implying that the interest rate should fall. A fall in the interest rates raises bond prices.

20b. Fear of inflation raises inflation expectations, which cause people to anticipate a rise in the nominal interest rate and thus a fall in the price of bonds. To escape the capital losses this would entail, people sell bonds, causing their price to fall.

22. Singapore could import goods, modify them, and then export them. The modification reflects the income generated by Singaporeans, but may be a modest fraction of the imports and exports.

24. The budget deficit must be financed from private saving and capital inflows. If capital inflows occur, they push up the exchange rate, which decreases exports and increases imports, creating a current account deficit. If there is enough financing from private saving, this won't happen. In this case, private saving increases, suggesting that perhaps capital inflows may not occur. Also, domestic investment decreases, implying that some private saving—which would have bought private bonds—is now available to buy government bonds, further reducing the need for foreign financing.

**Numerical Exercises**

N2. If 4 francs buy one dollar, and 1.5 marks buy one dollar, then 4 francs should buy 1.5 marks. Consequently, 1 franc should buy $1.5/4 = 0.375$ marks, or 1 mark should buy $4/1.5 = 2.67$ francs.

## Chapter 16:  Policy in an Open Economy

### Media Exercises

2a.   high (high interest rates create capital inflows such as those described); up the value of (the capital inflows increase demand for the dollar, pushing up its value); rise

2b.   Exporters discover that foreign currency received from sales abroad translates into fewer domestic dollars.

2c.   . . . to sell dollars. By selling dollars, the central bank decreases the excess demand for dollars that is pushing up the price of the dollar.

4.    . . . high interest rates to stop the dollar's fall . . .

6.    The central bank must be creating the rise in the interest rate as a reaction to the fall in the dollar.

8a.   The central bank must have been using reserves to buy dollars on the foreign exchange market to prevent the value of the dollar from falling.

8b.   If the international financial community is convinced that the dollar is overvalued, the central bank will need a huge amount of foreign exchange reserves to fight off speculators and prevent the dollar from falling.

10a.  The government, through its agent the central bank, is selling dollars on the foreign exchange market.

10b.  To get the dollars to sell, the government is selling bonds. The alternative is to print dollars, which increases the money supply and risks inflation.

12a.  Under a fixed exchange rate, higher domestic inflation would cause our export prices to rise relative to foreign competition, so our exports would fall. Similarly, imports become relatively cheaper, so our imports rise. These changes were prevented by a fall in the exchange rate.

12b.  Sharp declines in the value of exports would create a balance of payments deficit, which would decrease the value of the dollar, allowing exporters to be more competitive.

14a.  When the exchange rate moves toward a new equilibrium level, it often moves too far in the short run, overshooting its new equilibrium value.

14b.  If it falls too far, for example, the central bank can step in to buy dollars, preventing the overshoot.

14c.  Official intervention gets rid of some instability in the market that otherwise would inhibit economic activity.

16a. A fall in the exchange rate makes imported intermediate goods more expensive, thereby raising production costs of domestic goods and services.

16b. The devaluation will cause inflationary forces.

18a. The J curve taking hold usually means that the balance of trade is changing direction.

18b. Probably the bottom of the J curve

20a. The high interest rates caused capital inflows, which bid up the value of the dollar.

20b. Tight money causes the real interest rate to rise, decreasing aggregate demand and inhibiting price increases.

20c. A lower dollar increases demand for our exports.

22a. The French and German governments are both buying French francs.

22b. The disruption to the French economy is that the money supply is being decreased and the economy is being pushed into recession.

22c. The disruption to the German economy is that the German money supply is being increased, creating inflationary forces.

24. Expansion increases our income, which increases our imports and creates a balance of trade deficit. The rise in our income increases our demand for money, causing our interest rate to rise, which causes capital inflows. This bids up the value of our dollar, thereby decreasing exports and increasing imports, both of which create a balance of trade deficit.

## Chapter 17:   Purchasing Power Parity

### Media Exercises

2. The value of the Ukrainian currency would have risen relative to the value of the Russian currency as the Russians demanded Ukrainian currency on the foreign exchange market to buy the cheaper Ukrainian goods. This would have dampened the Russian demand for Ukrainian goods and led to more modest price increases of the goods themselves.

4. ... relative costs of living.

6. Fixing the exchange rate means the rate of money-supply growth is determined by the country to whom your exchange rate is fixed, so a policy of targeting on a money-supply growth rate requires that the exchange rate not be fixed.

8.  If inflation is lower in the United States than in Germany, PPP predicts that the value of the U.S. dollar should rise. People will buy U.S. dollars in anticipation of this.

10a. Yes. If the exchange rate is fixed, inflation higher than that of our trading partners should make our goods more expensive relative to those of foreigners, so our imports should rise. Similarly, because our exports will become more expensive to foreigners, our exports should fall.

10b. The government would raise the nominal interest rate to what the inflation warrants and beyond because this would raise the real interest rate, thus slowing aggregate demand and fighting inflation.

12.  ... inflation. Lowering the exchange rate can be accomplished by selling dollars on the foreign exchange market—which increases the money supply—or by lowering the interest rate, which is done by increasing the money supply. The increase in the money supply, in conjunction with the higher cost of imported intermediate goods and services because of the lower exchange rate, promotes inflation.

14.  ... our prices do not rise to offset this advantage.

16a. Tradeable goods and services in a country with an undervalued currency would be cheap to foreigners.

16b. Suppose a hamburger cost 2 dollars in the United States and 7 francs in France. The PPP exchange rate would be 2 dollars for 7 francs, or 3.5 francs per dollar.

16c. If the actual exchange rate is, say, 4 francs per dollar, then the dollar would be overvalued.

16d. Hamburgers and the associated service of preparing and serving them are not tradeable goods and services. Moreover, this is only one of many relevant goods and services.

18.  Maintaining the purchasing power of our currency at home means no inflation. By the PPP theorem, if we have a lower inflation than foreigners, our currency should appreciate.

20.  The PPP theory claims that tradeable goods should cost the same in all countries because otherwise people would buy from the cheaper country, pushing up its exchange rate until cost equality is obtained. It is stretching things to apply PPP to hamburgers: they cannot be considered tradeable goods because of the service component of their preparation and serving.

22a. The central bank could drive down the dollar's value by lowering interest rates to cut down on capital inflows or by selling dollars on the foreign exchange market.

22b. The policies above would drive down the nominal exchange rate, but they also involve higher money supply, which could increase prices. Higher prices wipe out any advantage of the lower dollar, leaving the real exchange rate unchanged.

24a. If inflation in Singapore is less than inflation in the United States, the value of the Singapore dollar must continually rise, according to PPP.

24b. If the value of the Singapore dollar climbs upward at a rate equal to the U.S. rate of inflation, inflation in Singapore should be kept around zero.

**Numerical Exercises**

N2. The PPP theorem says that the exchange rate should have changed by the difference between their two inflation rates. In this case, the U.S. dollar should have appreciated by $52 - 41 = 11\%$ to become $1.02 \times 1.11 = 1.13$ Canadian dollars.

N4a. PPP predicts the U.S. dollar should appreciate by 3 percent in each of these two years, from 1.0 U.S. dollar buys 1.1 Canadian dollars to 1.0 U.S. dollar buys $1.1 \times 1.06 = 1.17$ Canadian dollars.

N4b. Because the exchange rate has appreciated slightly more than this, the real exchange rate of the U.S. dollar in terms of Canadian dollars has risen by $1.2/1.17 = 2.6\%$.

N6. The real exchange rate should remain unchanged because (*a*) under a fixed exchange rate, inflation in Canada should rise to match inflation in the United States, and (*b*) under a flexible exchange rate, the exchange rate should flex to offset the difference in inflation rates.

---

## Chapter 18:   Interest Rate Parity

**Media Exercises**

2. ... higher interest rates. International capital flows have considerably dampened increases in domestic interest rates because foreigners are attracted by our higher rates and buy our bonds, implying that the interest rate will not rise by as much.

4. a currency devaluation; a currency devaluation; the guaranteed exchange rate is usually a bit lower than what the exchange rate is expected to be in future; a bit lower than

6a. A forward premium is the opposite of a forward discount: the exchange rate guaranteed in the future is higher than the current exchange rate because the exchange rate is expected to rise.

6b.   Speculators are determining the forward rate, which in this case involves a premium, so the speculators must have thought the currency would rise, not fall.

8a.   Suppose some local shock bumps up Canadian interest rates. To match U.S. interest rates, Canada will have to increase the money supply, which could create inflation. As inflation expectations rise, interest rates rise further, requiring further money-supply increases and creating a vicious cycle. The nominal interest rate will rise due to the inflation, and the higher inflation will lower our exchange rate—the worst of both worlds.

8b.   The situation seems a paradox because an increase in the interest rate should attract capital inflows and appreciate Canadian currency. This only works, however, for an increase in the real interest rate.

10a.  Falling interest rates should lower capital inflows, decreasing the demand for the dollar and lowering its value.

10b.  When the central bank buys bonds, it takes bonds out of the economy and replaces them with money.

10c.  In the short run, the purchase will lower interest rates, but in an inflationary environment an increase in the money supply could raise both inflation expectations and the interest rate in the longer run.

12a.  The Canadian dollar forward rate is the exchange rate guaranteed for the Canadian dollar for a future transaction. It is relevant here because a U.S. investor contemplating buying Canadian bonds must take into consideration what the value of the Canadian dollar will be when the bond matures.

12b.  U.S. investors were finding that the higher Canadian interest rate, less the implicit cost of guaranteeing a future Canadian dollar exchange rate was bigger than the risk premium required for investing in Canadian bonds. Consequently, they were buying lots of Canadian bonds, creating capital inflows that were bidding up the value of the Canadian dollar.

14.   The movement was an upward movement in the Canadian interest rate as the Bank of Canada sought to prevent the Canadian dollar from falling.

16.   Germany is a large enough world player that a rise in its real interest rate—due, for example, to higher borrowing—can raise the world real interest rate, causing the U.S. rate to rise.

18.   ... appreciate. Suppose the current rate is 4 francs per dollar, and the forward rate is 4.1 francs per dollar plus or minus a small amount to cover risk. If the actual future exchange rate turns out to be 4.1 francs per dollar, those who have promised to buy or sell dollars at that rate will be able to meet their contracts and pocket the risk premium. If the actual

future exchange rate turns out to be 3.9 francs per dollar, however, those who have promised to buy francs at 4.1 francs per dollar will make a killing, but those who promised to buy dollars at 4.1 francs per dollar will lose 0.2 francs on each dollar. The latter group would never have entered such a contract if they had expected the exchange rate to fall. The forces of supply and demand in this forward market ensure that the forward rate ends up being about where people expect the actual rate to be.

**Numerical Exercises**

N2.   IRP says that the foreign interest rate should equal our interest rate plus the expected rate of change of our exchange rate: in this case, 6% + 10% = 16%.

N4.   With a fixed exchange rate, inflation in Canada is the same as inflation in the United States, so Canada's nominal interest rate is 4% + 8% = 12%.

N6.   If both economies had the same inflation rate, the Canadian interest rate should be one percentage point higher than the U.S. interest rate, because of the risk premium. Instead, the Canadian rate is five percentage points lower than the U.S. rate, so the U.S. inflation must be six percentage points higher than Canada's inflation. This means that the U.S. exchange rate must be depreciating (relative to the Canadian dollar) by 6 percent per year.

N8.   Option (*a*) requires buying $600/1.04 = 577$ million yen, which costs $577/200 = 2.885$ million \$U.S. today. Option (*b*) requires $600/195 = 3.077$ million \$U.S. in one year's time, which requires $3.077/1.06 = 2.903$ million \$U.S. today. Option (*a*) is therefore cheaper.

N10.  Because of the three percentage point inflation difference, everyone should expect the U.S. dollar to depreciate by 3 percent during the year. Consequently, the forward rate should be about 4 less 3 percent $(.03 \times 4)$ equals 3.88 francs per dollar, less the reward for risk.

---

## Appendix B:   Additional Media Exercises

2.   Lower inflation means lower expected inflation and thus a lower interest rate.

4.   If Canadian inflation is falling relative to U.S. inflation, and the exchange rate is allowed to flex, it is possible for the Canadian interest rate to fall below the U.S. rate.

6.   ... interest rates higher. Presumably, the central bank is cushioning exchange rate movements with interest rate changes.

8.  If inflation is lowered, the interest rate will fall, meaning that the government will have lower interest payments on the national debt. Its budget deficit should fall and create some room for spending on other things—a fiscal dividend.

10. High inventory stocks mean that firms will cut back production to get rid of the high inventories, thereby creating a recession. A sharp inflationary spike will cause the central bank to cut back on the money supply and raise interest rates in order to attack the inflation by lowering aggregate demand, thereby pushing the economy into a recession.

12. A higher dollar could be engineered by raising the interest rate to increase capital inflows. The higher interest rate lowers aggregate demand, which is consistent with fighting inflation. A higher dollar could also be engineered by buying dollars on the foreign exchange market, which would decrease the money supply—also consistent with fighting inflation.

14a. Cutting the discount rate encourages banks to borrow from the Fed in order to increase reserves to make loans, resulting in an increase in the money supply. The money-supply increase lowers the interest rate and increases aggregate demand, thereby stimulating the economy.

14b. The lower interest rate lowers capital inflows, creating a balance of payments deficit and causing the exchange rate to fall.

14c. A lower dollar would be good for the economy because it will stimulate aggregate demand for domestically produced goods and services by making exports cheaper and imports more expensive. Since the economy is now "stalled," there is little danger that this will create inflation.

16. Lowering rates below their market-determined level will require increasing the money supply, which may cause inflation expectations. Because of this, the interest rate will rise, eliciting further money-supply increases. This vicious cycle could continue, resulting in high inflation and consequently a high nominal interest rate.

18a. The high U.S. money-supply growth foretells high U.S. inflation, which by PPP leads to a fall in the value of the U.S. dollar. Foreign investors will experience a loss if their bonds are denominated in U.S. dollars.

18b. The U.S. dollar is weakened because of the PPP result noted above and because investors sell their U.S. dollar assets, creating capital outflows that bid down the exchange rate.

20a. The fall in the dollar should make exports cheaper and imports more expensive, thus increasing exports and decreasing imports—both of which decrease the balance of trade deficit.

20b. The dollar may be falling because our inflation exceeds that of our trading partners, so there is no fall in the real exchange rate.

20c. If our growth falls, our demand for imports slows.

22. Currency devaluation does not create prosperity; high productivity does. Historically, currency devaluations usually occur because of high inflation.

24. A smaller deficit leaves more financing available for private investment; the interest rate should fall and private investment should increase. Furthermore, by national savings economists mean funds left over after the government has financed its deficit.

26. Crowding out forces may take some time to offset the initial multiplier effect.

28. natural rate of unemployment

30. Low inflation is what is meant by "soundness." If we keep our inflation low, holders of our currency will not experience a fall in the value of these currency holdings.

32a. Lower unemployment suggests that higher income would increase the demand for money, that inflation may arise, and that the Fed may tighten monetary policy to prevent unemployment from going too low—all of which spell higher interest rates and, consequently, lower bond prices.

32b. Reductions in the labor force cause the unemployment rate to fall; if this is the reason for the fall in the unemployment rate, the factors described in 32*a* are not relevant.

32c. the discouraged worker effect

34. Surging money-supply growth causes high inflation, which pushes up interest rates, causing major falls in the price of long-term bonds. If such an unpredictable inflationary environment were to appear, nobody would want to invest in long-term bonds.

36. The government is buying these military items and is taxing people (or selling bonds to these people) to reduce their demand for other things and to free up resources to produce these items. Moreover, higher interest rates also reduce aggregate demand for goods and services. Crowding out should come to mind; nonetheless, there will be some inflationary pressure if the economy is at full employment.

38. Although higher interest rates do raise costs, this is a one-time increase in costs. The major role of interest rates is to attack inflation by decreasing aggregate demand.

40. Without indexing, governments could increase taxes surrepticiously by creating inflation.

42.   ... greater than the economy's rate of growth of real income.

44a.  Low inflation should lower inflation expectations and cause the nominal interest rate to fall.

44b.  When interest rates are high because of high inflation, by spending the high interest payments, people are allowing the real value of their interest-earning assets to be eroded by inflation, so they are in effect drawing on capital.

46.   This advantage is true only of unexpected inflation. If the high inflation is expected, the interest payments on the debt will account for the erosion in the value of the principal.

48.   By increasing its money supply faster than the increase in the German money supply, Britain was bound to experience a higher inflation, which makes it impossible to have a fixed exchange rate.

50a.  If the government were truly successful in reducing its budget deficit, the decreased government demand for financing should lead to a lower interest rate without inflation. The market probably does not believe that the government would actually be able to reduce its deficit, implying that lower interest rates would be achieved only by increasing the money supply, an inflationary scenario.

50b.  Purchasing power parity suggests that higher inflation in Canada will lower its exchange rate. To avoid this loss, people start selling Canadian dollars.

52a.  Increase the money supply at a rate approximately equal to the real rate of growth of the economy.

52b.  The battle is lowering inflation; the war is getting employment back up to its natural rate.

52c.  Expectations of inflation have not yet fallen to the point where the economy can be pushed to a higher income level.

54.   If we are near full employment, increasing the money supply will increase inflation. If we borrow from abroad, we can use the foreign currency to buy the needed goods from abroad. If not, the foreign borrowing should increase the demand for the dollar, thereby raising its value and cutting down on domestic demand for goods and services because demand for exports falls and demand for import-competing goods and services falls. This offsets the inflationary pressure of the additional spending financed by the extra borrowing.

56a.  By overreacting to the current recession, policymakers will stimulate the economy too much, pushing it below the NRU and accelerating inflation.

To deal with this problem, policymakers will overreact in the opposite direction, pushing the economy back into recession. The peaks and troughs become ever greater because of the asymmetry of the Phillips curve.

56b. It is an argument for a policy rule to prevent the overreactions.

58.    Higher nominal interest rates cause capital inflows only if the real interest rate increases. Higher inflation causes a fall in unemployment only if that inflation is unexpected.

60.    Interest rates.

# Glossary

**Absolute Advantage.** The ability to produce a good or service with fewer resources than competitors. See also *comparative advantage*.

**Accelerationist Hypothesis.** Belief that an effort to keep unemployment below its natural rate results in an accelerating inflation.

**Accomodating Policy.** A monetary policy of matching wage and price increases with money supply increases so that the real money supply does not fall and push the economy into recession.

**AD.** Aggregate demand.

**Aggregate Demand.** Total quantity of goods and services demanded.

**Aggregate Demand Curve.** Combinations of the price level and income for which the goods and services market is in equilibrium, or for which both the goods and services market and the money market are in equilibrium.

**Aggregate Expenditure Curve.** Aggregate demand for goods and services drawn as a function of the level of national income.

**Aggregate Production Function.** An equation determining aggregate output as a function of aggregate inputs such as labor and capital.

**Aggregate Supply.** Total quantity of goods and services supplied.

**Aggregate Supply Curve.** Combinations of price level and income for which the labor market is in equilibrium. The short-run aggregate supply curve incorporates information problems and price/wage inflexibilities in the labor market, whereas the long-run aggregate supply curve does not.

**AS.** Aggregate supply.

**Appreciation.** Increase in the value of a currency.

**Arbitrage.** Transactions designed to make a sure profit from inconsistent prices.

**Asset.** Something that is owned; a financial claim or a piece of property that is a store of value.

**Automatic Stabilizer.** Any feature built into the economy that automatically cushions fluctuations.

**Autonomous Expenditure.** Elements of spending that do not vary systematically with variables such as GDP that are explained by the theory. See also *exogenous expenditure.*

**Average Propensity to Consume.** Ratio of consumption to disposable income. See also *marginal propensity to consume.*

**Average Propensity to Save.** Ratio of saving to disposable income. See also *marginal propensity to save.*

**Balance of Merchandise Trade.** The difference between exports and imports of goods.

**Balance of Payments.** The difference between the demand for and supply of a country's currency on the foreign exchange market.

**Balance of Payments Accounts.** A statement of a country's transactions with other countries.

**Balance of Trade.** See *balance of merchandise trade.*

**Balanced-Budget Multiplier.** The multiplier associated with a change in government spending financed by an equal change in taxes.

**Bank of Canada.** Canada's central bank.

**Barter.** A system of exchange in which one good is traded directly for another without the use of money.

**Base Year.** The reference year when constructing a price index. By tradition it is given the value 100.

**Beggar-my-neighbor Policy.** A policy designed to increase an economy's prosperity at the expense of another country's prosperity.

**Bellwether.** A signaling device.

**Bond.** A financial asset taking the form of a promise by a borrower to repay a specified amount (the bond's face value) on a maturity date and to make fixed periodic interest payments.

**Boom.** The expansionary part of a business cycle in which GDP is growing rapidly.

**Bretton Woods.** Site of a 1944 international monetary conference at which the postwar world fixed-exchange-rate system was structured and the International Monetary Fund (IMF) was created.

**Broad Definition of Money.** See *money.*

**Budget Deficit.** The excess of government spending over tax receipts.

**Business Cycle.** Fluctuations of GDP around its long-run trend, consisting of recession, trough, expansion, and peak.

**Capital.** (a) Physical capital: buildings, equipment, and any materials used to produce other goods and services in the future rather than being consumed today. (b) Financial capital: funds available for acquiring real capital. (c) Human capital: the value of people's education and experience that make them more productive.

**Capital Account.** That part of the balance of payments accounts that records demands for and supplies of a currency arising from purchases or sales of assets.

**Capital Consumption Allowance.**   See *depreciation*.

**Capital Flows.**   Purchase by foreigners of our assets (capital inflows) or our purchase of foreign assets (capital outflows).

**Capital Gain.**   An increase in the value of an asset.

**Capital Market.**   The market in which savings are made available to those needing funds to undertake investment projects. A financial market in which longer-term (maturity greater than one year) bonds and stocks are traded.

**Capital Mobility.**   A situation in which assets can easily be purchased by foreigners.

**Capital Stock.**   The total amount of plant, equipment, and other physical capital.

**Central Bank.**   A public agency responsible for regulating and controlling an economy's monetary and financial institutions. It is the sole money-issuing authority.

**Certificate of Deposit (CD).**   A bank deposit that cannot be withdrawn for a specified period of time. See also *term deposit*.

**Ceteris Paribus.**   Holding other things constant.

**Churn.**   See *creative destruction*.

**Circular Flow.**   Income payments to factors of production are spent to buy output. The receipts from these sales are used to pay factors of production, creating a circular flow of income.

**Classical Macroeconomics.**   The school of macroeconomic thought prior to the rise of Keynsianism.

**Clean Float.**   A flexible exchange rate system in which the government does not intervene.

**Closed Economy.**   An economy in which imports and exports are very small relative to GDP and so are ignored in macroeconomic analysis. Contrast with *open economy*.

**Cold-turkey Policy.**   Decreasing inflation by immediately decreasing the money growth rate to a new, low rate. Contrast with *gradualism*.

**Commercial Bank.**   A privately owned, profit-seeking firm that accepts deposits and makes loans.

**Comparative Advantage.**   A country has a comparative advantage over another country in the production of good A if to produce a unit of A it foregoes more of the production of good B than would the other country when it produces a unit of good A. Its efficiency in the production of good A relative to its efficiency in the production of good B is greater than is the case for the other country. See also *absolute advantage*.

**Complementary Policies.**   Policies that enhance each other.

**Constant Dollars.**   See *real*.

**Consumer Price Index (CPI).**   An index calculated by tracking the cost of a typical bundle of consumer goods and services over time. It is commonly used to measure inflation.

**Consumption Function.**   The relationship between consumption demand and disposable income. More generally, it refers to the relationship between consumption demand and all factors that affect this demand.

**Cost-benefit Analysis.**   The calculation and comparison of the costs and benefits of a policy or project.

**Cost-push Inflation.**   Inflation whose initial cause is cost increases rather than excess demand. See also *demand-pull inflation*.

**Countercyclical.**   Falling during expansions and rising during recessions. A countercyclical policy stimulates during a recession and contracts during an expansion.

**Coupon.**   The annual interest payment associated with a bond.

**Coupon Bond.**   Any bond with a coupon. Contrast with *discount bond*.

**Creative Destruction.**   The process whereby new technology creates new jobs and destroys old, less productive jobs.

**Credit Crunch.**   A decline in the ability or willingness of banks to lend.

**Credit Rationing.**   Restriction of loans by lenders so that not all borrowers willing to pay the current interest rate are able to obtain loans.

**Crowding Out.**   Decreases in aggregate demand that accompany an expansionary fiscal policy, dampening the impact of that policy.

**Current Account.**   That part of the balance of payments accounts that records demands for and supplies of a currency arising from activities that affect current income, namely imports, exports, investment income payments such as interest and dividends, and transfers such as gifts, pensions, and foreign aid.

**Current Dollars.**   A variable like GDP is measured in current dollars if each year's value is measured in prices prevailing during that year. In contrast, when measured in real or constant dollars, each year's value is measured in a base year's prices.

**Cyclical Unemployment.**   Unemployment that increases when the economy enters a recession and decreases when the economy enters a boom.

**Debt.**   See *national debt*.

**Debt Instrument.**   Any financial asset corresponding to a debt, such as a bond or a treasury bill.

**Deficit.**   See *budget deficit*.

**Deflation.**   A sustained decrease in the price level. The opposite of an inflation.

**Deflator.**   A price index used to deflate a nominal value to a real value by dividing the nominal value by the price deflator.

**Demand.**   An amount desired, in the sense that people are willing and able to pay to obtain this amount. Always associated with a given price.

**Demand Deposit.**   A bank deposit that can be withdrawn on demand, such as a deposit in a checking account.

**Demand Management Policy.**   Fiscal or monetary policy designed to influence aggregate demand for goods and services.

**Demand-pull Inflation.**   Inflation whose initial cause is excess demand rather than cost increases. See also *cost-push inflation*.

**Deposit Creation.** The process whereby the banking system transforms a dollar of reserves into several dollars of money supply.

**Deposit-switching.** Central bank switching of government deposits between the central bank and commercial banks.

**Depreciation.** (a) Of capital stock: decline in the value of capital due to its wearing out or becoming obsolete. (b) Of currency: decline in the exchange rate.

**Depreciation Allowances.** Tax deductions that businesses can claim when they spend money on investment goods.

**Depression.** A prolonged period of very low economic activity with large-scale unemployment.

**Devaluation.** Fall in the government-determined fixed exchange rate.

**Dirty Float.** A flexible exchange rate system in which the government intervenes.

**Discount Bond.** A bond with no coupons, priced below its face value; the return on this bond comes from the difference between its face value and its currrent price.

**Discounting.** Calculating the present value of a future payment.

**Discount Rate.** The interest rate at which the Fed is prepared to loan reserves to commercial banks.

**Discount Window.** The Federal Reserve facility at which reserves are loaned to banks at the discount rate.

**Discouraged Worker.** An unemployed person who gives up looking for work and so is no longer counted as in the labor force.

**Discretionary Policy.** A policy that is a conscious, considered response to each situation as it arises. Contrast with *policy rule*.

**Disequilibrium.** The absence of equilibrium. Disequilibrium implies excess demand or excess supply and pressure for change.

**Disposable Income.** Income less income tax.

**Dissaving.** Negative saving, a situation in which spending exceeds disposable income.

**Dividends.** Profits paid out to shareholders by a corporation.

**Economics.** The study of the allocation and distribution of scarce resources among competing wants.

**Effective Exchange Rate.** The weighted average of several exchange rates, where the weights are determined by the extent of our trade done with each country.

**Efficiency.** The ability to produce the things most wanted at the least cost.

**Efficiency Wage.** Wage that maximizes profits.

**Embodied Technical Change.** Technical change that can be used only when new capital embodying this technical change is produced.

**Endogenous.** Determined from within the system. Opposite of *exogenous*.

**Entitlement Program.**   A program such as social security, which is such that everyone meeting the eligibility requirements is entitled to receive benefits from the program, so that costs are not known in advance.

**Equation of Exchange.**   The quantity theory equation $Mv = PQ$.

**Equilibrium.**   A position in which there is no pressure for change, where demand and supply are equal.

**Equity.**   Ownership. Common stock represents equity in a corporation.

**Eurodollars.**   Deposits denominated in U.S. dollars but held in banks located outside the United States, such as in Canada or France.

**Excess Capacity.**   Unused production capacity.

**Excess Demand.**   A situation in which demand exceeds supply.

**Excess Reserves.**   Reserves of commercial banks in excess of those they are legally required to hold.

**Excess Supply.**   A situation in which supply exceeds demand.

**Exchange Rate, Nominal.**   The price of one currency in terms of another, in this book defined as number of units of foreign currency per dollar.

**Exchange Rate, Real.**   The nominal exchange rate corrected for price level differences.

**Exogenous.**   An adjective indicating that something is determined by forces unrelated to the theory determining the variables under investigation.

**Exogenous Expenditure.**   See *autonomous expenditure*.

**Export.**   Domestically produced good or service sold to foreigners.

**Face Value.**   The payoff value of a bond upon maturity. See *principal*.

**Factor of Production.**   A resource used to produce a good or service. The main macroeconomic factors of production are capital and labor.

**Fallacy of Composition.**   The incorrect conclusion that something that is true for an individual is necessarily true for the economy as a whole.

**Fed.**   See *Federal Reserve System*.

**Federal Funds Rate.**   The interest rate at which banks lend deposits at the Federal Reserve to one another overnight.

**Federal Open Market Committee (FOMC).**   Fed committee that makes decisions about open market operations.

**Federal Reserve Banks.**   The twelve district banks in the Federal Reserve System.

**Federal Reserve Board.**   Board of Governors of the Federal Reserve System.

**Federal Reserve System.**   The central banking authority responsible for monetary policy in the United States.

**Financial Intermediary.**   Any institution, such as a bank, which takes deposits from savers and loans them to borrowers.

**Financial Intermediation.** The process whereby financial intermediaries channel funds from lender/savers to borrower/spenders.

**Fine Tuning.** An attempt to maintain the economy at or near full employment by frequent changes in policy.

**Fiscal Policy.** A change in government spending or taxing designed to influence economic activity.

**Fixed Exchange Rate.** An exchange rate held constant by a government promise to buy or sell dollars at the fixed rate on the foreign exchange market.

**Flexible Exchange Rate.** An exchange rate whose value is determined by the forces of supply and demand on the foreign exchange market.

**Floating Exchange Rate.** See *flexible exchange rate.*

**FOMC.** See *federal open market committee.*

**Foreign Exchange.** The currency of a foreign country.

**Foreign Exchange Market.** A worldwide market in which one country's currency is bought or sold in exchange for another country's currency.

**Foreign Exchange Reserves.** A fund containing the central bank's holdings of foreign currency or claims thereon.

**45-Degree Line.** A line representing equilibrium in the goods and services market, on a diagram with aggregate demand on the vertical axis and aggregate supply on the horizontal axis.

**Forward Exchange Market.** A market in which foreign exchange can be bought or sold for delivery (and payment) at some specified future date but at a price agreed upon now.

**Fractional Reserve Banking.** A banking system in which banks hold only a fraction of their outstanding deposits in cash or in the form of deposits with the central bank.

**Free Trade.** The absence of any government restrictions on imports or exports, such as tariffs or quotas.

**Frictional Unemployment.** Unemployment associated with people changing jobs or quitting to search for new jobs.

**Full Employment.** The level of employment corresponding to the natural rate of unemployment.

**Full-Employment Output.** The level of output produced by the economy when operating at the natural rate of unemployment.

**Futures Contract.** A contract in which the seller agrees to provide something to a buyer at a specified future date at an agreed price.

**GATT.** General Agreement on Tariffs and Trade, an organization in which the world's countries have sought to negotiate agreements creating freer international trade.

**GDP.** See *gross domestic product.*

**GDP Deflator.** Price index used to deflate nominal GDP to real GDP by dividing nominal GDP by the GDP deflator.

**GNP.**   See *gross national product*.

**Gold Standard.**   A fixed exchange rate system in which a currency is directly convertible into gold.

**Goodhart's Law.**   Whatever measure of the money supply is chosen for application of the monetarist rule will soon begin to misbehave.

**Gradualism.**   A policy of decreasing the rate of growth of the money supply gradually over an extended period of time, so that inflation can adjust with smaller unemployment cost. Contrast with *cold-turkey policy*.

**Great Depression.**   The period of very high unemployment during the early 1930s.

**Gross Domestic Product.**   Total output of final goods and services produced within a country during a year.

**Gross National Product.**   Total output of final goods and services produced by a country's citizens during a year.

**Hedging.**   Reducing one's exposure to risk by buying and selling contracts for future delivery (of foreign currency, for example) at a price that is determined now.

**High-powered Money.**   See *money base*.

**Hoarding.**   See *labor hoarding*.

**Housing Start.**   A new house on which construction has just begun.

**Human Capital.**   The value of people's education, training, and experience that makes them more productive.

**Hyperinflation.**   Extremely high inflation.

**Hysterisis.**   Process by which the natural rate of unemployment is affected by past unemployment levels.

**IMF.**   See *International Monetary Fund*.

**Implicit Contract.**   An unwritten understanding between two groups, such as an understanding between an employer and employees that employees will receive a stable wage despite business cycle activity.

**Import.**   Foreign-produced good or service bought by us.

**Import Quota.**   Restriction on the quantity of a foreign good that can be imported.

**Impute.**   To assign a value to a good or service in place of a market value that is not available.

**Imputed Rent.**   The value of consumption services obtained by owning one's house rather than having to pay rent.

**Income.**   A flow of earnings over a period of time. Disposable income is income less taxes.

**Incomes Policy.**   A policy designed to lower inflation without reducing aggregate demand. Wage and price controls is an example.

**Index.**	A series of numbers measuring percentage changes over time from a base period. The index number for the base period is by convention set equal to 100.

**Indexing.**	Linking money payments to a price index to hold the real value of those money payments constant.

**Indirect Taxes.**	Taxes paid by consumers when they buy goods and services. A sales tax is an example.

**Inflation.**	A sustained increase in the general price level. The inflation rate is the percentage rate of change in the price level.

**Inflation Tax.**	The loss in purchasing power due to inflation eroding the real value of financial assets such as cash.

**Infrastructure.**	Basic facilities, such as transportation, communication, and legal systems, on which economic activity depends.

**Institutionally Induced Unemployment.**	Unemployment due to institutional phenomena such as the degree of labor force unionization, the level of discrimination, and government policies such as unemployment insurance programs, minimum wages, or regulations on business.

**Instrument.**	See *debt instrument*.

**Interest Rate Differential.**	The interest rate on our financial assets minus the interest rate on a foreign country's financial assets.

**Interest Rate, Nominal.**	Payment for the use of borrowed funds, measured as a percentage per year of these funds.

**Interest Rate Parity.**	Theory that real interest rates are approximately the same across countries except for a risk premium.

**Interest Rate, Real.**	Nominal interest rate less expected inflation.

**Intermediate Good.**	A good used in producing another good.

**International Monetary Fund (IMF).**	Organization originally established to manage the postwar fixed exchange rate system.

**International Reserves.**	See *foreign exchange reserves*.

**Inventory.**	Goods that a firm stores in anticipation of its later sale or use as an input.

**Investment Spending.**	Expenditures on capital goods including new housing. Financial "investments" and sales of existing assets are not included.

**Investment Tax Credit.**	A reduction in taxes offered to firms to induce them to increase investment spending.

**Keynesianism.**	The school of macroeconomic thought based on the ideas of John Maynard Keynes as published in his 1936 book *The General Theory of Employment, Interest, and Money*. A Keynesian believes the economy is inherently unstable and requires active government intervention to achieve stability.

**Labor Force.**	Those people employed plus those actively seeking work.

**Labor Hoarding.**   Not laying off redundant workers during a recession to ensure that skilled and experienced workers are available after the recession.

**Laffer Curve.**   Curve showing how tax receipts vary with the tax rate.

**Laissez Faire.**   A policy of minimum government intervention in the operation of the economy.

**Leading Indicator.**   A variable that reaches a turning point (a peak or a trough) before the economy reaches a turning point.

**Legal Reserve Requirement.**   See *reserve requirement*.

**Liquidity.**   Ease with which an asset can be sold on short notice at a fair price.

**Logarithmic Scale.**   A scale in which equal proportions are shown as equal distances so that, for example, a doubling from 2 to 4 is represented by one inch, as is a doubling from 4 to 8.

**M1.**   Narrow measure of money, consisting of cash, traveler's checks, and checkable deposits.

**M2.**   Broad measure of money, consisting of M1 plus various deposits that are less substitutable with cash.

**Macroeconomics.**   The study of the determination of economic aggregates such as total output and the price level.

**Make-work Project.**   A project, such digging holes and filling them up again, that has no useful purpose other than to make work.

**Marginal Propensity to Consume.**   Fraction of an increase in disposable income that is spent on consumption.

**Marginal Propensity to Import.**   Fraction of an increase in disposable income that is spent on imports.

**Marginal Propensity to Save.**   Fraction of an increase in disposable income that is saved.

**Marginal Tax Rate.**   Percent of an increase in income paid in tax.

**Market Efficiency.**   See *efficiency*.

**Market Mechanism.**   The system whereby using prices, the interaction of supply and demand allocates inputs and distributes outputs.

**Maturity.**   Time at which a bond can be redeemed for its face value.

**Medium of Exchange.**   Any item that can be commonly exchanged for goods and services.

**Menu Costs.**   The costs to firms of changing their prices.

**Microeconomics.**   The study of firm and individual decisions insofar as they affect the allocation and distribution of goods and services.

**Monetarism.**   School of economic thought stressing the importance of the money supply in the economy. Adherents believe that the economy is inherently stable so that policy is best undertaken through adoption of a policy rule.

**Monetarist Rule.** Proposal that the money supply be increased at a steady rate equal approximately to the real rate of growth of the economy. Contrast with *discretionary policy*.

**Monetary Aggregate.** Any measure of the economy's money supply.

**Monetary Base.** See *money base*.

**Monetary Policy.** Actions taken by the central bank to change the supply of money and the interest rate and thereby affect economic activity.

**Monetizing the Debt.** See *printing money*.

**Money.** Any item that serves as a medium of exchange, a store of value, and a unit of account. See *medium of exchange*.

**Money Base.** Cash plus deposits of the commercial banks with the central bank.

**Money Market.** A financial market in which short term (maturity of less than a year) debt instruments such as bonds are traded.

**Money Multiplier.** Change in the money supply per change in the money base.

**Money Rate of Interest.** See *interest rate, nominal*.

**MPC.** See marginal propensity to consume.

**Multiple Deposit Creation.** The process whereby the money multiplier operates.

**Multiplier.** Change in the equilibrium value of a variable of interest per change in a variable over which one has control. "The" multiplier is the change in equilibrium income per change in government spending.

**NAFTA.** North American Free Trade Agreement, negotiated in 1992 to extend the Canada/U.S. Free Trade Agreement to include Mexico.

**NAIRU.** Non-accelerating inflation rate of unemployment. See *natural rate of unemployment*.

**National Debt.** The debt owed by the government as a result of earlier borrowing to finance budget deficits. That part of the debt not held by the central bank is the publicly held national debt.

**National Income.** GDP with some adjustments to remove items that do not make it into anyone's hands as income, such as indirect taxes and depreciation. Loosely speaking, it is interpreted as being equal to GDP.

**National Income and Product Accounts.** The national accounting system that records economic activity such as GDP and related measures.

**National Output.** GDP.

**National Saving.** Private saving plus public saving. That part of national income that is not spent on consumption goods or government spending.

**Natural Rate of Unemployment (NRU).** The level of unemployment characterizing the economy in long-run equilibrium, determined by the levels of frictional, structural, and institutionally induced unemployment. At this rate of unemployment inflation should be constant, so it is sometimes called the non-accelerating inflation rate of unemployment, or NAIRU.

**Net Domestic Product.**   GDP minus depreciation.

**Net National Product.**   GNP minus depreciation.

**Net Exports.**   Exports minus imports.

**Net Investment.**   Investment spending minus depreciation.

**Neutrality of Money.**   The doctrine that the money supply affects only the price level, with no long-run impact on real variables.

**New Classicals.**   Economists who, like classical economists, believe that wages and prices are sufficiently flexible to solve the unemployment problem without help from government policy.

**New Keynesians.**   Economists who, like Keynes, believe that for good reason wages and prices are sticky and so prolong recessions, suggesting a need for government policy.

**Nominal.**   Measured in money terms, in current rather than real dollars. Contrast with *real*. See also *exchange rate, nominal* and *interest rate, nominal*.

**Notice Deposit.**   See *term deposit*.

**NOW Account.**   Negotiable order of withdrawal account, an interest-bearing bank account on which a special check called a negotiable order of withdrawal could be written. Because NOWs are not technically checks, by this means it was possible for banks to circumvent Fed regulations prohibiting payment of interest on checking accounts.

**NRU.**   See *natural rate of unemployment*.

**OECD.**   Organization for Economic Cooperation and Development, consisting of most of the world's developed economies.

**Official Settlements Account.**   An account within the balance of payments accounts showing the change in a country's official foreign exchange reserves. It is used to measure a balance of payments deficit or surplus.

**Okun's Law.**   Changes in employment give rise to greater-than-proportional changes in output, by a factor of about 2.5.

**OPEC.**   Organization of Petroleum Exporting Countries, a group of oil exporters that brought about the dramatic increases in oil prices during the 1970s.

**Open Economy.**   An economy that engages in a significant amount of trade. Contrast with *closed economy*.

**Open Market Operations.**   Buying or selling of bonds by the central bank.

**Opportunity Cost.**   The foregone value of an alternative not chosen, usually the most profitable alternative.

**Output Gap.**   The difference between full employment output and current output.

**Par Value.**   See *face value*.

**Paradox of Thrift.**   The result that an increase in saving by everyone causes a multiplied fall in income, which could end up decreasing aggregate saving.

**Participation Rate.**  Fraction of the non-institutionalized population over age fifteen that is in the labor force.

**Peak.**  The upper turning point of a business cycle, where expansion turns into a contraction.

**Permanent Income Hypothesis.**  Theory that individuals base current consumption spending on their perceived long-run average income rather than their current income.

**Phillips Curve.**  Relationship between inflation and unemployment.

**Plant and Equipment.**  Buildings and machines that firms use to produce output.

**Policy-ineffectiveness Proposition.**  Theory that anticipated policy has no effect on output.

**Policy Rule.**  A formula for determining policy. Contrast with *discretionary policy*.

**Political Business Cycle.**  A business cycle caused by policies undertaken to help a government be reelected.

**Potential Output or Potential GDP.**  Output produced when the economy is operating at its natural rate of unemployment.

**Present Value (PV).**  The value now of a future receipt or stream of receipts, calculated using a specified interest rate.

**Price Adjuster.**  A firm that reacts to excess supply or excess demand by adjusting price rather than quantity. Contrast with *quantity adjuster*.

**Price Flexibility.**  Ease with which prices adjust in response to excess supply or demand.

**Price Index.**  A measure of the price level calculated by comparing the cost of a bundle of goods and services in a given year with its cost in a base year. See also *index*.

**Price Level.**  A weighted average of prices of all goods and services where the weights are given by total spending on each good or service. Measured by a price index.

**Price Stickiness.**  Resistance of prices to change.

**Price System.**  See *market mechanism*.

**Principal.**  The original amount loaned, which is repaid plus interest. See *face value*.

**Printing Money.**  Purchase of bonds by the central bank.

**Private Saving.**  That part of disposable income not spent on consumption.

**Procyclical.**  Increasing during booms and decreasing during recessions.

**Production Function.**  A relationship showing how output varies with inputs.

**Productivity.**  Output per unit of input, usually measured as output per hour of labor.

**Progressive Tax.**  A tax in which the rich pay a larger percentage of income than the poor. Contrast with *regressive tax*.

**Proportional Tax.**  A tax taking the same percentage of income regardless of the level of income.

**Protectionism.**   Policy of tariffs or import quotas to protect domestic producers from foreign competition.

**Public Debt.**   See *national debt*.

**Publicly Held National Debt.**   See *national debt*.

**Pump Priming.**   A stimulating monetary or fiscal policy to set in motion an expansionary multiplier process.

**Purchasing Power Parity.**   Theory that says that over the long run exchange rate changes offset any difference between foreign and domestic inflation. This result assumes that the real exchange rate remains constant, something that is not true even in the long run.

**Quantity Adjuster.**   A firm that reacts to excess supply or excess demand by adjusting quantity rather than price. Contrast with *price adjuster*.

**Quantity Theory of Money.**   Theory that velocity is constant and so a change in money supply will change nominal income by the same percentage. Formalized by the equation $Mv = PQ$.

**Quota.**   See *import quota*.

**Ratio Scale.**   See *logarithmic scale*.

**Rational Expectations.**   Forecasts that are the best that can be made given the data available and knowledge of how the economy operates. Rational expectations implies random errors, no systematic errors.

**Reaganomics.**   The economic program of President Ronald Reagan, including tax cuts, restraint in spending except for defense spending, and less regulation.

**Real.**   Measured in base year, or constant, dollars. Contrast with *nominal*. See also following seven entries.

**Real Business Cycle Theory.**   Belief that business cycles arise from real shocks to the economy, such as technology advances and natural resource discoveries, and have little to do with monetary policy.

**Real Exchange Rate.**   See *exchange rate, real*.

**Real GDP.**   GDP expressed in base year dollars, calculated by dividing nominal GDP by a price index.

**Real Income.**   Income expressed in base year dollars, calculated by dividing nominal income by a price index.

**Real Money Supply.**   Money supply expressed in base year dollars, calculated by dividing the money supply by a price index.

**Real Rate of Interest.**   See *interest rate, real*.

**Real Wage.**   Wage expressed in base year dollars, calculated by dividing the money wage by a price index.

**Recession.**   Loosely speaking, a period of less-than-normal economic growth. Technically, a downturn in economic activity in which real GDP falls in two consecutive quarters.

**Regressive Tax.**   A tax in which the poor pay a larger percentage of income than the rich. Contrast with *progressive tax*.

**Relative Price.**   Ratio of the price of one item to the price of another.

**Required Reserves.**   Reserves that the central bank requires commercial banks to hold.

**Reserve Currency.**   A currency, frequently the U.S. dollar, that is used by other countries to denominate the assets they hold as international reserves.

**Reserve Ratio.**   See *reserve requirement*.

**Reserve Requirement.**   Fraction of total deposits that a commercial bank is required by the central bank to hold in the form of reserves.

**Reserves.**   Commercial banks' reserves consist of their holdings of cash and their balances in deposits with the central bank. See also *foreign exchange reserves, excess reserves, required reserves, reserve requirement*.

**Return.**   See *yield*.

**Risk.**   The degree of uncertainty associated with the return on an asset.

**Risk Premium.**   The difference between the yields of two bonds because of differences in their risk.

**Rule.**   See *monetarist rule*.

**Rules versus Discretion Debate.**   Argument about whether policy authorities should be allowed to undertake discretionary policy action as they see fit or should be replaced by robots programmed to set policy by following specific formulas. See *discretionary policy* and *policy rules*.

**Sales Tax.**   A tax levied as a percentage of retail sales.

**Say's Law.**   Belief that supply creates its own demand.

**SDR.**   Special Drawing Right, the name given to the "currency" of the IMF.

**Seasonal Adjustment.**   Adjustment to correct measures for changes that happen for seasonal reasons.

**Seigniorage.**   Funding available to the government through printing money.

**Speculator.**   Anyone who buys or sells an asset, such as a foreign currency, in the hope of profiting from a change in its price.

**Spot.**   For immediate payment and delivery, as opposed to future payment and delivery.

**Stagflation.**   Simultaneous existence of high inflation and high unemployment, or simultaneous existence of rising inflation and rising unemployment.

**Sterilization.**   Central bank action offsetting money supply changes automatically generated by a balance of payments surplus or deficit under a fixed exchange rate system.

**Stickiness.**   See *price stickiness* or *wage stickiness*.

**Structural Deficit.**   The budget deficit in excess of the deficit that in the long run keeps constant the ratio of the publicly held national debt to GDP. Sometimes this is defined merely as what the deficit would be if cyclical impacts on government spending and tax revenues were removed.

**Structural Unemployment.** Unemployment due to a mismatch between the skills or location of labor and the skills or location required by firms.

**Supply.** An amount made available for sale, always associated with a given price.

**Supply Side Economics.** View that incentives to work, save, and invest play an important role in determining economic activity by affecting the supply side of the economy.

**Tariff.** A tax applied to imports.

**Target.** A specific level of some economic variable that a policy attempts to maintain.

**Tax-related Incomes Policy (TIP).** Tax incentives for labor and business to induce them to conform to wage/price guidelines.

**Term.** See *term to maturity*.

**Term Deposit.** An interest-earning bank deposit that cannot be withdrawn without penalty until a specific time.

**Term to Maturity.** Period of time from the present to the redemption date of a bond.

**Term Structure of Interest Rates.** Relationship among interest rates on bonds with different terms to maturity.

**Terms of Trade.** The quantity of imports that can be obtained for a unit of exports, measured by the ratio of an export price index to an import price index.

**Time Deposit.** See *term deposit*.

**Time Series.** Observations on a variable over time.

**T-bill.** See *treasury bill*.

**Trade Deficit.** Deficit on the balance of merchandise trade.

**Tradeable.** Good or service that is capable of being traded.

**Transfer Payment.** A grant or gift that is not payment for services rendered.

**Transmission Mechanism.** The channels by which a change in the demand or supply of money affects aggregate demand for goods and services.

**Treasury Bill.** A short-term (less than one year) government discount bond.

**Trough.** The lower turning point of a business cycle, where a contraction turns into an expansion.

**Turning Point.** The trough or peak of a business cycle.

**Twin Deficits.** The trade deficit and the government budget deficit.

**Underground Economy.** Economic activity not observed by tax collectors and government statisticians.

**Unemployment Insurance.** A program in which workers and firms pay contributions and workers collect benefits if they become unemployed.

**Unemployment Rate.**   Fraction of the labor force that is not employed.

**User Cost of Capital.**   The implicit annual cost of investing in physical capital, determined by things such as the interest rate, the rate of depreciation of the asset, and tax regulations. What would be paid to rent this capital if a rental market existed for it.

**Value Added.**   The value of a firm's output less the value of intermediate goods bought from other firms.

**Velocity.**   The number of times during a year that the money supply turns over in supporting that year's economic activity, measured as the ratio of nominal income to the money supply.

**Wage Flexibility.**   Ease with which wages adjust in response to excess supply or demand.

**Wage/Price Controls.**   An incomes policy in which wages and prices are constrained by law not to rise by more than a specified percentage.

**Wage Stickiness.**   Resistance of wages to change.

**Wealth Effect.**   The effect on spending of a change in wealth caused by a change in the overall price level.

**World Bank.**   The International Bank for Reconstruction and Development, an international organization that provides long-term loans to developing countries to improve their infrastructure.

**Yield.**   The interest rate that makes the present value of a stream of future payments associated with an asset equal to the current price of that asset. Also called yield to maturity.

**Yield Curve.**   A graph showing how the yield on bonds varies with time to maturity.

**Zero-coupon Bond.**   See *discount bond*.

# Index

Microeconomics, 1, 11
Mitterrand, François, 319
Models, modeling, 2
Monetarist rule, 140–141, 142–144, 145
Monetarists, monetarism, 54, 116, 135,
    136, 147, 150, 178, 323, 334–335
  money supply, 148–149
Monetary aggregates, 125, 129–130, 131,
    132, 133, 134, 146, 148, 149, 177, 178,
    333
  types of, 122–124
*Monetary History of the United States,
    1867–1960, A* (Friedman and Schwarz),
    135
Monetary policy, 138(fig.), 143, 144, 145,
    167, 172, 195, 200, 204, 205–206, 207,
    212, 216, 220, 246, 253, 278, 320, 347–
    348
  effects of, 162–163
  and exchange rates, 258–260, 262–263,
    264, 289–290
  and fiscal policy, 116–117
  fixed exchange rate and, 275–276
  inflation and, 280–281, 316
  and interest rates, 155, 159–160, 164, 168,
    176–179, 180–181, 182, 185–186, 285,
    336–338
  and negative supply shock, 213, 217
  transmission mechanism and, 160–162
  and velocity, 149–150
Monetary shocks, 145, 177
Monetary targeting, 145, 177
Monetization of debt, 226, 232, 235
Money, 177, 308
  demand for, 342–343
  excess, 137, 139
  growth in, 201, 334, 335
  printing, 6, 115–116, 117
  role of, 121, 122–124, 136
  transactions, 129–130
Money base, 126
Money market, 156, 304, 305, 306–307
Money multiplier, 127–129, 130, 131,
    133–134, 151, 170, 236
Money neutrality, 64–65
Money supply, 6, 53, 64–65, 115–116,
    117, 122, 132, 152, 202, 217, 219, 220,
    260, 282, 317, 333, 353, 354, 355
  and aggregate demand, 191, 197
  and banking system, 125–126, 153
  bonds and, 127–129, 130–131, 164, 179,
    182, 319–320

controlling, 126–127, 212–215
and deficits, 130–131
and exchange rate, 257, 258, 276
and Federal Reserve System, 121, 145,
    177, 178
and foreign exchange, 255–256
growth in, 146–147, 151
and inflation, 7, 140–141, 190
and interest rates, 159, 175, 185
and monetarism, 148–149
and nominal interest rates, 213–214
politics and, 143, 151, 179–180
quantity theory and, 137–139
spending and, 160–161
Mortgage rates, 156, 162–163
MPC. *See* Marginal propensity to consume
Multipliers, 5, 46, 49–51, 56, 68–69, 74,
    115, 122, 170, 236, 318, 320. *See also*
    Money multiplier
  and government spending, 50–51, 61–62,
    112, 117
  income, 139, 147, 151, 152, 221
Multiplier process, 51, 55, 111, 160, 332
Municipal bond rate, 156
Mutual funds, 123

NAIRU. *See* Non-accelerating inflation
    rate of unemployment
National debt, 223–224, 226–227, 228
  and burdening future generations, 229–
    232
National income, 5, 11, 25, 65
  and aggregate demand, 45, 46, 48–49,
    50–51
National income accounts, 11
*National Income and Product Accounts,* 11
National saving, 107, 225, 242
  role of, 101–103
Natural rate of unemployment (NRU),
    35–36, 75, 78, 80, 89, 193, 194, 195,
    196, 201, 203, 208, 212, 213
  and Phillips curve, 190, 204, 209
Negotiable order of withdrawal (NOW)
    account, 125
New Classical school, 54, 65, 194
New Keynesian school, 54, 65, 82, 89, 194
New Zealand, 126, 209, 227, 293, 294,
    320, 342
Nixon, Richard, 200
Nominal interest rate, 171, 181, 182, 213–
    214, 240, 284, 286–289, 292, 338–340
  and inflation, 172, 173, 174–176, 283